21世纪英语专业系列教材

ENGLISH CULTURE

英语文化

（第二版）

王逢鑫　编著
By Wang Fengxin

图书在版编目(CIP)数据

英语文化(第二版)/王逢鑫编著. —北京：北京大学出版社，2010.9
(21世纪英语专业系列教材)
ISBN 978-7-301-17656-6

Ⅰ.英… Ⅱ.王… Ⅲ.英语—文化语言学—高等学校—教材 Ⅳ.H31

中国版本图书馆 CIP 数据核字(2010)第 161271 号

书　　　名：英语文化(第二版)
著作责任者：王逢鑫　编著
责 任 编 辑：孙　莹
标 准 书 号：ISBN 978-7-301-17656-6/H·2618
出 版 发 行：北京大学出版社
地　　　址：北京市海淀区成府路 205 号　100871
网　　　址：http://www.pup.cn
电　　　话：邮购部 62752015　发行部 62750672　编辑部 62754382　出版部 62754962
印 刷 者：北京宏伟双华印刷有限公司
经 销 者：新华书店
　　　　　787 毫米×960 毫米　16 开本　16.25 印张　450 千字
　　　　　2004 年 6 月第 1 版　2010 年 9 月第 2 版
　　　　　2021 年 10 月第 9 次印刷(总第 15 次印刷)
定　　价：45.00 元

未经许可，不得以任何方式复制或抄袭本书之部分或全部内容。
版权所有，侵权必究　　举报电话：010-62752024
　　　　　　　　　　　电子邮箱：fd@pup.pku.edu.cn

《21世纪英语专业系列教材》编写委员会

（以姓氏笔画排序）

王守仁　王克非　申　丹

刘意青　李　力　胡壮麟

桂诗春　梅德明　程朝翔

总　　序

北京大学出版社自2005年以来已出版《语言学与应用语言学知识系列读本》多种，为了配合第十一个五年计划，现又策划陆续出版《21世纪英语专业系列教材》。这个重大举措势必受到英语专业广大教师和学生的欢迎。

作为英语教师，最让人揪心的莫过于听人说英语不是一个专业，只是一个工具。说这些话的领导和教师的用心是好的，为英语专业的毕业生将来找工作着想，因此要为英语专业的学生多多开设诸如新闻、法律、国际商务、经济、旅游等其他专业的课程。但事与愿违，英语专业的教师们很快发现，学生投入英语学习的时间少了，掌握英语专业课程知识甚微，即使对四个技能的掌握也并不比大学英语学生高明多少，而那个所谓的第二专业在有关专家的眼中只是学到些皮毛而已。

英语专业的路在何方？有没有其他路可走？这是需要我们英语专业教师思索的问题。中央领导关于创新是一个民族的灵魂和要培养创新人才等的指示精神，让我们在层层迷雾中找到了航向。显然，培养学生具有自主学习能力和能进行创造性思维是我们更为重要的战略目标，使英语专业的人才更能适应21世纪的需要，迎接21世纪的挑战。

如今，北京大学出版社外语部的领导和编辑同志们，也从教材出版的视角探索英语专业的教材问题，从而为贯彻英语专业教学大纲做些有益的工作，为教师们开设大纲中所规定的必修、选修课程提供各种教材。《21世纪英语专业系列教材》是普通高等教育"十一五"国家级规划教材和国家"十一五"重点出版规划项目《面向新世纪的立体化网络化英语学科建设丛书》的重要组成部分。这套系列教材要体现新世纪英语教学的自主化、协作化、模块化和超文本化，结合外语教材的具体情况，既要解决语言、教学内容、教学方法和教育技术的时代化，也要坚持弘扬以爱国主义为核心的民族精神。因此，今天北京大学出版社在大力提倡专业英语教学改革的基础上，编辑出版各种英语专业技能、英语专业知识和相关专业知识课程的教材，以培养具有创新性思维的和具有实际工作能力的学生，充分体现了时代精神。

北京大学出版社的远见卓识，也反映了英语专业广大师生盼望已久的心愿。由北京大学等全国几十所院校具体组织力量，积极编写相关教材。这就是说，这套教材是由一些高等院校有水平有经验的第一线教师们制定编写大纲，反复讨论，特别是考虑到在不同层次、不同背景学校之间取得平衡，避免了先前的教材或偏难或偏易的弊病。与此同时，一批知名专家教授参与策划和教材审定工作，保证了教材质量。

当然，这套系列教材出版只是初步实现了出版社和编者们的预期目标。为了获得更大效果，希望使用本系列教材的教师和同学不吝指教，及时将意见反馈给我们，使教材更加完善。

航道已经开通，我们有决心乘风破浪，奋勇前进！

胡壮麟
北京大学蓝旗营

再 版 前 言

  1983年秋,我结束了在英国爱丁堡大学中文系的教学,返回祖国,重归北京大学英语系教书。在英国教英国学生学中文的经历,使我更加感到文化背景知识对学习语言的重要性。我回国后就在北京大学英语系开始上"英国概况"课。当时资料匮乏,去图书馆里找不到什么可以参考的东西,只好利用自己在英国教书时收集的材料编写讲义。最初,走的还是老路,教的还是老一套,讲英国历史和地理,再加上政治制度、教育制度和宗教知识。

  在教学过程中发现,同学们在中学里学过世界历史课和世界地理课,比较熟悉英国资产阶级革命和产业革命的内容,对重复的东西不感兴趣,而对比较陌生的基督教十分感兴趣。我与时俱进,不断修改教学内容。

  随着改革开放的深入,我增加了法律、经济和知识产权等方面的知识。我根据自己在国外教书和工作的经验,感到了解英语人名背后的文化内涵对人际交流十分有用,就在这方面的内容上花了很多时间,在教材中写了两章,占用了很大篇幅。此外,我在课堂上还通过自己的亲身经历,给同学们讲英美人的生活习惯和风土人情。我从"英国概况"讲起,其后增加了"美国概况"的内容,再后来发展到"英语文化"。我认为,教材需要不断修订,但是最好不包括时效太强而不断变化的资料性信息,内容还是包括相对稳定的常用知识比较好。80年代初,国内还没有普遍使用计算机,而现在已进入互联网时代,电脑已普及到千家万户。这次修订教材,我添加了"网络文化"一章,而将"英语人名"由两章压缩为一章。

  本书于2004年初版后,已经6次印刷,受到读者欢迎。本教材已列入"十一五"国家级规划教材。一些兄弟院校将这本书作为教材。我趁再版之际,对使用本教材的朋友们表示感谢,希望大家多多批评指正。

王逢鑫

2010年3月28日于北京海淀区蓝旗营小区

前　言

英语学习的重要性越来越显著。在英语教学改革中，人们越来越认识到语言教学必须与文化背景知识教学相结合。学习英语不仅要语法正确，而且要语用得体。学习英语国家文化知识与学习英语语言是同等重要的。掌握好相关文化背景知识既有利于语言学习，又有利于开阔视野，加深对世界的了解。在英语教学改革中加强文化知识教学，符合形势发展的需要，也符合英语教学自身的规律，并且促进学科建设和学科发展。

笔者自1983年起在北京大学英语系讲授英国概况、英语文化和希腊罗马神话等涉及英语文化知识的课程。二十余年来，撰写论文，编写教材，不断丰富、充实、调整和更新教学内容和方法，以适应社会发展和满足学生需求。教学效果良好，受到学生欢迎。这种将语言学习与文化学习结合的做法，对英语学习者是必不可少的启蒙教育和基础教育，使他们通过系统的学习，打下坚实的英语语言和文化知识基本功，有助于将来学习、工作和研究进一步发展。

本教材是笔者二十余年讲授英语文化知识课程心得、体会和经验的总结；也是笔者二十余年从事英国研究、美国研究和加拿大研究的成果体现。这门"英语文化"课的教学对象既包括英语专业学生，也包括大学英语通过六级考试的学生。笔者在长期教学过程中，为适应形势发展和满足学生需求，为促进学科建设和学科发展，不断丰富、充实、调整和更新教学内容和方法，对教材反复实践，反复修改，使之臻于完善。与国内同类教材相比较，本教材具有以下特点和创新：

1. 国内现有同类教材，多是"拿来主义"，直接选用外国教材、书籍或报刊文章，没有经过加工或修改。许多文章原本不是为教学目的而撰写的，这样凑成的教材从严格意义上讲，不能算是教材，因为它们没有考虑我国英语教学规律，也没有考虑我国学生实际需求。而本教材是笔者根据语言教学规律和社会实际需求用英语撰写的，内容循序渐进，难易程度恰当，注意科学性和实用性的结合。

2. 国内现有同类教材，大多内容陈旧，资料过时，甚至有时传达了错误信息。编写者只是将仅能收集到的资料拼凑在一起，没有经过去伪存真、去粗存精的加工过程，也没有经过实际教学的检验。本教材作者在编写过程中，收集了大量资料，阅读了大量文献，从中精选材料，认真写作，又在二十余年教学过程中反复实践，反复揣摩，反复思索，反复修改，精益求精，使之成为一本像样的教材。

3. 国内现有同类教材，内容大多是资料的堆积，没有注意语言教学与文化教学的结合，更没有注意语言学习内容与语言学习方法的结合。本教材是与基础阶段英语学习相配套的，可对初级或中级英语学习者进行启蒙教育和基本功训练。不但通过语言学习，让学生学习文化知识，而且通过传授文化知识，让学生学习语言。

4. 国内现有同类教材，内容大多是拼凑堆积而成，支离破碎，缺乏内在联系，不能进行系统的文化知识传授。本教材将我国英语学习者最需要掌握的文化背景知识，按照一定体系编写，让学生得到的是系统的、最必需的文化知识，为以后的学习、工作和研究奠定基础，铺平道路。

5. 国内现有的同类教材，内容大多没有考虑我国英语学习者的实际需求。本教材作者有四十多年丰富教学经验，有在国外大学教学和国际组织工作的经验，有在国外生活的经验，还有在国内担任笔译和口译工作的经验，深知涉外工作和文化交流中对英语语言和英语文化的需求，这样编写的教材有的放矢，针对性强。学生学习以后可以学以致用，理论联系实际。

6. 本教材作者多年从事英国研究、美国研究和加拿大研究，熟悉主要英语国家的历史与现状，在编写教材过程中，根据轻重缓急，能够选择对我国英语学习者最迫切需要掌握的英语文化知识，在有限的时间和有限的空间内教给学生尽量多的、有用的文化背景知识。

7. 本教材作者多年从事汉英两种语言的比较研究，并长期从事中国文化与西方文化的比较研究，熟悉汉英两种语言的异同之处，熟悉中西两种文化的异同之处。本教材引导学生注意英语文化与中国文化的差异，知己知彼，这将使他们在未来的学习和工作中，能够应付各种复杂多变的情况。

本教材涉及英语国家的政治、经济、法律、教育、媒体、宗教、社会、家庭等方面的文化背景知识。这是供普通高等教育和成人高等教育使用的基础阶段英语教材。用英语撰写，主要目的是让学习者通过简单、通俗易懂的英语，学习英语文化背景知识；面面俱到，点到为止，仅了解概况即可，并不深入展开。同时，还让学习者通过英语文化知识学习英语，提高学生的理解和表达能力。这不是一门涉及某一学科的专业课，它不同于用汉语讲授英语国家的政治、经济、法律、教育、媒体、宗教、社会、家庭等领域的内容。这门课涉及范围有一定的广度，但不要求有太专门的深度。

本教材共有18课，主要内容包括：

1. 英语语言（the English Language）——介绍作为国际语言的英语的历史与现状、使用范围，以及第一语言与第二语言、母语与外语。

2. 英语国家（the English-Speaking Countries）——介绍英国和美国等主要英语国家的概况，包括地理环境、名称、民族等基本情况。还介绍与英语国家关系密切的欧洲国家的概况。

3. 英语人名（the English Names）——介绍英语姓名的构成、命名的方法、姓氏的来历、姓名的含义、绰号以及称谓的方式。

4. 社会与家庭（Society and Family）——介绍英国和美国等主要英语国家的社会结构、家庭结构、亲属关系等内容。

5. 君主制度（the Monarchical System）——介绍以英国为代表的君主制政治特点、君主的权力、王室的构成、贵族制度等。比较君主制、君主立宪制、共和制和联邦制。

6. 议会制度（the Parliamentary System）——介绍西方议会与两院制，着重介绍英国议会和美国国会的选举、构成、权力与功能。

7. 选举制度（the Electoral System）——介绍西方的两党制，分析英国的工党与保守党，美国的共和党与民主党的轮流执政。着重介绍英国的大选和补缺选举，以及美国的总统选举。

8. 政府制度（the Governmental System）——介绍西方政府制度以及立法、行政与司法的三权分立。着重介绍英国内阁的产生与组成、首相的职能，以及公务员制度。并着重介绍美国联邦政府和州政府的组成和职能。还介绍其他政府形式,包括平民政府与军政府、临时政府以及联合政府。

9. **法律制度** (the Legal System)——介绍英国宪法和美国宪法以及刑法、民法。介绍法庭以及诉讼、审讯、陪审、判决和徒刑等过程。

10. **经济制度** (the Economic System)——介绍不同类型的经济,比较计划经济与市场经济;叙述经济发展的过程,分析传统经济与知识经济;介绍主要经济部门:生产部门与服务部门。

11. **收入与支出** (Income and Expenditure)——介绍货币形式与支付手段,国家收入(税收)、公司收入(利润)与个人收入(工资),各种费用支出,以及各种社会福利。

12. **商业与投资** (Commerce and Investment)——介绍商业活动形式,银行投资,以及其他投资活动,包括期货交易、房地产交易、股票与证券交易、彩票等。

13. **知识产权** (Intellectual Property)——介绍知识产权,包括专利、注册商标和版权,培养保护知识产权意识,反对侵权、盗版、剽窃等行为。

14. **教育制度** (the Educational System)——介绍教育制度,包括正规教育:初等教育、中等教育和高等教育;终身教育:成人教育、继续教育、学习化社会。

15. **大众传媒** (Mass Media)——介绍大众传媒的相关知识,包括报刊、广播、电视等,还介绍互联网的相关知识。

16. **宗教** (Religion)——介绍宗教的起源,特别是佛教、基督教和伊斯兰教的起源;着重介绍基督教的相关知识:耶稣基督,重大事件(耶稣蒙难和耶稣升天),圣诞节和复活节等宗教节日,天主教与新教,英国国教,神职人员,教堂等。结合中国实际,介绍佛教和道教的相关知识和说法。

自1983年以来,笔者一直坚持每年给北京大学英语系一年级本科生开设这门"英语文化"课程,从未间断。这门课程还曾经作为北京大学全校公共选修课,面对通过大学英语六级的学生,均收到良好效果。1999年,这门"英语文化"课程列为北京大学课程建设项目。2002年,本教材列入北京市高等教育精品教材建设工程项目。

笔者愿将这本积累我二十余年心血的教材,奉献给学习英语的广大读者。笔者更衷心地希望专家、学者以及使用本教材的教师和同学批评指正。

王逢鑫

2004年3月28日于北京海淀区蓝旗营小区

作者简介

王逢鑫,1939年生于山东省青岛市。1957年考入北京大学西方语言文学系英国语言文学专业,攻读英国语言文学。1962年毕业后留校任教。现任北京大学外国语学院英语系教授、博士生导师。1981年至1983年,曾在英国爱丁堡大学中文系讲授中国文学、语言和文化。曾三次在巴黎联合国教育、科学和文化组织总部工作,1980年担任同声传译,1990年担任笔译,1999年担任审校。1992年赴加拿大从事加拿大研究。学术领域涉及:语言学(语义学、词汇学、词典学、句法学、教学法、语言测试等)、英美文学(诗歌、小说、散文等)、跨文化研究(英国研究、加拿大研究等)、及翻译(口译与笔译)理论与实践。毕生从事教育事业和中外文化交流。主要论著有:

1) 《英语意念语法》,北京:北京大学出版社,1989
   《英语意念语法(修订版)》,北京:外文出版社,1999
   《王逢鑫文法语义篇》,台北:台湾经典传讯,2004
   《王逢鑫文法形式篇》,台北:台湾经典传讯,2004
2) 《英语情态表达法》,香港:香港商务印书馆,1990;台北:台湾商务印书馆,1991;北京:商务印书馆国际有限公司,1996
3) 《活用英语动词》,香港:香港商务印书馆,1990;台北:台湾商务印书馆,1991;北京:商务印书馆国际有限公司,1996
4) 《英汉意念分类词典》,北京:北京大学出版社,1991
   《常春藤 TOEFL 分类式字汇》,台北:台湾常春藤解析英语杂志社,1991
   《英语词汇分类联想学习法》,北京:外文出版社,2000
5) 《汉英口译教程》,北京:北京大学出版社,1992
6) 《英语词汇的魅力》,北京:北京大学出版社,1995
   《繁星组合英文学习法》,台北:台湾经典传讯,1999
   《英语词汇的魅力(修订版)》,北京:外文出版社,2003
   《王逢鑫词汇繁星篇(日常用语)》,台北:台湾经典传讯,2004
   《王逢鑫词汇组合篇(自然万象)》,台北:台湾经典传讯,2004
7) 《英语构词的玄妙》,北京:北京大学出版社,1997
   《英语构词的玄妙(修订版)》,北京:外文出版社,2003
8) 《汉英饮食文化词典》,北京:外文出版社,1998
9) 《英语同义表达法》,北京:外文出版社,1999
   《王逢鑫进阶文法同义表达(词汇 & 句法)》,台北:台湾经典传讯,2004
   《王逢鑫进阶文法同义表达(逻辑 & 特例)》,台北:台湾经典传讯,2004
10) 《英语模糊语法》,北京:外文出版社,2001

11)《英汉比较语义学》，北京：外文出版社，2001
12)《汉英旅游文化词典》，北京：北京大学出版社，2001
13)《高级汉英口译教程》，北京：外文出版社，2004
14)《英语文化》，北京：北京大学出版社，2004
15)《中国人最易犯的汉译英错误》，北京：中国书籍出版社，2008
16)《100个热门话题汉译英》，北京：北京大学出版社，2010

About the Author

Wang Fengxin, born in 1939, in Qingdao City, Shandong Province. In 1957, he was admitted to the Western Languages and Literature Department, Peking University, and majored in English language and literature. In 1962, he graduated from Peking University, and has since worked as a teacher in its English Department. He is now Professor and Ph. D. Supervisor of the English Department, College of Foreign Languages, Peking University. From 1981 to 1983, he taught Chinese literature, language and culture in the Chinese Department of Edinburgh University, U. K. He has worked for UNESCO headquarters in Paris three times, as simultaneous interpreter in 1980, as translator in 1990, and as reviser in 1999. He went to Canada to make Canadian studies in 1992. His academic areas involve linguistics, (including semantics, lexicology, lexicography, syntax, teaching methodology and language testing), English and American literature (including poetry, fiction and prose), cross-cultural studies (including British studies and Canadian studies), and translation and interpretation theory and practice. He has devoted himself to educational undertakings and cultural exchange between China and foreign countries. His principal works include:

1) *A Notional Grammar of English*, Beijing: Peking University Press, 1989
   A Notional Grammar of English (Revised Edition), Beijing: Foreign Languages Press, 1999; Taipei: Classic Communications Co., 2004
2) *English Modality*, Hong Kong: The Commercial Press (Hong Kong) LTD, 1990; Taipei: Taiwan Commercial Press, 1991; Beijing: The Commercial Press International LTD, 1996
3) *English Verbs*, Hong Kong: The Commercial Press (Hong Kong) LTD, 1990; Taipei: Taiwan Commercial Press, 1991; Beijing: The Commercial Press International LTD, 1996
4) *A Notional English-Chinese Lexicon*, Beijing: Peking University Press, 1991
   Ivy League TOEFL Lexicon, Taipei: Ivy League Analytical English, 1991
   How to Study English Vocabulary by Association, Beijing: Foreign Languages Press, 2000
5) *A Coursebook for Chinese-English Interpretation*, Beijing: Peking University Press, 1992
6) *The Appeal of English Words*, Beijing: Peking University Press, 1995; Taipei: Classic Communications Co., 1999
   The Appeal of English Words (Revised Edition), Beijing: Foreign Languages Press, 2003; Taipei: Classic Communications Co., 2004
7) *The Wonder of English Word-Making*, Beijing: Peking University Press, 1997
   The Wonder of English Word-Making (Revised Edition), Beijing: Foreign Languages Press, 2003
8) *A Chinese-English Lexicon of Cuisine Culture*, Beijing: Foreign Languages Press, 1998
9) *English Paraphrasing*, Beijing: Foreign Languages Press, 1999; Taipei: Classic Communications Co., 2004

10) *A Fuzzy Grammar of English*, Beijing: Foreign Languages Press, 2001
11) *English-Chinese Comparative Semantics*, Beijing: Foreign Languages Press, 2001
12) *A Chinese-English Lexicon of Tourism Culture*, Beijing: Peking University Press, 2001
13) *An Advanced Coursebook for Chinese-English Interpretation*, Beijing: Foreign Languages Press, 2004
14) *English Culture*, Beijing: Peking University Press, 2004
15) *Error Analysis in Chinese-English Translation*, Beijing: China Books Press, 2008
16) *Chinese-English Translation of 100 Hot Topics*, Beijing: Peking University Press, 2010

Abbreviations Used in This Book

a.	adjective	*n.*	noun
abbrev.	abbreviation	*prep.*	preposition
ad.	adverb	*prep. phrase*	prepositional phrase
AmE.	American English	sb	somebody; someone
BrE.	British English	sth	something
conj.	conjunction	*syn.*	synonym
e.g.	for example	usu.	usually
esp.	especially	*v.*	verb
etc.	et cetera	*v. phrase*	verb phrase

CONTENTS

Lesson One	The English Language	(1)
Lesson Two	The English-Speaking Countries	(11)
Lesson Three	The English Names	(28)
Lesson Four	Society and Family	(43)
Lesson Five	The Monarchical System	(54)
Lesson Six	The Parliamentary System	(65)
Lesson Seven	The Electoral System	(77)
Lesson Eight	The Governmental System	(91)
Lesson Nine	The Legal System	(103)
Lesson Ten	The Economic System	(115)
Lesson Eleven	Income and Expenditure	(131)
Lesson Twelve	Commerce and Investment	(143)
Lesson Thirteen	Intellectual Property	(156)
Lesson Fourteen	The Educational System	(167)
Lesson Fifteen	Mass Media	(180)
Lesson Sixteen	Network Culture	(195)
Lesson Seventeen	Religion (I)	(206)
Lesson Eighteen	Religion (II)	(219)
Partial Answers to Exercises		(229)
References		(240)

Lesson One

The English Language

A language is a system of communication used by the people of a particular country or a region for talking or writing purposes. A language system consists of a set of codes that are sounds and written symbols. People in one country or region may speak a different language from those in another country or region. We often have the difficulty of communicating with people who speak a different language. This forms the language barrier. That's why we have to learn a foreign language that is spoken by the people from another country.

Most languages have both oral or spoken, and written forms. Take English for example. Oral English is its spoken form while written English is its written form. But a few languages have only spoken forms, but lack written ones.

A modern language is a language that is still spoken today while a dead language is a language that is no longer spoken. Latin is a dead language, which is the language of the ancient Romans.

English is spoken by the English-speaking people or by the English-speaking population as their mother tongue. When we say mother tongue, we refer it to the language that we learned from our parents when we were children. Mother tongue is in contrast to foreign language. It can also be called native tongue or native language. Native language is in contrast to non-native language. When you speak more than one language, there is a difference between your first language and second language. Your first language, or L1 for short, is the language you first learned as a child. First language is another way of saying mother tongue or native language. In contrast to your first language, your second language or L2 for short, is not the language you first learned when you were a child, but the language you learned later, and you use at work, at school or for business purposes. A second language is not a native language in a country, but it is widely used as a medium of communication, for instance, in education and in government. It is usually used alongside another language or other languages.

English-speaking countries include Britain, the United States, Canada, Australia, New Zealand, Ireland, South Africa and several Caribbean countries. The English-speaking population or the English-speaking people are called native speakers of English. They have learned English as their first language, rather than a foreign language. They think in English and use it naturally. The English language used in the English-speaking countries varies as to its pronunciation, vocabulary and grammar. So there are different types of regional English like British English and American English. They are the two most popular kinds of English in the world.

British English (BrE., for short) is the English language used in Britain. It consists of many regional kinds of English. For example, people in London, Newcastle, Glasgow and Manchester speak English in different ways. American English (AmE., for short) is the English language used in the United States. It consists of many regional kinds of English. For example, people in New England, New York City and the South of the United States speak English in different ways. An Americanism is a word, phrase, sound or expression, which is characteristic of and typical of American English.

In areas where English is not the only language spoken, the people speak English as Anglophone. Canada is a bilingual country. The Canadian people consist of the Anglophone people who speak Canadian English and the Francophone people who speak Canadian French. Both English and French are official languages of Canada.

Official language refers to the language that is used in the formal situations such as government, law courts, newspapers, TV programmes, broadcasting, etc. However, there may be more than one official language in a multilingual country. For example, the Republic of Singapore has four official languages: English, Chinese, Malay and Tamil. Usually, the national language, which is the main language and standard language of a country, is also the official language.

English is spoken by people as their second language in some Commonwealth countries, which were former British colonies such as Fiji, Singapore, India and Nigeria. They teach English as a second language at school. The course of Teaching English as a Second Language is simply called TESL. English used to be the official language in some countries or regions such as India, Pakistan, Sri Lanka, Bangladesh, Malaysia, Singapore and Hong Kong in Asia, and Nigeria, Zambia, Uganda and the Sudan in Africa.

English is not only spoken by native speakers of English as their first language and by the above-mentioned people who speak English as their second language, but also spoken by the people of other parts of the world as a foreign language. A foreign language is a language, which is not a native language in a country. It is taught as a school subject but not used as a medium of instruction in schools, or as a language of communication within a country, for example, in government, business or industry. English is described as a foreign language in France, Germany, Spain, China, Japan, etc.

There are different varieties of English. For instance, Japan English includes expressions for things and concepts that are unique in Japan. They are mainly found in tourism, trade and commerce. Japan English is understood and accepted by the native speakers of English, for it is appropriate in its use. Japan English is generally realized at the lexical level. The Chinese people have to introduce to the world the special things and concepts found only in China with the help of China English. As a new variety of English, China English has become more and more intelligible and acceptable to the native speakers of English, for it is used appropriately. China English is also realized mainly at the lexical level. And it is restricted to such areas of political affairs, economy, tourism and traditional culture. But when some Chinese first learn English, they tend to speak Chinese English or Chinglish which is not accepted by the native speakers of English, for it is not appropriate in its use. As Chinglish is uneducated and error-inflicted, it has a derogatory sense.

Some uneducated workers, visiting seamen and traders in Western African and Southeast Asian countries speak in Pidgin English when they communicate with English-speaking people. A pidgin is a language that is a mixture of two other languages. It is not usually anyone's native language, but is used when people from two different countries do business with each other. So, Pidgin English is a language containing elements of English and the local languages used in these areas. A local language exists in or belongs to a particular area or district.

Diplomats, businessmen and scholars all over the world use English as an international language for communication. The English language is widely used in commercial and tourist centres, banks, stock exchanges, airports, and hotels in most countries and at international meetings, gatherings and conferences.

The history of English is conventionally divided into three periods usually called Old English or Anglo-Saxon, Middle English and Modern English. The earliest period began with the migration of certain Germanic tribes from the European Continent to Britain in the 5th century A. D., and it continued until the end of the 11th century or a bit later. The period of Middle English lasted roughly from the 12th through the 15th century. The period of Modern English extended from the 16th century to our present day. English is considered as the first international language for historical reasons. The expansion of English to other countries began in earnest in the 17th century, with the successful colonization of the eastern seaboard of North America, later spread by colonization both directly from Britain and from the United States. So the wide use of English in the world is a result of the great impact of the United Kingdom in the 19th century and that of the United States in the 20th century.

English, as an international language, or a world language, or even a global language, no longer belongs only to the native speakers of English. English has several dialects due to geographical reasons, for example, American English, British English, Australian English, Indian English, etc. There has appeared such a word as english, which implies it is a common language universally used. English can also be in the plural form. So the word "Englishes" implies the variety and diversity of the English language.

English, as an international language, is widely used in global trade market and world cultural circles. English has also shown its importance in the following four areas:
    1) the global audio-visual market and especially satellite TV;
    2) the Internet and computer-based communication, including language-related and document handling software;
    3) technology transfers and associated processes in economic globalization; and
    4) English language-study industry.

Together with French, Spanish, Russian, Arabic and Chinese, English is used as one of the six working languages in the United Nations and its subordinate organizations such as UNESCO, which stands for the United Nations Educational, Scientific and Cultural Organization.

English, as a natural language used by many people in the world, is different from Esperanto that is an artificial international language. It was invented by a Polish doctor, Ludovic Zamenhof (1859 – 1917). This invented language consists of parts of several languages, and was designed to help people from different countries communicate easily with one another. However, as it is an artificial language without culture and literature as its foundation, it falls short of the original expectations, and is seldom adopted in practical use.

Many non-native speakers of English study English as a foreign language. For instance, there are many Chinese students who are learning English. Chinese as their mother tongue is their source language, while English as their foreign language is their target language. In doing translation, source language refers to the language from which one translates, whereas target language refers to the language into which one translates. If a person translates a book from English into Chinese, English is the source language of the book and Chinese is its target language. A language may take a word from another and changes it into a part of its vocabulary. The words borrowed from other languages are called loanwords. The language from which a word is borrowed may also be referred to as the source language of the loanword. Sometimes, people study a third language by means of a second language or foreign language, which forms a medium language. For instance, if a Chinese student learns Swahili, an African language, by means of English, then English is his medium language while Swahili is his target language.

Some language students major or specialize in English. So English is their major or speciality. People learn English for Special Purposes(ESP, for short), for instance, some students learn business English. It is the English language used in business. Those non-English majors like science students learn English as service English. In China, the service English taught at universities and colleges is called College English.

Language is an instrument for communication. There are two ways of communication, that is, verbal means and non-verbal means. The verbal means of communication includes oral or spoken form and written form. So the students of English learn oral English or spoken English, and also learn written English. The non-verbal means of communication includes body language, signs and diagrams. Body language, including facial expressions and gestures, is the way in which people show their feelings or thoughts to other people by means of the position or movements of their bodies rather than with words. A sign is a mark or shape, which always has a generally-known meaning. A diagram is a simple drawing consisting mainly of lines. It often serves to explain how something works. As a sign and a diagram both have particular meanings, they can be used as non-verbal means of communication.

Words and Expressions

language *n*. a system of communication which consists of a set of sounds and written symbols that are used by the people of a particular country or a region for talking or writing 语言 *e.g.* the English language 英语语言

code *n*. any system of signs or symbols which has a meaning 代码;语码

language barrier *n*. a language problem which prevents two people or groups from agreeing or communicating with each other 语言障碍

foreign language *n*. a language which is spoken by the people from another country 外语

oral language *also* **spoken language** *n*. the spoken form, rather than the written form, of a language 口语 *e.g.* oral English; spoken English 英语口语

written language *n*. the written form, rather than the spoken form, of a language 书面语 *e.g.* written English 英语书面语

modern language *n*. a language that is still spoken at the present time 现代语言 *e.g.* modern English 现代英语

dead language *n*. a language that is no longer in use 不再通用的语言

Latin *n*. a dead language which the ancient Romans used to speak 拉丁语
English-speaking people *also* **English-speaking population** *n*. native speakers of English 母语是英语的人
mother tongue *also* **native tongue, native language** *n*. the language which people learned from their parents when they were children 母语；本族语 *syn*. **first language** 第一语言
non-native language *n*. the language which is not a person's native language 非本族语
first language *also* **L1** (*abbrev*.) *n*. the language which a person first learned as a child 第一语言
second language *also* **L2** (*abbrev*.) *n*. the language which people learned later than their first language 第二语言
medium of communication *n*. sth that people can use to communicate 交流媒介
English-speaking country *n*. a country in which English is spoken by people as their first language 英语国家
Canada *n*. a country in North America 加拿大
Australia *n*. a country in Oceania 澳大利亚
New Zealand *n*. a country in Oceania 新西兰
Ireland *n*. a country in the northwest of Europe 爱尔兰
South Africa *n*. a country located in the south of Africa, whose official full name is the Republic of South Africa 南非
Caribbean country *n*. any country in the Caribbean Sea 加勒比海国家
pronunciation *n*. the way in which a word of a language is usu. pronounced 发音
vocabulary *n*. the words in a language 词汇
grammar *n*. the rules of a language, relating to the way in which one can put words together in order to make sentences 语法
regional English *n*. the English language used in a special region 地区英语
British English *also* **BrE**. (*abbrev*.) *n*. the English language which is used in Britain 英国英语
American English *also* **AmE**. (*abbrev*.) *n*. the English language which is used in the United States 美国英语
London *n*. capital of the United Kingdom 伦敦
Newcastle *n*. a city in the north of England, U.K. 纽卡斯尔
Glasgow *n*. a city in Scotland, U.K. 格拉斯哥
Manchester *n*. a city in the northwest of England, U.K. 曼彻斯特
New England *n*. an area in the east of the United States 新英格兰
New York City *n*. a big city in the United States 纽约市
Americanism *n*. a word or phrase used in American English, but not in the standard English in Britain 美国词语
Anglophone *n*. the English language spoken by people in areas in which English is not the only language spoken 在英语不是唯一通行语言的地区的英语
bilingual *a*. involving or using two languages 双语的 *e.g*. bilingual country 双语国家
Canadian English *n*. the English language used in Canada 加拿大英语
Francophone *n*. the French language spoken by people in areas in which French is not the only language spoken 在法语不是唯一通行语言的地区的法语
Canadian French *n*. the French language used in Canada 加拿大法语
official language *n*. the legally-recognized language which is used in the formal situations such as government, law courts, newspapers, TV programmes, broadcasting, etc. 官方语言
multilingual *a*. involving or using many languages 多语的 *e.g*. multilingual country 多语国家
Republic of Singapore *n*. a southeastern Asian country 新加坡共和国
Malay *n*. the language of the Malays, which is also one of the four official languages of the Republic of Singapore 马来语

Tamil *n*. the language of the Tamils, which is also one of the four official languages of the Republic of Singapore 泰米尔语

national language *n*. the main language and standard language of a country, which is also the official language 国家语言

Commonwealth *n*. an international organization formed by Britain and countries which were once part of the British Empire 英联邦

colony *n*. a country or region controlled by a more powerful country, which uses the colony's resources in order to increase its own power or wealth 殖民地

Fiji *n*. a country of many islands in the South Pacific Ocean 斐济

Nigeria *n*. a country in Africa 尼日利亚

Teaching English as a Second Language *also* **TESL** (*abbrev.*) *n*. 作为第二语言的英语教学

India *n*. a country in South Asia 印度

Pakistan *n*. a country in South Asia 巴基斯坦

Sri Lanka *n*. a country in South Asia 斯里兰卡

Bangladesh *n*. a country in South Asia 孟加拉国

Malaysia *n*. a country in Southeast Asia 马来西亚

Zambia *n*. a country in East Africa 赞比亚

Uganda *n*. a country in East Africa 乌干达

the Sudan *n*. a country in North Africa 苏丹

Japan English *n*. a variety of English which includes expressions for things and concepts that are unique in Japan 日本英语

China English *n*. a variety of English which includes expressions for things and concepts that are unique in China 中国英语

intelligible *a*. understandable; that can be understood 可以理解的

acceptable *a*. that can be accepted 可以接受的

Chinese English *also* **Chinglish** *n*. the English spoken by some Chinese when they first learn English, which is not appropriate in use and not accepted by the native speakers of English 中国式英语

pidgin *n*. a language which is a mixture of two other languages, used when people from two different countries do business with each other 洋泾浜

Pidgin English *n*. a language containing elements of English and the local languages used in certain areas 洋泾浜英语

local language *n*. a language used in a particular area 地方语言

international language *n*. a language which is commonly used on an international scale 国际语言

Old English *also* **Anglo-Saxon** *n*. the language which was spoken in England between the 5th century A.D. and the Norman Conquest 古英语;盎格鲁撒克逊语

Middle English *n*. the English language which was spoken from the 12th century to the 15th century 中世纪英语

Modern English *n*. the English language which has been used since the 16th century 现代英语

Germanic *a*. that is used to describe the ancient culture and people of northern Europe, and the language they spoke, from which the modern Scandinavian languages and English, German and Dutch derive 日耳曼民族的 *e.g.* Germanic mythology 日耳曼神话

tribe *n*. a group of people of the same race, who share the same customs, religion, language, or land, esp. when they are not considered to have reached a very advanced level of civilization 部落 *e.g.* Germanic tribe 日耳曼部落

European Continent *also* **Old Continent**, **the Continent** *n*. the mainland of Europe, esp. central and southern Europe 欧洲大陆;旧大陆;大陆

colonization *n*. turning a place, area or country into a colony 殖民开拓;殖民化
seaboard *n*. the land along the coastline of a country, close to the sea, used esp. of the coast in North America 沿海地区 *e.g.* the eastern seaboard of North America 北美的东部沿海地区
world language *n*. a language which is commonly used on a worldwide scale 世界语言
global language *n*. a language which is commonly used on a global scale 全球通用语
dialect *n*. a form of a language which is spoken by a particular group of people, esp. those living in one area, which has different pronunciations, words, and grammar from other forms of the language 方言
Australian English *n*. the English language used in Australia 澳大利亚英语
Indian English *n*. the English language used in India 印度英语
english *n*. English written in small letter, as a common language which is universally used 英语(注意:这个词不要随意用,仅用于特殊情况,否则视为错误。)
Englishes *n*. English written in the plural form, implying the varieties of the English language 英语(注意:这个词不要随意用,仅用于特殊情况,否则视为错误。)
audio-visual market *n*. the market involving the sale of both recorded sound and pictures 视听产品市场
satellite TV *n*. television transmitted by television 卫星电视
Internet *n*. a large computer network that links smaller computer networks worldwide 互联网
technology transfer *n*. the transfer of the ownership of technology from one person or institution to another person or institution 技术转让
English language-study industry *n*. the teaching and learning of English, considered as an industry 英语语言教学产业
working language *n*. a language used by an international organization or international conference 工作语言
United Nations also **UN** (*abbrev.*) *n*. an international organization with many member countries, aiming at encouraging international peace, cooperation and friendship 联合国
United Nations Educational, Scientific and Cultural Organization also **UNESCO** (*abbrev.*) *n*. an international organization under the UN, which is aimed at promoting the international cooperation in education, science and culture 联合国教育、科学与文化组织;联合国教科文组织
natural language *n*. the language as a native language used by people in their everyday life, which is in contrast to artificial language 自然语言 *syn*. **ordinary language** 普通语言
artificial language *n*. a language invented by man for the sake of promoting international communication, which, in contrast to natural language, doesn't exist as a native language with culture and literature as its foundation 人造语言
Esperanto *n*. an artificial international language invented by Ludovic Zamenhof for the purpose of helping people from different countries to communicate easily with one another 世界语
Ludovic Zamenhof (1859-1917) *n*. a Polish doctor, who invented Esperanto 柴门霍夫
non-native speaker of English *n*. a person whose mother tongue is not English 母语不是英语的人
source language *n*. the language from which one translates, or from which a loanword comes, which is in contrast to target language 源语
target language *n*. the foreign language which one learns, or the language into which one translates, which is in contrast to source language 目标语;目的语
medium language *n*. a second language or a foreign language, by means of which one learns a third language 媒介语
Swahili *n*. an African language 斯瓦希里语
loanword *n*. a word taken into a language from another 借词;外来语
English for Special Purposes also **ESP** (*abbrev.*) *n*. the English language taught, learned and used for special purposes, like tourism and foreign trade 专门用途英语
business English *n*. the English language used in business, which is a kind of English taught and learnt for

a special purpose 商务英语

service English n. the English language learned by the non-English majors 公共英语

College English n. the service English taught at universities and colleges in China 大学英语

verbal means of communication n. communication by way of words in oral or written form 言语性交流手段

non-verbal means of communication n. communication by ways other than words in spoken and written forms, including body language, signs and diagrams 非言语性交流手段

body language n. the use of bodily movements and signs as a way of expressing one's feelings or intentions without using words 身体语言；体态语

facial expression n. expression on the face 面部表情

gesture n. a movement that a person makes with a part of his body, esp. his hands or his head, to express emotion or information, either instead of speaking or while he is speaking 姿势；手势

sign n. a mark or shape with a particular meaning 符号

diagram n. a simple drawing consisting mainly of lines, which is often used to explain how sth works 图解

primitive a. of the earliest stage of development, esp. of life or of human beings 原始的

ape n. a large monkey without a tail or with a very short tail, such as a gorilla or chimpanzee 猿

gorilla n. a kind of ape 大猩猩

chimpanzee n. a kind of ape 黑猩猩

division of labour n. a way of organizing a society or a household so that each member has a particular task to do and therefore contributes to the running of the society or household 劳动分工

vocal sound n. sound made by the use of human voice 嗓音

derivative a. that is not new or original but has been developed from sth else 模仿的；缺乏创意的

community n. people who live in a particular area and who are alike in some way 社会；社区；群体 e.g. primitive community 原始群体

sign language n. a method of communicating by using movements of human hands and arms 手语 e.g. sign language of deaf and dumb people 聋哑人手语

Additional Knowledge

What is Language?

It is language, more obviously than anything else, that distinguishes man from the rest of the animal world. At one time it was common to define man as a thinking animal, but we can hardly imagine thought without words. More recently, man has often been described as a tool-making animal; but language itself is the most remarkable tool that man has invented, and is the one that makes all the others possible. The most primitive tools, admittedly, may have appeared earlier than language; the higher apes sometimes use sticks for digging, and have even been observed to break sticks for this purpose. But tools of any greater sophistication demand the kind of human co-operation and division of labour which is hardly possible without language. Language, in fact, is the great machine tool which makes human culture possible.

A human language is a signaling system. As its materials, it uses vocal sounds. It is important to remember that basically a language is something that is spoken: the written language is secondary and derivative. In the history of each individual, speech is learned before writing, and there is good reason for believing that the same was true in the history of the race. There are primitive communities that have speech without writing, but we know of no human society, which has a written language without a spoken one. Such things as the sign language of deaf and dumb people are not exceptions to this rule; even if used by people who cannot speak, and have never been able to speak, these languages are derived from the spoken language of the community around them.

Exercises

I. Explain each of the following:
1) English-speaking country
2) mother tongue
3) British English
4) Canadian French
5) regional English
6) official language
7) bilingual country
8) Anglophone
9) Pidgin English
10) local language
11) english
12) Englishes
13) working language
14) Esperanto
15) target language
16) medium language
17) Swahili
18) English major
19) science student
20) service English
21) business English
22) College English
23) oral English
24) written English
25) body language
26) facial expression
27) gesture
28) code
29) sign
30) diagram

II. Tell what each of the following stands for:
Model: TV → television
1) L1 →
2) L2 →
3) TESL →
4) ESP →
5) BrE. →
6) AmE. →
7) IT →
8) PC →
9) CBD →
10) UFO →

III. Give another way or other ways of saying each of the following:
Models: oral language → spoken language
mother tongue → native tongue, native language
1) English-speaking population →
2) Chinglish →
3) Anglo-Saxon →
4) Old Continent →
5) ordinary language →

IV. Answer the following questions:
1) In what ways does British English differ from American English?
2) What are the official languages of Canada?
3) Who speak English as their second language?
4) Can you give the names of some Asian countries?

5) Can you give the names of some countries in Africa where they used to have English as their official language?
6) Does the Japanese people speak English as their second language?
7) What is the difference between China English and Chinese English?
8) Is Chinglish acceptable to the native speakers of English?
9) Why is English considered as an international language?
10) For what reason has English become the first international language?
11) What are the three kinds of people who speak English?
12) Can you tell in what areas English is widely used?
13) What are the six working languages of the United Nations?
14) Can you give the original full name of UNESCO?
15) Who invented Esperanto?
16) Where is Poland?
17) What are the two ways of communication?
18) What does the verbal means of communication include?
19) What does the non-verbal means of communication include?
20) What does body language include?

Lesson Two

The English-Speaking Countries

The first English-speaking country is Britain where the English language was originated. Its official full name is the United Kingdom of Great Britain and Northern Ireland. Its official simple form is the United Kingdom. And U. K. is the shortened or abbreviated word of United Kingdom.

The British Empire is a historical conception, with a broader sense than the United Kingdom. It used to cover a larger territory, including Britain itself and its former colonies. Now Britain and some of its former colonies have formed the British Commonwealth of Nations, which can be simply called the British Commonwealth, or the Commonwealth. It is an international organization in which Britain and other member countries carry out political and economic consultation and cooperation. The Commonwealth consists of the United Kingdom, other English-speaking countries like Canada, Australia, and New Zealand, African countries like Nigeria, Zambia, Uganda and the Sudan, Asian countries like India, Pakistan, Sri Lanka, and Singapore, and American countries in the West Indies.

Britain is made up of four parts. They are England, Scotland, Wales and Northern Ireland. The first three nations constitute Great Britain, located on the largest island of the British Isles. Geographically, the British Isles refer to the group of islands on the northwest of Europe, which includes Great Britain, Ireland, and the smaller islands around them. In the geographical sense, Great Britain is a name frequently-used to refer to the island consisting of England, Scotland and Wales, which together with Northern Ireland make up the United Kingdom. But Great Britain is often incorrectly used to refer to the political state, officially called the United Kingdom of Great Britain and Northern Ireland. Normally, people simply call it Britain. So, Britain in the political sense may include Northern Ireland, which is actually part of the United Kingdom. As to the Irish Island, it refers to the whole of Ireland. On its northern part is located Northern Ireland which is a part of the United Kingdom, while on its southern part is located the Republic of Eire or the Republic of Ireland which has been an independent country since 1949.

Look at the first chart:

Britain and Its People

Country	Nationality		
Britain	the British; the British people	He/She is British.	He/She is a Briton. (*BrE.*) He/She is a Britisher. (*AmE.*)
England	the English; the English people	He is English.	He is an Englishman. She is an Englishwoman.
Scotland	the Scots; the Scottish; the Scottish people	He is Scottish.	He is a Scot/Scotsman. She is a Scot/Scotswoman.

Country	Nationality		
Wales	the Welsh; the Welsh people	He is Welsh.	He is a Welshman. She is a Welshwoman.
Northern Ireland	the Irish; the Irish people	He is Irish.	He is an Irishman. She is an Irishwoman.

The British population consists of the English people, the Scottish people, the Welsh people and the Irish people. Some scholars say that Britain is one kingdom of four countries or four nations, because many of the Scots, Welshmen and Irishmen still have a strong sense of national independence. So we mustn't refer to a Scotsman, a Welshman or an Irishman as an Englishman, which will annoy them greatly. They dislike being called English even if they live in England. A Briton is a person who comes from Great Britain or who is a citizen of the United Kingdom. And a Britisher also refers to a person who comes from Great Britain or who is a citizen of the United Kingdom, and it is an informal word found only in American English, but not used by the British people. An Englishman is a British male citizen born in England or a British male citizen of English parent or parents. An Englishwoman is such a British female citizen. A Scot is a person who comes from Scotland. A Scotsman is a male who comes from Scotland. And a Scotswoman is a female who comes from Scotland. A Welshman is a male who comes from Wales. And a Welshwoman is a female who comes from Wales. An Irishman is a man who comes from the Republic of Ireland, or Northern Ireland which is a part of the United Kingdom. And an Irishwoman is a woman who comes from the Republic of Ireland or Northern Ireland.

Look the second chart:

The Four Countries of Britain and Their Languages

Country	Languages
England	English
Scotland	English & Gaelic by Scottish Celts
Wales	English & Welsh
Northern Ireland	English & Gaelic by Irish Celts

Celtic, as a general term, is used to refer to a group of related languages which are or were once spoken in Scotland, Wales, Ireland and some other areas. Gaelic, as a specific term, is used to refer to any of the Celtic languages, especially that of Scotland, or that of Ireland. The Gaelic language spoken in Ireland is also called Erse.

Celts are people from Scotland, Wales, Ireland and some other areas. The Celts from Scotland are called Scottish Celts. And the Celts from Ireland are called Irish Celts.

Wales is a bilingual country with two official languages, Welsh and English. Welsh is the language spoken by the Welsh people in some parts of Wales.

In Britain, when people talk about the Continent, they mean the European Continent, that is, the mainland of Europe, especially Western Europe. The European Continent is also called the Old Continent, which is in contrast to the New Continent—the American Continent. Between Britain and the European Continent there is the English Channel or the Channel. It is the narrow area of water between England and France, which joins the North Sea to the Atlantic

Ocean. Historically, the Old World refers to the eastern hemisphere of the world, especially Asia, Europe and Africa. When the British people say the Far East, they mean China, Japan and the other countries of East and Southeast Asia. They loosely call the area comprising Egypt, Iran and the countries between them the Middle East or the Near East.

The American Continent, including North America, Central America and South America, is called the New Continent or the New World. Between Britain and America there is the Atlantic Ocean, which can be simply called the Atlantic.

Another important English-speaking country is the United States which is located in North America. Its official full name is the United States of America. It can be simply called the United States. The British call it the States. Its shortened form is U. S. A. or U. S. It can also be called America. Actually, America is a big conception. It may refer to the whole American Continent, including North America, Central America and South America. America, as a whole continent, is bounded throughout by the Atlantic Ocean on the east and the Pacific Ocean on the west. When America is used only to refer to the United States, it is disliked by the people from other countries of North, Central and South America. Latin America refers to the countries of South America, Central America and Mexico, because Spanish or Portuguese that was developed from Latin is the official language in these countries.

The United States is a country of multi-cultures and multi-races. An American is a person who comes from the United States. In a broad sense, an American can also refer to a person from North, Central or South America. A Yank is a person from the United States, which is a slightly offensive word used mainly in British English. A Yankee also refers to a citizen from the United States, and especially a person born or living in the northern or northeastern states of the United States, which is a word used mainly in American English. The original inhabitants of America were called Native Americans, or American Indians. The shortened form of American Indian is Amerindian. A Native American or an American Indian is a person from one of the first groups of people who lived in America before white people arrived there. These expressions are used especially about people from South America and sometimes considered offensive. In the 17th century, the colonists from Britain came to settle in North America and colonized it. In the 18th century, the colonists traded slaves from Africa. The American Blacks are called African Americans or Afro-Americans. An African American or an Afro-American is a black American whose family originally came from Africa, especially as slaves. In the 19th century and the 20th century, there were several immigration tides. Immigrants from every corner of the world came to settle in the United States. People who originally came from Mexico or whose family originally came from Mexico are called Chicanos; while people who originally came from Latin America or whose family originally came from Latin America, are called Latinos. Immigrants from Asian countries are called Asian Americans. Those Americans of Chinese descent are called Chinese Americans. Those Chinese Americans who were born in the United States are called American-born Chinese, or ABC for short.

Canada is another English-speaking country, which is located to the north of the United States in North America. Australia and New Zealand are two English-speaking countries, which are located in Oceania or Oceanica. Ireland is also an English-speaking country, which is a neighbouring country of Britain. It is located in the southern part of the Irish Island. South Africa is also an English-speaking country, which is located in the southern part of Africa. Its official full name is the Republic of South Africa.

Look at the third chart:

Other Main English-Speaking Countries

Country	Nationality		Official Languages
America	the Americans; the American people	an American	English
Australia	the Australians; the Australian people	an Australian	English
Canada	the Canadians; the Canadian people	a Canadian	English, French
Ireland	the Irish; the Irish people	an Irishman/Irishwoman	Irish, English
New Zealand	the New Zealanders; the New Zealand people	a New Zealander	English

Geographically, the Western countries refer to those countries located in the western part of the world, mainly in Europe and North America. Politically and ideologically, the Western countries originally referred to the non-Communist countries of Europe and North America. It may also constitute a contrast in culture with the Oriental countries, especially China. The Western Powers have become a political term, referring to such countries as the United States, Britain, Canada, Australia, France, Germany, Italy and Japan. These countries have loosely formed a political and economic alliance. Very often, people use a general term "the West", to refer to the Western countries. Western culture refers to the way in which the people of Europe and North America live, especially to their political and economic systems, attitudes and technology. Westernization refers to bringing to other countries the customs, habits, ideas, behaviours, attitudes and business methods that are typical of Europe and the United States. Traditionally, Britain and the United States have had close relationships with the European Continental countries. European Union is an organization of European countries that have joint policies on matters such as trade, agriculture and finance. NATO is an abbreviation of the North Atlantic Treaty Organization. It is a military organization formed by a group of countries including the United States, Canada, Britain, France, Germany, Spain, Italy and several other European countries. They have agreed to give military support to one another if they are attacked.

Some European countries are multilingual countries. Switzerland and Belgium are both trilingual countries. Switzerland has French, German and Italian as its official languages. Belgium has French, Dutch and German as its official languages.

Look at the fourth chart:

The Main European Countries

Country	Nationality		Official Languages
Austria	the Austrians; the Austrian people	an Austrian	German

Country	Nationality		Official Languages
Albania	the Albanians; the Albanian people	an Albanian	Albanian
Belgium	the Belgians; the Belgian people	a Belgian	French, Dutch, German
Bulgaria	the Bulgarians; the Bulgarian people	a Bulgarian	Bulgarian
Czech	the Czechs; the Czech people	a Czech	Czech
Denmark	the Danes; the Danish; the Danish people	a Dane	Danish
Finland	the Finns; the Finnish; the Finnish people	a Finn	Finnish
France	the French; the French people	a Frenchman/Frenchwoman	French
Germany	the Germans; the German people	a German	German
Greece	the Greeks; the Greek people	a Greek	Greek
Holland, the Netherlands	the Dutch; the Dutch people	a Dutch/Dutchman/Dutchwoman; a Hollander; a Netherlander	Dutch
Hungary	the Hungarians; the Hungarian people	a Hungarian	Hungarian
Italy	the Italians; the Italian people	an Italian	Italian
Luxembourg	the Luxembourgers; the Luxembourg people	a Luxembourger	German
Norway	the Norwegians; the Norwegian people	a Norwegian	Norwegian
Poland	the Poles; the Polish people	a Pole	Polish
Portugal	the Portuguese; the Portuguese people	a Portuguese	Portuguese
Romania	the Romanians; the Romanian people	a Romanian	Romanian

Country	Nationality		Official Languages
Russia	the Russians; the Russian people	a Russian	Russian
Slovakia	the Slovaks; the Slovakians; the Slovakian people	a Slovak; a Slovakian	Slovak
Spain	the Spaniards; the Spanish; the Spanish people	a Spaniard	Spanish
Sweden	the Swedes; the Swedish; the Swedish people	a Swede	Swedish
Switzerland	the Swiss; the Swiss people	a Swiss	French, German, Italian
Turkey	the Turks; the Turkish people	a Turk	Turkish

Words and Expressions

the United Kingdom of Great Britain and Northern Ireland *n*. the official full name of Britain 大不列颠及北爱尔兰联合王国

the United Kingdom *also* **U. K.** (*abbrev*.) *n*. the official simple form of the United Kingdom of Great Britain and Northern Ireland 联合王国

U. K. *n*. the abbreviated word of the United Kingdom 联合王国

Great Britain *also* **GB** (*abbrev*.) *n*. the island consisting of England, Scotland and Wales, which together with Northern Ireland makes up the United Kingdom 大不列颠

Britain *n*. the geographical areas of England, Wales and Scotland; or the political state, with its official full name as the United Kingdom of Great Britain and Northern Ireland 不列颠;英国

Northern Ireland *n*. a component part of the United Kingdom of Great Britain and Northern Ireland, which is located in the north of the Irish Island 北爱尔兰

shortened word *also* **abbreviated word**, **abbreviation** *n*. a word made by leaving out some of the letters or a short form of a phrase by using only the first letters of each word 缩略词

the British Empire *n*. a historical conception, with a broader sense than the United Kingdom, covering a larger territory, including Britain itself and its former colonies 英帝国

the British Commonwealth of Nations *also* **the British Commonwealth**, **the Commonwealth** *n*. an association of Britain and some of its former colonies which still have political, economic and other links with one another 英联邦

the West Indies *n*. a group of islands extending in a curve between North and South America 西印度群岛

England *n*. a part of the United Kingdom, located in the south of the British Isles 英格兰

Scotland *n*. a part of the United Kingdom, located in the north of the British Isles 苏格兰

Wales *n*. a part of the United Kingdom, located in the southwest of the British Isles 威尔士

the British Isles *n*. the group of islands on the northwest of Europe, which includes Great Britain, Ireland, and the smaller islands around them 不列颠群岛

the Irish Island *n*. an island of the British Isles, in the southern part of which is located the Republic of Ireland, and in the northern part of which is located Northern Ireland, a component part of the United Kingdom 爱尔兰岛

the Republic of Eire *also* **the Republic of Ireland** *n*. a country located in the southern part of the Irish Island 爱尔兰共和国

chart *n*. a diagram, picture, or graph which makes information easy to understand 图表

nationality *n*. the country which a person belongs to 国籍

nation *n*. a country, together with its political and social structure; the people who live in a country 国家；民族

British *a*. that belongs or relates to Britain 英国的 *e.g.* the British people 英国人民

the British *also* **the British people** *n*. the people who come from or live in Britain 英国人民

Briton *BrE*. *n*. a person who comes from Britain 英国人

Britisher *AmE*. *n*. a person who comes from Britain 英国人

English *a*. that belongs or relates to England, or to its people or language 英格兰的；英格兰人的；英语的 *e.g.* the English people 英格兰人民; the English language 英语语言

the English *also* **the English people** *n*. the people who come from or live in England 英格兰人民

Englishman *n*. a man who comes from England 英格兰男人

Englishwoman *n*. a woman who comes from England 英格兰女人

Scottish *a*. that belongs or relates to Scotland, or to its people 苏格兰的；苏格兰人的 *e.g.* the Scottish people 苏格兰人民

the Scottish *also* **the Scottish people**, **the Scots** *n*. the people who come from or live in Scotland 苏格兰人民

Scot *n*. a person who comes from Scotland 苏格兰人

Scotsman *n*. a man who comes from Scotland 苏格兰男人

Scotswoman *n*. a woman who comes from Scotland 苏格兰女人

Welsh *a*. that belongs or relates to Wales, or to its people or language 威尔士的；威尔士人的；威尔士语的 *e.g.* the Welsh people 威尔士人民; the Welsh language 威尔士语

the Welsh *also* **the Welsh people** *n*. the people who come from or live in Wales 威尔士人民

Welshman *n*. a man who comes from Wales 威尔士男人

Welshwoman *n*. a woman who comes from Wales 威尔士女人

Welsh *n*. the language spoken by the Welsh people in some parts of Wales 威尔士语

Irish *a*. that belongs or relates to the Republic of Ireland or to Northern Ireland which is part of the United Kingdom, or to its people or language 爱尔兰的；爱尔兰人的；爱尔兰语的 *e.g.* the Irish people 爱尔兰人民; the Irish language 爱尔兰语

the Irish *also* **the Irish people** *n*. the people who come from or live in the Republic of Ireland or Northern Ireland 爱尔兰人民

Irishman *n*. a man who comes from the Republic of Ireland or Northern Ireland 爱尔兰男人

Irishwoman *n*. a woman who comes from the Republic of Ireland or Northern Ireland 爱尔兰女人

Irish *n*. the language spoken by the Irish people 爱尔兰语

national independence *n*. the independence of a nation that has its own government and is not ruled by any other country 民族独立

citizen *n*. a person of a particular country, who is legally accepted as belonging to that country 公民 *e.g.* British citizen 英国公民

Celtic *also* **the Celtic languages** *n*. a group of related languages which are or were once spoken in Scotland, Wales, Ireland and some other areas 凯尔特语

Gaelic *also* **the Gaelic language** *n*. a language spoken by people in parts of Scotland and Ireland, belonging to the Celtic languages 盖尔语

Erse *n.* the Gaelic language spoken in Ireland 爱尔兰盖尔语
Celts *n.* people from Scotland, Wales, Ireland and some other areas, who speak Celtic 凯尔特人
Scottish Celts *n.* the Celts from Scotland, who speak Gaelic 苏格兰凯尔特人
Irish Celts *n.* the Celts from Ireland, who speak Erse 爱尔兰凯尔特人
the European Continent *also* **the Continent** *n.* the mainland of Europe, esp. Western Europe 欧洲大陆
the Old Continent *n.* another way of saying the European Continent, which is in contrast to the New Continent 旧大陆
the English Channel *also* **the Channel** *n.* the narrow area of water between England and France, which joins the North Sea to the Atlantic Ocean 英吉利海峡
the North Sea *n.* the shallow water area between the east coast of Britain and the European Continent 北海
the Atlantic Ocean *also* **the Atlantic** *n.* one of the great oceans of the globe, separating the Old World and the New World 大西洋
the Old World *n.* the eastern hemisphere of the world, esp. Asia, Europe and Africa 旧大陆
the Far East *n.* the countries in Asia east of India, such as China, Japan, the Democratic People's Republic of Korea, the Republic of Korea and all the Southeast Asian countries, in contrast to the Middle East and the Near East, so called from the point of view of the British people 远东
the Middle East *also* **the Near East** *n.* a part of Asia, including Iran and all the countries in Asia which are to the west and southwest of Iran, in contrast to the Far East, so called from the point of view of the British people 中东;近东
the Near East *n.* another way of saying the Middle East 近东
the American Continent *also* **the New Continent** *n.* the land mass of North America, Central America and South America 美洲大陆;新大陆
the New Continent *n.* another way of saying the American Continent 新大陆
the New World *n.* the western hemisphere of the world, esp. the land mass of North and South America 新大陆 *syn.* **the American Continent, the New Continent** 美洲大陆;新大陆
the United States of America *also* **U.S.A.** (*abbrev.*) *n.* the official full name of America, which is located in North America 美利坚合众国
U.S.A. *n.* the abbreviated word of the United States of America 美国
the United States *also* **U.S.** (*abbrev.*) *n.* the official simple form of the United States of America 美利坚合众国;美国
U.S. *n.* the abbreviated word of the United States of America 美国
the States *n.* a way of saying the United States, often so called by the British people 美国 *syn.* **the United States** 美国
America *n.* a simple form of saying the United States of America 美国;or the whole American Continent, including North America, Central America and South America 美洲
the Pacific Ocean *also* **the Pacific** *n.* the largest water area on the globe, lying between Asia and Australia on the west, and North and South America on the east 太平洋
Latin America *n.* the countries of South America, Central America and Mexico, where Spanish or Portuguese that was developed from Latin is the official language in these countries 拉丁美洲
multi-cultures *n.* a situation in which there exist many cultures in a country or society with equal rights and opportunities and with none of them being ignored or regarded as unimportant 多元文化
multi-races *n.* a situation in which there exist many racial groups in a country or society 多种族
American *n.* a person who comes from North, Central or South America, esp. a person who comes from the United States 美洲人;美国人
Yank *n.* a person from the United States, which is a slightly offensive word used mainly in British English 美国佬

Yankee *n*. a person from the United States 美国佬; esp. a person from the northern and northeastern United States 美国北方佬

Native American *also* **American Indian, Amerindian** *n*. an original inhabitant of America, a person from one of the first groups of people who lived in America before white people arrived there 美洲印第安人; 美国印第安人

American Indian *n*. another way of saying Native American 美洲印第安人; 美国印第安人

Amerindian *n*. the shortened form of American Indian 美洲印第安人; 美国印第安人

colonist *n*. a person who starts a colony or who is one of the first group of people to settle in it 殖民者

colonize *v*. turn a place, area or country into a colony 将……开拓为殖民地

slave *n*. a person who belongs to sb else as their property and has to work for them 奴隶 *e.g.* to trade slaves from Africa 从非洲贩卖奴隶

American Black *also* **African American, Afro-American** *n*. a black person living in the United States who comes from Africa or whose family originally came from Africa 美国黑人

African American *also* **Afro-American** *n*. a black American whose family originally came from Africa, esp. as slaves 非洲裔美国人

Afro-American *n*. another way of saying African American 非洲裔美国人

immigration *n*. the coming of people into a country in order to live and work there 移民

immigration tide *n*. the coming of large numbers of people into a country in order to live and work there 移民浪潮

immigrant *n*. a person who has come to settle in a country from another 移民

Chicano *n*. an American citizen who originally came from Mexico or whose family originally came from Mexico 墨西哥裔美国人

Latino *n*. an American citizen who originally came from Latin America or whose family originally came from Latin America 拉美裔美国人

Asian American *n*. an American citizen who originally came from an Asian country or whose family originally came from an Asian country 亚洲裔美国人

Chinese American *n*. an American citizen who originally came from China or whose family originally came from China 美籍华人; 华裔美国人

American-born Chinese *also* **ABC** (*abbrev.*) *n*. a Chinese American who was born in the United States 美国出生的华人

ABC *n*. an abbreviation of American-born Chinese 美国出生的华人

descent *n*. family origin 血统; 祖籍 *e.g.* Chinese descent 中国血统

Oceania *also* **Oceanica** *n*. a geographical area of the south and central Pacific Ocean 大洋洲

the Republic of South Africa *n*. the official full name of South Africa 南非共和国

Western country *n*. a country in the western part of the world, esp. one in North America or Europe 西方国家

Communist country *n*. a country which followed the principles of communism, like the former Soviet Union and other eastern European countries 共产主义国家

non-Communist country *n*. a country which is not a Communist country 非共产主义国家

Oriental country *also* **Eastern country** *n*. a country in the eastern part of the world, esp. an Asian country like China 东方国家

Power *n*. a country which has influence and control 大国; 强国 *e.g.* Western Powers 西方大国; 西方列强

alliance *n*. a close agreement or connection made between countries, groups, families, etc. for a shared purpose or for the protection of their interests 同盟 *e.g.* political alliance 政治同盟; economic alliance 经济同盟

the West *n*. a general term for the Western countries 西方国家

Western culture *n*. the way in which the people of Europe and North America live, esp. their political and economic systems, attitudes and technology 西方文化

Westernization *n*. introducing into a society, a place, a system, or a country ideology and behaviour which are common in Europe and the United States, so that people who originally had different traditions change their habits or attitudes 西方化;西化

the European Union also **E. U.** (*abbrev*.) *n*. an organization of European countries which have joint policies on matters such as trade, agriculture and finance 欧盟

the North Atlantic Treaty Organization also **NATO** (*abbrev*.) *n*. a military organization formed by a group of countries including the United States, Canada, the United Kingdom and several other European countries 北大西洋公约组织

NATO *n*. an abbreviation of the North Atlantic Treaty Organization 北约

Austria *n*. a European country 奥地利

Austrian *a*. that belongs or relates to Austria, or to its people 奥地利的;奥地利人的 *e.g.* the Austrian people 奥地利人民

the Austrians also **the Austrian people** *n*. the people who come from or live in Austria 奥地利人民

Austrian *n*. a person who comes from Austria 奥地利人

Albania *n*. a European country 阿尔巴尼亚

Albanian *a*. that belongs or relates to Albania, or to its people or language 阿尔巴尼亚的;阿尔巴尼亚人的;阿尔巴尼亚语的 *e.g.* the Albanian people 阿尔巴尼亚人民;the Albanian language 阿尔巴尼亚语

the Albanians also **the Albanian people** *n*. the people who come from or live in Albania 阿尔巴尼亚人民

Albanian *n*. a person who comes from Albania 阿尔巴尼亚人;or the language spoken by the Albanian people 阿尔巴尼亚语

Belgium *n*. a European country 比利时

Belgian *a*. that belongs or relates to Belgium, or to its people 比利时的;比利时人的 *e.g.* the Belgian people 比利时人民

the Belgians also **the Belgian people** *n*. the people who come from or live in Belgium 比利时人民

Belgian *n*. a person who comes from Belgium 比利时人

Bulgaria *n*. a European country 保加利亚

Bulgarian *a*. that belongs or relates to Bulgaria, or to its people or language 保加利亚的;保加利亚人的;保加利亚语的 *e.g.* the Bulgarian people 保加利亚人民;the Bulgarian language 保加利亚语

the Bulgarians also **the Bulgarian people** *n*. the people who come from or live in Bulgaria 保加利亚人民

Bulgarian *n*. a person who comes from Bulgaria 保加利亚人;or the language spoken by the Bulgarian people 保加利亚语

Czech *n*. a European country 捷克

Czech *a*. that belongs or relates to Czech, or to its people or language 捷克的;捷克人的;捷克语的 *e.g.* the Czech people 捷克人民;the Czech language 捷克语

the Czechs also **the Czech people** *n*. the people who come from or live in Czech 捷克人民

Czech *n*. a person who comes from Czech 捷克人;or the language spoken by the Czech people 捷克语

Denmark *n*. a European country 丹麦

Danish *a*. that belongs or relates to Denmark, or to its people or language 丹麦的;丹麦人的;丹麦语的 *e.g.* the Danish people 丹麦人民;the Danish language 丹麦语

the Danes also **the Danish**, **the Danish people** *n*. the people who come from or live in Denmark 丹麦人民

Dane *n*. a person who comes from Denmark 丹麦人

Danish *n*. the language spoken by the Danish people 丹麦语

Finland *n*. a European country 芬兰

Finnish *a*. that belongs or relates to Finland, or to its people or language 芬兰的;芬兰人的;芬兰语的 *e.*

  g. the Finnish people 芬兰人民；the Finnish language 芬兰语
the Finns *also* **the Finnish, the Finnish people** *n*. the people who come from or live in Finland 芬兰人民
Finn *n*. a person who comes from Finland 芬兰人
Finnish *n*. the language spoken by the Finnish people 芬兰语
France *n*. a European country 法国
French *a*. that belongs or relates to France, or to its people or language 法国的；法国人的；法语 *e.g.*
  the French people 法国人民；the French language 法语
the French *also* **the French people** *n*. the people who come from or live in France 法国人民
Frenchman *n*. a man who comes from France 法国男人
Frenchwoman *n*. a woman who comes from France 法国女人
French *n*. the language spoken by the French people 法语
Germany *n*. a European country 德国
German *a*. that belongs or relates to Germany, or to its people or language 德国的；德国人的；德语 *e.g.*
  the German people 德国人民；the German language 德语
the Germans *also* **the German people** *n*. the people who come from or live in Germany 德国人民
German *n*. a person who comes from Germany 德国人；or the language spoken by the German people 德语
Greece *n*. a European country 希腊
Greek *a*. that belongs or relates to Greece, or to its people or language 希腊的；希腊人的；希腊语的 *e.g.*
  the Greek people 希腊人民；the Greek language 希腊语
the Greeks *also* **the Greek people** *n*. the people who come from or live in Greece 希腊人民
Greek *n*. a person who comes from Greece 希腊人；or the language spoken by the Greek people 希腊语
Holland *also* **the Netherlands** *n*. a European country 荷兰
Dutch *a*. that belongs or relates to Holland, or to its people or language 荷兰的；荷兰人的；荷兰语的 *e.g.*
  the Dutch people 荷兰人民；the Dutch language 荷兰语
the Dutch *also* **the Dutch people** *n*. the people who come from or live in Holland 荷兰人民
Dutch *also* **Hollander, Netherlander** *n*. a person who comes from Holland 荷兰人
Dutchman *n*. a man who comes from Holland 荷兰男人
Dutchwoman *n*. a woman who comes from Holland 荷兰女人
Dutch *n*. the language spoken by the Dutch people 荷兰语
Hungary *n*. a European country 匈牙利
Hungarian *a*. that belongs or relates to Hungary, or to its people or language 匈牙利的；匈牙利人的；匈牙
  利语的 *e.g.* the Hungarian people 匈牙利人民；the Hungarian language 匈牙利语
the Hungarians *also* **the Hungarian people** *n*. the people who come from or live in Hungary 匈牙利人民
Hungarian *n*. a person who comes from Hungary 匈牙利人；or the language spoken by the Hungarian
  people 匈牙利语
Italy *n*. a European country 意大利
Italian *a*. that belongs or relates to Italy, or to its people or language 意大利的；意大利人的；意大利语的
  e.g. the Italian people 意大利人民；the Italian language 意大利语
the Italians *also* **the Italian people** *n*. the people who come from or live in Italy 意大利人民
Italian *n*. a person who comes from Italy 意大利人；or the language spoken by the Italian people 意大利语
Luxembourg *n*. a European country 卢森堡
Luxembourg *a*. that belongs or relates to Luxembourg, or to its people 卢森堡的；卢森堡人的 *e.g.* the
  Luxembourg people 卢森堡人民
the Luxembourgers *also* **the Luxembourg people** *n*. the people who come from or live in Luxembourg 卢森堡
  人民
Luxembourger *n*. a person who comes from Luxembourg 卢森堡人

Norway n. a European country 挪威

Norwegian a. that belongs or relates to Norway, or to its people or language 挪威的；挪威人的；挪威语的 e.g. the Norwegian people 挪威人民；the Norwegian language 挪威语

the Norwegians also **the Norwegian people** n. the people who come from or live in Norway 挪威人民

Norwegian n. a person who comes from Norway 挪威人；or the language spoken by the Norwegian people 挪威语

Poland n. a European country 波兰

Polish a. that belongs or relates to Poland, or to its people or language 波兰的；波兰人的；波兰语的 e.g. the Polish people 波兰人民；the Polish language 波兰语

the Poles also **the Polish people** n. the people who come from or live in Poland 波兰人民

Pole n. a person who comes from Poland 波兰人

Polish n. the language spoken by the Polish people 波兰语

Portugal n. a European country 葡萄牙

Portuguese a. that belongs or relates to Portugal, or to its people or language 葡萄牙的；葡萄牙人的；葡萄牙语的 e.g. the Portuguese people 葡萄牙人民；the Portuguese language 葡萄牙语

the Portuguese also **the Portuguese people** n. the people who come from or live in Portugal 葡萄牙人民

Portuguese n. a person who comes from Portugal 葡萄牙人；or the language spoken by the Portuguese people 葡萄牙语

Romania n. a European country 罗马尼亚

Romanian a. that belongs or relates to Romania, or to its people or language 罗马尼亚的；罗马尼亚人的；罗马尼亚语的 e.g. the Romanian people 罗马尼亚人民；the Romanian language 罗马尼亚语

the Romanians also **the Romanian people** n. the people who come from or live in Romania 罗马尼亚人民

Romanian n. a person who comes from Romania 罗马尼亚人；or the language spoken by the Romanian people 罗马尼亚语

Russia n. a European country 俄罗斯；俄国

Russian a. that belongs or relates to Russia, or to its people or language 俄罗斯的；俄罗斯人的；俄语的 e.g. the Russian people 俄罗斯人民；the Russian language 俄语

the Russians also **the Russian people** n. the people who come from or live in Russia 俄罗斯人民

Russian n. a person who comes from Russia 俄罗斯人；or the language spoken by the Russian people 俄语

Slovakia n. a European country 斯洛伐克

Slovakian a. that belongs or relates to Slovakia, or to its people or language 斯洛伐克的；斯洛伐克人的；斯洛伐克语的 e.g. the Slovakian people 斯洛伐克人民；the Slovakian language 斯洛伐克语

the Slovaks also **the Slovakians, the Slovakian people** n. the people who come from or live in Slovakia 斯洛伐克人民

Slovak also **Slovakian** n. a person who comes from Slovakia 斯洛伐克人

Slovak n. the language spoken by the Slovakian people 斯洛伐克语

Spain n. a European country 西班牙

Spanish a. that belongs or relates to Spain, or to its people or language 西班牙的；西班牙人的；西班牙语的 e.g. the Spanish people 西班牙人民；the Spanish language 西班牙语

the Spaniards also **the Spanish, the Spanish people** n. the people who come from or live in Spain 西班牙人民

Spaniard n. a person who comes from Spain 西班牙人

Spanish n. the language spoken by the Spanish people 西班牙语

Sweden n. a European country 瑞典

Swedish a. that belongs or relates to Sweden, or to its people or language 瑞典的；瑞典人的；瑞典语的 e.g. the Swedish people 瑞典人民；the Swedish language 瑞典语

the Swedes also **the Swedish, the Swedish people** n. the people who come from or live in Sweden 瑞典人民

Swede *n*. a person who comes from Sweden 瑞典人
Swedish *n*. the language spoken by the Swedish people 瑞典语
Switzerland *n*. a European country 瑞士
Swiss *a*. that belongs or relates to Switzerland, or to its people 瑞士的;瑞士人的 *e.g.* the Swiss people 瑞士人民
the Swiss *also* **the Swiss people** *n*. the people who come from or live in Switzerland 瑞士人民
Swiss *n*. a person who comes from Switzerland 瑞士人
Turkey *n*. a European country 土耳其
Turkish *a*. that belongs or relates to Turkey, or to its people or language 土耳其的;土耳其人的;土耳其语的 *e.g.* the Turkish people 土耳其人民;the Turkish language 土耳其语
the Turks *also* **the Turkish people** *n*. the people who come from or live in Turkey 土耳其人民
Turk *n*. a person who comes from Turkey 土耳其人
Turkish *n*. the language spoken by the Turkish people 土耳其语
multilingual country *n*. a country where many languages are spoken 多语国家
trilingual country *n*. a country where three languages are spoken, often as official languages 三语国家
CPC *n*. the abbreviation of the Communist Party of China 中国共产党
initial letters *n*. a word composed of the first letters of the words in a word group or phrase 首字母合成词
initialism *n*. a word composed of the first letters of the words in a word group or phrase, with each of its first letter read separately 首字母缩略词
acronym *n*. a word composed of the first letters of the words in a word group or phrase, which can be read as one word 首字母拼音词
Red Cross *n*. the emblem of the International Red Cross for the relief of the sick and wounded in war-times, famine or natural disaster 红十字
International Red Cross *also* **the Red Cross**, **IRC**（*abbrev.*）*n*. an international organization which helps people who are suffering because of war, famine, or natural disaster 国际红十字会
IRC *n*. the initialism of International Red Cross 国际红十字会
World Trade Organization *also* **WTO**（*abbrev.*）*n*. an international organization for the coordination of world trade 世界贸易组织
WTO *n*. the initialism of World Trade Organization 世贸组织
International Olympic Committee *also* **IOC**（*abbrev.*）*n*. an international organization for the coordination of the world sports events 国际奥林匹克委员会
IOC *n*. the initialism of International Olympic Committee 国际奥委会
refugee *n*. sb who has been forced to leave their country because there is a war there or because of their political or religious beliefs 难民
International Refugee Organization *also* **IRO**（*abbrev.*）*n*. an international organization for the relief of the refugees who suffer in war-times or who are persecuted for their political or religious beliefs 国际难民组织
IRO *n*. the initialism of International Refugee Organization 国际难民组织
Test of English as a Foreign Language *also* **TOEFL**（*abbrev.*）*n*. an American standardized test 以英语作为外语的测试
TOEFL *n*. the acronym for Test of English as a Foreign Language 托福考试
Graduate Record Examination *also* **GRE**（*abbrev.*）*n*. an American standardized test 研究生成绩考试
GRE *n*. the acronym for Graduate Record Examination 研究生成绩考试;GRE 考试
severe acute respiratory syndrome *also* **SARS**（*abbrev.*）*n*. a terrifying epidemic and infectious disease 严重急性呼吸系统综合症;非典型性肺炎
SARS *n*. the acronym of severe acute respiratory syndrome 萨斯;非典

epidemic disease *n.* a disease which affects a large number of people and which spreads quickly 流行病

infectious disease *n.* a disease which can be passed from one person to another by infection, esp. in the air 传染病

acquired immuno-deficiency syndrome *also* **AIDS** (*abbrev.*) *n.* a kind of disease 获得性免疫缺陷综合症

AIDS *n.* the acronym of acquired immuno-deficiency syndrome 艾滋病

Additional Knowledge

Initial Letters

U.N. is an abbreviation of the United Nations, U.S.A. is an abbreviation of the United States of America, and CPC is an abbreviation of the Communist Party of China. This kind of abbreviation is formed by a set of initial letters, that is, by the first letter of each word in order.

Initial letters may form a word composed of the first letters of the words in a word group or phrase, especially in the case of the name of something. There are two kinds of initial letters, including initialism and acronym. In an initialism, each first letter is read separately. For example, U.K., an abbreviation of the United Kingdom, is formed by initialism.

The other form of initial letters is acronym. In an acronym, all the first letters can be read as one word. For instance, UNESCO is a short form of United Nations Educational, Scientific, and Cultural Organization, and NATO is a short form of the North Atlantic Treaty Organization. They are both acronyms.

Many international organizations have their fixed abbreviations. To name but a few, IRC stands for International Red Cross, WTO for World Trade Organization, IOC for International Olympic Committee, and IRO for International Refugee Organization.

Initial letters are widely used. For instance, TOEFL stands for Test of English as a Foreign Language, and GRE for Graduate Record Examination.

SARS is an abbreviation of severe acute respiratory syndrome, which is a terrifying epidemic and infectious disease. Another example of acronym used in medicine is AIDS, which stands for acquired immuno-deficiency syndrome.

Exercises

I. Explain each of the following:
   1) initialism
   2) acronym
   3) British Empire
   4) British Commonwealth
   5) Irish Island
   6) Republic of Eire
   7) the English people
   8) the British people
   9) Englishman
   10) Briton
   11) Northern Ireland
   12) Old Continent
   13) English Channel
   14) New Continent
   15) Old World
   16) New World
   17) Far East
   18) Middle East

19) Oriental countries
20) the States
21) Western Powers
22) America
23) Latin America
24) Spanish
25) Portuguese
26) Amerindian
27) Afro-American
28) American-born Chinese
29) Austria
30) Australia

II. Tell what each of the following initial letters stands for, and tell whether it is an initialism or an acronym:

Models: CPC → Communist Party of China(initialism)
UNESCO → United Nations Educational, Scientific and Cultural Organization (acronym)

1) U. K.
2) U. N.
3) U. S. A.
4) IRC
5) WTO
6) NATO
7) GRE
8) TOEFL
9) IOC
10) IRO

III. Fill in the blanks:

Model: A Luxembourger is a person from _____, whose official language is _____.
→
A Luxembourger is a person from <u>Luxembourg</u>, whose official language is <u>German</u>.

1) A Czech is a person from _____, whose official language is _____.
2) A Turk is a person from _____, whose official language is _____.
3) A Portuguese is a person from _____, whose official language is _____.
4) A Dane is a person from _____, whose official language is _____.
5) A Swede is a person from _____, whose official language is _____.
6) A Russian is a person from _____, whose official language is _____.
7) A Greek is a person from _____, whose official language is _____.
8) A German is a person from _____, whose official language is _____.
9) A Slovak is a person from _____, whose official language is _____.
10) A Finn is a person from _____, whose official language is _____.
11) A Romanian is a person from _____, whose official language is _____.
12) A Pole is a person from _____, whose official language is _____.
13) A Frenchman is a person from _____, whose official language is _____.
14) A Dutch is a person from _____, whose official language is _____.
15) A Spaniard is a person from _____, whose official language is _____.

IV. Fill in the blanks:

Model: The Republic of Singapore has _____, _____, _____ and _____ as its official languages.
The Republic of Singapore has <u>English</u>, <u>Chinese</u>, <u>Malay</u> and <u>Tamil</u> as its official languages.

1) Wales has _____ and _____ as its official languages.
2) Canada has _____ and _____ as its official languages.

3) Belgium has _____, _____ and _____ as its official languages.
4) Switzerland has _____, _____ and _____ as its official languages.
V. Give another way or other ways of saying each of the following:
Models: abbreviation → abbreviated word, shortened word
　　　　the Republic of Eire → the Republic of Ireland
1) the Commonwealth →
2) the Celtic languages →
3) the Gaelic language →
4) the Continent →
5) the Channel →
6) the Atlantic →
7) the New Continent →
8) the States →
9) the Pacific →
10) American Indian →
11) African American →
12) Oceanica →
13) Eastern country →
14) the Red Cross →
VI. Answer the following questions:
1) Where was the English language originated?
2) What is the official full name of Britain?
3) What is the official full name of U.S.A.?
4) What are the two forms of initial letters?
5) Where is Sri Lanka located?
6) Where is the Sudan located?
7) Where is the West Indies located?
8) What are the four nations that make up Britain?
9) Where is Great Britain located?
10) What does Britain refer to? What does Great Britain refer to?
11) What are the two parts of Ireland?
12) Where is the Republic of Ireland located?
13) When did the Republic of Ireland become an independent country?
14) What does the British population consist of?
15) Why does a Welshman dislike being called an Englishman?
16) Can you give the two ways of calling a man from Scotland?
17) What are the official languages of Wales?
18) What is the water area between Europe and America called?
19) What are the main Western countries?
20) What are the official languages of Switzerland?
21) What is the official full name of South Africa?
22) Where is Australia? Where is Austria?
23) What are the official languages of Latin American countries?

24) What were the original inhabitants of America called?
25) When did the colonists from Britain come to settle in North America and colonize it?
26) Where did the Chicanos come from?
27) Where did the Latinos come from?
28) Can you give the four ways of calling a man from Holland?
29) What are the official languages of Belgium?
30) What is the official language of Austria?

Lesson Three

The English Names

  An English full name consists of a person's first name and last name. Sometimes there is a middle name between the first name and the last name.
  The first name is a person's given name by his or her parents at some point after the birth of the child. It is also called a person's forename or personal name. The first name is informal, which is usually used among family members or close friends and colleagues. If we say we are all on first-name terms with John, it means we call him by his first name, which is a sign of a friendly informal relationship. The common English given names are John, Robert, Thomas, William, Alice, and so on.
  In Christian countries, the Christian name is often used for the first name. Soon after a child is born, it is christened. That is, the child is given a Christian name by its godfather and godmother at a Christian religious ceremony like baptism. So in Britain, a person's first name is also called a baptismal name. We may say the child was baptized or christened by the name of John or Mary. Parents often give their children names after the people in *the Bible*. Such biblical names as Adam, Abraham, Daniel, David, Paul and Peter are first names, which are most commonly used.
  In modern times in the English-speaking countries there has been a strong trend towards using surnames as given names, for example, Beverley, Bradley and Ryan. The surnames themselves are from a variety of sources. There are also many vocabulary words, such as Jade, Summer and Hope, which are used as given names.
  There are such first names as Ivan, which originated from Russian names. There are such first names as Louis, which originated from French names. There are such first names as Carlos, which originated from Spanish names. And there are such first names as Albert, Adolph, Carl and Karl, which originated from German names.
  To show endearment, people tend to use pet names. A pet name is a special name that people use to address a close friend or a family member. When people show their endearment for a child, they use the child's pet name, which is also called infant name or childhood name. They shorten men's names like Alfred into Alf; Alexander into Alec or Alex; David into Dave or Davy; Donald into Don; Edward into Ed, Eddy, Eddey or Eddie; Frederick into Fred, Freddy or Freddie; Harold into Harry; Michael into Mike; Richard into Dick; Robert into Bob or Bobby; Samuel into Sam or Sammy; Thomas into Tom, Tommy or Tommie; and William into Bill, Billy or Billie. They shorten women's names like Elizabeth into Liz, Lizzy, Lizzie and Libby or Bess, Bessie, Bette, Betty, Beth and Betsy; and Catherine or Katherine into Cathy, Kate, Katy, Katie, Kay, Kathy and Kitty. In English, the suffix "-y" or "-ie" shows endearment.
  When some English first names are put together, they may have special meanings. "Tom, Dick and Harry" refers to "ordinary people". "Darby and Joan" means "a pair of

happy aged couple".

To show endearment, people also tend to use nicknames. A nickname is an informal name for someone, especially one that is used by their friends or relations. It is often a funny name for someone as a joke. Nicknames can be used to describe a person's physical significance, for example, Fatty for a fat boy, and Shorty for a short man. A nickname can also be one altered from a person's real name, for instance, Hurry for Harry. A nickname can also be called a by-name.

Some nicknames refer to certain part of people, which is different from others, for example, Heads, Neck, Legg, Foot and Shanks. These nicknames became surnames later. There are also other examples relating to a person's physical characteristics, like Barefoot, Broadhead, Bullhead, Chaffin, Garnham, Redhead, Sheepshanks, and Vidler. And the above-mentioned nicknames also turned into surnames later.

The last name is a person's family name or surname, which is common to all members of the family. It is formal and often used on official occasions or with people you do not know well. The first name can be used as an informal form of address. But the family name is often used with a form of address before it. Usually it cannot be used as a form of address.

English family names have their origins. England was mainly a rural society in the Middle Ages. There were no large cities. Some groups of people lived within the walls of a castle or nearby. Some others lived in small villages. The people had only one name. And the number of different names was not large. The popular names were John, Robert, Thomas, and William for men, and Alice for women. Some biblical names such as Adam, Abraham, Daniel, David, Paul and Peter, came later.

In a typical medieval village where there lived not many people, there might be only five or ten Johns, a similar number of Williams and might be two or three Roberts or Thomases. So it became necessary to distinguish people of identical names from one another. If two villagers were talking about a person called John, misunderstanding would arise if each had a different John in mind. Distinctions often needed to be made between this John and that John in their conversation. Such qualifications as place of residence, patronym, occupation, personal description and physical features might be added to a person's name.

In the rush of conversation the little, unimportant words could drop out or be slurred over so that John from the hill became John hill, and the other persons could be John dale, John Robert's son, John William's son, John smith, John tailor, John long and John bald. The capital letters that we now associate with surnames are only scribal conversations introduced later on.

These distinctions were a step toward surnames. Gradually, people had a second name, like Hill or Robertson, and the second name became part of their full names. When the second name was fixed and hereditary in an individual family and passed down from one generation to the next, it became a surname.

It is interesting to find out that there are some English family names relating to colour terms such as Black, Brown/Browne, Green/Greene, Grey/Gray and White. Actually, Black and Brown were originally nicknames describing the ancestor's hair that was black or brown. Likewise, White was originally a nickname describing the ancestor's face that was white.

Some animals' names are also used to describe a person's character or physical features, for example, Bird, Bull, Eagle, Fish, Fox and Wolf. There are also relevant English family names derived from animal names such as Bird, Bull, Eagle/Eagles, Fish, Fox, Lamb, Vidler, and Wolf/Wolfe.

In English, there are such family names as Bush, Cherry, and Wood, which are relating to plant names.

There are English family names relating to monarchy and peerage, such as King, Queen, Prince, Duke, Marquis, Earl/Earle, Viscount and Baron.

In Britain, Jones is a familiar surname. There are a great number of people whose family name is Jones. When people refer to a certain type of people, they often use Jones to represent the special kind of people, which may not be annoying. For instance, when people want to criticize those who compete with their neighbours socially, especially by buying the same expensive new things that they buy, they use the expression "to keep up with the Joneses". This expression is usually used in a derogatory sense. Besides, people sometimes say "Mrs. Jones' room" as a euphemism to refer to "ladies' room".

In the United States, the five most common last names are Smith, Johnson, Williams, Jones and Brown.

The order of the Chinese names is just the other way round. Chinese family names or surnames go before the given names or forenames.

Some English-speaking people have a middle name between their first and last names. The middle name can be considered as the second of a person's given name or forename. With a middle name, a person can distinguish himself or herself from another person in the family who happens to have the same first name. Take George Bernard Shaw for example. Bernard is the middle name. A middle name can also be given at random, for instance, after a famous person appearing in the newspaper or on television. However, not everyone has a middle name.

The second name is a person's last name, plus the middle name which goes before the last name.

The initials of a person are the set of capital letters, which represent the person's full name in order. For instance, if a man's full name is John Bernard Robertson, his initials will be J. B. R. And in this case, J. B. R. stands for John Bernard Robertson. A single initial can be the first letter of a person's first name. For example, we may address Mr John Smith as Mr J. Smith in written form, by using the initial of his first name.

An alias is a name by which a person is called at other times, in other places, or on other occasions. It can be a false name used by a person who is doing something criminal. For instance, Peter Smith alias John Simpson, means Peter Smith who is also called John Simpson. His real name is Peter Smith, but he sometimes goes by the alias of John Simpson.

Many writers or authors write under a pen name or a pseudonym which is an assumed name. Its French way of saying is nom de plume. Pen names or pseudonyms are names used or taken by writers instead of their real names. O. Henry is the pen name of William Sydney Porter. Mark Twain is the pen name of Samuel Langhorne Clemens. George Eliot is the pen name of Mary Ann Evans. Very often people know the writers by their pen names rather than by their real names.

An English name may denote a person's social or family background. Sometimes when you first get acquainted with a stranger and know his name, you may guess his background from his name. This is very important in public relations, which may help you to shorten the distance between you and your new acquaintance.

Those names beginning with Mac or Mc are usually Scottish surnames. For instance, McArthur, MacDonald, McMichael, or McMillan may well be the surname of a Scot or of a person whose ancestor was from Scotland. Actually, "mac" is the Gaelic for "son of". So, MacDonald originally had the meaning of "the son of Donald", just like the surname Donaldson which originally had the meaning of "the son of Donald". Other familiar surnames of Scottish origin include Campbell, Fraser and Steward/Stewart/Stuart.

Since the Irish language is also Gaelic, there are some Irish surnames also beginning with Mac or Mc. For instance, McCarthy, MacMahon, McMullan, or McNamara may well be the surname of an Irishman or of a person whose ancestor was from Ireland.

Some familiar English and Welsh surnames like Edwards, Jones, Owen, Thomas and Williams, are of Welsh origin.

People may sometimes use figures, such as Henry Ford II, to show the generation he belongs to.

Some people like to drop names. Name-dropping is a practice of casually mentioning the names of famous or powerful persons one is supposed to know, so as to impress others. These people are usually called name-droppers.

The form of address is the way people call or address a person in speech or writing. In informal situations, the way of addressing a familiar person is simply to call him or her by his or her first name.

The official or formal way of addressing a person is using his or her surname with a proper form of address before it. Mr, which is an abbreviation of Mister, refers to all men. It is a title that comes before the first name and the surname of a man, or just before his surname, for instance, Mr John Brown, or Mr Brown. Mr can also be a title for certain men who are in official positions, like Mr Chairman, and Mr President.

Miss is a form of addressing all unmarried women, young or old, or addressing married women for professional reason. Such professional women like lawyers, professors, doctors, actresses, writers, and newspaper or TV reporters keep the title "Miss" for they had gained their reputations before they got married.

When a woman gets married, she usually changes her surname into her husband's surname. Mrs is used to call such a married woman, who has given up her maiden name that is her original surname before her marriage and adopted her husband's surname. Mrs usually comes before a married woman's own first name and her husband's surname, or just before her husband's surname. For example, if Mary Smith is married to John Brown, she'll change her name into Mary Brown. And she may be addressed as Mrs Mary Brown or Mrs Brown. When people address this couple, they often say Mr and Mrs John Brown, or just say Mr and Mrs Brown. But many women like the saying: Mrs and Mr Brown.

Due to the influence of Women's Lib in the last few decades, many women, married or unmarried, prefer to use Ms as a form of addressing themselves. This title comes before a woman's first name and her maiden name, or just before her maiden name, as in the case of Mary Smith, who can be addressed as Ms Mary Smith, or Ms Smith.

A form of address often goes together with a person's full name or surname. In a monarchy, the king, the queen, the emperor or the empress is directly addressed as Your Majesty, while any of them is indirectly addressed as His Majesty or Her Majesty. Their plural forms are Your Majesties and Their Majesties respectively. When we say "Their Majesties have arrived", we mean "Both the king and the queen, or the emperor and the empress, have arrived". We can also add names after His or Her Majesty, for instance, Her Majesty Queen Elizabeth II.

Royal Highness or Highness is the title used to refer to a prince or a princess respectively. A prince or a princess is directly addressed as Your Royal Highness or Your Highness, while he or she is indirectly addressed as His Royal Highness/His Highness, or as Her Royal Highness/ Her Highness.

A form of address may be an honorary title like Lord Alfred Tennyson, Sir Isaac Newton, and Lady Catherine. Lord and Lady are titles prefixed to the names of such peers as marquises, earls, viscounts or barons in Britain.

A form of address may also be an official title like President Obama, Chairman Mao, or Premier Zhou; or a military title like Marshal Montgomery, General Taylor, Colonel Baker or Major Smith. Lady can also be part of an official title of respect, as in the case of Lady President or Lady Mayoress.

Excellency is a title given to the president or the chairman of a country, the premier or the prime minister of a government, the minister of a ministry, the governor who is appointed to govern a province or a state, the ambassador to a foreign country, and a high-rank officer or a high official, and her husband or his wife, and also a person who holds a high position in the church. They are directly addressed as Your Excellency and are indirectly referred to as His Excellency or Her Excellency. We can add a position of the person who is addressed after this form of address, for instance, His Excellency the American Ambassador to China.

Professor and Doctor can be an academic title, which can be used as a form of address, for instance, Professor Johnson or Doctor Robertson. Doctor, which is often abbreviated into Dr, can be a title referring to a medical doctor who has been trained in medical science, or an academic person who has received the highest university degree.

In British English, sir and madam, in small letter, are polite forms of address respectively for men and women one does not know personally. However, in American English, they can be used to get the attention of a man or a woman, especially of an old man or an old woman whose name you don't know. Such forms of address can be used separately and don't necessarily go with a person's family name. They can also serve as a way of addressing a military officer or a police officer to show respect. Miss can be used as a polite form of address to a young woman by shop assistants, taxi-drivers, waiters, or hotel staff.

Mister can be used as a form of address to a man, by children or trades people. Sir can be used as a form of address by school children to a male teacher. Miss can be used as a form of address by school children to a female teacher.

Such names of occupation as doctor and nurse can be used as forms of address. The names of a few other occupations like porter and waiter are sometimes used as forms of address, though some people may consider that this is impolite. However, most names of occupation cannot be used in this way. For instance, teacher cannot be used as a form of address.

Sometimes we may meet a person who has more than one title. If we want to address him or her with all his or her titles, we must be careful of the order. For example, there is a person named John Smith, who is a professor, a doctor and also a Sir. We may address him Professor, Doctor Sir John Smith.

Words and Expressions

full name *n.* the whole of a person's name, consisting of the first name and the last, and sometimes the middle 全名

first name *also* **given name, forename, personal name** *n.* the first part of the people's names which were given to them when they were born 名字

last name *n.* the last part of a person's name, which is the surname name 姓氏;姓

middle name *n.* the name which comes between the first name and the surname name 中名

given name *n.* a person's first name, which they are given at birth in addition to their surname; used esp. in American English 名字

forename *n.* another way of saying a person's first name 名字

personal name *n.* another way of saying a person's first name 名字

John *n.* a common English first name for men 约翰

Robert *n.* a common English first name for men 罗伯特

Thomas *n.* a common English first name for men 托马斯

William *n.* a common English first name for men 威廉

Alice *n.* a common English first name for women 艾丽斯

Mary *n.* a common English first name for women 玛丽

Adam *n.* a common English first name for men 亚当

Abraham *n.* a common English first name for men 亚伯拉罕

Daniel *n.* a common English first name for men 丹尼尔

David *n.* a common English first name for men 大卫;戴维

Paul *n.* a common English first name for men 保罗

Peter *n.* a common English first name for men 彼得

Christian name *n.* a name which is given to sb when they are born or when they are christened 教名

Christian country *n.* a country with Christianity as its official religion 基督教国家

christen *v.* give a baby a name during the Christian ceremony of baptism, as a sign that the baby is now a member of the Christian Church 给……起教名

ceremony *n.* a set of formal and traditional actions and words which are performed or spoken at a special occasion 典礼;仪式 *e.g.* religious ceremony 宗教仪式;Christian ceremony 基督教仪式

baptism *n.* a Christian religious ceremony in which sb is sprinkled with water or goes under water as a sign that they have become spiritually pure and that they have become Christians 洗礼;浸礼

godfather *n.* a man who agrees to take responsibility for the religious upbringing of sb when they are baptized in a Christian church 教父

godmother *n.* a woman who agrees to take responsibility for the religious upbringing of sb when they are

baptized in a Christian church 教母
baptismal name *n*. the name given to a person at baptism 教名
the Bible *n*. the holy book of Christianity 圣经
biblical name *n*. a name found in *the Bible* 圣经人名
surname *also* **last name** *n*. the name sb shares with other members of their family 姓氏;姓
Beverley *n*. an English first name for men coming from a surname 贝弗利
Bradley *n*. an English first name for men coming from a surname 布拉德利
Ryan *n*. an English first name for men coming from an Irish surname 瑞安
Jade *n*. an English first name for women, which is borrowed from the word for the semi-precious stone 杰德
Summer *n*. an English first name for men, which is borrowed from the word for the season between spring and autumn 萨默
Hope *n*. an English first name for men, which is borrowed from the word for the feeling of confidence that what people want to happen might happen 霍普
Ivan *n*. a man's first name of Russian origin 伊凡
Louis *n*. a man's first name of French origin 路易斯
Carlos *n*. a man's first name of Spanish origin 卡洛斯
Albert *n*. a man's first name of German origin 艾伯特
Adolph *n*. a man's first name of German origin 阿道夫
Carl *also* **Karl** *n*. a man's first name of German origin 卡尔
pet name *n*. a special name which people use to address a close friend or a family member 爱称;昵称
child's pet name *also* **infant name, childhood name** *n*. a special name which people use to call a baby or a child 小名;乳名
Alfred *n*. an English first name for men 艾尔弗雷德
Alf *n*. a short form of Alfred 阿尔夫
Alexander *n*. an English first name for men 亚历山大
Alec *n*. a short form of Alexander 亚历克
Alex *n*. a short form of Alexander 亚历克斯
Dave *n*. a short form of David 戴夫
Davy *n*. a short form of David 戴维
Donald *n*. an English first name for men 唐纳德
Don *n*. a short form of Donald 唐
Edward *n*. an English first name for men 爱德华
Ed *n*. a short form of Edward 埃德
Eddy *also* **Eddey, Eddie** *n*. a short form of Edward 埃迪
Frederick *n*. an English first name for men 弗雷德里克
Fred *n*. a short form of Frederick 弗雷德
Freddy *also* **Freddie** *n*. a short form of Frederick 弗雷迪
Harold *n*. an English first name for men 哈罗德
Harry *n*. a short form of Harold 哈里
Michael *n*. an English first name for men 迈克尔
Mike *n*. a short form of Michael 迈克
Richard *n*. an English first name for men 理查德
Dick *n*. a short form of Richard 迪克
Bob *n*. a short form of Robert 鲍勃
Bobby *n*. a short form of Robert 博比

Samuel *n.* an English first name for men 塞缪尔
Sam *n.* a short form of Samuel 萨姆
Sammy *n.* a short form of Samuel 萨米
Tom *n.* a short form of Thomas 汤姆
Tommy *also* **Tommie** *n.* a short form of Thomas 汤米
Bill *n.* a short form of William 比尔
Billy *also* **Billie** *n.* a short form of William 比利
Elizabeth *n.* an English first name for women 伊丽莎白
Liz *n.* a short form of Elizabeth 利兹
Lizzy *also* **Lizzie** *n.* a short form of Elizabeth 利齐
Libby *n.* a short form of Elizabeth 利比
Bess *n.* a short form of Elizabeth 贝丝
Bessie *n.* a short form of Elizabeth 贝西
Bette *n.* a short form of Elizabeth 贝特
Betty *n.* a short form of Elizabeth 贝蒂
Beth *n.* a short form of Elizabeth 贝思
Betsy *n.* a short form of Elizabeth 贝齐
Cathy *n.* a short form of Catherine 卡西
Kate *n.* a short form of Katherine 凯特
Katy *also* **Katie** *n.* a short form of Katherine 凯蒂
Kay *n.* a short form of Katherine 凯
Kathy *n.* a short form of Katherine 凯西
Kitty *n.* a short form of Katherine 基蒂
suffix *n.* a letter or group of letters which is added to the end of a word in order to form a new word, often of a different word class 后缀
Tom, Dick and Harry *n.* ordinary people 普通百姓；张三、李四、王五
Darby and Joan *n.* a pair of happy aged couple 老两口
nickname *n.* an informal name for sb, esp. one that is used by their friend or relations 外号；绰号
Fatty *n.* a nickname for a fat boy 胖子
Shorty *n.* a nickname for a short man 矮子
real name *n.* a true and actual name, not a false name 真名；实名
Hurry *n.* a nickname for Harry 赫里
by-name *n.* a secondary name like a nickname or an assumed name 别名；外号；绰号；化名
Heads *n.* a surname coming from a nickname 黑兹
Neck *n.* a surname coming from a nickname 尼克
Legg *n.* a surname coming from a nickname 莱格
Foot *n.* a surname coming from a nickname 富特
Shanks *n.* a surname coming from a nickname 尚克斯
Barefoot *n.* a surname coming from a nickname 贝尔富特
Broadhead *n.* a surname coming from a nickname 布罗德黑德
Bullhead *n.* a surname coming from a nickname 布尔黑德
Chaffin *n.* a surname coming from a nickname, which means "bald" 查芬
Garnham *n.* a surname coming from a nickname, which means "moustache" 加纳姆
Redhead *n.* a surname coming from a nickname 雷德黑德
Sheepshanks *n.* a surname coming from a nickname 希普尚克斯
Vidler *n.* a surname coming from a nickname, which means "face of a wolf" 维德勒

family name also **surname** n. a person's last name, which is shared by all members of the family 姓氏；姓

form of address n. way of calling sb by their name or title when talking or speaking to them 称谓

the Middle Ages n. the period between about 1100 AD and 1500 AD in European history; or sometimes in a wider sense, beginning with the fall of the West Roman Empire in 476 AD, and closing with the discovery of America and the Renaissance of the 15th century 中世纪

medieval a. that relates to or dates from the period between 1100 AD and 1500 AD in European history 中世纪的

castle n. a large building with thick, high walls, which was built by kings, queens or other important people in former times, esp. for protection during wars and battles 城堡

dale n. valley 山谷

Dale n. an English surname, coming from the word "dale" in the sense of "valley" 戴尔

smith n. a worker in metal 铁匠

Smith n. an English surname, coming from the occupational name "smith" in the sense of "a worker in metal" 史密斯

tailor n. a person who makes clothes 裁缝

Tailor also **Taylor** n. an English surname, coming from the occupational name "tailor" in the sense of "a person who makes clothes" 泰勒

Taylor n. an English surname, which is a variant of Tailor 泰勒

Hill n. an English surname, coming from the place name "hill" 希尔

Robertson n. an English surname, coming from "son of Robert" 罗伯逊

colour term n. a word which denotes a colour 色彩词

Black n. an English surname, coming from a nickname describing the ancestor's hair that was black 布莱克

Brown also **Browne** n. an English surname, coming from a nickname describing the ancestor's hair that was brown 布朗

Green also **Greene** n. an English surname, coming from the word "green" which means "young, fresh and immature" 格林

Grey also **Gray** n. an English surname, coming from a nickname describing the ancestor's hair that was grey 格雷

White n. an English surname, coming from a nickname describing the ancestor's face that was white 怀特

Bird n. an English surname, coming from the word "bird" 伯德

Bull n. an English surname, coming from the word "bull", which means "strong and willful" 布尔

Eagle also **Eagles** n. an English surname, coming from the word "eagle" 伊格尔

Fish n. an English surname, coming from the word "fish" 菲什

Fox n. an English surname, coming from the word "fox", which means "sly" 福克斯

Lamb n. an English surname, coming from the word "lamb", which means "tamely" 兰姆

Wolf also **Wolfe** n. an English surname, coming from the word "wolf" 沃尔夫

Bush n. an English surname, coming from the word "bush" 布什

Cherry n. an English surname, coming from the word "cherry" 彻里

Wood n. an English surname, coming from the word "wood" 伍德

monarchy n. a system in which a monarch reigns over a country and in which the next monarch will be another member of the same family 君主制

peerage n. rank of a peer, who is a member of any of the five noble ranks, including duke, marquis, earl, viscount and baron 贵族爵位

king n. a man who is the head of his kingdom 国王

King n. an English surname, coming from the word "king" 金

queen *n*. a woman who is the head of her kingdom 女王；or a woman who is the wife of the king 王后
Queen *n*. an English surname, coming from the word "queen" 奎因
prince *n*. a male member of a royal family, esp. the son of the king or queen of a country 王子；亲王
Prince *n*. an English surname, coming from the word "prince" 普林斯
duke *n*. a nobleman with a rank just below that of a prince 公爵
Duke *n*. an English surname, coming from the word "duke" 杜克
marquis *n*. a nobleman with a rank just below that of a duke 侯爵
Marquis *n*. an English surname, coming from the word "marquis" 马奎斯
earl *n*. a nobleman with a rank just below that of a marquis 伯爵
Earl *also* **Earle** *n*. an English surname, coming from the word "earl" 厄尔
viscount *n*. a nobleman with a rank just below that of an earl 子爵
Viscount *n*. an English surname, coming from the word "viscount" 怀康特
baron *n*. a nobleman with a rank just below that of a viscount 男爵
Baron *n*. an English surname, coming from the word "baron" 巴伦
Jones *n*. an English and Welsh surname, which is of Welsh origin 琼斯
keep up with the Joneses *v. phrase* try to have all the same possessions as one's friends and neighbours, and to do all the same things as them, because they do not want to seem inferior to their friends or neighbours 与朋友/邻居攀比
Mrs. Jones' room *n*. a euphemistic expression in the sense of "ladies' room" 女卫生间
Williams *n*. an English and Welsh surname, which is of Welsh origin 威廉斯
George Bernard Shaw (1856 – 1951) *n*. an English playwright and novelist 萧伯纳
Sir *n*. an honorary title, which is used before the first name of a baronet or a knight 爵士 *e.g.* Sir Isaac Newton 艾萨克·牛顿爵士
Sir Winston Leonard Spencer Churchill (1874 – 1965) **n.** the former British Prime Minster (1940 – 1945；1951 – 1955) 温斯顿·伦纳德·斯潘塞·丘吉尔爵士
alias *n*. a name by which a person is called at other times, in other places, or on other occasions；or a false name 别名；化名
false name *n*. a name which is not a person's real name 假名字
assumed name *n*. false name 假名字
pen name *also* **pseudonym** *n*. a name under which a writer or author uses on books or articles instead of his or her real name 笔名
nom de plume *n*. the French way of saying "pen name" 笔名
O. Henry (1862 – 1910) *n*. the pen name of William Sydney Porter, an American novelist 欧·亨利
Mark Twain (1835 – 1910) *n*. the pen name of Samuel Langhorne Clemens, an American novelist 马克·吐温
George Eliot (1819 – 1880) *n*. the pen name of Mary Ann Evans, an English novelist 乔治·艾略特
background *n*. a person's family, social class, experience, and education 背景 *e.g.* social background 社会背景；family background 家庭背景
public relations *n*. the state of the relationship of a person or an organization with the public 公共关系；公关
McArthur *n*. a Scottish surname, which means "the son of Arthur" 麦克阿瑟
MacDonald *n*. a Scottish surname, which means "the son of Donald" 麦克唐纳
Donaldson *n*. an English surname, which means "the son of Donald" 唐纳森
McMillan *n*. a Scottish surname, which means "the son of the bald-head person" 麦克米伦
Campbell *n*. a Scottish surname, which means "crooked mouth" 坎贝尔
Fraser *n*. a Scottish surname 弗雷泽
Steward *n*. a Scottish surname, which means "the keeper of a household" 斯图尔德

Stewart also **Stuart** n. an Scottish surname, which is a variant of Steward 斯图尔特

McCarthy n. an Irish surname, which means "the son of Craddock" in its Irish form 麦卡锡

McMahon n. an Irish surname, which means "the son of Bear" 麦克马洪

McMullan n. an Irish surname, which is the Irish form of McMillan 麦克马伦

McNamara n. an Irish surname, which means "the son of Hound of the Sea" 麦克纳马拉

Edwards n. an English and Welsh surname, which is of Welsh origin 爱德华兹

Owen n. an English and Welsh surname, which is of Welsh origin 欧文

Thomas n. an English and Welsh surname, which is of Welsh origin 托马斯

Henry Ford II (1917–1987) n. an American industrialist 亨利·福特第二

drop names v. phrase mention the names of famous or powerful people one is supposed to know, as so to impress others 提及名人以抬高身价

name-dropping n. a habit of referring often to famous people as though they were friends, so as to impress people who are listening 提及名人以抬高身价的做法

name-dropper n. a person who often mentions the names of famous or powerful people he is supposed to know, as so to impress others 提及名人以抬高身价者

form of address also **address form** n. a title or rank used to call a person in speech or writing 称谓；称呼

Mr n. a form of address, which is an abbreviation of Mister, used before a man's name referring to him 先生

Miss n. a form of address, used before the name of a girl or an unmarried woman, or to a married woman for professional reason 小姐

professional woman n. a woman who has a job which requires special training and which has a fairly high status, like a lawyer, a professor, a doctor, an actress, a writer, and a newspaper or TV reporter 职业妇女 syn. **career woman** 职业妇女；**working woman** 工作妇女

Mrs n. a form of address, used before the name of a married woman who has given up her maiden name and adopted her husband's family name 太太；夫人

maiden name n. the surname of a woman she had had before she got married and took her husband's surname 娘家姓

Women's Liberation also **Women's Lib** n. a term of the 1960's for the women's rights movement, which advocates that women should have the same social and economic rights and privileges as men 妇女解放运动

Women's Lib n. an informal expression of Women's Liberation 妇女解放运动

Ms n. a form of address, used before a woman's first name and her maiden name 女士

emperor n. a man who rules an empire 皇帝

empress n. a woman who rules an empire 女皇；or the wife of an emperor 皇后

Your Majesty n. the form of directly addressing a king, queen, emperor or empress 国王/皇帝陛下；陛下

His Majesty n. the form of indirectly addressing a king or emperor 国王/皇帝陛下

Her Majesty n. the form of indirectly addressing a queen or empress 女王/王后/女皇/皇后陛下 e.g. Her Majesty Queen Elizabeth II 伊丽莎白女王二世陛下

Your Royal Highness also **Your Highness** n. the form of directly addressing a prince or princess 王子/亲王殿下；公主殿下

His Royal Highness also **His Highness** n. the form of indirectly addressing a prince 王子/亲王殿下

Her Royal Highness also **Her Highness** n. the form of indirectly addressing a princess 公主殿下

princess n. a female member of a royal family, usu. the daughter of a king, queen, emperor or empress 公主；or the wife of a prince 王妃

honorary title n. the title given to sb as a sign of respect or honour for a special reason 荣誉称号

Lord n. a title used before the name of a marquis, earl, viscount or baron in Britain 勋爵

Lord Alfred Tennyson (1809–1892) 艾尔弗雷德·丁尼生勋爵

President n. the leader, and often also ruler or chief governing official, of many modern countries which do not have a king or queen 总统

President Obama *n*. Barack Obama (1961-), the 45th President of the United States 巴拉克·奥巴马;奥巴马总统

Premier *also* **Prime Minister** *n*. the leader of the government of a country 总理;首相

military title *n*. the title used to refer to the officers, esp. those of high rank, in the armed forces of a country 军衔

marshal *n*. an officer who has the highest rank in an army or an air force 元帅

Marshal Montgomery *n*. Bernard Montgomery (1887-1976), a marshal of the British Army, and also a viscount 伯纳德·蒙哥马利;蒙哥马利元帅

general *n*. a person who holds a high officer's rank in the armed forces, usu. in the army 将军

colonel *n*. a senior officer in the army or air force 上校

major *n*. an officer in the army of medium rank 少校

mayoress *n*. a woman who holds the office of mayor 女市长; or the wife of a mayor 市长夫人; or other woman helping a mayor or mayoress to perform mayoral duties 市长女助理

Lady *n*. an official title of respect for a female president or a mayoress 阁下 *e.g.* Lady President 女总统阁下; Lady Mayoress 女市长阁下;市长夫人阁下;市长女助理阁下

Your Excellency *n*. the form of directly addressing an official of very high rank 阁下

His Excellency *n*. the form of indirectly addressing a male official of very high rank 阁下 *e.g.* His Excellency the American Ambassador to China 美国驻华大使阁下

Her Excellency *n*. the form of indirectly addressing a female official of very high rank 阁下

ministry *n*. a government department which deals with a particular area of administration within a country 部 *e.g.* Ministry of Education 教育部

minister *n*. a person who is in charge of a particular government department 部长;大臣 *e.g.* Foreign Minister 外交部长;外交大臣

governor *n*. a person who governs or controls a place 地方长官 *e.g.* governor of the state of California 加利福尼亚州州长

ambassador *n*. a diplomat of the highest rank who is the official representative of his or her country in a foreign country 大使 *e.g.* China's ambassador to the United States 中国驻美大使

professor *n*. a person who has the highest rank of the teachers in a department in a British university 教授; a teacher in an American or Canadian university or college 大学教师

Professor *n*. an academic title, which can be used as a form of address 教授

Doctor *also* **Dr** (*abbrev.*) *n*. an academic title referring to a medical doctor who has been trained in medical science 医生;大夫 *e.g.* Doctor Norman Bethune 诺尔曼·白求恩大夫; or an academic person who has received the highest university degree, which can be used as a form of address 博士

sir *BrE* *n*. a polite form of address for men one does not know personally 先生; or a form of address by school children to a male teacher 老师

madam *BrE* *n*. a polite form of address for women one does not know personally 女士;太太

Miss *n*. a form of address by school children to a female teacher 老师

international organization *n*. an organization formed by different countries 国际组织

inter-governmental organization *n*. an organization formed by governments of various countries 政府间组织

specialized agency *n*. an administrative organization run by a government or an international organization, which is in charge of a specialized field of work 专门机构

Food and Agriculture Organization of the United Nations *also* **FAO** (*abbrev.*) *n*. an international organization under the UN, which tries to solve the problems concerning food and agriculture in the world, esp. in the developing countries 联合国粮食及农业组织

FAO *n*. the initialism of Food and Agriculture Organization of the United Nations 粮农组织

World Health Organization *also* **WHO** (*abbrev.*) *n.* an international organization under the UN, which is aimed at guiding and coordinating the medical work of the whole world 世界卫生组织

WHO *n.* the initialism of World Health Organization 卫生组织

Universal Postal Union *also* **UPU** (*abbrev.*) *n.* an international organization which is aimed at promoting the international cooperation in postal affairs 万国邮政联盟

UPU *n.* the initialism of Universal Post Union 万国邮联

International Monetary Fund *also* **IMF** (*abbrev.*) *n.* an international organization under the UN, which is aimed at promoting the international cooperation in monetary issues 国际货币基金组织

IMF *n.* the initialism of International Monetary Fund 货币基金

World Meteorological Organization *also* **WMO** (*abbrev.*) *n.* an international organization under the UN, which is aimed at promoting the international cooperation in meteorology 世界气象组织

WMO *n.* the initialism of World Meteorological Organization 气象组织

International Labour Organization *also* **ILO** (*abbrev.*) *n.* an international organization, which is aimed at promoting full employment and improvement of living standards, promoting the cooperation between capital and labour, and protecting the health of the workers 国际劳工组织

ILO *n.* the initialism of International Labour Organization 劳工组织

International Civil Aviation Organization *also* **ICAO** (*abbrev.*) *n.* an international organization which is aimed at promoting the international cooperation in civil aviation 国际民用航空组织

ICAO *n.* the initialism of International Civil Aviation Organization 民航组织

International Maritime Organization *also* **IMO** (*abbrev.*) *n.* an international organization which is aimed at promoting the international cooperation in maritime affairs 国际海事组织

IMO *n.* the initialism of International Maritime Organization 海事组织

Untied Nations Development Programme *also* **UNDP** (*abbrev.*) *n.* an international organization under the UN, which provides the developing countries with financial and social assistance for their development 联合国开发计划署

UNDP *n.* the initialism of Untied Nations Development Programme 开发署

United Nations International Children's Emergency Fund *also* **UNICEF** (*abbrev.*) *n.* the former full name of United Nations Children Fund 联合国国际儿童紧急基金会

United Nations Children Fund *also* **UNICEF** (*abbrev.*) *n.* an international organization under the UN, which tries to solve the problems concerning the under-nourishment, diseases and education of the children in the developing countries 联合国儿童基金会

UNICEF *n.* the acronym of United Nations Children Fund 联合国儿童基金会

non-governmental organization *also* **NGO** (*abbrev.*) *n.* an organization which is formed by non-governmental groups of different countries 非政府组织

NGO *n.* the initialism of non-governmental organization 非政府组织

Additional Knowledge

International Organizations

International organizations are those formed by different countries. The biggest and most important international organization is the United Nations, or the U. N., for short. It was formed after World War II, with about 200 member countries belonging to it now. It tries to encourage international peace, cooperation and friendship.

The United Nations has many inter-governmental organizations and specialized agencies under it. Among them the important ones are United Nations Educational, Scientific and Cultural Organization (UNESCO, for short), Food and Agriculture Organization of the United Nations (FAO, for short), World Health Organization (WHO, for short), Universal Postal Union (UPU, for short), International Monetary Fund (IMF, for short), World Meteorological Organization (WMO, for short), International Labour Organization (ILO, for short), International Civil Aviation Organization (ICAO, for short), and International Maritime Organization (IMO, for short).

There are also many other organization and specialized agencies under the United Nations. Among them there are UNDP whose full name is Untied Nations Development Programme, and UNICEF whose former full name is United Nations International Children's Emergency Fund and whose present full name is United Nations Children Fund.

The above international organizations are formed by governments of various countries. There are also many non-governmental organizations, which can be shortened into NGO. These organizations are formed by non-governmental groups of different countries.

Exercises

I. Explain each of the following:
  1) first name
  2) Christian name
  3) biblical name
  4) pet name
  5) nickname
  6) last name
  7) surname
  8) patronym
  9) middle name
  10) second name
  11) real name
  12) assumed name
  13) pseudonym
  14) pen name
  15) nom de plume
  16) name-dropper
  17) form of address
  18) maiden name
  19) Miss
  20) Mrs
  21) Ms
  22) Lord
  23) Sir
  24) Lady
  25) Your Excellency

II. Give the original form of each of the following pet names:
  Model: Don → Donald
  1) Betty →
  2) Bill →
  3) Bobby →
  4) Dick →
  5) Eddie →
  6) Fred →
  7) Lizzie →
  8) Mike →
  9) Sam →
  10) Tom →

III. Tell which of the following is a surname of Scottish origin, which of the following is a surname of Welsh origin, and which of the following is a surname of Irish origin:
  1) Campbell →
  2) Edwards →
  3) Fraser →
  4) Jones →
  5) McArthur →
  6) Williams →

7) Owen →   8) Stuart →
9) MacDonald →   10) Mulligan →

IV. Tell what each of the following initial letters stands for:
Models: CPC → Communist Party of China
         UNESCO → United Nations Educational, Scientific and Cultural Organization
1) IMF →   2) WHO →
3) FAO →   4) UPU →
5) WMO →   6) ILO →
7) ICAO →   8) IMO →
9) UNDP →   10) UNICEF →

V. Answer the following questions:
1) What is an English full name made up of?
2) Can you give a few common English names?
3) When did a person get his or her Christian name?
4) Among whom is a person's first name usually used?
5) Can you give five names for men from the Bible?
6) What does the English suffix"-y" or"-ie" show?
7) When do you usually use a person's family name?
8) Did an Englishman have his last name in the medieval times?
9) What were the popular English names for men in the Middle Ages?
10) What were the main origins of English surnames?
11) Which is a first name and which is a surname among such names as Daniel, Daniels and Danielson?
12) Which is a first name and which is a surname among such names as Donald, Donaldson and MacDonald?
13) Please give some English surnames which are originated from place names.
14) Please give some English surnames which are originated from patronyms.
15) Please give some English surnames which are originated from occupational names.
16) Please give some English surnames which are originated from original nicknames.
17) Can you give some English surnames which are relating to colour terms?
18) Can you give some English surnames which are relating to animal names?
19) What is the difference between an English name and a Chinese name in order?
20) What is the real name of Mark Twain?
21) What is the pen name of William Sydney Porter?
22) What is the pseudonym of Mary Ann Evans?
23) Why do we say an English name may denote a person's social or family background?
24) Can you give some Scottish surnames beginning with Mac or Mc?
25) Can you give some Irish surnames beginning with Mul?
26) Is McNamara a Scottish surname or an Irish surname?
27) Do you think name-dropping is a good thing?
28) What is the way of addressing a familiar person on informal occasions?
29) What is the official way of addressing a person?
30) How do you address a person you don't know personally?

Lesson Four

Society and Family

Society refers to the people who live in a country or region, their organizations, and their way of life. The social structure and social framework of a country are changing from time to time. In Britain and the United States, great changes took place in the 20th century. Among the main social changes during the second half of the 20th century, were a lower birth rate and longer life expectancy. This is reflected in a growing proportion of elderly people. Now people in these countries often talk about the ageing society, in which 10% or more than 10% of the population are over 60 years old. Birth rate refers to the number of babies born for every 100 or every 1,000 people in a specified area over a particular period of time. There are several contributory factors to the falling birth rate in recent years. The trend towards later marriage and postponing having children has led to an increase in the average age of women giving birth. More people prefer to have smaller families than in the past, which has caused a significant decline in the proportion of families with four or more children. Family planning is the practice of using contraception to control the number of children people have. More widespread and effective contraception has made it easier for people to plan families. Besides, the greater prevalence of voluntary sterilization for both men and women also forms a factor leading to low birth rate.

Life expectancy or the expectation of life is the length of time which a person is normally likely to live. Women usually have a longer life expectancy than men. At birth, the expectation of life for a man in Britain is now over 74 years and for a woman nearly 80 years, compared with 49 years for men and 52 years for women in 1901. There has been a decline in mortality at most ages, particularly among children. Mortality, mortality rate, or death rate is the number of deaths for every 100 or every 1,000 people in a particular year in a particular place. The decline in the mortality rate reflects many factors, including better nutrition, rising standards of living, advances in medical science, better working conditions, and the smaller size of families.

The average household size in these countries has fallen from 3.1 to 2.5 in the last decade. Fewer people are living in the traditional family of a married couple with dependent children, while many more people are living on their own. The declining average household size also reflects growth in the elderly and in one-parent families, and the preference for smaller families.

Such English-speaking countries as Britain, America, Canada and Australia are all multi-racial and multi-cultural societies. In these countries, people of many different nationalities and cultures live together. America used to be considered as a melting pot of races since its beginning, where people of different nations and races gradually got mixed together.

A family is a group of one or usually two adults and their children living in the same home. In the English-speaking countries such as the United States, Britain and Canada, the family is still very much alive. It is considered as the basic unit of the society. In a family, people who live together are related to each other by blood or marriage. A man and a woman who are married form a married couple. The husband and wife are basic members of a family. Most American and British couples have two or three children, though bigger families or larger families are not unusual. The fundamental family pattern is the nuclear family. It consists of parents and their dependent or minor children only, but does not include any less close relations. Usually, the family group occupies one household.

A minor is a person who is still legally a child. In Britain and the United States, people are minors until they reach the age of eighteen. The minors are usually dependent on and looked after by their parents. When they grow up, typically at the age of 18, they are fully responsible in law for their actions. In most cases, they will leave their parents and live independently. So middle-aged people and elderly people generally do not live with their married children. However, parents usually keep in close contact with their grown children and take great interest in their grandchildren. Of course, in some families the non-dependent children still live together with their parents. In such English-speaking countries as the United States and Britain, there are very few extended families that are often found in parts of Africa and in old China. An extended family is a family structure with three or four generations living under the same roof, where uncles, aunts and cousins are regarded as close relations with an obligation to help and support each other.

Generation refers to the group of people in a family who share the same position in its history and structure. For instance, a person and his or her brothers, sisters and cousins belong to the same generation. So do their parents, aunts and uncles. Between older and younger people, there exist differences in ideas, feelings, attitudes, behaviours and interests. Such a difference between two generations is called generation gap. In many families, there is generation gap between parents and their teenage children, which often causes them to misunderstand, argue with and even be unfriendly to one another. How to bridge the generation gap has become a serious social problem.

Most families are headed by a married couple. Ideally, Mother and Father have an equal voice in making decisions. That's the ideal, but obviously not all households are run this way. In many families, Father's word is law. In many others, Father leaves home early in the morning before his children get up, and goes back home late in the night after they fall asleep. So the children rarely see their father when they are awake. In this case, Mother takes care of the children and becomes the major decision-maker of the family matters. But in some families, there exist tensions, arguments, hostilities and even conflicts between husband and wife. In many cases, their conflicts develop and finally lead to the failure of their marriage. And this will be unfavourable to their children when they are growing up.

In some families, one parent, either Father or Mother, is absent as a result of divorce, separation or desertion. The family with one parent absent for the above-mentioned reasons turns into a single-parent family, which is also called a one-parent family or a lone-parent family. In such a family, Mother or Father has to bring up the children on her or his own. As the dependent children have to live with their lone parents, they lack either maternal love or paternal love, and often meet with psychological problems and obstacles which are also not favourable to their growth and development.

Divorce is the legal ending of a marriage between husband and wife, so that they are free to marry again. As divorce is on the increase, there is a higher divorce rate. Separation is a legal arrangement by which a married couple live apart but do not end the marriage. As many people fail in their first marriages, divorce and separation have become much more common in recent decades. Many divorced people do eventually remarry, with men more likely than women to remarry following divorce. Desertion is an instance in which the husband leaves his wife and children, and no longer helps or supports them. The deserted wife has to take care of the children by herself.

Marriage is a legal union between a man and a woman as husband and wife. The traditional marriage pattern is that a married couple legally live together and give birth to their children. But there is a tendency that fewer people are getting married. A man and a woman may cohabit or live together without marriage or before marriage. This is called cohabitation. In this case, the man and the woman are no longer bound by the traditional marriage pattern. In the United States and Britain, cohabitation has become much more common. As cohabitation before marriage is increasingly widespread, many women can be found to cohabit with their future husbands before marriage.

Dink is the abbreviation of Double/Dual Income, No Kids. It is also called Dinky, which is the abbreviation of Double/Dual Income, No Kids Yet. A dink family refers to a married young couple who both earn a lot of money but don't want to have their own child. Now there have appeared more and more dink families. Children are no longer the link to maintain a couple's marriage. A dink is one of such two young people who are married to each other. Usually, they are highly educated. With their higher educational background, they have higher pay. As they have no children, they can spend all their earnings on their own consumption. Instead of cooking in their own kitchen, they often go out to eat in the restaurant. In their leisure time, they don't have to worry about their housework. As they don't shoulder the responsibility of brining up children, they have more leisure and comfort of their own, and they have plenty of money and time for making holidays.

In the past, women in Britain and in the United States didn't have the equal social status as men. In the 1960's, Women's Libbers started a social and political movement which aimed to achieve women's liberation by organizing groups and campaigns and by causing individual women and men to change their attitudes. Women's Liberation, which was also simply called Women's Lib, was the ideal that women should have the same social and economic rights and privileges as men. In this women's rights movement, they advocated gender equality and promoted other feminist issues. The effects of the movement included an explosion in working females and the controversial advocacy of "abortion rights". As a result, women have obtained many political and legal rights previously open only to men. The economic and domestic lives of women have been transformed since then. Women are no longer confined to their homes to do housework and look after children. Now the growth of part-time and flexible working patterns has allowed more women to combine raising a family with paid employment. Women now make up over 40% of the workforce in employment. Many of them are running their own businesses. However, women are still under-presented in some occupations and at senior levels. For example, fewer than 5% of company directors are women.

Kin, kinfolk or kindred refers to a person's family and relatives. A person's near kin is closely related to him while his distant kin or remote kinfolk is not closely related to him. Kinship is a family relationship, an interrelationship between family members and their relatives. Kinship contains filiation, spouseship and consanguinity.

Filiation is the blood relationship between parents and their children or their offspring, including the relationships between father and son, father and daughter, mother and son, and mother and daughter.

Spouseship is the marriage relationship between husband and wife, like the relationships between grandfather and grandmother, father and mother, uncle and aunt, son and daughter-in-law, and son-in-law and daughter. The in-laws are a colloquial term for the close relatives of a person's wife or husband. For instance, father-in-law is a man's wife's father or a woman's husband's father. Mother-in-law is a man's wife's mother or a woman's husband's mother. Son-in-law is a person's daughter's husband and daughter-in-law is a person's son's wife.

Consanguinity is the blood relationship of family members, apart from filiation. It can be a relationship between different generations, like the relationships between grandparent and grandchild, and uncle/aunt and nephew/niece. As a special consanguinity, sibling refers to the blood relationship between two people with the same parents, including the relationships between elder brother and younger brother, elder brother and younger sister, elder sister and younger brother, and elder sister and younger sister.

Consanguinity can refer to a person's paternal relatives, or relatives on his father's side, like the relationship between paternal grandfather and grandchild, or between a person and his paternal cousin. Consanguinity can also refer to a person's maternal relatives, or relatives on his mother's side, like the relationship between maternal grandfather and grandchild, or between a person and his maternal cousin. People are not allowed to marry within certain degrees of consanguinity.

Words & Expressions

society *n*. people in general, considered with regard to the structure of laws, organizations, etc., that makes it possible for them to live together, or a particular broad group of people who share laws, organizations, customs, etc. 社会

way of life *also* **life-style** *n*. the conditions, behaviour, and habits which are typical of a particular person or a group of people, or are chosen by them 生活方式

structure *n*. the way in which sth is made, built, or organized, with all its different parts or aspects forming a particular shape, pattern, or system 结构 *e.g.* social structure 社会结构

framework *n*. a structure which forms a support or frame for sth 框架 *e.g.* social framework 社会框架

life expectancy *also* **the expectation of life** *n*. the average number of years which a person is expected to live 预期寿命

birth rate *n*. the number of births for every 100 or every 1,000 people in a particular year in a particular place 出生率

elderly *a.* a polite word for "old", often used to refer to old people 老年的 *e.g.* elderly people 老年人
the elderly *n.* the old people, the aged people, or the elderly people 老年人
ageing society *also* **aging society** *n.* a society in which 10% or more of the population are over 60 years old 老龄化社会
contributory *a.* that causes sth to happen 促成的 *e.g.* contributory factor 诱因
marriage *n.* the relationship between a man and a woman as husband and wife 婚姻 *e.g.* later marriage 晚婚; failure of one's marriage 婚姻失败
postpone *v.* move to some later time 推迟 *e.g.* to postpone having children 推迟要孩子
family *n.* a group of people that consists of parents and their children 家庭 *e.g.* family pattern 家庭模式; family structure 家庭结构; family matter 家庭事务; or children, esp. young children 子女; 孩子 *e.g.* big/large family 多子女; small family 少子女
start a family *v. phrase* begin to have children 开始要孩子
raise a family *v. phrase* bring up children 抚养孩子; 生儿育女
plan families *v. phrase* control the number of children born in a family and the time of their birth by the use of any of various contraceptive methods 计划生育
family planning *n.* the practice of using contraception to control the number of children people have 计划生育
contraception *n.* the use of contraceptives to prevent a woman from becoming pregnant during sexual intercourse 避孕 *e.g.* widespread and effective contraception 广泛而有效的避孕
contraceptive *n.* a device which is used, or a pill which is taken, in order to prevent a woman from becoming pregnant during sexual intercourse 避孕器具; 避孕药
contraceptive method *also* **contraceptive technique** *n.* a method of technique which prevents a woman from becoming pregnant during sexual intercourse 避孕方法
prevalence *n.* the fact that sth is widespread and occurs commonly 普遍; 盛行
sterilization *n.* making a person or an animal unable to produce young 绝育 *e.g.* voluntary sterilization 自愿绝育
mortality *also* **mortality rate**, **death rate** *n.* the rate or number of deaths caused by a particular thing, happening among a certain kind of people, within a particular period of time or on a particular occasion 死亡率
nutrition *n.* the process of taking food or nutrients into the body and absorbing them 营养
standards of living *n.* the level of comfort and wealth which people have in a particular society or country 生活水平
medical *a.* relating to medicine or to the care of people's health 医学的 *e.g.* medical science 医学科学
working conditions *n.* the conditions in which people work, like heating, hygiene, safety, etc., and which also affect the quality of people's job 工作条件
household *n.* all the people in a family or a group who live together in a house 家庭 *e.g.* household size 家庭规模
married couple *n.* husband and wife 已婚夫妇
dependent child *n.* a child who depends on his or her parents for food, clothing, money, etc. 受赡养子女
non-dependent child *n.* a child who doesn't depend on his or her parents for food, clothing, money, etc. 不受赡养的子女
single parent *also* **lone parent** *n.* a parent who is bringing up a child on his or her own, because the other parent is not living with them 单亲
one-parent family *also* **single-parent family**, **lone-parent family** *n.* a family in which a single parent or lone parent brings up a child on his or her own 单亲家庭
preference *n.* the desire to have, do, or choose one thing rather than another, because people like it

better, or because it is more convenient for them 优先考虑；偏爱

multi- a prefix added to the beginning of nouns and adjectives, which means "many" 多 *e.g.* multi-racial society 多种族社会；multi-cultural society 多文化社会

nationality *n.* a large group of people with the same race, origin, language, etc. 民族；the membership of a nation by a person, esp. when abroad 国籍

melting pot *n.* a place in which people of different nations and races gradually get mixed together 熔炉

nuclear family *n.* a family consisting only of parents and their children, but not including aunts, uncles, cousins, etc. 核心家庭

minor *n.* a person who is still legally a child 未成年人

minor child *n.* a child who is below the age at which it is fully responsible in law for its actions 未成年子女 *syn.* **dependent child** 受赡养子女

relation *also* **relative** *n.* a member of one's family 亲属；亲戚 *e.g.* close/near relation；close/near relative 近亲；distant relation/relative 远亲

extended family *n.* a family group which includes relatives such as uncles, aunts, and grandparents, as well as parents, children, and brothers and sisters 外延家庭；大家庭

generation *n.* all the members of a family of about the same age 一辈人；一代人；a period of time in which a human being can grow up and have a family, about 25 or 30 years 一代

generation gap *n.* the difference in ideas, feelings, and interests between older and younger people, esp. considered as causing lack of understanding 代沟 *e.g.* to bridge/narrow the generation gap 消除代沟

teenage *a.* aged between 13 and 19 years 十几岁的 *e.g.* teenage people 十几岁的人们

divorce *n.* the formal ending of a marriage between husband and wife 离婚 *e.g.* divorce rate 离婚率

separation *n.* a legal arrangement by which a married couple live apart but do not end the marriage 离异

desertion *n.* an instance in which the husband leaves his wife and children without help or support 遗弃

desert *v.* leave sb and no longer help or support them 遗弃 *e.g.* deserted wife 被遗弃的妻子

tension *n.* the feeling which is produced in a situation when people are anxious and do not trust each other, and when there is a possibility of sudden violence or conflict 紧张

argument *n.* the act of disagreeing with sth or questioning whether it is correct 争论

hostility *n.* the state of extreme unfriendliness 敌对

conflict *n.* serious disagreement and argument about sth important 冲突

paternal *a.* relating to a father 父亲的；or the father's side of a family 父亲一方的 *e.g.* paternal love 父爱；paternal relative 父亲一方的亲戚

maternal *a.* relating to a mother 母亲的；or the mother's side of a family 母亲一方的 *e.g.* maternal love 母爱；maternal relative 母亲一方的亲戚

cohabit *v.* live together without marriage or before marriage 同居

cohabitation *n.* the state in which an unmarried couple live together as though married 同居

dink *n.* the abbreviation of Double/Dual Income, No Kids, which means either member of married partnership in which both members have a job and there are no children 丁克族

dinky *n.* the abbreviation of Double/Dual Income, No Kids Yet 丁克族 *syn.* **dink** 丁克族

dink family *n.* a married young couple who both earn a lot of money but don't want to have their own child 丁克家庭

Women's Libber *n.* an informal expression for a woman who is active in the Women's Liberation movement 妇女解放运动积极分子

advocate *v.* support a particular action or plan publicly 倡导

advocacy *n.* the act of supporting a particular action or plan publicly 主张 *e.g.* controversial advocacy 有争议的主张

gender *n.* a formal word which expresses the fact of being male or female 性别 *e.g.* gender equality 性别

平等

feminism *n*. the political belief which women should have the same rights, power, and opportunity that men have, and that the present situation should be changed to give them equality with men 女权主义

feminist *a*. relating to feminism 女权主义的 *e.g.* feminist issue 女权问题

abortion *n*. a woman's ending of her pregnancy and loss of the baby 堕胎 *e.g.* abortion rights 堕胎权利

workforce *n*. the total number of people in a country or region who are physically able to do a job and are available for work 全体劳动力; or the total number of people who are employed by a particular company 全体员工

under-presented *a*. rarely shown 很少露面的

kin *also* **kinfolk, kindred** *n*. a person's family and relatives 亲属 *e.g.* near kin 近亲 *syn*. **near relative/relation, close relative/relation** 近亲; distant kin/remote kinfolk 远亲 *syn*. **distant relative/relation** 远亲

kinship *n*. the relationship which exists between members of the same family 亲属关系

filiation *n*. the blood relationship between parents and their children or offspring 亲嗣关系

offspring *n*. a formal word for "children", being both the singular form and the plural form 子女

spouseship *n*. the marriage relationship between husband and wife 配偶关系

in-laws *n*. members of a person's husband's or wife's family 姻亲

father-in-law *n*. a man's wife's father 岳父; or a woman's husband's father 公公

mother-in-law *n*. a man's wife's mother 岳母; or a woman's husband's mother 婆婆

son-in-law *n*. a person's daughter's husband 女婿

daughter-in-law *n*. a person's son's wife 儿媳

consanguinity *n*. the relationship by birth 血缘关系

sibling *n*. a formal word for the blood relationship between two people with the same parents, like brothers and sisters 兄弟姐妹关系

paternal relative *n*. a relative on a person's father's side 父亲一方的亲戚

maternal relative *n*. a relative on a person's mother's side 母亲一方的亲戚

language study *n*. the study or learning of a language 语言研究; 语言学习

linguistic study *n*. the study or research of the linguistic knowledge 语言学研究

English learning *n*. the study or the learning of English as a language 英语学习

English study *n*. the study or the research of English culture, or the culture of English-speaking countries 英语文化研究

simultaneously *ad*. at the same time 同时

cross-cultural study *n*. the study dealing with or involving two or more different cultures 跨文化研究

English culture *n*. the culture of English-speaking countries such as Britain, United States, Canada, Australia and New Zealand 英语文化

definition *n*. a statement explaining the meaning of a word or expression 定义

classification *n*. the activity or process of classifying things into different types 分类

scope *n*. the whole area which an activity, topic, or piece of work deals with or includes 范围

extent *n*. the size or scale of a situation or difficulty 程度

range *n*. the total number of things which an activity or influence includes or involves 领域

social *a*. relating to society and the way it is organized, and to the way that the various groups within society depend on each other 社会的 *e.g.* social ideology 社会思想

intellectual *a*. involving a person's ability to understand or deal with ideas and information 智力的 *e.g.* intellectual wealth 智力创造的财富; 精神财富

spiritual *a*. relating to people's deepest thoughts and beliefs, rather than to their bodies and physical surroundings 精神的 *e.g.* spiritual civilization 精神文明

level *n*. the amount of sth at a particular time 水平

layer *n.* the different parts of ideas, systems, people's personalities, etc., and the way that they are added together or hide each other 层次

subjective *a.* influenced by or based on personal opinions and feelings rather than on facts 主观的 *e.g.* subjective will 主观意愿

ideological *a.* relating to principles, beliefs, or philosophy, esp. to a particular set of political beliefs held by a person, party, or country 思想的 *e.g.* ideological culture 思想文化

values *n.* the moral principles and beliefs that a person or a group of people think are important in life and that they tend to live their lives by 价值观 *e.g.* human values 人的价值观

way of thinking *n.* the manner or method of thinking 思维方式

aesthetics *n.* a branch of philosophy concerned with study of the concept of beauty 美学

morality *n.* the idea that some forms of behaviour are right, proper, and acceptable and that other forms of behaviour are bad or wrong, either in a person's own opinion or in the opinion of society 道德

ethics *n.* the idea or moral belief which influences the behaviour, attitudes, and philosophy of life of a group of people 伦理

religious *a.* relating to or connecting with religion in general or one particular religion 宗教的 *e.g.* religious feelings 宗教感情

psychology *n.* the kind of mind that a particular person, a type of person or a group of people have, which causes them to think or behave in the way that they do 心理 *e.g.* national psychology 国民心理

material *a.* concerned with the real world and physical objects, rather than with the abstract or the spiritual world 物质的；有形的；实体的 *e.g.* material production 物质生产

immaterial *a.* not having material form; without substance 无形的；非物质的 *e.g.* The body is material, but the soul is immaterial. 身体是有形的，而灵魂是无形的。

visible *a.* that can be seen 可以看见的 *e.g.* visible outcome 可以看见的成果

invisible *a.* that can't be seen 看不见的

tangible *a.* clear enough or definite enough to be easily seen, felt or noticed 可以触摸到的 *e.g.* tangible outcome 可以触摸到的成果

intangible *a.* not clear enough or definite enough for people to see, feel, or notice easily 触摸不到的

civilization *n.* a human society which has its own highly developed social organization, culture, and way of life that makes it distinct from other societies 文明 *e.g.* human civilization 人类文明

code *n.* a set of ideas by a group of people about the proper way to behave 准则 *e.g.* code of conduct 行为准则

Additional Knowledge

What Is Culture?

Language study refers to the study or learning of a language; while linguistic study refers to the study or research of the linguistic knowledge.

English learning refers to the study or the learning of English as a language; while English study refers to the study or the research of English culture, or the culture of English-speaking countries.

When we study a language, we study its culture at the same time. We make language study and cultural study simultaneously. When we study a foreign language, we study the culture of the concerning country at the same time. We make a cross-cultural study.

English culture refers to the culture of English-speaking countries such as Britain, the

United States, Canada, Australia and New Zealand.

What is culture? Scholars differ in its definition. There are more than 250 definitions concerning culture. There are various ways of its classification.

In consideration of its scope, extent or range, culture can be taken in a narrow sense and in a broad sense. Culture in a narrow sense refers to the social ideology or to the intellectual wealth in education, philosophy, art and literature.

Culture in a broad sense refers to the total sum of the material wealth and the intellectual wealth which have been created in the whole process of human social and historical development, or to the way of life, or life-style.

In consideration of its level or layer, culture can be classified at three levels. The first level is material culture which is processed and transformed by human subjective will. The second level is system culture which includes political system, economic system, legal system, artistic and literary works, human interrelation, customs and habits, and behaviour. The third level is ideological culture which includes human values, way of thinking, aesthetics, morality, ethics, religious feelings and national psychology.

There is a different way of classifying culture at four levels. They are:

1) the outcome or result of material production, including science and technology;

2) the productive relations including social system, political system, economic system, legal system and religious system;

3) the material(visible or tangible) outcome of spiritual civilization, including architecture, painting, sculpture, artistic and literary works; and

4) the immaterial(invisible or intangible) outcome of spiritual civilization, including ideology, habits and customs, and values.

There is also a way of classification of culture at two levels. That is culture with a big C and culture with a small c. Culture with a big C refers to art and literature, music, architecture, philosophy, and scientific and technological achievements which reflect various aspects of human civilization. And culture with a small c refers to habits and customs, way of life, code of conduct, social organization, and human interrelation which are a series of characteristics.

Exercises

I. Explain each of the following:
1) society
2) birth rate
3) life expectancy
4) ageing society
5) family
6) family planning
7) contraception
8) sterilization
9) mortality
10) nutrition
11) standards of living
12) working conditions
13) household
14) household size
15) married couple
16) dependent child
17) multi-racial society
18) multi-cultural society
19) nationality
20) melting pot

21) nuclear family
22) close relation
23) minor
24) extended family
25) generation
26) generation gap
27) divorce
28) separation
29) desertion
30) lone parent
31) tension
32) argument
33) conflict
34) paternal love
35) maternal love
36) marriage
37) cohabitation
38) dink
39) dink family
40) Women's Libber
41) Women's Liberation
42) abortion
43) kin
44) kinship
45) remote kinfolk
46) filiation
47) offspring
48) spouseship
49) consanguinity
50) in-laws

II. Give another way or other ways of saying each of the following:
Models: ageing society → aging society
　　　　elderly people → the elderly; old people; aged people
1) the expectation of life →
2) mortality rate →
3) minor child →
4) large family →
5) contraceptive method →
6) single-parent family →
7) Double Income, No Kids →
8) dinky →
9) Women's Lib →
10) kinfolk →
11) close kin →
12) distant kin →
13) relative on one's father's side →
14) relative on one's mother's side →

III. Answer the following questions:
1) Please give some examples showing the main social changes during the second half of the 20th century in Britain.
2) Why has there been a falling birth rate in recent years in Britain?
3) What has made it easier for people to plan families?
4) What is the relationship between voluntary sterilization for both men and women and a low birth rate?
5) Who usually have a longer life expectancy, men or women?
6) Why has there been a decline in mortality in recent years in Britain?
7) What factors have contributed to the decline in the mortality rate?
8) Who are the members of a traditional family?
9) Who do people prefer smaller families?
10) Why was the United States compared to a melting pot?
11) What is the fundamental family pattern in the United States now?
12) What does a nuclear family consist of?
13) Until when does a child usually stay with his or her parents in Britain?
14) Do the middle-aged people and elderly people generally live with their married children in the United States?

15) Where are extended families often found?
16) Do a person and his or her cousins belong to the same generation?
17) Do you think generation gap is a serious social problem in China?
18) Do Mother and Father equally have the final say on family matters in most American families?
19) Who takes care of the dependent children in a one-parent family?
20) Why does the dependent child in a one-parent family tend to have psychological problems?
21) Why is the failure of a married couple's marriage unfavourable to the growth and development of their dependent children?
22) What is the difference between divorce and separation?
23) Why have divorce and separation become much more common in recent decades in the United States?
24) Which of the divorced couple is more likely to remarry after divorce, man or woman?
25) Why is there a tendency that fewer people are getting married?
26) Why do more men and women tend to cohabit without marriage or before marriage?
27) What do dink and dinky respectively stand for?
28) What was the aim of the Women's Liberation movement in the 1960's?
29) What were the effects of the Women's Liberation movement in the 1960's?
30) What does sibling refer to?

Lesson Five

The Monarchical System

    For historical reason, countries in the world vary in their political systems.

    The United Kingdom is a constitutional monarchy. A monarchy is a monarchical state, which is governed by the monarchical system with a monarch as its supreme ruler. In this political system, power resides in the personage of an individual and is passed from one generation to the next through lines of inheritance. In Britain, the power of the monarch is limited by the country's constitution. The legal authority is given to Parliament, and the executive authority to the government.

    There are mainly two kinds of monarchy in the world. They are kingdom and empire. Generally speaking, a kingdom is a country or a state with a single supreme ruler, while an empire is a group of countries or states that are all controlled by the ruler or the government of one particular country. A male supreme ruler of a kingdom is the king while a female supreme ruler is the queen. But a queen can also be the wife of a king. A male supreme ruler of an empire is the emperor while a female supreme ruler is the empress. But an empress can also be the wife of an emperor. A king or an emperor is not elected, but is born into a royal family. The emperor of Japan is called Mikado.

    A crown is a circle made of gold and decorated with precious jewels, worn by a king and queen, or an emperor and empress on their heads in an official ceremony. So a crown is a sign or symbol of royal power. If a man is crowned, he has a crown placed on his head at a special ceremony and is given the power and status of king or emperor. If a woman is crowned, she has a crown placed on her head and becomes a queen or empress. So a crowned head is a king, queen, emperor or empress who is the ruler of their country. The Crown or the crown refers to the monarchy as represented by a monarch as the head. The crown can also be the office or power of a monarch. So the crown is regarded as an institution concerned with the government of a kingdom or an empire, rather than as an individual king or emperor. The monarch can also be called the crown while any member except the monarch is called the subject. So the subjects of a country are the people who are born and live there, or who have the right to live there. A sovereign is another way of saying a monarch, who has the highest level of authority in a country. A throne is a special chair that a king, queen, emperor or empress sits on in important ceremonies or on important official occasions. When a man comes to the throne, he becomes a king or an emperor. When a woman comes to the throne, she becomes a queen or an empress. If a person is on the throne, he or she is ruling or reigning in a kingdom or empire. So people may refer to the throne as a way of referring to the position of being king, queen, emperor or empress.

    Royalty refers to the royal family as a whole, or to all the members belonging to the royal family. A male member of the royal family who is not the king or the emperor is a prince. In Britain, the son or grandson of the sovereign is called a prince. The heir to the throne is called the Crown Prince, who will become the next king or emperor. In Britain, the Prince of Wales is the title often given to the heir to the throne, who is the eldest son of the king or queen. He will next rule the country. The wife of the Crown Prince has the title of Crown Princess. A Crown Princess can also be a princess who will be queen of her country when the present king or queen dies. Consort is the wife or husband of the ruling monarch. Prince Consort is the title often given to the husband of a reigning queen. A female member of the royal family who is not the queen or the empress is a princess. In Britain, the daughter or granddaughter of the sovereign, or the wife of a prince, is called a princess. Princess Royal is the title often given to the eldest daughter of the sovereign. A dowager is a woman who holds a title because of her late husband's important position. So the queen dowager is the widow of the former king while the empress dowager is the widow of the former emperor. In other words, she may well be the mother of the present king or emperor. In Britain, Queen Mother is the mother of a ruling king or queen, now referring to Queen Elizabeth II's mother in Britain. In some countries, a man can legally have more than one wife. The woman who lives with and has sex with a man but is of lower status than his wife is called a concubine. In some empires, an emperor may have an empress and many imperial concubines in his palace.

In a monarchy, the hereditary system is practiced. The power is passed on from an older to a younger person in the same family, from father to child, from one generation to the following generation. A monarchy has a hereditary head and a hereditary privileged class. This privileged class is called the aristocracy. It is a class of people whose families have a high social rank and who hold special titles. The aristocracy is made up of aristocrats whose family has a high social rank. An aristocrat usually has a title and some privileges. In Britain, the aristocracy is also called the nobility. Those people of noble birth or rank belong to the nobility. A member of the nobility is called a noble, either a nobleman or a noblewoman. In a hereditary system, the aristocracy is divided into the following ranks: duke, marquis/marquess, earl/count, viscount, baron and baronet. In Britain, a male member of one of the above ranks is called a peer. The whole body of peers is called peerage. A peeress is a female peer, or the wife of a peer, or the widow of a peer. The son or daughter of a peer can inherit a peerage. Then he or she is a hereditary peer or peeress. A Lord is a nobleman who has such a high rank in the British nobility as marquis/marquess, earl/count, viscount and baron. Lord is the title used in front of the name of a marquis, earl/count, viscount or baron. Lord may also be the title of a male life peer, for instance, Lord Owen. A Lady is a noblewoman who has such a high rank in the British nobility as marquise/marchioness, countess, viscountess or baroness. Lady is the title used in front of the name of a noblewoman, or of the wife and daughter of a nobleman. Lady may also be the title of a female life peer, for instance, Lady Thatcher.

In contrast to an aristocrat who is a hereditary peer, a commoner is a member of the common people who don't have any privileges or titles. A commoner can be elevated or raised to the peerage, that is, he or she can be made a life peer. This is an honorable title, which is granted only to the person himself or herself and is not inherited by his or her heir. In Britain, the King or the Queen may confer a knighthood on a person. Then he becomes a knight, with a rank of honor, lower than that of a baronet. A baronet is a member of the lowest hereditary titled order in Britain below a baron but above a knight. A baronet and a knight have the title "Sir" used before the first name with or without the surname, for instance, Sir Isaac Newton, and Sir Isaac, and Sir Winston Churchill or Sir Winston.

A monarchy with a hereditary head and a hereditary privileged class is in contrast to a republic like the United States, Canada, France and China. A republic is a country with a system of government in which the elected representatives of the people hold the supreme power with a non-hereditary head that is an elected President. That is to say, the republican form of government distinguishes from a monarchy in that it has an executive where the supreme leader is an elected President instead of a hereditary ruler. The system of government of a republic is based on the idea that every citizen has equal status, so that there is no king or queen, no emperor or empress, and no aristocracy. The government of a republic is usually elected by the people.

Britain is a united kingdom with a centralized central government. It is different from a federation. A federation is a federal country or a union of states, which consists of a group of states controlled by a central government. For instance, the United States is a federal country. And Switzerland is also a federal country. In this political system, the central government deals with things concerning the whole country, and makes decisions on such important things as foreign affairs and national defense. But each individual state has its own local powers and laws, and retains control of many internal matters.

The supreme leader of a country is called the Head of State, who is the chief representative of the country. In Britain, Queen Elizabeth II is its Head of State. Her counterpart in the United States is its President. The supreme leader of a government is called the Head of Government. In Britain, the Prime Minister is its Head of Government; but in the United States, the President also acts as its Head of Government.

The United Kingdom is a constitutional monarchy, with a king or a queen as its nominal Head of State. The king or the queen is a constitutional ruler, whose power is restricted or limited by the constitution.

U.K. monarchy is a secular institution, which is temporal and worldly. A secular power or a temporal power is not concerned with spiritual or religious affairs. It is in contrast to the Church, which is concerned with spiritual or religious affairs.

In Britain, the monarch is either the king or the queen. As his or her absolute power has been reduced, he or she has no real power in hand. The Queen reigns, but does not rule. Although every new law must receive the Royal Assent, the Queen never refuses this. She is usually advised by the Prime Minister and unfailingly follows the will of Parliament. But today, the Queen is still a symbol of national unity.

The Queen's royal title is: "Elizabeth the Second, by the Grace of God of the United Kingdom of Great Britain and Northern Ireland and of Her other Realms and Territories Queen, Head of the Commonwealth, Defender of the Faith".

The Queen personifies the State. In law, she is:

1) head of the executive;

2) an integral part of the legislature;

3) head of the judiciary;
4) the commander-in-chief of the all the armed forces of the Crown; and
5) the "supreme governor" of the established Church of England.

The succession of the monarch is "male before female". Sons of the Sovereign have precedence over daughters in succeeding to the throne. The general order of succession is the eldest son, the eldest son's descendant, the second son, the eldest daughter, the eldest daughter's descendant, the brother. When a daughter succeeds, she becomes Queen Regnant, and has the same power as a king. The consort of a king takes her husband's rank and style, becoming Queen. The constitution does not give any special rank or privileges to the husband of a Queen Regnant. In Britain, the husband of Queen Elizabeth II has the title of Prince of Edinburgh. The monarch must have an intermarriage with aristocracy of any nation.

The Sovereign succeeds to the throne as soon as his or her predecessor dies. He or she is at once proclaimed at an Accession Council. The Sovereign's coronation follows the accession after a convenient interval. A coronation is the ceremony in which a king or queen is crowned. The ceremony takes place at Westminster Abbey in London, in the presence of representatives of the Houses of Parliament and all the great public organizations in Britain. The Prime Ministers and leading members of the other Commonwealth nations and representatives of other countries also attend.

The Sovereign has several official residences. Buckingham Palace is the official London residence of the sovereign. Windsor Castle is an official residence of the sovereign in Windsor, Berkshire. And Holyrood House, or properly the Palace of Holyrood House, is a large mansion in Edinburgh, Scotland, used as a residence by members of the royal family when visiting Scotland.

Words and Expressions

monarchy *also* **monarchical system** *n*. a system in which a monarch reigns over a country and in which another member of the same family will be the next monarch 君主制 *e.g.* constitutional monarchy 君主立宪制

monarch *n*. a royal person like a king or an emperor who reigns over a country 君主

monarchical *a*. relating to a monarch 君主的 *e.g.* monarchical state 君主国

constitution *n*. the system of laws and rules which formally states people's rights and duties 宪法

legal authority *n*. the power and right relating to the judgment in a court of law 司法权

executive authority *n*. the power and right to carry out decisions 行政权

supreme *a*. at the highest level in a particular organization or system 最高的;至高无上的 *e.g.* supreme ruler 最高统治者

kingdom *n*. a country or a state with a single supreme ruler 王国

empire *n*. a group of countries or states which are all controlled by the ruler or the government of one particular country 帝国 *e.g.* the British Empire 英帝国

emperor *n*. a male supreme ruler of an empire 皇帝

empress *n*. a female supreme ruler of an empire 女皇;or the wife of an emperor 皇后

Mikado *n*. the emperor of Japan 日本天皇

crown *n*. a circle made of gold and decorated with precious jewels, worn by a king and queen, or an emperor and empress on their heads at an official ceremony 王冠;皇冠

crowned head *n*. a king, queen, emperor or empress who is the ruler of their country 君主
the Crown *also* **the crown** *n*. the monarchy as represented by a monarch as the head 王位; or the monarch 君主
the subject *n*. any member except the monarch in a country 臣民
the subjects *n*. the people who are born and live in a country or who have the right to live there 国民
sovereign *n*. another way of saying a monarch, who has the highest level of authority in a country 最高统治者; 君主
throne *n*. a special chair which a king, queen, emperor or empress sits on at important ceremonies or on important official occasions 宝座; the position of being king, queen, emperor or empress 王位
come to the throne *v. phrase* become a king or an emperor, a queen or an empress 登基; 即位
be on the throne *v. phrase* rule or reign in a kingdom or empire 在王位
royal *a*. that belongs to, or is connected with a monarch, or a member of his or her family 王室的; 皇家的
royal family *n*. a king and a queen, or an emperor and an empress, and the members of their family 王室; 皇家
royalty *n*. the royal family as a whole, or all the members belonging to the royal family 王室全体成员; 皇家全体成员
Crown Prince *n*. a prince who will be king or emperor of his country when the present monarch dies 王储; 皇储
Crown Princess *n*. the wife of the Crown Prince 王妃; or a princess who will be queen of her country when the present king or queen dies 女王储
Prince of Wales *n*. the title often given to the heir to the throne in Britain, who is the eldest son of the king or queen, and will next rule the country 威尔士亲王
consort *n*. the wife or husband of the ruling monarch 在位君主的配偶
Prince Consort *n*. the title often given to the husband of a reigning queen 在位女王的丈夫
princess *n*. a female member of the royal family who is not the queen or the empress 公主; 王妃; 亲王夫人
Princess Royal *n*. the title often given to the eldest daughter of the sovereign 长公主; 大公主
dowager *n*. a woman who has received a title from her dead husband 享有亡夫爵位称号的贵妇
queen dowager *n*. the widow of the former king 王太后
empress dowager *n*. the widow of the former emperor 皇太后
Queen Mother *n*. the mother of a ruling king or queen, now referring to Queen Elizabeth II's mother in Britain 王太后
concubine *n*. a woman who lives with and has sex with a man but is of lower status than his wife 妾
imperial concubine *n*. a woman who lives with and has sex with an emperor but is of lower status than his empress 皇妃
hereditary *a*. that is passed on as a title, position or right from parent to child 世袭的 *e.g.* hereditary head 世袭首领; hereditary ruler 世袭统治者
hereditary system *n*. the system practiced in a monarchy, in which the power is passed on from an older to a younger person in the same family, from father to child, from one generation to the following generation 世袭制度
privilege *n*. a special right or advantage which is given to only one person or group and which puts them in a better position than other people 特权
privileged *a*. having special rights, advantages or opportunities which most other people do not have 有特权的
privileged class *n*. a group of people who have special rights which most other people do not have 特权阶级 *e.g.* hereditary privileged class 世袭特权阶级
aristocracy *n*. a class of people whose families have a high social rank and who hold special titles 贵族阶级

aristocrat *n*. a member of the aristocracy, who usually has a title and some privileges 贵族
nobility *n*. the aristocracy with noble birth or rank in Britain 贵族阶级
noble *n*. a member of the nobility, who has a title such as "Duke" or "Baron" 贵族
nobleman *n*. a male member of the nobility 男贵族
noblewoman *n*. a female member of the nobility 女贵族
duchess *n*. a noblewoman with the same title as a duke 女公爵; or the wife of a duke 公爵夫人; or the widow of a duke 公爵遗孀
marquis *also* **marquess** *n*. a nobleman with a rank just below that of a duke 侯爵
marquise *also* **marchioness** *n*. a noblewoman with the same title as a marquis 女侯爵; or the wife of a marquis 侯爵夫人; or the widow of a marquis 侯爵遗孀
earl *also* **count** *n*. a nobleman with a rank just below that of a marquis in Britain 伯爵
count *n*. a European nobleman with a rank just below that of a marquis, who has the same rank as an English earl 伯爵
countess *n*. a noblewoman with the same title as an earl or count 女伯爵; or the wife of an earl or count 伯爵夫人; or the widow of an earl or count 伯爵遗孀
viscountess *n*. a noblewoman with the same title as a viscount 女子爵; or the wife of a viscount 子爵夫人; or the widow of a viscount 子爵遗孀
baroness *n*. a noblewoman with the same title as a baron 女男爵; or the wife of a baron 男爵夫人; or the widow of a baron 男爵遗孀
peer *n*. a male member of one of the peerage in Britain 贵族
peeress *n*. a female peer 女贵族; or the wife of a peer 贵族夫人; or the widow of a peer 贵族遗孀
hereditary peer *n*. the son of a peer who can inherit a peerage 世袭贵族
hereditary peeress *n*. the daughter of a peer who can inherit a peerage 世袭女贵族
Lord *n*. a nobleman who has such a high rank in the British peerage or the title of a male life peer 勋爵 *e.g.* Lord Owen 欧文勋爵
Lady *n*. a noblewoman who has such a high rank in the British peerage or the title used in front of the name of a noblewoman, or the title of a female life peer 女勋爵 *e.g.* Lady Thatcher 撒切尔女勋爵
commoner *n*. a member of the common people who don't have any privileges or titles 平民
life peer *n*. a person who is given a title such as "Lord" which he can use for the rest of his life but which he cannot pass on to his eldest son when he dies 终身贵族; 新封贵族
knighthood *n*. a title which is given to a man by the King or the Queen in Britain for his outstanding achievements or his service to his country 爵士
knight *n*. a person who has been given a knighthood, the title "Sir", which is lower than that of a baronet 爵士
baronet *n*. a member of the lowest hereditary titled order in Britain below a baron but above a knight, who has the title "Sir" 准男爵
Sir *n*. the title used before the first name with or without the surname of a baronet and a knight 爵士
Sir Isaac Newton *also* **Sir Isaac** (1642–1727) *n*. English natural philosopher, who established the theory of gravitation to explain the motions of the earth and the moon 艾萨克·牛顿爵士; 艾萨克爵士
Sir Winston Churchill *also* **Sir Winston** (1874–1965) *n*. the former Prime Minster of the United Kingdom in 1940–1945, and 1951–1955, whose full name is Sir Winston Leonard Spencer Churchill 温斯顿·伦纳德·斯潘塞·丘吉尔爵士; 温斯顿·丘吉尔爵士; 温斯顿爵士
republic *n*. a country whose system of government is based on the idea that every citizen has equal status, so that there is no king or queen and no aristocracy 共和国
executive *n*. the part of the government of a country which is concerned with carrying out decisions or orders 行政部门

supreme leader *n.* the person who is at the highest level in a particular organization or system 最高领导人；最高领袖

elected President *n.* a person who has been elected to the presidency but has not officially started to carry out the duties as a president 当选总统

united kingdom *n.* a kingdom formed by different areas joined together 联合王国

central government *n.* the government of a whole country, in contrast with a local government which governs local areas 中央政府

centralized *a.* relating to a system of government or organization by which one central group of people gives out instructions to all the other regional groups 集权的 *e.g.* centralized central government 中央集权政府

state *n.* one of the areas or divisions in a country such as the United States or India, which is made up of a number of areas or divisions that each have control over many of their own affairs （美国的）州；（印度的）邦

federal country *n.* a country consisting of a group of states controlled by a central government, which deals with things concerning the whole country, such as foreign policy 联邦制国家

federal *a.* belonging or relating to the federal system, in which a central government deals with things concerning the whole country 联邦制的

federation *n.* a federal country or a union of states, which consists of a group of states controlled by a central government 联邦；联邦制国家

Head of State *n.* the supreme leader of a country, who is the chief representative of the country 国家元首

counterpart *n.* a person who has a similar function or position in another place or organization 对应的人

Head of Government *n.* the supreme leader of a government 政府首脑

nominal *a.* that is supposed to have a particular identity or status, but in reality does not have it 名义的 *e.g.* nominal Head of State 名义国家元首

constitutional *a.* officially allowed by the constitution of a particular country 宪法规定的

constitutional ruler *n.* the ruler who is officially allowed by the constitution of a particular country 宪法规定的统治者

secular *a.* that has no connection with religion or churches 世俗的；非宗教的 *syn.* **temporal, worldly** 世俗的

secular institution *n.* an institution which has no connection with religion or churches 世俗制度

secular power *also* **temporal power** *n.* the power which has no connection with religion or churches 世俗权力

temporal *a.* relating to practical material affairs as opposed to religious affairs 尘世的；世俗的

worldly *a.* relating to this life and ordinary activities, rather than to spiritual or eternal things 今世的；世俗的

absolute power *n.* the complete power of a monarch over his or her country 绝对权力；无限权力

reign *v.* be the king or queen, esp. without holding real power 在王位 *e.g.* The Queen reigns, but does not rule. 女王在位，而无实权。

assent *n.* agreement to a suggestion or idea, esp. after careful consideration 同意；赞成；批准

Royal Assent *n.* agreement by the king or queen 国王/女王批准

unity *n.* the state of people being in agreement and acting together for a particular purpose 统一；团结 *e.g.* national unity 国家统一；民族团结

grace *n.* the kindness which God shows to human beings because He loves them 恩典 *e.g.* the grace of God 上帝的恩典

realm *n.* a country which has a king or queen as its head of state 王国

territory *n.* the land which is controlled by a particular country or ruler 领土；a country or region which controlled by another country 领地

head of the executive n. the person who is responsible for the part of the government of a country which is concerned with carrying out decisions or orders 行政首脑

legislature n. the group of people in a country who have the power to make and pass laws 立法机构

judiciary n. the branch of authority in a country which is concerned with justice and the legal system 司法部门

head of the judiciary n. the person who is responsible for the branch of authority in a country which is concerned with justice and the legal system 司法部门首脑

commander-in-chief n. an officer who is in charge of all the forces fighting in a particular area or taking part in a particular operation 总司令；最高统帅

armed forces n. military forces of a country, usu. the army, navy and air force 武装部队

succession n. the act, process or right of being the next person to have an important job or position 继承 e.g. succession of the monarch 王位继承

have precedence over v. phrase treat as being more important and deal with before the others 优先于

succeed to the throne v. phrase be the next king or queen 继承王位

regnant a. ruling, esp. (of a queen) in her own right and not as the wife of a king 执政的 e.g. Queen Regnant 执政的王后

Prince of Edinburgh n. the title of the husband of Queen Elizabeth II in Britain 爱丁堡亲王

intermarriage n. the marriage between people from different social, racial or religious groups 联姻；通婚

predecessor n. the person who held a position before sb else 前任；前辈

accession n. the act of taking up a position of authority, esp. as the ruler of a country 登基；即位；就职

council n. a specially organized meeting which is attended by a particular group of people 会议

Accession Council n. a specially organized meeting for the accession of a king or queen 登基典礼

coronation n. the ceremony in which a king or queen is crowned 加冕礼 e.g. the Sovereign's coronation 君主加冕礼

Westminster Abbey n. one of the leading landmarks of London, being a fine early English church in Westminster, where almost all the English sovereigns have been crowned since the 11th century, and where many famous Englishmen and Englishwomen are buried 威斯敏斯特大教堂

residence n. a big and impressive house in which a person lives 住宅；府邸 e.g. official residence 官邸

Buckingham Palace n. the official London residence of the British Sovereign 白金汉宫

Windsor Castle n. an official residence of the British Sovereign in Windsor, Berkshire 温莎城堡

Windsor n. a town in Berkshire, England, which is famous for its castle as an official residence of the British Sovereign 温莎

Berkshire n. a midland county of England, famous for its beautiful scenery 伯克郡

the Palace of Holyrood House also **Holyrood House**, **Holyrood** n. a large mansion in Edinburgh, Scotland, used as a residence by members of the British royal family when visiting Scotland 霍利鲁德行宫

politics n. the work and ideas that are connected with governing a country or a town; and also a profession and a means of winning and keeping governmental control 政治

politician n. a person whose job is politics, esp. one who is a member of parliament or who is involved in some way in governing a country 从政者; or sb who is skilled at dealing with people in a way which is advantageous to themselves or at using a system to their own advantage 政客；玩弄权术者

political affair n. an affair related to politics 政治事务

neutral a. without strong feelings or opinions on either side of a question or argument 中立的 e.g. neutral sense 中性意义

derogatory a. having a low opinion of 贬低的 e.g. derogatory sense 贬义

commendatory a. having a high opinion of 赞扬的 e.g. commendatory sense 褒义

statesman *n.* an important and experienced political leader or government leader, esp. one who is widely known and respected 政治家;国务活动家

elder statesman *n.* an old and respected person, usually no longer in a position of power who is often asked for advice because of his or her long experience in politics 资深政治家;政界元老

political party *n.* a political organization whose members all have the same basic aims and beliefs, usu. an organization which tries to get its members elected to the government of a country or an area 政党

party politics *n.* the political actions carried out by or for a political party 党派政治

Additional Knowledge

Politics

In the West, politics refers to the work and ideas that are connected with governing a country or a town. It is often considered as a profession and a means of winning and keeping governmental control. Those who are engaged in political activities are called politicians. As their business is politics, they are concerned with political affairs. Very often a politician is a person who has been elected to a parliament or to a position in government. In this case, it has a neutral sense. But sometimes people use the word "politician" in a derogatory sense, which means a person who is skilled at dealing with people in a way that is advantageous to himself or herself or at using a system to his or her own advantage. However, the word "statesman" has a commendatory sense. It refers to an important and experienced political leader or government leader, especially one who has earned public respect as being wise, honorable and fair-minded. An elder statesman is an old and respected person, usually no longer in a position of power. But he is often asked for advice because of his or her long experience in politics.

In a Western country, people hold different political ideas, views and beliefs. A group or an association of people with the same political aims, opinions and beliefs may form a political party. A person who has joined a political party is a member of the party. And a person who supports a political party is a supporter of the party. The members of the political party try to win elections. Party politics refers to the political actions carried out by or for a political party.

Exercises

I. Explain each of the following:
   1) monarch
   2) monarchy
   3) constitutional monarchy
   4) king
   5) emperor
   6) Mikado
   7) crown
   8) coronation
   9) subject
   10) sovereign
   11) prince
   12) Prince of Wales
   13) princess
   14) Princess Royal
   15) widow
   16) queen dowager
   17) imperial concubine
   18) aristocracy

19) nobility
20) peerage
21) Lord
22) Lady
23) knighthood
24) Sir
25) federation
26) Head of State
27) Head of Government
28) Queen Regnant
29) Prince of Edinburgh
30) constitution

II. Give the converse word for each of the following words:
   Models: man → woman
           husband → wife
   1) king →
   2) emperor →
   3) Crown Prince →
   4) reigning queen →
   5) nobleman →
   6) peer →
   7) marquis →
   8) count →
   9) viscount →
   10) baron →

III. Look at the following list of words and find out which are members of the royalty, and which are members of the nobility:
   aristocrat, baron, baroness, baronet, consort, count, countess, crown prince, crown princess, duchess, duke, earl, emperor, empress dowager, empress, imperial concubine, king, marquis, marquise, monarch, noble, nobleman, noblewoman, peer, peeress, prince, princess, queen dowager, queen, viscount, viscountess
   1) Members of the royalty: monarch,
   2) Members of the nobility: noble,

IV. Answer the following questions:
   1) What is the difference between a kingdom and an empire?
   2) What is a queen?
   3) What is an empress?
   4) When is a king or queen crowned?
   5) What does royalty refer to?
   6) What is a Crown Prince?
   7) What is an empress dowager?
   8) Who is Queen Mother in Britain?
   9) Is an emperor allowed to have more than one wife?
   10) Who is directly addressed as Your Majesty in a monarchy?
   11) Who is indirectly addressed as Her Royal Highness?
   12) What is the hereditary system in a monarchy?
   13) What are the different ranks of the aristocracy?
   14) What is a peer?
   15) What is a hereditary peer?
   16) What is a life peer?
   17) What is a knight?
   18) What is a baronet?
   19) In what ways does a republic differ from a monarchy?
   20) Is Britain a federal country? Is Switzerland is federal country?

21) Who is the Head of State in Britain? Who acts as its counterpart in the United States?
22) Who acts as the Head of Government in Britain? Who acts as its counterpart in the United States?
23) How do you understand "The Queen reigns, but does not rule"?
24) Where does British Sovereign's coronation take place?
25) Who are present at British Sovereign's coronation?

Lesson Six

The Parliamentary System

In the Western countries, the legislature goes to the parliament or the congress; the executive goes to the government, and the judiciary goes to the Supreme Court.

The legislature of a country is the law-making body or institution. It is formed by a group of people who have the power to make, pass and change laws. In Britain, the legislature is the Parliament with its two Houses, which is also called the Houses of Parliament. In other words, the Parliament is the law-making body of Britain and its supreme authority. The Parliament usually adopts a two-house system. It is a system of the national law-making body with two branches: the Upper House or the Upper Chamber, and the Lower House or the Lower Chamber. The Upper House is usually grander but smaller, less representative, and less powerful than the other. The British Upper House is called the House of Lords, while the British Lower House is called the House of Commons. The American counterpart of the British Parliament is the Congress. In the United States, the Congress is made up of the Senate as its Upper House and the House of Representatives as its Lower House.

In Britain, the House of Lords can be simply called the Lords or the House. It used to be the assembly of members of the nobility and bishops in the Parliament. It is the less powerful of the two parts of the British Parliament. The members of the House of Lords are not elected by the people. They consist of Lords Spiritual and Lords Temporal. The Lords Spiritual are the Archbishops of Canterbury and York, the Bishops of London, Durham and Winchester, and the 21 next most senior diocesan bishops of the Church of England. The Lords Temporal used to be formed by:

1) hereditary peers of England, Scotland, Great Britain and the United Kingdom, but not including the peers of Ireland;

2) life peers created to assist the House in its judicial duties, which are Lords of Appeal or Law Lords; and

3) other life peers.

The work of the House of Lords is largely complementary to that of the House of Commons. It includes examining and revising bills from the Commons, and discussing important matters, which the Commons cannot find time to debate. It also acts in a legal capacity as a final court of appeal. The House usually sits or meets regularly for four days a week, with an average of 150 days in the year.

Since Tony Blair came to power as Prime Minister, he started a reform in 1997 on the formation of the Upper House. In 1999, he abolished 600 seats originally belonging to hereditary peers from the House of Lords.

The House of Lords acts as an advisory body to the government, but nearly always passes the bills presented to it by the Commons. The bill then goes to the Sovereign and receives the Royal Assent. After that, it becomes an Act of Parliament and is Law.

The House of Lords is the final court of appeal for civil cases in Britain, and for criminal cases in England, Wales and Northern Ireland. As the House of Lords also serves as the highest court in the land, the decision made in the House cannot be changed. Lords of Appeal or Law Lords are peers in the House of Lords who sit as the highest court of appeal, including the Lord Chancellor, and any peers who have held high judicial office or have themselves been Lord Chancellor. Lord Chancellor, or Lord High Chancellor as its full title, is the chief legal officer and also a member of the Cabinet. He acts as the Speaker of the House of Lords.

The House of Commons can also be called the Commons Chamber or the Chamber of Commons. It can be shortened as the Commons or the House. It is the assembly of elected representatives of the Parliament. It is the more powerful of the two parts of the British Parliament, whose members are called Members of Parliament. A Member of Parliament is a person who has been elected by the adult population of a particular town or district to represent them in the House of Commons. A Member of Parliament can be simply called an MP.

The main functions of the Parliament are to pass laws; to provide, by voting for taxation, the means of carrying on the work of government; to scrutinize government policy and administration, including proposals for expenditure; and to debate the major issues of the day. Parliament sits at Westminster. A meeting of the Parliament is called a sitting while a series of meetings of the Parliament is called a session. So a session is a period of time during which the Parliament regularly holds its meetings. A particular parliament is a particular period of time in which a parliament is doing its work, between two elections or between two periods of holiday. The House of Commons sits for about 175 days in the year and it is not in session during the summer months. The House has a maximum term of five years, at the end of which a general election must be held. The House meets regularly for five days each week. And each sitting officially starts from 14:30 in the afternoon to 22:00 at night from Mondays to Thursdays, and from 11:00 in the morning to 16:30 in the afternoon on Fridays. As the Commons is made up of opposing parties, all new bills must be passed by a majority vote. When a formal vote takes place, the MPs will divide into two groups, for the motion or against it, and go to one of two special corridors to cast or record their vote. The voting lobbies are called division lobbies. As the Members of Parliament have many duties apart from actually attending debates in the Chamber of the House, their days are very full. As 22:00 draws near, a vote may be called. When a vote is going to take place, a bell is rung to summon MPs to the voting lobbies. This bell is called Division Bell. When this Division Bell is rung, the MPs who are not actually attending the debate must hurry to vote. Sometimes, MPs can be seen running to the House of Commons across Parliament Square.

A bill is a plan for a possible new law. The process of passing a public bill goes through three readings. Each new bill must be presented or read three times to the Commons and passed by a majority vote on both the second and third readings. The bill does not become law at once. Before that, it must go through the same process in the House of Lords.

The government ministers from the ruling party sit on the front row of the fitted benches in the Commons Chamber. The leading members from the Opposition sit on the front row opposite the government ministers. Either of the two rows of seats is called the frontbench. These two groups of people are seated on opposite sides of the House facing each other. They are called Front Benchers. All other MPs who do not hold an official position in the Government or in the Opposition must find a seat wherever they can in the backbenches. They are called Back Benchers or Backbench MPs. An independent or neutral MP who belongs neither to the Government nor to the Opposition, sits on the crossbenches, which are at one end of the chamber at right angles to the main benches of the Government and the Opposition. Such an MP is called a crossbencher. The man who is elected by all the parties to control the proceedings in the House of Commons is called the Speaker. He is the only person who has a permanent seat and controls business in the Commons Chamber. A parliamentarian is a Member of Parliament who is an expert on the rules and procedures of Parliament and takes an active part in debates.

In the United States, the legislative branch or the law-making body is called the Congress. The federal laws are made by the Congress. It is made up of two houses—the Senate and the House of Representatives. The Senate is often referred to as the Upper House. It is the smaller but more important part of the Congress in the United States. It has the power to make laws. A senator is a member of the Senate in the United States. The Senate is composed of two senators from each state. So there are altogether one hundred senators. They are elected for six-year terms. Every two years, one-third of them will be reelected.

The House of Representatives can be simply called the House. It is the assembly of elected representatives in the central government of the United States. It is the less powerful of the two parts of the Congress. The population of each state determines its representation. So while the smallest states have only one representative each, the representation of the biggest states like California may have nearly 50 representatives. The entire House is elected every two years. A Congressman is a male member and a Congresswoman is a female member of the American Congress, especially of the House of Representatives. The person who controls business in the U. S. Congress is called the Speaker.

The job of the American Congress is to make laws. Before a bill or a proposed law becomes enacted, it must be approved by both houses of the Congress and by the President. The powers of the Congress and its limitations are specified in the Constitution.

The American Congress differs from the British Parliament chiefly in the fact that it does not contain the executive. The executive is the part of a government that is responsible for making sure that new laws and other decisions are carried out in the way they have been planned. The American President and his Cabinet are not members of the House, while the British Prime Minister and his Cabinet are members of the House. The Congress cannot commandingly ask a question of the President except in an impeachment proceeding. When the President is thought to have committed a serious crime, especially one against the State, he will be accused or impeached. If the Congress refuses to pass an Administration bill, there is no "crisis". The President in that case does not resign nor does he dissolve the Congress and force a new election.

In the U. S. Government the people are represented in two ways by the Congress and in another by the President. Each has the right and the means to appeal directly to the people for support against the other, and they do. The effect is that the struggle between the executive and the Congress varies between open hostility and an armed truce, even when the President's party is in control of the Congress. Another situation that cannot occur in a parliament arises when the people choose a President of one party and a Congress of another, putting the executive and the legislative branches automatically in opposition to one another.

The U.S. Congress is therefore more irresponsible than the British Parliament, for the members of the President's party can vote against an Administration proposal without voting to have the President resign. This lack of responsibility encourages demagogues in the Congress to play for headlines, since the party in power does not feel that strict discipline is a matter of life and death.

Executive is opposed to legislature and judiciary. In the United States, the judicial branch is composed of the federal courts. They are the District Courts, where trials are conducted; the Courts of Appeals; and the Supreme Court. One of the unusual features of the American judicial system is the power of the courts to declare legislation unconstitutional and, therefore, null and void. Federal laws are unconstitutional if they are in excess of the Congress's authority, or if they would infringe upon individual rights protected by the Constitution. State laws are unconstitutional if they conflict with federal laws or with that state's constitution. United States laws are in some way controlled or affected by all three branches of government. This is one example of the government's system of "checks and balances", by which each branch prevents improper actions by the other branches.

The building in which the United Kingdom Parliament works is called the Houses of Parliament, while the building in which the United States Congress works is called the Capitol.

Words & Expressions

parliament n. a group of people who meet in a particular place to make or change the laws of their country 议会

parliamentary a. that is connected with a parliament 议会的

parliamentary system n. the political system in which a group of elected representatives regularly meet to make or change the laws of their country 议会制

the Supreme Court n. the highest court of law 最高法院

law-making body also **law-making institution** n. a group of people who make laws 立法机构

the British Parliament n. the law-making body of Britain and its supreme authority 英国议会

two-house system n. the system of the national law-making body with two parts: the Upper House and the Lower House, of which one is more powerful than the other 两院制

the Houses of Parliament n. the British Parliament which consists of two parts: the House of Lords and the House of Commons 英国议会; or the building in London where the House of Lords and the House of Commons do their work 英国议会大厦

house also **chamber** n. a group of people who make laws and govern a country 议院

the Upper House also **the Upper Chamber** n. one of the two branches of a parliament, esp. the one which is grander but smaller, less representative, and less powerful in the British Parliament 上议院; 上院

the House of Lords *also* **the Lords, the House** *n*. the Upper House of the British Parliament 上议院；上院；贵族院

court of appeal *n*. a court in Britain, which deals with appeals against legal judgments 上诉法院 *e.g.* the final court of appeal 最终上诉法院

civil *a*. that exists or occurs within a country and involves the relationship between the different groups of people 民事的 *e.g.* civil case 民事案件

criminal *a*. that is connected with crime or with the punishment of crime 刑事的 *e.g.* criminal case 刑事案件

the Lower House *also* **the Lower Chamber** *n*. one of the two branches of a parliament, esp. the one that is larger, more representative, and more powerful in the British Parliament 下议院；下院

the House of Commons *also* **the Commons Chamber, the Chamber of Commons, the Commons, the House** *n*. the more powerful of the two parts of parliament in Britain, to which members are elected by the adult population of the country 下议院；下院；众议院；平民院

Lords Spiritual *n*. a collective term for those bishops in the Church of England, who are members of the House of Lords (上议院的) 宗教议员

Archbishop of Canterbury *n*. the spiritual leader of the Church of England, and also the Primate of All England 坎特伯雷大主教

Archbishop of York *n*. the Primate of England 约克大主教

bishop *n*. a clergyman of high rank in the Christian Church who is in charge of all the clergymen of lower rank in a particular area like a city or a district 主教

diocesan *a*. belonging or relating to a bishop's district for which he is responsible 主教教区的 *e.g.* diocesan bishop.主教教区主教

Durham *n*. an ancient city in Britain, famous for its noble cathedral and a castle 达勒姆

Winchester *n*. an ancient city in Britain, famous for its old cathedra and a castle 温彻斯特

the Church of England *n*. the established Protestant Church in England, and the official state religion of England 英国国教会；英国国教

Lords Temporal *n*. a collective term for all those peers in the House of Lords who are not Lords Spiritual (上议院的)世俗议员

Lords of Appeal *also* **Law Lords** *n*. peers in the House of Lords who sit as the highest court of appeal, including the Lord Chancellor and any peers who have held high judicial office or have themselves been Lord Chancellor 上诉法院法官议员

Lord High Chancellor *also* **Lord Chancellor** *n*. the title of the chief legal officer and also a member of the Cabinet, who acts as the Speaker of the House of Lords 上院议长兼大法官

Tony Blair (1953-) *n*. British Prime Minister 托尼·布莱尔

advisory body *n*. a group of people who regularly give suggestions and help to other people or organizations, esp. about a particular subject or area of activity 咨询机构

bill *also* **proposed law** *n*. a plan for a possible new law 议案；提案 *e.g.* to examine a bill 审议提案；to revise a bill 修改提案；to pass a bill 通过提案

Member of Parliament *also* **MP** (*abbrev.*) *n*. a person who has been elected by the adult population of a particular town or district to represent them in the House of Commons 下院议员

policy *n*. a general set of ideas or plans which has been officially agreed on by people in authority and which is used as a basis for making decisions, esp. in politics, economy or business 政策 *e.g.* government policy 政府政策

scrutinize *v*. look at sth very carefully, often in order to find out some information about it or from it 检查 *e.g.* to scrutinize government policy 检查政府政策；to scrutinize government administration 检查政府行政工作

vote *n.* a choice made by a particular person or group at a meeting or in an election 投票；选举 *e.g.* majority vote 多数选票

the ruling party *also* **the party in power** *n.* the political party which takes charge of a country's affairs by winning an election 执政党

the opposition party *n.* a political party which forms part of a parliament, but is not in the government 反对党 *syn.* the opposition 反对党

the Opposition *n.* the biggest opposition party, or a group of opposition parties which form part of a parliament, but are not in the government 最大的反对党

opposing parties *n.* the political parties with two opposing ideas which are too different to fit into the same system or plan 对立的政党

public bill *n.* a bill which affects the general public 公共议案

reading *n.* one of the three stages of presentation and discussion of a new bill in the parliament before it can be passed as law 读议案 *e.g.* to go through three readings 经过三读；first reading 一读议案；second reading 二读议案；third reading 三读议案

summon *v.* order sb to come 召集 *e.g.* to summon MPs 召集议员

motion *n.* a formal proposal which the people present discuss and then vote on 动议 *e.g.* for the motion 赞成动议；against the motion 反对动议

lobby *n.* the area which is behind the main door of a large building and which has corridors and staircases leading off it 前厅 *e.g.* voting lobbies 投票厅；division lobbies 分组投票厅

division *n.* a formal vote in the House of Commons, when MPs divide into two groups, for the motion or against it, and go to one of two special corridors called division lobbies to cast or record their vote 分组投票

cast one's vote *also* **record one's vote** *v. phrase* make one's choice or state one's opinion, esp. officially at a meeting or in an election, for example, by raising one's hand or writing on a piece of paper 投票

cast one vote *v. phrase* make a choice or decision by voting 投一票

Division Bell *n.* the bell rung to summon MPs to the voting lobbies when a vote is going to take place 分组投票钟声

Parliament Square *n.* the square in front of the Houses of Parliament in London 议会广场

Westminster *n.* an alternative term for the Houses of Parliament, esp. in the sense of the government of the day 威斯敏斯特

sit *v.* meet regularly and carry out the work officially 开例会

sitting *n.* one of the occasions when the Parliament meets regularly in order to carry out is work 例会

session *n.* a series of meetings of the Parliament 一系列会议；or a period of time during which the Parliament regularly holds its meetings 会期 *e.g.* to be in session 正在开会；to be not in session 休会

parliament *n.* a particular period of time in which a parliament is doing its work, between two elections or between two periods of holiday 议会任期

general election *n.* an election held throughout the United Kingdom on a particular day to elect a government 大选；普选

minister *n.* a person who is in charge of a particular government department 部长；大臣 *e.g.* government minister 政府部长；政府大臣

the frontbench *n.* one of the two front benches or rows of sets in the House of Commons, to the right and left of the Speaker, which are occupied respectively by ministers of the current government and equivalent members of the Opposition 前座

Front Bencher *n.* an MP entitled to sit on one of the frontbenches in the House of Commons 前座议员

the backbench *n.* the bench in the back of the House of Commons, where sit the MPs who do not hold any official position or special office in the Government or in the Opposition 后座

Back Bencher *also* **Backbench MP** *n*. an MP who does not hold any official position or special office in the Government or in the Opposition and who must find a seat wherever they can in the backbenches 后座议员

the crossbench *n*. the bench at one end of the chamber at right angles to the main benches of the Government and the Opposition, which is occupied by an MP who does not regularly support any particular political party 中立议员席位

crossbencher *n*. an independent or neutral MP who belongs neither to the Government nor to the Opposition, who sits on the crossbench 中立议员 *syn*. **independent MP** 独立议员; **neutral MP** 中立议员

independent MP *n*. an MP who does not represent any political party 无党派议员; 独立议员

neutral MP *n*. an MP who does not regularly support any particular political party 中立议员

the Speaker *n*. the person who is elected by all the parties to preside over meetings and control the proceedings in the Parliament 议长

seat *n*. a place as an MP, which is a result of gaining the most votes in an election 席位 *e.g.* permanent seat 永久席位

parliamentarian *n*. an MP who is an expert on the rules and procedures of Parliament and takes an active part in debates 资深议员

the Congress *n*. the elected group of politicians that is responsible for making federal laws in the United States 美国国会

the Senate *n*. the Upper House of the U.S. Congress, which is smaller but more important than the Lower House, the House of Representatives 参议院

senator *n*. a member of the Senate in the United States 参议员

the House of Representatives *also* **the House** *n*. the Lower House of the U.S. Congress, which is bigger but less important than the Upper House, the Senate 众议院

assembly *n*. a gathering of people 集会

representative *n*. a person who has been chosen to act or make decisions on behalf of another person or a group of people 代表 *e.g.* elected representative 当选代表

representation *n*. the state of having one or more representatives in a parliament, who can vote or make decisions on behalf of other people 代表

California *n*. one of the biggest states in the United States 加利福尼亚

Congressman *n*. a male member of the U.S. Congress, esp. of the House of Representatives 男国会议员; 男众议员

Congresswoman *n*. a female member of the U.S. Congress, esp. of the House of Representatives 女国会议员; 女众议员

the Speaker *n*. the person who controls business in the U.S. Congress 美国国会议长

Cabinet *n*. a group of the most senior and powerful ministers in a government, or advisers to a president, who meet regularly to discuss and decide policies 内阁 *e.g.* Cabinet member/member of the Cabinet 内阁成员

impeachment *n*. the trial of a public official, esp. in the United States, for a serious crime committed in office 弹劾 *e.g.* impeachment proceeding 弹劾程序

impeach *v*. charge a government official or politician with committing a serious crime, esp. in the United States 弹劾

Administration *n*. the government of a country, esp. that of the United States 政府; 美国政府 *e.g.* Administration bill 政府提案; Administration proposal 政府建议

crisis *n*. a situation where sth, such as people's confidence in a person, is so heavily attacked or questioned that there is serious doubt whether it will continue to exist 危机 *e.g.* crisis of confidence 信任危机

resign *v*. give up a job or a position 辞职

dissolve *v*. formally end or break up an organization or an institution, esp. the Parliament or the Congress, so that elections for a new Parliament or Congress can be held 解散 *e.g.* to dissolve the Congress 解散国会

hostility *n*. a behaviour which is unfriendly or aggressive, esp. towards particular people or ideas that one disagrees with or disapproves of 敌视 *e.g.* open hostility 公开敌视

truce *n*. an agreement between two people or groups of people to stop fighting or quarrelling for a short time 停战 *e.g.* armed truce 军事停战

demagogue *n*. a political leader who tries to win support by appealing to people's emotions rather than by rational arguments, which has a derogatory sense 蛊惑民心的政客;煽动家

headline *n*. the title of a newspaper story printed in large letters at the top of the story, esp. on the front page 报纸(头版)标题

headlines *n*. the main points of the news which are read on radio or television 新闻提要

play for headlines *v. phrase* try to become famous by getting a lot of publicity from the media about sth 企图成为新闻人物

discipline *n*. the practice of making people obey strict rules of behaviour and of punishing them when they do not obey rules 纪律 *e.g.* strict discipline 严格纪律

a matter of life and death *n*. an extremely serious and dangerous matter 生死攸关的事情

federal court *n*. a court belonging or relating to the federal country, rather than to one of the states within it 联邦法院

district court *n*. a court belonging or relating to an area of a country or town treated as an administrative unit 地方法院

legislation *n*. the act or process of passing a law 立法

unconstitutional *a*. that is against the constitution 违反宪法的

null and void *a*. legally invalid 无效的

federal law *n*. a law passed by the federal law-making body 联邦法律

state law *n*. a law passed by the state law-making body 州法律

in excess of *prep. phrase* more than a particular amount 超过

infringe upon *v*. interfere with people and do not allow them the freedom they are entitled to 侵犯 *e.g.* to infringe upon one's right 侵权

right *n*. sth which people are morally or legally entitled to do it or to have it 权利 *e.g.* individual right 个人权利

checks and balances *n*. a political system of the United States to deal with the relationship among the three branches of legislature, executive and judiciary, in which each branch prevents improper actions by the other branches 制约与均衡

Capitol *n*. the building in Washington where the U.S. Congress meets 美国国会大厦;or a similar building for each particular state of the United States 美国各州议会大厦

power *n*. the official authority and permission to do sth 权;权力;权限

legislative power *n*. the official authority to make and pass laws 立法权

federal administration *n*. another way of saying federal government 联邦政府

the Parliament of Canada *n*. the law-making body of Canada, which consists of the Crown, the Senate and the House of Commons 加拿大议会

money bill *n*. a bill concerning finance 财政议案

review *v*. examine a situation, method or procedure in order to decide whether to make any changes in it 审议 *e.g.* to review a bill 审议提案

legislation *n*. the laws which are passed by a government or state concerning a particular situation or thing

法律 e.g. proposed legislation 提议的法律; to introduce one's own legislation 提出自己的法律

constituency n. a town or area which is officially allowed to elect sb to represent them in parliament 选区

majority n. the difference between the number of votes or parliamentary seats which the winner gets in an election or vote and the number of votes or parliamentary seat which the next person or party gets 多数选票 e.g. simple majority 简单多数选票

election n. an organized process in which people vote to choose a person or group of people to represent them in parliament, on a committee, etc., or to hold an official position such as president or chairman of a group 选举 e.g. federal election 联邦选举

Governor General n. a person who is sent to a former colony as the chief representative of the country which used to control that colony 总督

exercise v. use authority, rights, or responsibilities effectively 行使 e.g. to exercise executive power 行使行政权

prerogative n. a special privilege or power which sb has or is allowed to have 特权 e.g. to exercise the prerogative 行使特权

confidence n. a strong belief in the ability of a person, plan, etc. to do what is needed effectively and successfully 信任 e.g. to enjoy the confidence 得到信任; to lose the confidence 失去信任

duty n. all the work which sb has to do because it is part of their job or their position in society 职责 e.g. parliamentary duty 议会职责

ministerial a. belonging or relating to a government minister 部长的 e.g. ministerial responsibility 部长责任

Additional Knowledge

Canada's Legislature and Executive

All the legislative powers of Canada's federal administration are vested in the Parliament of Canada, which consists of the Crown, the Senate and the House of Commons. The Canadian Head of State is Queen Elizabeth II. In Canada, the Governor General, who is appointed on the recommendation of the Prime Minister, represents the Queen. Bills may originate either in the Senate or in the House of Commons. In practice, however, important bills originate in the House of Commons; any money bill must originate in the Commons.

The 104-seat Senate was designed as an institution whose members would represent the various regions of Canada. The Governor General on the recommendation of the Prime Minister appoints the members of the Senate. The 104 senators' job is to review bills passed in the House of Commons and to take a "second look" at proposed legislation. They also introduce their own legislation.

The 295 members of the House of Commons are elected in as many constituencies by simple majority for a maximum of five years. These elected representatives gather to make laws affecting all Canadians. Any Canadian citizen, male or female, who has reached the age of 18, is entitled to vote in a federal election.

The Governor General, who exercises all the prerogatives of the Canadian Crown, is the source of executive power. In practice, the Prime Minister and other members of the Cabinet exercise executive power as the Government. The Cabinet comprises the Prime Minister, who is leader of the party enjoying the confidence of the popularly elected House of Commons, and his personally chosen ministers. The Cabinet members are members of

Parliament and their responsibility as such often requires them to give priority to their parliamentary duties despite their ministerial responsibilities.

The Cabinet, or the Government, is responsible only to the House of Commons. If it loses the confidence of the majority in the House, it is called upon to resign, in which case the defeated Prime Minister is expected to recommend that the Governor General dissolve the Parliament and call a general election.

Exercises

I. Explain each of the following:
1) legislature
2) parliament
3) congress
4) executive
5) judiciary
6) the Supreme Court
7) two-house system
8) the Upper House
9) the Lower Chamber
10) the House of Lords
11) the House of Commons
12) the Senate
13) the House of Representatives
14) Lords Spiritual
15) Lords Temporal
16) court of appeal
17) Act of Parliament
18) advisory body
19) civil case
20) criminal case
21) Lords of Appeal
22) Lord Chancellor
23) Member of Parliament
24) Westminster
25) opposing parties
26) sitting
27) session
28) bill
29) reading
30) division lobbies
31) Division Bell
32) the ruling party
33) the Opposition
34) the frontbenches
35) Front Bencher
36) the backbenches
37) Back Bencher
38) the crossbenches
39) crossbencher
40) independent MP
41) neutral MP
42) the Speaker of the Commons Chamber
43) parliamentarian
44) senator
45) Congressman
46) Congresswoman
47) the Speaker of the U.S. Congress
48) impeachment
49) Administration bill
50) crisis
51) resign
52) dissolve the Congress
53) Administration proposal
54) demagogue
55) play for headlines
56) discipline
57) unconstitutional
58) infringe upon individual rights
59) the system of "checks and balances"
60) the Capitol

II. Give another way or other ways of saying each of the following:
Model: the Parliament → the Houses of Parliament
1) the Upper Chamber →
2) the Lower House →

3) the House of Lords →
4) the House of Commons →
5) Law Lords →
6) Lord High Chancellor →
7) MP →
8) proposed law →
9) the party in power →
10) the opposition party →
11) Backbench MP →
12) the House of Representatives →

III. Fill in the blanks:
   Model: The Canadian Parliament consists of two houses, which are ____ and ____. →
       The Canadian Parliament consists of two houses, which are the Senate and the House of Commons.
   1) The British Parliament consists of two houses, which are _____ and _____.
   2) The U.S. Congress consists of two houses, which are _____ and _____.
   3) The members of the House of Lords consist of Lords _____ and Lords _____.
   4) In the United States, the judicial branch consists of the _____ Courts, which are the _____ Courts, where trials are conducted; the Courts of _____; and the _____ Court.

IV. Look at the following words and find out which are related to the British Parliament and which are related to the U.S. Congress:
   Archbishop of Canterbury, Archbishop of York, Back Bencher, backbench, Capitol, Congressman, Congresswoman, crossbench, crossbencher, Front Bencher, frontbench, House of Commons, House of Lords, House of Representatives, Houses of Parliament, Lord High Chancellor, Lords of Appeal, Lords Spiritual, Lords Temporal, Member of Parliament, MP, Parliament Square, parliamentarian, Senate, senator, Speaker, Westminster
   1) The British Parliament: Parliament,
   2) The U.S. Congress: Congress,

V. Answer the following questions:
   1) What is the parliamentary system?
   2) What institution in Britain has the power to make, pass and change laws?
   3) What is the difference between the Upper House and the Lower House?
   4) What is the name of the British Upper House? What is the name of the British Lower House?
   5) What is the American counterpart of the British Parliament?
   6) What is the British counterpart of the American Senate?
   7) What is the American counterpart of the British House of Commons?
   8) What is the function of the House of Lords?
   9) What institution acts as a final court of appeal?
   10) How often does the House of Lords meet each week?
   11) How long does the House of Lords sit in the year?
   12) Who started a reform in 1997 on the formation of the House of Lords?
   13) How many seats in the House of Lords were abolished in 1999?
   14) Who acts as the Speaker of the House of Lords?
   15) Which is the more powerful of the two branches of the British Parliament?
   16) What are the main functions of the Parliament?

17) Where is the Parliament situated?
18) What is a sitting? What is a session?
19) How often does the House of Commons meet each week?
20) How long does the House of Commons sit in the year?
21) How long does each sitting of the Commons last each day?
22) Is the Commons in session during the summer months?
23) How long is it between the two general elections in Britain?
24) Why must a new bill be passed by a majority vote in the Commons?
25) What are the voting lobbies called in the Commons?
26) When is Division Bell rung?
27) Why can some MPs be seen running to the House of Commons across Parliament Square when Division Bell is rung?
28) How many readings must a bill go through before it becomes law?
29) Who sit on the frontbenches in the House of Commons?
30) Who sit on the backbenches in the House of Commons?
31) Who sit on the crossbenches in the House of Commons?
32) Who has a permanent seat in the House of Commons?
33) What institution makes the federal laws in the United States?
34) How many senators are there in the Senate?
35) How long is the term of a Senate?
36) Which is the more powerful branch of the British Parliament, the House of Lords or the House of Commons?
37) Which is the more powerful branch of the American Congress, the Senate or the House of Representatives?
38) What determines the representation of the House of Representatives?
39) Is California a big or small state in the U.S.?
40) What is the function of the U.S. Congress?
41) Who have the right to approve the proposed law before it becomes enacted?
42) Where are the powers and limitations of the Congress specified?
43) In what way does the American Congress differ from the British Parliament?
44) Do the American President and his Cabinet constitute members of the Congress? Do the British Prime Minister and his Cabinet constitute members of the Parliament?
45) Can the U.S. Congress commandingly ask a question of the President? When can the Congress ask a question of the President in a commanding way?
46) Is there crisis when the U.S. Congress refuses to pass an Administration bill?
47) Does the U.S. President resign or dissolve the Congress and force a new election if there is crisis?
48) How are the people represented in the U.S. Government?
49) Why is the American Congress more irresponsible than the British Parliament? What is the result of such lack of responsibility?
50) Under what circumstances are state laws unconstitutional in the U.S.?

Lesson Seven

The Electoral System

In a Western country like Britain, there are various kinds of election. In a general election, the voters of the whole country choose their national parliament, while in a local election, the voters in a district choose their local council.

In Britain, the House of Commons is a representative assembly elected by voters or electors through a general election and by-elections.

A general election takes place after a Parliament has been dissolved and a new one summoned by the Sovereign. But sometimes, the Prime Minister may call a snap election to take place before the expiry of the five-year term of the Parliament. In that case, it is a sudden and unexpected decision made by the Prime Minister in his favour to have an election to take place beforehand. But under ordinary circumstance, the political parties launch campaigns and the government officials organize the election for several weeks. The general election is a massive undertaking and all the voters in the country must be notified.

A by-election is a special election held between regular elections. It is an election of a new Member of Parliament in a single constituency, which takes place when a vacancy occurs in the Commons as a result of the death or resignation of an MP, or when an MP is given a peerage.

The United Kingdom is divided into 659 constituencies. A constituency is a district with its own elected representative in the Parliament. The constituency may also refer to the body of voters living in that district. Each constituency chooses one member to the House of Commons. This member is called Member of Parliament or MP, who will occupy one seat in the Parliament. The Member of Parliament will go to the House of Commons to represent his or her constituency. Every MP must be responsible for their constituency. Every constituency has a returning officer to oversee the voting and make sure that the votes are counted correctly. If the result of the election is very close, the official in charge may order a recount.

Suffrage refers to the right to vote in political elections. In Britain, universal adult suffrage refers to the right of all adults to vote. The British women have struggled for their suffrage, that is, for their equal right to vote as men have. A suffragette was a woman who was involved in the campaign for women to be given the right to vote in Britain in the early 20th century.

A voter or an elector is a person who votes or who has the right to vote in a political election. The electorate refers to all the people in a country or in an area who have the right to vote in an election. On polling day, each voter or elector goes to cast one vote at a polling station. Every voter writes their choice on a ballot paper. After making a choice, they put the ballot paper into a ballot box. The electors can vote by post, or by proxy. The postal vote is sent by the electors who have to be away from their constituency on polling day, while the proxy vote is made by a person on behalf of an elector when that elector is unable to go to the polling station for such reasons as disability and long-term illness. If a person is a British subject, who is over the age of eighteen, he or she may vote. Besides, the voter must live for a fixed period of time in any constituency. But there are a few exceptions to this, the strangest one being the Queen. As the Sovereign is considered to be above politics, the Queen has no right to vote. Members of the House of Lords also have no right to vote. Criminals and lunatics have no right to vote. The person who applies for election to the Parliament is a candidate. The candidate must be aged 21 or over 21.

The present electoral system is based on the existence of organized political parties, each laying rival policies before the electorate. Now the two main political parties in Britain are the Labour Party and the Conservative Party. Many trades unions support the Labour Party. Trades unions were originally formed in the early 19th century to try to change the long hours of work, disgraceful conditions and low rates of pay in factories. Unions of many different types of workers were formed. They gained in strength through the 20th century and are now a strong force, negotiating pay and working conditions with the employers.

Traditionally, the two major parties held different views in some issues. But now their differences are getting smaller and smaller. And even they don't make much difference in their political views. They come to power in rotation.

Major parties are big parties with more members and supporters while minor parties are small parties with fewer members and supporters. The majority party is the party, which has won most of the seats in the Parliament, and is usually in power. The minority party is the party, which has a few seats in the Parliament, and is usually out of power.

Whenever there is a general election or a by-election, the political parties may set up candidates for election; any other citizen who wishes to stand for an election may also stand as an independent candidate or non-party candidate.

The party which wins the majority of seats (although not necessarily the majority of votes) in a general election, or which is able to command a majority of supporters in the House of Commons, forms the Government.

By tradition, the leader of the majority party is appointed as Prime Minister by the Sovereign. The Prime Minister is responsible for making the Cabinet. The Cabinet is a group of the most senior and powerful ministers in the government, who meet regularly to discuss and decide policies.

The largest minority party with the next largest number of seats, becomes the official Opposition, with its own leader who has the title of "Leader of Her Majesty's Opposition". And the leader of the Opposition also has a cabinet but since it is not in power it is called the "Shadow Cabinet".

In the United States, each state is divided into congressional districts for the purpose of electing representatives. The districts within a state are approximately equal in population. One representative is elected from each district. One of the representative's major obligations is protecting the interests of the people in his or her district.

In the United States, the more exciting election is the presidential election. The

President of the United States is the title of America's chief executive, chosen by the presidential election every four years. Theoretically, any "natural born" citizen over age 35 and with 14 years' residency is eligible. To date, all the presidents have been white males with political backgrounds. Most of them have been Protestants.

Americans participate in the campaign to select their nation's President. So in the presidential year, an election for president is held.

The first step in choosing a party's presidential candidate is the primary. In most countries, the party picks the candidate. But in the United States, voters who declare support for one party or another get to choose from the list of candidates. Campaigning against other members of the same party, a candidate must win enough state primaries to give him or her a majority of delegates at the party convention in the summer of the presidential year. In primaries, voters simply indicate which delegate they support at the ballot box.

In the summer before the election, each of the major political parties holds a convention. The party conventions are one of the great set pieces of American politics. The Republicans hold the Republican Party Convention, while the Democrats hold the Democratic Party Convention. Delegates from every state meet together to choose candidates for President and Vice-President. The number of delegates from each state is determined by the population and its support for that party in previous elections. The way of choosing delegates varies from state to state. In some states, delegates are elected by the voters. In others, they are appointed by a state party convention or by state political leaders.

After routine formalities, convention business usually begins with the creation and acceptance of a party platform. A platform is a very general statement of the party's philosophy, goals and position on issues of national and international concern. A majority of the convention delegates must vote for the various planks of the platform in order for them to be accepted. A plank refers to any of the main principles of the policy or programme of a political party. The next business of the convention is the nomination of prospective presidential candidates. Then, the delegates get down to the serious work of choosing their party's presidential candidate. His primary qualification is the ability to get elected, but the delegates also consider a nominee's integrity, philosophy, and talent for leadership.

When nominations are completed, votes are taken alphabetically by state. Several roll calls may be necessary before one nominee wins the majority of votes needed to become the party's candidate. In the early balloting, many delegations withhold their support from serious contenders by voting for a prominent politician from their own state, called a favourite son. This device makes it possible for state delegations to negotiate with major contenders by agreeing to switch their votes in exchange for some political favour or governmental position. Eventually, enough deals are made so that one man receives a majority of the votes.

By this stage, the party normally knows who has won. The delegates from each state formally choose their champion to go forward as presidential candidate. The candidate with the most delegates wins, and normally secures the support of party rivals. Once the presidential candidate is selected, his running mate, that is the vice-presidential candidate, must be chosen. Usually, the delegates give their presidential candidate the choice of his running mate. The winning candidate names a vice-presidential running mate. Traditionally, a party's presidential and vice-presidential candidates come from different sections of the country and have somewhat different political views. Thus, the party achieves what is called a balanced ticket, a combination of candidates that will appeal to many different blocs of voters.

Actual campaigning for the election traditionally begins on Labour Day. From then on, the rival candidates square up for the presidential campaign proper. Policies are refined, often to take into account the supporters of the candidates who have been eliminated. From that time until Election Day, voters are bombarded with political materials from all sides by radio, television, newspapers, and personal communications. This stage of the campaign is shorter than the slog through the state primaries. So each candidate tries to convince a majority of the American voters that he is best qualified to lead the country for the next four years. Since he has only two months in which to do this, a very concentrated campaign is necessary. All the resources of modern communication are used to acquaint voters with the candidates' views and personalities. The various candidates who participate in the presidential election have to raise funds for their campaigns. Most campaign funds come from private contributions. This, unfortunately, means that the man who gets elected has many "friends" who expect political favours in return for their financial help.

To preserve free democratic elections, the rights of all candidates are carefully guarded. They may speak their minds openly, even to the extent of severely criticizing the viewpoints of other candidates, without fear of punishment. This right prevails even when an opponent is an incumbent who is currently holding office.

In the final weeks, the contenders typically concentrate their attention on the big so-called "swing states" as they battle it out for the critical Electoral College votes. The Electoral College refers to the people as a group who vote for electors.

The first Tuesday after the first Monday in November is the Election Day. On that day, some 100 million voters are likely to cast their ballots for President and Vice-President. Some members of the Congress and many state and local officials are also selected at this time.

The President and Vice-President are not actually chosen by popular votes but by electoral votes. That is, they are not elected directly by the voters. Each state has a number of Electoral College members who actually vote for the President on behalf of the people. The Electoral College also selects the Vice-President. When a citizen casts his vote for a presidential candidate, he is really choosing electors. Each elector is expected, although not obliged, to vote for the candidate who wins the majority of popular votes in his state.

The number of Electoral College electors allotted to each state is equal to the total number of representatives and senators who represent that state in the Congress. Thus, states with larger populations have more electoral votes. In fact, the number of the Electoral College members reflects the state's representation in the Congress. The candidate who receives a majority of the votes in a particular state wins all of that state's Electoral College members, that is, he receives all of that state's electoral votes. The other candidates get none. It is possible for a presidential candidate to win a majority of popular votes but not a majority of electoral votes, thereby losing the election. This can happen if his opponent wins by small margins in states with many electoral votes and loses by large margins in states with few electoral votes. It is also possible that an elector expected to vote for one candidate will exercise his constitutional right to vote for someone else. However, since electors are prominent members of their respective parties, this rarely happens. This method of choosing the United States President has been criticized as archaic and undemocratic, but states with small populations do not want to change it because they have a great proportional vote in the Electoral College than they would have if the President were chosen by popular vote. To be elected, candidates for President and Vice-President must receive a majority of the votes in the Electoral College. If no candidate receives a majority, the House of Representatives chooses the President from the top three candidates, and the Senate chooses the Vice-President from the top two candidates having the highest number of electoral votes.

Once a candidate gets a majority of Electoral College members from across the states, the election is over in the public's mind. But in fact, the Electoral College members do formally meet and vote for the President and the state results are counted before the full Congress in January. The person who is selected as the President remains the elected President until his inauguration. The newly-elected President is inaugurated in January during a solemn, nationally-televised ceremony. He then moves into the White House and starts his presidency, that is his four-year term of office as President. He appoints members of his Cabinet, and begins the difficult task of trying to persuade the Congress to help him fulfill his campaign promises.

In the U. S. presidential election, because campaigning is extremely expensive and because a candidate must receive a majority of the electoral votes to be elected, presidential politics has, to a large extent, been limited to two major parties: the Democratic Party and the Republican Party. A great number of votes are needed to win a national election. No candidate can hope to survive by appealing to one or two classes of voters, such as farmers or businessmen. Because of the need for broad appeal, the philosophies of both parties take a middle course so as not to alienate any large blocs of voters. Even so, the Democratic Party is generally supported by workers, farmers and liberals, while the Republican Party gets most of its support from businessmen, professionals and the more conservative voters. Each party has a familiar symbol: for the Democrats it is a donkey, and for the Republicans an elephant. These symbols were created by Thomas Nast, a famous 19th-century political cartoonist. The Republican Party is also called the GOP, which stands for the Grand Old Party. Many people see little difference between these two political parties. They think both parties are controlled by corporate interests, and their legislative programmes are practically indistinguishable. Since the two major parties are not extremely different, no sudden shift in national policy results from a change in government. Change can be detected only with the passage of time as the new administration becomes accustomed to its powers and responsibilities.

Besides the two major parties, third parties also participate in the presidential campaign. Although no third-party candidate has ever won a presidential election, third-parties have often played an important role by focusing attention upon particular issues and influencing the policies of the two major parties.

Words & Expressions

electoral system *also* **voting system** *n*. the system in connection with an election, including the intention for an election, the happening in an election, and the result from an election 选举制度

election *n*. the act or process of choosing a representative by vote to take an official, esp. a political, position 选举 *e.g.* free democratic election 自由民主选举；to win the election 在选举中获胜；to lose the election 在选举中失利

voter *n*. a person who has the legal right to vote in an election, esp. a political election 选民 *syn.* **elector, constituent** 选举人

local election *n*. an election which takes place in a small area like a county or a city of a country 地方选举

local council *n*. a group of people who are elected to run a particular town, borough, city, or county 地方政务委员会

elector *n*. a person who has the right to vote in an election 选举人 *syn.* **voter, constituent** 选民

by-election *n*. an election held in a single constituency between one general election and the next, because an MP has retired or died, or because he has been transferred to the House of Lords 补缺选举

party *n*. a political organization whose members all have the same basic aims and beliefs, usu. an organization which tries to get its members elected to the government of a country or state 党 *e.g.* political party 政党

campaign *n*. a planned set of activities which people deliberately carry out over a period of time in order to produce a particular result, esp. in order to achieve social or political change 有计划的活动；运动 *e.g.* election campaign 竞选活动；presidential campaign 总统竞选

notify *v*. inform sb officially about sth 通知

vacancy *n*. a position which is not being held by anyone and which people can apply for 空缺

constituency *n*. a political administrative district whose voters elect a single MP to represent them in the House of Commons 选区；or all the qualified electors and constituents who live in a district 全体选民

constituent *n*. a person who lives in a particular constituency, esp. sb who is able to vote in an election 选民 *syn.* **voter, elector** 选举人

returning officer *n*. the officer who is responsible for arranging an election in a particular town or district and who formally announces the result 选举监察人

oversee *v*. watch to see that work is properly done 监督；监察

count the votes *v. phrase* add up the votes in order to find how many there are 数选票

recount *n*. a second or further count, esp. of votes in an election when the result is very close between two or more candidates 重新计算(选票)

suffrage *n*. the right which people have to vote in order to choose a government or a national leader in political elections 选举权

universal suffrage *n*. the right which all adults have to vote in Britain 普遍选举权

adult suffrage *n*. the right that all adults have to vote in Britain 成人选举权

universal adult suffrage *n*. the right which all adults have to vote in Britain 成人普遍选举权

suffragette *n*. a woman involved in the campaign for women to be given the right to vote in Britain in the early 20th century 争取妇女选举权的女子

electorate *n*. all the people in a country or in an area who have the right to vote in an election 全体选民

polling day *n*. a day appointed for electors to cast their votes at polling stations in an election 投票日

polling station *n*. a building or other place where people go to vote in an election 投票站

ballot *n*. the process or system of secret voting 无记名投票 *e.g.* secret ballot 无记名投票；to cast one's

ballot 投票
ballot paper *n.* a special slip of paper on which an elector records his vote in a political election, which has the names of the candidates and their parties printed on it 选票
ballot box *n.* the box into which ballot papers are put after people have voted 投票箱
proxy *n.* the authority to represent sb else in voting in an election 代理投票权
postal vote *n.* a vote sent by the electors who have to be away from their constituency on polling day 邮寄投票 *syn.* **vote by post** 邮寄投票
proxy vote *n.* a vote made by a person on behalf of an elector when that elector is unable to go to the polling station for some reason 代理投票 *syn.* **vote by proxy** 代理投票
disability *n.* a permanent physical or mental injury or illness which restricts the way that sb can live their life 残疾;残障
politics *n.* the actions or activities which people use to achieve power in a country, society, or organization or which ensure that power is used in a particular way 政治 *e.g.* above politics 超越政治; American politics 美国政治
criminal *n.* a person who has committed an illegal action 罪犯
lunatic *n.* a person who is mentally ill 精神病患者
the Labour Party *n.* the political party in Britain which believes particularly in the importance of a socialist economy with state ownership and control rather than private ownership 工党
the Conservative Party *n.* the political party in Britain which believes particularly in the importance of a capitalist economy with private ownership rather than state control 保守党
trade union *also* **trades union** *n.* an organization of workers which represents them and has the aim of improving such things as the working conditions, pay, and benefits of its members 工会
major party *n.* a more important political party with more members and supporters 大党
minor party *n.* a less important political party with fewer members and supporters 小党
supporter *n.* a person who supports a political leader or a political party 支持者;拥护者
majority party *n.* the party which wins the majority of seats in the Parliament and which forms the government 多数党
minority party *n.* the party which wins less than half of the seats in the Parliament 少数党
independent candidate *n.* a candidate who does not represent any political party 独立候选人
non-party candidate *n.* a candidate who does not belong to any political party 无党派候选人
win a seat *v. phrase* get a place as an MP 赢得席位 *e.g.* to win the majority of seats 赢得多数席位
appoint *v.* choose formally a person for a particular post 任命
the Cabinet *n.* the executive group of ministers, usu. about 20 in number, who are chosen by the Prime Minister to determine government policies, exercise supreme control of government and coordinate government departments 内阁 *e.g.* to make/form the Cabinet 组阁
the official Opposition *n.* the leading opposition party which forms part of the parliament, but which is not in the government 最大反对党
Leader of Her Majesty's Opposition *n.* the title of the leader of the official Opposition 女王陛下反对党领袖
the Shadow Cabinet *n.* the team of ministers in the Opposition, who would probably form the Cabinet if their party won the next general election 影子内阁
congressional *n.* belonging to or relating to the U.S. Congress 国会的 *e.g.* congressional district 国会议员选区
presidential election *n.* the campaign held every four years, in which Americans participate to select their nation's President 总统选举
the President of the United States *n.* the title of America's chief executive, chosen by the presidential election every four years 美国总统

theoretically *ad*. saying or thinking that although sth is supposed to be true or to happen in the way stated, it may not in fact be true or happen in that way 从理论上讲

"natural born" citizen *n*. a citizen who was born in this country 本国出生的公民

residency *n*. the period of time during which a person lives in a place 居留期；居住期

eligible *a*. qualified or suitable to take part in sth, receive it, or be connected with it 有资格的

to date *prep. phrase* until the present time 迄今；到目前为止

political background *n*. a person's education and experience relating to politics 政治背景

Protestant *n*. a member of any of the Christian bodies, which separated from the Roman Catholic Church in the 16th century, or of their branches formed later 新教徒

presidential year *n*. the year in which presidential election is held 总统选举年

presidential candidate *n*. one of the people who stand in the election for the position of the president 总统候选人

primary *also* **state primary** *n*. an election in an American state in which people vote for sb to become a candidate for a political office 预选

party convention *n*. a large gathering of members of a political party who meet to discuss the business of their party 党代表大会

Iowa *n*. one state of the United States of America, on the right bank of the Mississippi River 衣阿华州

caucus *n*. the meeting of a small group of people within a political party, at which they discuss important matters 政党核心会议 *e.g.* caucus system "政党核心会议"制度

the Republican Party *n*. one of the two main political parties in the United States of America 共和党

Republican *n*. a member or supporter of the Republican Party in the United States of America 共和党人

the Democratic Party *n*. one of the two main political parties in the United States of America 民主党

Democrat *n*. a member or supporter of the Democratic Party in the United States of America 民主党人

Vice-President *n*. the person who holds the rank or title, which is next in importance to the President 副总统

formality *n*. a procedure or action which has to be done 例行公事 *e.g.* routine formality 惯例

platform *n*. a programme including the main policies and aims of a political party, *esp*. as stated before an election 纲领 *e.g.* party platform 党纲

plank *n*. the main principle, on which a political party bases it campaign, or its main aim 政纲要点

nomination *n*. an official suggestion of sb as a candidate in an election 提名

nominate *v*. formally suggest a person as a candidate in an election 提名

nominee *n*. a person who is nominated 被提名者

prospective *a*. expected or intended; likely to be or become 可能成为……的

primary *a*. that is extremely important 主要的 *e.g.* primary qualification 主要资格

integrity *n*. the quality of being honest and firm in a person's moral principles 正直；廉正

take votes *v. phrase* make one's choice in an election by writing on a piece of paper 投票表决

roll call *n*. the act of checking which of the members of a group are present by reading aloud a list of their names 点名

balloting *n*. voting in which people mark a piece of paper to indicate the person they choose in an election 投票 *e.g.* early balloting 早期投票 *syn*. **voting** 投票

contender *n*. a person who competes with other people in an election 竞选者 *e.g.* major contender 主要竞选者；serious contender 严肃的竞选者

favourite son *n*. the son who is most loved by his parents 宠儿；or a person who is expected to win 最有希望获胜者

political favour *n*. the treatment in political affairs by showing special kindness or giving special privileges 政治上的照顾

governmental position *n*. a job or a post in a government 政府职务
champion *n*. a person who has won the first prize in a competition 冠军; or a person who has beaten everyone else in a contest, fight or election 优胜者
rival *n*. a person who competes with other people in the same field or for the same aim, for instance, in an election 竞争者; 对手 *e.g.* party rival 党内竞选对手; rival candidate 作为竞选对手的候选人
winning candidate *n*. a candidate who has won in an election 获胜的候选人
running mate *n*. a person with whom another is trying to get elected to a pair of political positions of greater and less importance 竞选伙伴; esp. the vice-presidential candidate 副总统候选人
ticket *n*. a list of people supported by one political party in an election 候选人名单
balanced ticket *n*. a combination of candidates that will appeal to many different blocs of voters 候选人组合
Labour Day *n*. a day when workers make a public show with marches, meetings, etc., which is the first Monday in September in North America 劳工节
square up for *v. phrase* face an opponent with determination 正视
proper *a*. emphasizing that sth is definitely a part of a particular place, object, etc. in order to distinguish it from other things which are sometimes regarded as part of it and sometimes not 本身的 *e.g.* the presidential campaign proper 总统竞选本身
Election Day *n*. the day when the presidential election takes place, which is the first Tuesday after the first Monday in November 总统选举日
be bombarded with *v. phrase* be asked aggressive questions one after another 被连珠炮似地提问
slog *n*. a difficult piece of work which needs a lot of effort 困难而费力的工作
raise funds *v. phrase* manage to get the amount of money needed for a particular purpose 筹集资金
funds *n*. amounts of money that are available to be spent, esp. money that is given to a person or organization for a particular purpose 基金 *e.g.* campaign funds 竞选基金
contribution *n*. sth, esp. money, that is given in order to help to make an undertaking successful 捐献; 捐款 *e.g.* private contribution 私人捐款
guard the right *v. phrase* protect the right 捍卫权利
speak one's mind openly *v. phrase* say openly what one thinks about a situation, rather than keeping it a secret or being afraid 直陈自己的看法
opponent *n*. a person who is against another person in a disagreement, fight, contest, or game 对手
incumbent *n*. a person who is currently holding office 现任者
swing *n*. a sudden or extreme change, esp. in people's attitudes, beliefs, or political opinions 突变 *e.g.* swing state 形势突变的州
battle *v*. fight 战斗 *e.g.* to battle it out for 为争夺……战斗到底
critical *a*. extremely important 关键的
the Electoral College *n*. the people as a group who vote for electors that act as representatives for each state, and elect the President and Vice-President 总统选举团
popular votes *n*. the votes cast directly by the voters 民众选票 *e.g.* to win the majority of popular votes 赢得多数民众选票
electoral votes *n*. the votes cast by the Electoral College 选举团选票
archaic *a*. old-fashioned or out-of-date 过时的
undemocratic *n*. that is not based on the idea that everyone should have equal rights and should be involved in making important decisions 不民主的
the full Congress *n*. the meeting of the Congress with all its members present 国会全体会议
inauguration *n*. a special ceremony with which a new official or leader of an organization, such as a President, is introduced 就职典礼

inaugurate v. introduce a new official or leader of an organization, such as a President with a special ceremony 为……举行就职典礼

televise v. broadcast a programme so that it can be seen on television 用电视播放 e.g. nationally-televised ceremony 全国电视直播的典礼

the White House n. the official home of the American President in Washington D.C. 白宫

presidency n. the position or function of a President 总统职位; or the period of time during which a person acts as the President 总统任期

middle course v. a moderate course of action which lies between two opposite and extreme courses 中间道路 e.g. to take a middle course 走中间道路

alienate v. make unfriendly or unsympathetic 使疏远; 使异化

bloc n. a group of people in power that have similar political aims and interests and that act together over some issues 集团 e.g. a bloc of voters 一伙选民

liberal n. a person who is in favour of people having a lot of political freedom 自由主义者

symbol n. sth which seems to represent sth else 象征

donkey n. the symbol of the Democrats 驴(民主党人)

elephant n. the symbol of the Republicans 象(共和党人)

Thomas Nast (1840-1902) n. a famous 19th-century political cartoonist 托马斯·纳斯特

the Grand Old Party also **the GOP** (abbrev.) n. another name of the Republican Party 共和党

corporate a. relating to business corporations 公司的 e.g. corporate interests 公司利益

programme n. a list of planned activities, or plan for future action 纲领 e.g. legislative programme 立法纲领; election programme 竞选纲领

practically ad. almost; nearly; virtually 几乎

indistinguishable a. difficult to tell which is which because of the similarity of two things 难以区别的

third party n. a political party which doesn't belong to the two major parties and takes the middle course 第三党

voting n. a method of making a decision in which each person involved indicates their own choice, and the choice which most people support is accepted 投票

the first-past-the-post system n. a system of voting in elections by which the person who got the most votes in each constituency is elected to the parliament 得票最多者当选的选举制度

proportional representation n. a system of voting in elections by which all political parties, small as well as large, are represented in the parliament according to the proportion of votes they receive, rather than having to get a majority of the votes in each voting area 比例代表制

horseracing n. the sport of racing horses 赛马 e.g. horseracing track 赛马跑道

post n. a post which marks the finishing point on a horseracing track 终点柱 e.g. winning post/finishing post 终点柱

finishing point n. the place on the track or course where the race officially ends 终点

term n. a word or expression with a specific meaning, esp. one that is in relation to a particular subject 术语 e.g. sports term 体育术语

Additional Knowledge

Two Types of Voting System

Voting is a method of making a decision in which each person involved indicates their own choice, and the choice which most people support is accepted. A voting system is a system in connection with an election, including the intention for an election, the happening in an election, and the result from an election. In Britain, the voting system is associated with a general election and a local election. Every voter casts one vote in a secret ballot for the candidate they wish to support. The vote is normally made in person at a polling station.

There are mainly two types of voting system or electoral system. They are the first-past-the-post system and the proportional representation.

In the first case, the candidate with the most votes is elected and will become the representative of a particular district. "First past the post" is originally a colloquial phrase from horseracing. A post marks the finishing point on a horseracing track. The first horse which passes the post is the winner. People often use sports terms to describe the events in an election, for both activities are competitive. "First past the post" is used mainly in British English to describe an election. The first-past-the-post system in political elections is the system in which the winner is the person with more votes than any other candidate, even though the winner may receive only a small proportion of the total number of votes.

In the second case, the final result depends on the percentage of the vote that each party received in an election. Proportional representation is a system of voting in elections in which each political party is represented in the parliament in proportion to the number of people who vote for it in an election. In Britain, there is no proportional representation, as in some other countries.

Exercises

I. Explain each of the following:
1) election
2) general election
3) local election
4) local council
5) by-election
6) call a snap election
7) constituency
8) vacancy
9) resignation
10) constituenty
11) returning officer
12) suffrage
13) universal adult suffrage
14) suffragette
15) electorate
16) polling day
17) polling station
18) ballot paper
19) ballot box
20) proxy
21) proxy vote
22) postal vote
23) disability
24) criminal
25) lunatic
26) the Cabinet
27) minority party
28) the official Opposition
29) the Shadow Cabinet
30) presidential election
31) the President of the United States
32) "natural born" citizen
33) residency
34) eligible
35) Protestant
36) presidential year
37) primary
38) party convention
39) caucus
40) Vice-President

41) party platform
42) plank
43) nomination
44) presidential candidate
45) nominee
46) roll call
47) politician
48) favourite son
49) political favour
50) governmental position
51) party rivals
52) vice-presidential running mate
53) balanced ticket
54) Labour Day
55) presidential campaign
56) Election Day
57) raise funds
58) campaign funds
59) private contributions
60) incumbent
61) swing state
62) the Electoral College
63) popular votes
64) electoral votes
65) proportional vote
66) the full Congress
67) the elected President
68) inauguration
69) the White House
70) presidency

II. Give another way or other ways of saying each of the following:
Model: contender → rival; opponent
1) the electoral system →
2) voter →
3) cast one's vote →
4) vote by post →
5) proxy vote →
6) balloting →
7) vice-presidential candidate→

III. Fill in the blanks:
Model: A Cabinet member is a member of the _____.
→ A Cabinet member is a member of the Cabinet.
1) An elector is a member of the _____.
2) A constituent is a member of the _____.
3) A Republican is a member of the _____.
4) A Democrat is a member of the _____.
5) A senator is a member of the _____.
6) An Electoral College elector is a member of the _____.

IV. Answer the following questions:
1) What is the difference between a general election and a local election in Britain?
2) What is the difference between a general election and a by-election?
3) When does a general election take place in Britain?
4) Who can call a snap election before the expiry of the five-year term of the British Parliament?
5) How many constituencies is the United Kingdom divided into?
6) Who does an MP represent?
7) What is the work of a returning officer?
8) Under what circumstances may the official in charge order a recount in an election?
9) Did the British women have the equal right to vote as the men had in the late 19th century?
10) When does a voter put his or her ballot paper into a ballot box?

11) What are the requirements of a British voter?
12) Who have no right to vote in Britain?
13) Why does the British Queen have no right to vote?
14) What is the minimum age of a candidate who can apply for the British parliamentary election?
15) Which party is responsible for forming the Government in Britain?
16) Who is appointed as Prime Minister by the British Sovereign?
17) Who is responsible for making the Cabinet in Britain?
18) What is the job of the British Cabinet?
19) Which party becomes the official Opposition in Britain?
20) Who has the title of "Leader of Her Majesty's Opposition"?
21) Who forms the Shadow Cabinet in Britain?
22) Why is each state divided into congressional districts in the United States?
23) How many representatives are elected from a congressional district?
24) What are the obligations of a representative from his or her congressional district?
25) How often does the American presidential election take place?
26) Who is eligible to be the American President theoretically?
27) Has there ever been any American President who is black?
28) Has there ever been any American President who is a woman?
29) Has there ever been any American President who doesn't have any political background?
30) Has there ever been any American President who is not a Protestant?
31) What do the Americans do in the presidential year?
32) Who actually choose the presidential candidate in the United States, the political party leaders or the voters?
33) What do the American voters do in state primaries?
34) What determines the number of delegates from each state at a party convention in the United States?
35) How are the party convention delegates chosen in the United States?
36) What is the first business of a party convention after routine formalities? What is its second business? And what is its third business?
37) What are the qualifications of a presidential candidate?
38) What may be necessary before one nominee wins the majority of votes needed to become a party's candidate?
39) Who chooses a party's vice-presidential candidate?
40) Does a party's presidential candidate come from the same state with his running mate? Do they usually have the same political views?
41) When does the actual presidential campaign begin?
42) How long is it between Labour Day and Election Day?
43) Why is a very concentrated campaign necessary for a presidential candidate?
44) How does a presidential candidate raise funds for his campaigning in most cases?
45) What does it mean since a presidential candidate receives private contributions in the presidential election?

46) Can you give some examples of the resources of modern communication?
47) Can a presidential candidate severely criticize the viewpoint of another candidate who is now in office?
48) Who are also elected on Election Day apart from the President and Vice-President in the United States?
49) When does the American presidential election take place?
50) Are the American President and Vice-President chosen by popular votes or electoral votes?
51) Who actually vote for the American President on behalf of the people?
52) Who is a citizen really choosing when he casts his ballot for a presidential candidate in the United States?
53) How many Electoral College electors are allotted to each state in America?
54) What does the number of the Electoral College members reflect?
55) Can it be possible for an American presidential candidate to lose the election when he wins a majority of popular votes but not a majority of electoral votes?
56) Why has the conventional method of choosing the American President been criticized as archaic and undemocratic?
57) Why do these states with small populations not want to change the current method of choosing their President?
58) When is the presidential election over in the public's mind?
59) When dose the newly-elected President's inauguration take place?
60) What does the American President do after he is inaugurated?
61) Why has the U. S. presidential politics been limited to the Democratic Party and the Republican Party?
62) Can a presidential candidate win a national election just by appealing to one or two classes of voters?
63) Why do the philosophies of both the Democratic Party and the Republican Party take a middle course?
64) From whom does the Democratic Party get most of its support?
65) From whom does the Republican Party get most of its support?
66) What is the symbol of the Democratic Party?
67) What is the symbol of the Republican Party?
68) Who created the symbols of the Democratic Party and the Republican Party?
69) What is another name for the Republican Party?
70) Has any third-party candidate ever won a presidential election in the United States?

Lesson Eight

The Governmental System

A government refers to a group of people who are responsible for governing a country or an area at a particular time. The British Government is officially called Her Majesty's Government. It is the body of ministers responsible for the conduct of national affairs.

When the general election is complete in Britain, the political party with an overall majority of members of the House of Commons forms the new government and begins its work. The chief executive of the Government is the Prime Minister. The Prime Minister is the Head of Government, who is appointed by the Sovereign. By tradition, the Prime Minister is also First Lord of the Treasury and Minister for the Civil Service. All the other ministers are appointed by the Sovereign on the recommendation of the Prime Minister.

The British Government has the Cabinet as its centre. The Cabinet headed by the Prime Minister is the group of the most important government ministers responsible for government administration and policy. The members of the Cabinet are the Prime Minister's closest colleagues. They are personally selected by the Prime Minister and can be dismissed by him. They may include the holders of departments and non-departmental offices, such as the Chancellor of the Exchequer, who is often called the Chancellor; the Secretary of State for Home Affairs, who is often called the Home Secretary; and the Secretary of State for Defence, who is often called the Defence Secretary. The Cabinet meets in private and its proceedings are strictly confidential. The cabinet meeting is usually held in 10 Downing Street, which is the official residence of the Prime Minister. Sometimes, the Prime Minister may have a cabinet reshuffle which is an interchange of the posts or responsibilities of the cabinet ministers.

The British Cabinet headed by the Prime Minister plays an important role in political life. The Cabinet members are all important political figures. They are also Members of Parliament who are high up in their party. The task of the British Cabinet as a whole is to decide what policy to submit to the Parliament, to carry it out at once when it is agreed by the Parliament, and to see that the government departments function efficiently. It is also the Cabinet's job to watch over the state of national economy. The Cabinet in Britain bridges a gap between "executive" and "legislature", and practises "collective responsibility". They all stick together and support the final consensus. The British Cabinet is different from the American Cabinet in that the latter consists of experts from universities, and law officers without experience in winning elections or serving the Congress.

In Britain, departmental ministers who are in charge of government departments are responsible for national policies. The holder of a government department is known as Minister, Secretary of State or Secretary. Non-departmental ministers are holders of various traditional offices, with no or few departmental duties. A minister without portfolio is a non-departmental minister. Portfolio is a formal use, referring to a minister's responsibility for a particular area of a government's activities. In Britain, a minister without portfolio is a Cabinet Minister without responsibility for a particular department. But he is available to act as an envoy on special mission, or perform special duties, which the Prime Minister may wish to entrust to him.

The composition of the British Government can vary both in the number of ministers and in the titles of some offices. New ministerial offices may be created, others may be abolished, and functions may be transferred from one minister to another.

The British executive consists of government departments and agencies, local authorities, public corporations, independent bodies and other bodies. Government departments and agencies are responsible for national administration; local authorities are responsible for local services; public corporations are responsible for operating particular nationalized industries; independent bodies are responsible for regulating the privatized industries; and other bodies are subject to ministerial control.

To keep the stability of the society and the consistency of the national policy, the civil service is exercised in Britain and many other countries. It is a system in which civil servants remain to serve in the governmental offices for a long time. They usually have a lifelong job with a high pay so as to prevent corruption. They are in charge of everyday routine and day-to-day work in the governmental offices. Their job is to assist government ministers, but they themselves are not policy-makers, nor are they decision-makers. They are politically impartial, remaining neutral and independent in political inclinations. But the government ministers may make decisions on the data provided by the civil servants.

In Britain, the civil service consists of all the government departments which administer the affairs of the country, and all the civil servants who work in them. But it doesn't include the members of such armed forces as the Navy, Army and Air Force. Nor does it include the Members of Parliament, the members of law courts and officers, or the members of religious organizations.

Downing Street is the name of a street in central London. 10 Downing Street is the official home of the British Prime Minister and 11 Downing Street is the official home of the Chancellor of the Exchequer. So Downing Street is a term used for the British Prime Minister or the British Government. Whitehall is the name of a street in central London, near which there are many important government officers. So Whitehall is a term used to refer to the British Government itself.

The United States Government is organized differently from the British Government. From the Constitution, the United States Government derives all its power. The U.S. Constitution is the basic law that protects the inhabitants of this nation from arbitrary actions by the Federal Government or any individual state. The Constitution defines three distinct branches of the national government of the United States. They are the legislative branch—the Congress, which enacts laws; the executive branch with the President as its chief, who approves and enforces laws; and the judicial branch—the courts, which determine their validity and interpret laws. The Administration is part of the U.S. Government that manages public affairs during the period of office of a President.

The United States President is the Head of State and also the Head of Government. As the nation's chief executive, he must see that all national laws are carried out.

Naturally, he has a large staff of advisers and other employees to assist him. The most important group of advisers is called the Cabinet, which includes the heads of the eleven departments of the executive branch. They are chosen by the President with the advice and consent of the Senate. The Secretary of State or the State Secretary is the head of the State Department, that is U. S. government department of foreign affairs. The President also appoints ambassadors and other consular heads, as well as judges of the federal courts. The Vice-President is the only other elected person in the executive branch. His chief constitutional duty is to preside over the Senate. His most important function is to succeed to the presidency upon the death, resignation, or disability of the President.

The central government is the government of the whole country, which is in contrast to a local government. In the United States, the Federal Government is the central government. A centralized central government is a government by which one central group of people gives out instructions to all the other regional groups. A decentralized central government is a government by which some departments or branches are moved away from a central administrative area to other places around the country.

In the United States, state governments form the Federal Government. The division of powers between the states and the central government is known as the federal system. So the Federal Government is decentralized. As a single national authority, the Federal Government does such things as dealing with foreign nations, establishing a uniform monetary system, and regulating commerce between the states. Other governmental responsibilities, such as public school systems, local police, fire protection and local roads, are left to the states and their subdivisions.

Most of the state governments in the United States are quite similar to the Federal Government or the central government. Each is headed by an elected executive called a governor. The legislature may be called a general assembly or by some other name, but it generally functions much as the Congress does. Almost all of the state legislatures also have two houses. The state court systems generally follow the three-level federal court plan, which provides for a trial court, an appellate court, and a supreme court.

A local government is a smaller governmental organization, which governs a smaller area like a city or a county. In the United States, a state government is a local government. A regional government is a local government, which governs the areas outside the capital. A provincial government is a regional government, which governs a province far away from the capital. A municipal government or municipality is the local government of a city or a town, which has the authority to appoint a local council and local officials to administer its internal affairs.

In America, states are divided into smaller governmental units, such as cities, towns, counties, and villages. These units have some legislative authority, which they receive from the state, and they are responsible for local control within their boundaries. There are local governments at different levels, which are systems of administration of such units as a district, a county or a city, formed by elected representatives of the people who live there.

Judging from who are in power, government can be divided into civilian government and military government. Civilian government is prevalent in most countries, where those in power are people who are not serving in the armed forces or in the police force. But in some countries where the political situation is not secure or stable, army officers often stage a coup. It is a sudden unconstitutional action, and often a violent change of the government. They usually abolish the constitution, overthrow the existing civilian government, get rid of the president, seize power for themselves, form a military government and practise dictatorship. Generally, the army leader who has launched the coup d'état and obtained the power by force will become the dictator with total power over the country and use the power in a cruel way.

A caretaker government is a government, which holds office only for a short period of time between the end of one government and the start of another. Similarly, a caretaker cabinet has power only for a short period of time between the end of one cabinet and the appointment of a new one.

A provisional government is a government that has been arranged and appointed for the present time. It is intended to exist for only a short time before the election and likely to be changed after the election.

A minority government is a government, which has fewer seats in a parliament than the combined opposition parties have.

When the result of an election shows that no single party has got more than half of the seats in the Parliament and no single party is in position to form the government, two or more than two parties may take the action of temporary alliance and form a coalition government. Since the end of the Second World War, especially in the last two or three decades, there has been a tendency of political pluralism in the West. The former pattern of two major parties has been broken in many countries. Very often it is difficult to find two major parties in one country. There have appeared quite a few minor parties which can hardly win a majority vote in an election. So it is impossible for a single party to become a majority party and form the cabinet. Two or even more small parties have to form a coalition government through a temporary alliance. National government is a kind of coalition government, especially one that is formed during a crisis, like a crisis of confidence.

The White House is the official home of the American President in Washington D.C. It is also used to mean the American President or the people who work with the President on government business, for instance, his advisers. The Pentagon is the building in Washington, which is the headquarters of the U.S. Department of Defense. The military officers of high rank work there and direct the U.S. armed forces. It is also used to refer to the military leaders who work there and the decisions which they make.

Words & Expressions

Her Majesty's Government n. the official name of the British Government (英国)女王陛下政府

the Treasury n. the government department in Britain and some other countries which deals with the country's finances (英国)财政部

First Lord of Treasury n. the Minister who is in charge of the Treasury (英国)首席财政大臣

the civil service n. the institution in Britain and in many other countries, which consists of all the government departments that administer the affairs of a country 文官部;文职部门;or all the people who are employed in these government departments 全体文职官员;全体公务员

civil servant n. a person who is employed in the civil service 文官;文职官员;公务员

government department *also* **department** *n*. one of the sections of a government which is responsible for the administration of a particular area of policy（政府的）部；司；署；局；处；科

non-departmental office *n*. the position of a non-departmental minister 无所任大臣的公职

Minister for the Civil Service *n*. the Minister who is in charge of the Civil Service in Britain（英国）文官部大臣

the Chancellor of the Exchequer *also* **the Chancellor** *n*. the special title for the minister in the British Government who makes decisions about finance and taxes（英国）财政大臣

the Secretary of State for Home Affairs *also* **the Home Secretary** *n*. the member of the British Government who is in charge of the Home Office（英国）内务大臣

the Secretary of State for Defence *also* **the Defence Secretary** *n*. the member of the British Government who is in charge of the Ministry of Defence（英国）国防大臣

in private *prep. phrase* without other people being present 秘密地；私下地

proceedings *n*. a series of actions which happen in a particular place, esp. in a planned or controlled way 事件过程；程序

confidential *a*. that is to be kept secret or private and should not be discussed with other people 保密的 *e.g.* strictly confidential 严格保密的

Downing Street *n*. the name of a street in central London 唐宁街；or a term used to refer to the British Prime Minister or the British Government 唐宁街

10 Downing Street *n*. the official residence of the British Prime Minister 唐宁街10号

reshuffle *n*. a reorganization of people or things, esp. of jobs within a government 改组 *e.g.* cabinet reshuffle 内阁改组

interchange *n*. the act or process of exchange of people, things or ideas 调换 *e.g.* interchange of the posts the cabinet ministers 内阁部长职务的调换

figure *n*. a person who is well-known and important in some way 人物 *e.g.* political figure 政治人物

consensus *n*. general agreement amongst a group of people about a subject or about how sth should be done 同意；一致意见 *e.g.* the final consensus 最后一致意见

departmental minister *n*. a minister who is in charge of a government department and responsible for the national policy in a particular area in Britain 有所任大臣

Secretary of State *n*. a government minister in Britain（英国）国务大臣

Secretary *n*. a minister who is in charge of one of the main government departments in Britain, such as foreign affairs or defence（英国）大臣；the head of one of the main government departments in the United States, appointed by the President（美国）部长 *e.g.* the Foreign Secretary（英国）外交大臣；the Secretary of Defence（英国）国防大臣；the Secretary of Defense（美国）国防部长；the Treasury Secretary（美国）财政部长

non-departmental minister *n*. a minister who has no or few departmental duties in the British Government（英国）无所任大臣

portfolio *n*. a minister's responsibility for a particular area of a government's activities 大臣/部长的职责

minister without portfolio *n*. a person who is given the rank of minister without being given responsibility for any particular area of a government's activities 不管部大臣；不管部部长

envoy *n*. a person who is sent as a messenger, esp. from one government to another 使者 *e.g.* special envoy 特使；envoy on special mission 承担特殊使命的使者

ministerial *a*. belonging to or relating to a government minister or ministry 部长的；部的 *e.g.* ministerial office 部长的公职；ministerial control 部的控制

government agency *n*. an administrative organization responsible for national administration, usu. run by a government 政府分支机构

local authorities *n*. official organizations or government departments of a small area of a country, which have the power to make decisions and have the responsibility for local services 地方政府部门；地方当局

corporation *n*. the organization which is responsible for running a particular town or city and looking after the people who live there 市政当局

public corporation *n*. a government organization which is responsible for operating the affairs in a particular area 公共机构

nationalize *v*. change the ownership of a company or industry so that it is no longer private but owned by the state and controlled by the government 使……国有化 *e.g.* nationalized industry 国有化工业

independent body *n*. an organization responsible for regulating the affairs in a particular area, which does not receive money from the government 独立机构

regulate *v*. control an activity or process, usu. by means of rules or laws 调节；控制；调控

privatize *v*. change the ownership of a company, industry, or service which is owned and controlled by the state, so that it becomes private and owned by an individual or group 使……私有化 *e.g.* privatized industry 私有化工业

be subject to *v. phrase* have to obey; be under the control of 受……制约

corruption *n*. dishonesty and illegal behaviour by people in positions of authority or power 腐化；腐败 *e.g.* to prevent corruption 防止腐败

impartial *a*. not involved directly in a particular situation, and therefore able to consider it and give an opinion about it fairly 不偏不倚 *e.g.* politically impartial 政治上不偏不倚的

inclination *n*. a feeling which makes a person act or want to act in a particular way without thinking or reasoning 倾向 *e.g.* political inclination 政治倾向

11 Downing Street *n*. the official home of the Chancellor of the Exchequer or the Chancellor 唐宁街11号

Whitehall *n*. the name of a street in central London, which contains many important government officers; or a term used to refer to the British Government itself 白厅

arbitrary *a*. that is done without consideration for the wishes of the people affected and cannot be prevented or changed 武断的；霸道的 *e.g.* arbitrary action 武断的行动

centralized *a*. relating to a system of government or organization by which one central group of people gives out instructions to all the other regional groups 集权的 *e.g.* centralized central government 中央集权政府

decentralize *v*. move some departments or branches away from a central administrative area to other places around the country 分散（政府）权力

decentralized *a*. relating to a system of government or organization by which some departments or branches are moved away from a central administrative area to other places around the country 分权的 *e.g.* decentralized central government 中央分权政府

the Secretary of State also **the State Secretary** *n*. the head of the State Department which is the government department dealing with foreign affairs in the United States（美国）国务卿

the State Department *n*. the department of the U.S. Government which deals with foreign affairs, with the Secretary of State as its head（美国）国务院

ambassador *n*. an important official who is sent by his or her government to live in a foreign country and to represent his or her own country's interests there 大使

consul *n*. an official who is sent by his or her government to live in a foreign city in order to look after and protect all the people and businesses there that belong to his or her own country 领事

consular *a*. involving or relating to a consul or to the work of a consul 领事的；领事职责的 *e.g.* consular head 领事

state government *n*. the government of a state in the United States（美国）州政府

the Federal Government *n*. the central government of the United States（美国）联邦政府

the central government *n*. the government of a whole country, which is in contrast to local government 中央

政府

the federal system *n.* a system which consists of a group of states controlled by a central government that deals with things concerning the whole country, such as foreign policy, but leaves the local affairs to the state governments 联邦制

uniform *a.* the same all over; not different or varying in any way; regular 一样的；一致的；统一的 *e.g.* a uniform monetary system 统一的货币制度

monetary *a.* relating to or concerned with money 货币的 *e.g.* monetary system 货币制度

public school *AmE. n.* a free local school in the United States, which is controlled and paid for by the government, for children who study there but live at home（美国）公立走读学校

fire protection *n.* keeping people or things safe from fire 防火

subdivision *n.* an area, part, or section of sth that is itself a part of sth larger 分支；分区；分部

local government *n.* a smaller governmental organization, which governs a smaller area like a city or a county 地方政府

regional government *n.* a local government, which governs the areas outside the capital 地区政府

provincial government *n.* a regional government, which governs a province far away from the capital 省政府

municipal *a.* belonging to or associated with a city or town which has its own local government 城市的；市政的

municipal government *also* **municipality** *n.* the local government of a city or a town 市政府

executive *n.* the part of the government of a country that is concerned with carrying out decisions or orders, as opposed to the part that makes laws, or the part that deals with criminals 行政部门

governor *n.* a person who is responsible for the political administration of a region, esp. of a state in the United States（美国）州长

general assembly *n.* the law-making body of a state in the United States（美国）州议会

trial *n.* a formal legal process in which a judge and jury decide whether sb is guilty of a particular crime by questioning them and considering the evidence 审讯；审判

court *n.* a place where legal matters are decided by a judge and jury or by a magistrate 法庭；法院 *e.g.* trial court 审判庭

appellate court *AmE. n.* a court of appeal 上诉法庭；上诉法院

supreme court *n.* a court at the highest level in a particular legal organization or system 最高法院

civilian *n.* a person who is not a member of the armed forces 平民；文职人员

civilian government *n.* a government in which the people in power are not serving in the armed forces or in the police force 文官政府；平民政府

coup *also* **coup d'état** *n.* an action by a group of people, often army officers, to get rid of the president or government of a country and to seize power for themselves 政变 *e.g.* to launch/stage a coup 发动政变

military government *n.* a government led by army officers instead of civilians 军人政府；军政府

dictatorship *n.* complete and absolute power or authority which is held by a dictator or a political group 独裁；专制；专政 *e.g.* to practise dictatorship 实行专政

dictator *n.* a ruler who has complete power in a country, esp. power which was obtained by force 独裁者；专制者；专政者

caretaker government *n.* a government which holds office only for a short period of time between the end of one government and the start of another 看守政府

caretaker cabinet *n.* a cabinet which has power only for a short period of time between the end of one cabinet and the appointment of a new one 看守内阁

provisional *a.* for the present time only; suitable now, but likely to be changed 临时的

provisional government *n.* a government which has been arranged and appointed for the present time 临时政府

minority government *n.* a government with fewer seats in a parliament than the combined opposition parties 少数党政府

pluralism *n.* the existence of a variety of different people, opinions, or principles within the same society, system, or philosophy 多元化 *e.g.* political pluralism 政治多元化

coalition government *also* **coalition** *n.* a government formed from the alliance of normally opposed political parties, esp. at the time of crisis, as during war 联合政府

national government *n.* a coalition government, esp. one that is formed during a crisis, like a crisis of confidence 国民政府

crisis *n.* a situation where sth, such as people's confidence in sb or sth else, is so heavily attacked or questioned that there is serious doubt whether it will continue to exist 危机 *e.g.* crisis of confidence 信任危机

the White House *n.* the official residence of the American President in Washington D.C.; or the American President or his advisers 白宫

Washington D.C. *n.* the capital of the United States 华盛顿哥伦比亚特区

D.C. *n.* the initial letters for the District of Columbia 哥伦比亚特区

the Pentagon *n.* the building in Washington, which is the headquarters of the U.S. Department of Defense; and which is also used to refer to the military leaders who work there and the decisions which they make 五角大楼

the Department of Defense *also* **the Defense Department** *n.* the U.S. government department in charge of national defence （美国）国防部

Marxism *n.* the political philosophy based on the writings of Karl Marx, which states that the struggle between people of different social classes is the most important part of history, and believes that people will develop through socialism towards a communist society 马克思主义

Marxist *n.* a person who believes in Marxism 马克思主义者

communism *n.* the political belief that the state should own and control the means of producing everything, so that all levels of society can be made equal because everyone will do as much as they can get as much as they need 共产主义

the Communist Party *also* **the communist party** *n.* the political party set up by the communists 共产党

Communist *also* **communist** *n.* a person who believes in communism or who is a member of a communist party 共产主义者；共产党员；共产党人

socialism *n.* a set of political beliefs and principles whose general aim is to create a system in which everyone has an equal opportunity to benefit from the country's wealth, usu. by having the country's main industries owned by the state 社会主义

the Socialist Party *also* **the socialist party** *n.* the political party set up by the socialists 社会党

socialist *n.* a person who believes in socialism or who is a member of the socialist party 社会主义者；社会党员；社会党人

nationalism *n.* a political belief that the country where people live should form an independent nation or that their country is better than others are 民族主义；国家主义

the Nationalist Party *also* **the nationalist party** *n.* the political party formed by the nationalists 民族主义党；国家主义党；国民党

nationalist *n.* a person who believes in nationalism or who is a member of a nationalist party 民族主义者；国家主义者；民族主义党员；国家主义党员；国民党员

radical party *n.* a political party which holds that there should be very great or extreme changes in society 激进党

conservative party *n.* a political party which is often opposed to a great or sudden change in the established order of society 保守党

moderate party *n.* a political party which keeps neutral and holds the opinions that are not extreme 温和党

Additional Knowledge

Political Parties

In Western countries, there are various kinds of political parties with different aims, beliefs and principles.

Those who hold that change is caused by the struggle between social classes are Marxists. Their ideology is Marxism. Those who hold that the state should own and control the means of production and all people are equal are communists. Their ideology is communism. They believe that the goods and wealth produced should be shared according to the principle "from each according to his ability, to each according to his needs". The political party set up by the communists is called the communist party.

Some people hold that the economy of a country should be controlled by the state and wealth should be shared equally. Such people are socialists. There are various kinds of socialists. For instance, the members of the Labour Party in Britain are often referred to as Socialists. Socialism is their ideology. And there are various kinds of socialism. The socialists are aimed at public ownership of the means of production and the establishment of a society in which every person is equal. The political party set up by the socialists is called the socialist party.

Those who hold that the country where they live should form an independent nation or that their country is better than others are nationalists. Their ideology is nationalism. The political party formed by the nationalists is called the nationalist party.

According to their divergent political views, ideas and beliefs, political parties can be divided into radical, moderate and conservative parties. Their distinction is made on the basis of their various attitudes towards the existing social system, that is, whether they want to maintain or change the present social system. A radical party favours great political change and thorough social reform. Usually its members hold extreme views and opinions. A conservative party is often opposed to a great or sudden change in the established order of society. Usually its members also hold extreme views. They are in favour of existing methods and ideas and only gradual change. They are against state control of industry. And a moderate party keeps neutral and holds the opinions that are not extreme. It is a party with moderate views and opinions. In most cases, it is a third party, which takes the middle road. Its members are usually concerned with slow, limited or small reforms in a system, rather than with sudden or large changes.

Exercises

I. Explain each of the following:
   1) government
   2) Her Majesty's Government
   3) executive
   4) First Lord of the Treasury
   5) Minister for the Civil Service
   6) non-departmental office
   7) the Chancellor of the Exchequer
   8) the Secretary of State for Home Affairs

9) the Secretary of State for Defence
10) proceeding
11) confidential
12) 10 Downing Street
13) reshuffle
14) political figure
15) departmental minister
16) Secretary of State
17) non-departmental minister
18) minister without portfolio
19) portfolio
20) envoy
21) government department
22) government agency
23) local authorities
24) public corporation
25) independent body
26) civil service
27) civil servant
28) corruption
29) Downing Street
30) 11 Downing Street
31) Whitehall
32) arbitrary
33) the Federal Government
34) the Administration
35) the State Department
36) central government
37) local government
38) consul
39) centralized central government
40) decentralized central government
41) state government
42) monetary system
43) public school
44) fire protection
45) subdivision
46) governor
47) general assembly
48) trial court
49) appellate court
50) supreme court
51) regional government
52) provincial government
53) municipal government
54) civilian
55) civilian government
56) military government
57) coup
58) unconstitutional action
59) dictatorship
60) dictator
61) caretaker government
62) caretaker cabinet
63) provisional government
64) minority government
65) coalition government
66) pluralism
67) national government
68) crisis of confidence.
69) Washington D. C.
70) the Pentagon

II. Give another way or other ways of saying each of the following:
Model: Secretary of State → Secretary, Minister
1) the Home Secretary (U. K.) →
2) the Defence Secretary (U. K.) →
3) the Chancellor (U. K.) →
4) the State Secretary (U. S.) →
5) government department →
6) appellate court (U. S.) →
7) municipality →
8) coup →
9) stage a coup →
10) coalition →

III. Fill in the blanks:
Model: Buckingham Palace in London is the official residence of the _____.
→ Buckingham Palace in London is the official residence of the British Sovereign.
1) 10 Downing Street in London is the official residence of the _____.
2) 11 Downing Street in London is the official residence of the _____.

3) The White House is the official residence of the _____.
IV. What does each of the following stand for?
   Model: The Pentagon can be used to refer to _____.
   → The Pentagon can be used to refer to the U.S. Department of Defense.
   1) Downing Street can be used to refer to _____.
   2) Whitehall can be used to refer to _____.
   3) The White House can be used to refer to _____.
V. Answer the following questions:
   1) What is the official name of the British Government?
   2) What party forms the new government in Britain?
   3) Who is the chief executive of the British Government?
   4) Who is the Head of Government in Britain?
   5) Who appoints the British Prime Minister?
   6) What are the other posts of the British Prime Minister by tradition?
   7) Who appoints the other ministers in Britain?
   8) What is the relationship between the British Government and the Cabinet?
   9) Who leads the Cabinet in Britain?
   10) What is the relationship between the Prime Minister and the Cabinet members?
   11) Who selects the Cabinet members and who can dismiss them?
   12) Where does the British Prime Minister usually hold his cabinet meeting?
   13) Where is the official residence of the Prime Minister in London?
   14) What is a cabinet reshuffle?
   15) What is the task of the British Cabinet as a whole?
   16) What is the difference between the British Cabinet and the American Cabinet?
   17) Does the British Cabinet consist of experts and law officers?
   18) What is the difference between a departmental minister and a non-departmental minister?
   19) Is a minister without portfolio a departmental minister or a non-departmental minister?
   20) What is a minister without portfolio available to do?
   21) Is the number of ministers in the British Government fixed?
   22) What does the British executive consist of?
   23) What are the British government departments and agencies responsible for?
   24) What are the British local authorities responsible for?
   25) What organizations are responsible for operating particular nationalized industries in Britain?
   26) What organizations are responsible for regulating the privatized industries in Britain?
   27) Why are the civil servants highly paid in Britain?
   28) What is the job of the civil servants?
   29) Are the civil servants policy-makers and decision-makers?
   30) What are the political inclinations of the civil servants?
   31) Who are not included in the British civil service?
   32) Are the British Government and the American Government organized in the same

way?
33) Where does the United States Government derive all its power?
34) What is the basic law of the United States?
35) What are the three distinct branches of the American Government defined by the Constitution?
36) Who is the Head of State of the United States? Who is its Head of Government?
36) Who is the head of the U. S. State Department?
37) What is the chief constitutional duty of the American Vice-President?
38) Under what circumstances can the American Vice-President succeed the President?
39) What is the central government of the United States?
40) What are the responsibilities of the Federal Government?
41) Who leads a state government in the United States?
42) What is the state legislature called in the United States?
43) Does the American state legislature also have two houses?
44) Does a caretaker government hold office for a long period of time?
45) Will a provisional government still exist after the election?

Lesson Nine

The Legal System

    Constitution is the basic law of a country. It is a system of laws, rules and principles, according to which a country is organized and governed with regard to such fundamental matters as legislative, executive and judicial power and authority. The constitution of a country formally states the rights and duties of its people. There are various types of constitution. It can be divided into written constitution and unwritten constitution. The United States has a written constitution while Britain has an unwritten constitution. The British Constitution, unlike that of most other countries, is not set out in any single document. The British Constitution is formed partly by statute, partly by common law, and partly by conventional law. Statute is a law passed by Parliament or a similar law-making body and written down formally. Common law is a law developed from old customs and from decisions made by judges, but not created by Parliament. Conventional law, which is also called conventions, refers to rules and practices which are not legally enforceable, but which are regarded as indispensable to the working of government. The British Constitution can be altered by Act of Parliament, or by general agreement, and is thus adaptable to changing political conditions. Act of Parliament is a law which has been passed by the House of Commons and House of Lords and given the Royal Assent. If a parliamentary bill receives royal assent, the king or queen agrees to it and signs it so that it becomes law. The judiciary interprets statutes and determines common law.

    The U. S. Constitution is the basic law from which the United States Government derives all its power. It is the law which protects the inhabitants of this nation from arbitrary actions by the Federal Government or any individual state. The Bill of Rights is formed by the first ten amendments to the Constitution of the United States, and it is probably its most significant and far-reaching portion. The Bill of Rights guarantees individual liberties: freedom of speech, religion and assembly, the right to a fair trial, the security of one's home. Every time when the situation of the country changed, the U. S. Congress would amend or revise its constitution in order to improve it. An amendment to the constitution is a passage, which is added to the constitution for its alteration and improvement. The Bill of Rights was added to the U. S. Constitution in 1791. Since then, the Constitution has been amended only sixteen times, and one of these amendments merely repealed another. Most of the others have made only slight changes in the basic law. These later amendments record America's struggle for equality and justice for all of its people. They abolish slavery, prohibit any denial of rights because of race or colour, grant the vote to women and to citizens of the District of Columbia, and enfranchise citizens at the age of 18.

    Justice is the legal system of a country for the purpose of making sure that people obey the laws and that punishment is given to those people who violate the laws. Justice administration is the management of the legal system. Law-enforcement agencies or officials are those such as the police and government legal departments that are responsible for making sure that people do not break the laws of a country.

The law is a system of rules which a society or government develops over time in order to deal with business, agreements, social relationships, and crimes such as theft, murder, or violence.

The two main branches of the law in most countries are the criminal law and the civil law. The former deals with wrongs affecting the community for which the State may prosecute in the criminal courts, while the latter is about deciding disputes between two parities, including individuals, administrative authorities, and commercial organizations.

The criminal law deals with such crimes as treason, espionage, conspiracy, murder, arson, poisoning, violence against the person, sexual offences, robbery, theft, burglary, kidnapping, fraud, forgery, corruption, bribery, libel, perjury, and criminal damage. Treason is the crime of betraying one's own country, for example, by helping its enemies or trying to overthrow its government. Espionage is the activity of finding out the political, military, or industrial secrets of a country. Conspiracy is the crime of planning in secret to do something illegal, usually for political reasons. Murder is the crime of killing a person deliberately and unlawfully. Arson is the crime of deliberately setting fire to something, especially a building. Poisoning is the act or crime of deliberately killing a person or making a person very ill by means of poison. Violence is a behaviour which is meant to hurt or kill people, for example, hitting or kicking or using guns or bombs. Robbery is the crime of stealing money or property from a bank, a shop, or a train, often by using force, violence or threats. Theft is the act or crime of stealing things from a person. For instance, car theft is the crime of stealing a car from a person. Burglary is the crime of breaking into a building and stealing things. Kidnapping is the taking away of a person by force, usually in order to demand money from his or her family, employers, or government. Fraud is the crime of gaining money or other benefits by deceit or trickery. Forgery is the crime of copying or making money, documents, or paintings, so that they look genuine in order to deceive people. Corruption is the dishonest and illegal behaviour by people in positions of authority or power. Bribery is the crime of influencing the behaviour or judgment of someone in a position of power unfairly or illegally by offering them money, favours or gifts. Libel is the act or crime of writing something in a book or a newspaper which wrongly damages someone's reputation, and which is therefore against the law. Perjury is the crime of telling a lie intentionally after promising solemnly to tell the truth, especially in a court of law.

The civil law is the part of a country's set of laws, which is concerned with the private affairs of citizens, rather than crime. The main subdivisions of civil law are the family law, the law of property, the law of intellectual property, the law of contract, the law of torts, the administrative law, the law of labour, the mercantile law and the company law. The family law includes the laws governing marriage, divorce, adoption, the welfare of children and other family matters. The law of property governs the ownership of property, the creation and administration of trusts, and the disposal of property on death. The law of intellectual property deals with patent cases, copyright cases and other intellectual property matter. The law of contract regulates the sale of goods, loans, partnerships, insurance and guarantees. The law of torts deals with non-contractual wrongful acts suffered by one person at the hands of another. Tort is a wrongful but not criminal act, which can be dealt with in a civil court of law. The administrative law is concerned with the powers of the State. The law of labour is related to employment, and the protection of labour force. And the mercantile law regulates trade, business and bankruptcy. And the company law is related to companies, which is designed to meet the need for proper regulation of business, to maintain open markets and to create safeguards for those wishing to invest in companies or do business with them.

A law court, a court of law, a legal court, or a court, is a place where legal matters are decided by a judge and jury or by a magistrate. The supreme court is the most important court of law in certain countries. A court of appeal is a court which deals with appeals against legal judgments in Britain and some other countries. In Britain, the House of Lords is the final court of appeal for all other courts. A criminal court is a law court which deals with criminal offences. A civil court is a law court which deals with civil cases. A juvenile court is a court of law which deals with crimes committed by young people who are not yet old enough to be considered as adults.

The law is enforced by law-enforcement officials or judicial officials. A judge is a public judicial official who has the power to decide questions brought before a court of law and make decisions about how the law should be applied to people. For example, a judge can give his judgment about how a person who has been found guilty of a crime should be punished. A magistrate or a Justice of the Peace is an official who acts as a judge in law courts which deal with less serious crimes or disputes, and decides whether cases are important enough to be passed on to higher courts.

Accusation is a formal legal charge which a person has committed a crime. Prosecution is the bringing of a criminal charge against a person. A prosecutor is a person, and often a lawyer, who brings a criminal charge against an accused person and tries to prove in a trial that the accused person who is on trial is guilty. The accused refers to the person or group of people being charged with doing wrong or breaking the law and being tried in a court for a particular crime.

Trial is a formal legal process in which a judge and jury decide whether an accused person is guilty of a particular crime by questioning the accused person and considering the evidence. In a trial, a witness is sometimes called to a court of law and gives evidence, telling what he or she knows about a crime or other event.

A conviction is the decision which is taken when someone is found guilty in a court of law. If a person is guilty, he is officially stated to have committed a crime or offence. As a rule, the guilty party should clearly have to pay all the costs. When the person charged with a crime is stated guilty, he may plead guilty or not guilty. That is, he may officially say in a court of law that he has or has not committed the crime.

If a person is convicted, the court decides on the most appropriate sentence. A sentence in a law court is the punishment which a person receives after being found guilty of a crime. It can also be the statement or order which fixes the punishment given by a law court. When the judges make the decisions, they take into account the facts of the offence, the circumstances of the offender, any previous convictions or sentences and any statutory limits on sentencing. The defence lawyer may make a speech in mitigation. A life sentence is a legal punishment in which a criminal is sent to prison for the rest of his or her life. In the United States, a person can be sentenced to death for treason. In Britain, a person may serve a life sentence for murder. Other criminals have to receive a heavy or a light sentence. Whether they are given a long or a short sentence depends on how serious their offences are.

An appeal is a formal request to a court of law for an earlier decision to be changed, or for a fine or sentence to be reduced. If a person appeals to a higher court of law against the conviction or sentence made by a lower court of law, he or she formally asks the higher court to change the decision or reduce the sentence. The court may accept the appeal and change the former decision or reduce the sentence. The court may also reject or turn down the appeal.

In 1966, the U. S. Supreme Court made a landmark decision in the Miranda vs. Arizona case. The Miranda Decision requires law enforcement officials to tell anyone taken into custody that: (1) He has the right to remain silent. (2) Anything he says can and will be used against him. (3) He has the right to have his lawyer present while being questioned. (4) If he cannot afford a lawyer, the Court will appoint one to represent him. Now Miranda is often used to refer to the continuing concern for the rights of the accused.

Punishment is an act or a way of punishing a person who has done something wrong, for example, committed a crime. Penalty is a legal punishment. Death penalty is the punishment of death used in some countries for people who have committed serious crimes such as murder. Capital punishment is another way of saying death penalty. It was originally the execution of a criminal by hanging. This was abolished in Britain in 1965, but can still, at least in theory, be the punishment awarded for treason. In the United States, the state of California has also abolished the death penalty. In Britain, capital punishment has been replaced by life imprisonment, which usually means imprisonment for a minimum of 20 years. In Western countries, some people who hold liberal views are opposed to capital punishment. Imprisonment is locking a person in prison, usually as a punishment for a crime. Life imprisonment is a punishment given to a criminal which means that the criminal must spend the rest of his or her life in prison.

Legal advice or legal counsel is the activity of giving people advice about legal affairs.

Legal aid is the financial help and assistance given by the government or another organization to the disadvantaged group of people who are in need but cannot afford to pay for a lawyer when they have trouble and need advice in legal affairs. Very often, a lawyer in a court case provides legal aid free to people too poor to pay for the services.

The citizens of a country are supposed to have equal rights. They should all be equal in the eyes of the law. They also have their duties and obligations to abide by the laws. They should perform their civic duties in the same spirit that they accept their lawful rights. A law-abiding citizen is in the habit of obeying the laws. The first duty of the state is to ensure that law-abiding people are protected.

Words & Expressions

legal *a.* involved in the law, the knowledge of the law, or the use of the law 法律的;法学的 *e.g.* legal matter 法律事务

constitution *n.* the system of laws and rules which formally states people's rights and duties, and according to which a country is governed 宪法

the judiciary *n.* the branch of authority in a country which is concerned with justice and the legal system 司法部门

judicial *a.* relating to the judgment in a court of law 司法的 *e.g.* judicial power 司法权;judiciary official 司法官员 *syn.* **law-enforcement official** 司法官员

law *n.* a rule which is supported by the power of government and which controls the behaviour of members of a society 法律 *e.g.* basic law 基本法

written constitution *n.* a rigid constitution, which is recorded or expressed in writing rather than verbally 成文宪法

unwritten constitution *n.* a flexible constitution, which is known about, accepted or understood by everyone without being officially laid down 不成文宪法

statute *n.* a law passed by Parliament or a similar law-making body and written down formally 成文法

statutory *a.* consisting of, or done because of, laws which have been formally written down 成文法的 *e.g.* statutory limit 成文法的限制

common law *n.* the system of law, esp. in Britain, which is based on old customs and on decisions made by judges, rather than on written laws passed by Parliament 普通法;习惯法;判例法

conventional law *also* **conventions** *n.* the rules and practices which are not legally enforceable, but which are regarded as indispensable to the working of government 习俗;惯例

act *n.* a law passed by the government 法令;法规

Act of Parliament *also* **Act** *n.* a British law which has been passed by the House of Commons and House of Lords and given the royal assent 议会法案

royal assent *n.* the official signing of an Act of Parliament by the sovereign, as a result of which it becomes law 国王/女王批准

bill of rights *n.* a written statement of the most important rights of the citizens of a country 人权法案

amendment *n.* a passage which is added to a law, or rule, in order to change its wording and improve it 修正案 *e.g.* to move/suggest an amendment 提出修正案;to debate an amendment 辩论修正案;to pass an amendment 通过修正案

federal *a.* belonging or relating to the central government of a federal country rather than to one of the states within it 联邦的 *e.g.* federal government 联邦政府

far-reaching *a.* having a very wide influence and affecting a great number of things 深远的

liberty *n.* the freedom to live one's life in the way that they want, esp. without a lot of interference from others 自由 *e.g.* to guarantee individual liberties 保证个人自由

freedom *n.* the right to express any political or religious opinion and live or act without the government or another country interfering 自由 *e.g.* freedom of speech 言论自由;freedom of religion 宗教自由;freedom of assembly 集会自由

trial *n.* a formal legal process in which a judge and jury decide whether sb is guilty of a particular crime by questioning them and considering the evidence 审判;审讯 *e.g.* to hear a trial 听取审讯;fair trial 公正审判

repeal *v.* officially put an end to a law 废除 *e.g.* to repeal a law 废除法律

enfranchise *v*. give sb the right to vote in elections 给予投票权 *e.g.* to enfranchise citizens at age 18 给予年满 18 岁公民投票权

criminal law *n*. the law that deals with wrongs affecting the community for which the State may prosecute in the criminal courts 刑法

criminal court *n*. a law court which deals with criminal offences 刑事法庭

crime *n*. an illegal action for which a person can be punished by law 罪；罪行；犯罪 *e.g.* to commit a crime 犯罪

criminal *n*. a person who has committed a crime or an illegal action 罪犯

wrong *n*. action or behaviour which is not morally right or correct 错误；邪恶；坏事

prosecute *v*. bring a criminal charge against sb in a court of law 起诉

prosecution *n*. the bringing of a criminal charge against a person 起诉

the prosecution *n*. all the lawyers who are responsible for bringing criminal charges against sb and trying to prove that they are guilty in a trial 原告方；控方

prosecutor *n*. a lawyer who tries to prove in a trial that the person who is on trial is guilty 起诉人

offence *n*. a crime, esp. one which breaks a particular law and requires a particular punishment 违法；犯罪 *e.g.* criminal offence 刑事犯罪；sexual offence 性犯罪

offender *n*. a person who has committed a crime 违法者；罪犯

treason *n*. the crime of betraying of a person's country, for example, by helping its enemies or by trying to overthrow its government 叛国罪；叛逆罪

espionage *n*. the action or work of finding out secrets, esp. the political secrets of a country 间谍活动；间谍罪

conspiracy *n*. the secret planning of doing sth against the law 密谋；谋反

murder *n*. the deliberate and unlawful killing of a person 谋杀

arson *n*. the crime of setting fire to property 纵火；放火

poisoning *n*. the act or crime of putting poison into or onto sth, for the purpose of harming or killing people 投毒

robbery *n*. the crime of taking the property of a person or organization illegally, esp. by using force or threats 抢劫 *e.g.* bank robbery 抢银行

theft *n*. the act or crime of stealing sth from a person or a place 偷窃；盗窃 *e.g.* car theft 盗窃汽车

burglary *n*. the crime of entering into a building by force with the intention of stealing 入室盗窃罪

kidnapping *n*. the taking away of a person illegally, and usu. by force, in order to demand money from his or her family, employers, or government 绑架

fraud *n*. the act of deceitful behaviour for the purpose of making money, which may be punishable by law 诈骗

forgery *n*. the act of making a copy of sth like money, documents or paintings for the purpose of deceiving people 伪造

corruption *n*. a dishonesty, esp. by people in positions of power 贪污；腐败

bribe *v*. offer sb money or sth valuable, in order to persuade them to do sth 贿赂；行贿

bribery *n*. the act or crime of offering money or sth valuable to sb in order to persuade them to do sth 贿赂

libel *n*. the act or crime of making a printed or written statement which says unfairly bad things about a person and may make others have a low opinion of him or her 诽谤

perjury *n*. the crime of lying in a court of law 伪证罪

damage *n*. physical harm which is caused to sth, esp. harm which stops it working properly or makes it look less good 损坏；破坏 *e.g.* criminal damage 刑事破坏

civil law *n*. the law about deciding disputes between two parities, including individuals, administrative authorities, and commercial organizations 民法

civil court *also* **civil court of law** *n*. a law court which deals with civil cases 民事法庭

the family law *n*. a subdivision of the civil law, dealing with such family affairs as marriage, divorce, adoption, and the welfare of children 家庭法

adoption *n*. the act of taking sb else's child into one's family for ever and taking on the full responsibilities in law of a parent 收养

the law of property *n*. a subdivision of the civil law, dealing with the ownership of property, the creation and administration of trusts, and the disposal of property on death 财产法

property *n*. all the things belonging to a person, esp. land, buildings or both together 财产

trust *n*. an amount of money, property, etc. which sb owns, usu. by inheriting it, and which is kept and invested for them by a group of people or an organization 信托财产

disposal *n*. the act or process of getting rid of sth which is no longer needed or wanted 处理 *e.g.* disposal of property 财产处理

intellectual property *n*. the intellectual achievements of a person's mental work including patent and copyright 知识产权

the law of intellectual property *n*. a subdivision of the civil law, dealing with patent cases, copyright cases and other intellectual property matter 知识产权法

the law of contract *n*. a subdivision of the civil law, dealing with the sale of goods, loans, partnerships, insurance and guarantees 合同法

tort *n*. sth that a person does or fails to do which harms sb else and for which the person can be sued for damages 民事侵权行为

the law of torts *n*. a subdivision of the civil law, dealing with non-contractual wrongful acts suffered by one person at the hands of another 民事侵权法

contractual *a*. being in the form of a contract or being agreed in a contract 合同性的 *e.g.* non-contractual wrongful act 非合同性侵权行为

the administrative law *a*. a subdivision of the civil law, concerned with the powers of the State 行政法

the law of labour *n*. a subdivision of the civil law, related to employment, and the protection of labour force 劳动法

mercantile *a*. relating to merchants and trading 商业的

the mercantile law *n*. a subdivision of the civil law, dealing with trade and business 商业法

company law *n*. a subdivision of the civil law, dealing with the law relating to companies, which are designed to meet the need for proper regulation of business, to maintain open markets and to create safeguards for those wishing to invest in companies or do business with them 公司法

dispute *n*. disagreement about the facts or truth of sth 争端

justice *n*. the system which a country or other group of people uses in order to make sure that people obey laws and that punishment is given to those people who break the law 司法

justice administration *n*. the management of the legal system 司法管理

violate the law *v. phrase* break the law 违犯法律;违法 *syn*. **disobey the law**, **cheat the law** 违法

law-enforcement agency *n*. an organization like the police or a government legal department that is responsible for making sure that people do not break the laws of a country 执法机构

law-enforcement official *n*. a person from the police or a government legal department that is responsible for making sure that people do not break the laws of a country 执法官员

law court *also* **court of law**, **legal court**, **court** *n*. a place where law cases are heard and judged 法院;法庭

judge *n*. a public official who has the power to decide questions brought before a court of law 法官

magistrate *also* **Justice of the Peace** *n*. an official who judges cases in a small court of law 地方法官;治安法官

supreme court *n*. the highest and most important court of law in certain countries 最高法院 *e.g.* U.S. Supreme Court 美国最高法院

court of appeal *n*. a higher legal court where people can formally ask to change the decision made by a lower court 上诉法院

juvenile court *n*. a court of law which hears the case of young person aged 10 to 16 少年法庭；未成年人法庭

accusation *n*. charging a person with doing wrong or breaking the law 控告

the accused *a*. the person or group of people being tried in a court for a particular crime 被起诉人

charge *n*. a formal accusation, made by an authority such as the police, that a person is guilty of a crime and has to stand trial in a court of law 指控；罪名 *e.g.* legal charge 法律罪名；criminal charge 刑事罪

guilty *a*. being officially stated to have committed a crime or offence 有罪的 *e.g.* guilty party 有罪的一方

evidence *n*. the information which is used in a court of law to try to prove sth and which is obtained from documents, objects, or witnesses 证据

witness *n*. sb who tells in a court of law what they saw happen or what they know about a person 证人

jury *n*. a group of usu. 12 people chosen to hear all the details of a case in a court of law and give their decision on it 陪审团 *e.g.* jury service 陪审团服务

juror *n*. a member of a jury 陪审员

conviction *n*. the act of proving or declaring that a person is guilty of a crime after a trial in a court of law 定罪；宣判有罪

convict *v*. find a person guilty of a crime in a court of law 定罪；宣判有罪

plead *v*. declare in official language that one is in a state of 承认 *e.g.* How do you plead? 你认罪吗？

plead guilty *v. phrase* officially say in a court of law that one has committed the crime 认罪；服罪

plead not guilty *v. phrase* officially say in a court of law that one has not committed the crime 不认罪；不服罪

sentence *n*. an order given by a judge which fixes a punishment for a criminal declared to be guilty in court 判刑 *e.g.* appropriate sentence 合适的量刑；heavy sentence 重刑；light sentence 轻刑；long sentence 长期徒刑；short sentence 短期徒刑；to reduce the sentence 减刑

sentence *v*. give a punishment to sb 判刑 *e.g.* to sentence sb to death 判处死刑；be sentenced to five years in prison 被判处5年徒刑

defence *n*. the person who has been accused of a crime in a trial and his or her lawyers 被告方 *e.g.* defence lawyer 被告方律师

defendant *n*. a person who has been accused of a crime in a case in a court of law 被告

in mitigation *prep. phrase* making a crime easier to understand and excuse, usu. in the hope that the court will decide to punish the person responsible less severely 减轻罪责

life sentence *n*. a legal punishment in which a criminal is sent to prison for the rest of his or her life 无期徒刑 *e.g.* to serve a life sentence 服无期徒刑

appeal *n*. a formal request to a higher court of law for an earlier legal decision to be changed 上诉 *e.g.* to make/lodge an appeal 提出上诉；to accept the appeal 接受上诉；to reject/turn down the appeal 拒绝上诉

landmark *n*. an event, idea, or stage in a process which people think is very important and different and will be remembered for a long time in the future 里程碑；标志物 *e.g.* to make a landmark decision 做出里程碑式的判决

the Miranda vs. Arizona case *n*. a case in which Miranda sued the government of the state of Arizona in 1966 米兰达诉亚利桑那州案

Miranda Decision *n*. the decision made by the U.S. Supreme Court on the Miranda vs. Arizona case in 1966 米兰达判决

custody *n*. the state of being arrested and kept in prison until the trial in a court of law 被拘留;被监禁 *e.g.* to take sb into custody 拘留;监禁
punishment *n*. an act or a way of punishing a person who has done sth wrong 惩罚;惩处;处罚
penalty *n*. a legal punishment 刑罚
death penalty *n*. the punishment of death used in some countries for people who have committed serious crimes 死刑
capital punishment *n*. another way of saying death penalty, which involves the legal killing of a person who has committed a serious crime such as murder 极刑
imprisonment *n*. locking a person in prison, usually as a punishment for a crime 监禁;关押
life imprisonment *n*. a punishment given to a criminal which means that the criminal must spend the rest of his or her life in prison 终身监禁
liberal *a*. 自由的;开明的 *e.g.* to hold liberal views 持有自由观点
legal advice *also* **legal counsel** *n*. the activity of giving people advice about legal affairs 法律咨询
legal aid *n*. the services of a lawyer in a court case provided free to people too poor to pay for them 法律援助
citizen *n*. a person who belongs to a particular country by birth or by being naturalized, gives loyalty to it, and expects protection from it, whether he or she actually lives there 公民
abide by *v*. accept a law, agreement, or decision, and behave in accordance with it 遵守 *e.g.* to abide by the law 守法 *syn*. **to keep the law, to obey the law, to follow the law, to comply with the law** 遵守法律;守法; to abide by the court's decision 服从法庭判决
civic *a*. of a city or of its citizens 公民的 *e.g.* civic duty 公民责任
lawful *a*. allowed by law, or admitted by law to be the stated thing 合法的 *e.g.* lawful right 合法权利
law-abiding *a*. always obeying the law 守法的 *e.g.* law-abiding citizen 守法公民
obey *v*. do what one is told or advised to do by sb in a position of power, or act in accordance with laws or orders 服从;遵守 *e.g.* to obey the law 遵守法律
ensure *v*. make sure 确保
contend *v*. compete or struggle with sb for sth in order to win or achieve it 竞争;对立 *e.g.* contending party 对立的一方
case *n*. a set of events needing inquiry or action by the police or a similar body, or a question to be decided in a court of law 案件 *e.g.* legal case 法律案件; criminal case 刑事案件
verdict *n*. the official decision made by a jury in a court of law at the end of a trial, esp. about whether the accused is guilty or not guilty 裁决 *e.g.* to give/reach/deliver/return a verdict 做出裁决; majority verdict 多数裁决
plaintiff *n*. a person who brings a legal case against sb in a court of law 原告
unanimous *a*. all agreeing about sth or all voting for the same thing 全体一致的 *e.g.* unanimous verdict 全体一致的裁决
retrial *n*. a second trial which sb has, because the jury at the first trial could not reach a decision or because the first trial was not properly conducted 重审;复审
panel *n*. a small group of people who are chosen, for example, to discuss or give their opinions on a particular subject in public, or to hear evidence and make a decision 专门小组 *e.g.* jury panel 陪审团
pool *n*. a number of people who are deliberately collected together to be used or shared by several people or organizations 一伙人 *e.g.* a pool of potential jurors 一组潜在的陪审员
register *n*. an official list or record of names, objects, events, etc. 登记册 *e.g.* electoral register 选民登记册
at random *prep. phrase* without a definite plan, pattern, or purpose 任意地;随意地

Additional Knowledge

The Jury

A jury is a group of people, usually twelve people, who are selected to listen to the facts about a crime and to the evidence put before them in a court of law. Members of the jury must decide which of the contending parties is right or, in criminal cases, whether the accused has committed a crime. The jury is responsible for deciding whether the person accused is guilty or not by delivering a verdict. The verdict is the official decision at the end of a trial in a law court as to whether the accused is guilty or where the plaintiff or the defendant was right. Normally, the jury's verdict is a unanimous one; but it may also be a majority verdict, provided that there are not more than two people who disagree. If agreement cannot be reached, or the first trial was not properly conducted, there must be a retrial. If some members of the jury were bribed, the judge would order a retrial. A jury is independent of the judiciary and any attempt to interfere with its members is a criminal offence. The judge is not allowed to direct the jury to return a verdict of guilty or not guilty.

Jury panels are generally selected from a pool of potential jurors before the start of a trial. Both the prosecution and the defence may object to particular jurors. People between the ages of 18 and 70 whose names appear on the electoral register are, with certain exceptions, liable for jury service and their names are chosen at random. These jury panels may include several hundred people where courts are busiest. From these panels, twelve jurors are selected to hear each trial. Many people find jury service an interesting and rewarding experience and look forward to being called again. Jurors usually spend two weeks on duty and are then discharged and a new panel selected.

Exercises

I. Explain each of the following:
1) constitution
2) written constitution
3) unwritten constitution
4) statute
5) common law
6) conventional law
7) Act of Parliament
8) Royal Assent
9) the Bill of Rights
10) liberty
11) freedom of speech
12) freedom of religion
13) freedom of assembly
14) trial
15) amendment
16) justice
17) justice administration
18) law
19) law-enforcement agency
20) law-enforcement official
21) crime
22) criminal law
23) civil law
24) treason
25) espionage
26) conspiracy
27) murder
28) arson
29) poisoning
30) violence
31) robbery
32) theft

33) burglary
34) kidnapping
35) fraud
36) forgery
37) corruption
38) bribery
39) libel
40) perjury
41) the family law
42) the law of property
43) the law of intellectual property
44) the law of contract
45) the law of torts
46) the administrative law
47) the law of labour
48) the mercantile law
49) the company law
50) law court
51) judge
52) jury
53) magistrate
54) supreme court
55) court of appeal
56) appeal
57) criminal court
58) civil court
59) juvenile court
60) accusation
61) prosecution
62) prosecutor
63) the accused
64) witness
65) conviction
66) plead guilty
67) plead not guilty
68) sentence
69) life sentence
70) Miranda vs. Arizona
71) Miranda Decision
72) punishment
73) penalty
74) capital punishment
75) imprisonment
76) life imprisonment
77) legal advice
78) legal aid
79) disadvantaged group of people
80) civic duty

II. Give another way or other ways of saying each of the following:
Models: appellate court → court of appeal
court of law → law court, legal court, court
1) conventions →
2) Justice of the Peace →
3) law-enforcement official →
4) turn down the appeal →
5) violate the law →
6) death penalty →
7) legal counsel →
8) civil court of law →
9) abide by the law →
10) ensure →

III. Answer the following questions:
1) What is the difference between written constitution and unwritten constitution?
2) What are the three component parts of the British Constitution?
3) How many amendments to the U.S. Constitution are included in the Bill of Rights?
4) What is the importance of the Bill of Rights in the life of the American people?
5) How many times has the U.S. Constitution been amended?
6) When was the Bill of Rights added to the U.S. Constitution?
7) What are the two main branches of the law in most countries?
8) What does the criminal law deal with?
9) What does the civil law deal with?
10) What are the main subdivisions of the civil law?

11) What is the final court of appeal for all other courts in Britain?
12) Who enforce the law?
13) What is the difference between a judge and a magistrate?
14) What should a judge take into consideration when he makes a conviction?
15) What will the court do if a person cannot afford a lawyer?
16) When was capital punishment abolished in Britain?
17) Who are opposed to capital punishment in Western countries?
18) Who need legal aid in legal affairs?
19) What is the characteristic of a law-abiding citizen?
20) Why is it the first duty of the state to ensure that law-abiding people are protected?

Lesson Ten

The Economic System

There are three contrasting types of economic systems in which individual economic units can interact with one another. The three basic ways may be described as the traditional system, the administered system and the market system.

In a traditional society, production and consumption patterns are governed by tradition. A person's position within the economic system is fixed by his or her parentage, religion and custom. Transactions also take place on the basis of tradition. People belonging to a certain group or caste may have an obligation to care for other persons, provide them with food and shelter, care for their health, and provide for their education. In a traditional system, every decision is made on the basis of tradition alone. So progress may be difficult to achieve. A stagnant society may result.

The administered system is an administrative control by some agency over all transactions. This agency will issue edicts or commands as to how much of each good and service should be produced, exchanged and consumed by each economic unit. Central planning may be one way of administering such an economy, which is called planned economy. In a system where planned economy is practiced, production, distribution and consumption are all controlled by the government. The central plan, drawn up by the government, shows the amounts of each commodity produced by the various firms and allocated to different households for consumption. This is an example of complete planning of production, exchange, and consumption for the whole economy.

In a market system, individual economic units are free to interact with each other in the marketplace. It is possible to buy commodities from other economic units or sell commodities to them. In a market, transactions may take place via barter or money exchange. In a barter economy, real goods or concrete goods are traded against each other. A person can exchange an ax with another person for five sheep. Obviously, finding somebody who wants to trade an ax in exchange for five sheep may not always be an easy task. As a barter economy can lead to difficulties for the traders, the introduction of money as a medium of exchange makes transactions much easier. In the modern market economy, goods and services are bought or sold for money. Under such an economic system, production, distribution and consumption are adjusted by market.

Economy consists of three parts, that is, the primary sector, the secondary sector and the tertiary sector. The primary sector is the section of the economy concerned with the extraction of raw materials and the provision of agricultural crops and animal produce. The secondary sector, which is also called the industrial sector, is mainly concerned with the manufacture of goods. The primary sector and the secondary sector make up goods-producing sectors. They mainly contain agriculture, mining, manufacture and construction. In some countries, oil and gas extraction, quarrying, forestry, husbandry, fishing and hunting also belong to good-producing sectors.

The tertiary sector which is also called the service sector forms the section of the economy containing the service industry or the third industry. The service industry offers service by putting producers in touch with consumers, instead of producing or manufacturing goods by themselves, and it belongs to immaterial economy in nature. The service sector consists of distributive services, consumer services, producer services, business services, and nonprofits and government services. In some developed countries, the tertiary sector has become the major sector of the economy. The above-mentioned three sectors of the economy actually reflect the three stages of economic growth.

Distributive services are concerned with the distribution of resources and products. They contain logistics, wholesale, retail trade, communications, real-estate business, and public utilities. Logistics refers to the planning and organization of the distribution of materials, including ordering, transportation, storage, warehousing, loading and unloading, packing, processing and delivery. The distribution of goods, including food and drink, to their point of sale by road, rail, air and sea is a major economic activity. Wholesale is the activity of buying and selling goods in large quantities and therefore at cheaper prices, especially the activity of selling goods to shopkeepers who then sell them to the public. Retail trade, retail business, or retail is the activity of selling goods to the public, usually in small amounts. The large wholesalers and retailers operate, either directly or through contractors, extensive distribution networks. Generally, retail goods are sold in ordinary shops or stores to the public. Buyers and customers can do shopping in a nearby shop or store, a department store, a supermarket, a shopping center or a shopping mall. A shop or store is a place where things are sold. A department store is a large shop which is divided into a lot of different sections and which sells many different kinds of goods. A supermarket is a large shop which sells all kinds of food and household goods. People can walk round the supermarket and take items off the shelf themselves, and pay for them all together at the check-out counter before they leave. A hypermarket is an extremely large supermarket where people can buy a very wide range of products. A chain store is a department store or a supermarket which is part of a chain of shops or stores. A shopping centre is an area in a town where a lot of shops have been built close together. A shopping mall or a mall is a specially built covered area containing shops and restaurants between which people can walk, and where cars are not allowed. Communications refer to the various ways of traveling and moving goods or people between places by means of roads or railways, or sending information between places by radio or telephone. Telecommunications refer to the business or process of receiving or sending messages by television, radio, telephone or telegraph. Real-estate business is the business of selling immovable property, such as houses, buildings and land. Public utility is a useful service for the public, including water supply, natural gas supply, electricity or power supply, and bus service. It is an important service which is provided for everyone and paid for by everyone.

Consumer services are concerned with consumption and intended to serve consumers. They contain catering trade, hotel trade, laundry, dry-cleaning establishment, repairs, resorts, travel, tourism, and entertainment. Catering trade is the business of providing food and drink for a large number of people at a public or private party or in other social events. Hotel trade is the business of managing a hotel, which provides rooms for people to stay in for a short time and also provides meals for them, in return for payment. Laundry is a firm or business which washes and irons clothes, sheets and towels for people. Now many people go to have their clothes in a launderette or a laundromat. It is a shop where there are coin-operated washing machines and driers, which the public can use to wash and dry their clothes. Dry-cleaning establishment is a dry-cleaning shop where clothes and other things made of cloth can be dry-cleaned by using a liquid chemical instead of water. Repair refers to the act or business of mending a machine, a car, a piece of clothing, or other thing which has been worn, broken or damaged or is not working property, for the purpose of making them work again. DIY which is an abbreviation of "do-it-yourself", is the activity of making or repairing things yourself, instead of buying things ready-made or paying a workman to do the work for you. There are a lot of DIY shops where people can rent tools and buy parts needed for them to make or fix things themselves. Resorts are places where a lot of people go and make holidays. Travel refers to going from one place to another, especially to a distant place, or going to several places, especially in foreign countries. The travelers often go to a travel agency or a travel bureau to book their tickets or hotel accommodation. A travel agency is a business which makes arrangements for people's holidays and journeys. Tourism is the business of providing tourists with services such as hotels, restaurants, and sightseeing trips on holiday. Tourists are people who visit interesting places for pleasure, especially when they are on holiday. The natural beauty of scenic spots has great appeal for tourists. But there is a growing interest in heritage, arts and culture. Tourist attractions also include museums, art galleries, historic buildings and monuments, and theatres, as well as shopping, sports and business facilities. In recent years, business travel has got a growing share of the tourism market. It includes attendance at conferences, exhibitions, trade fairs and other business sites. Entertainment refers to the act or profession of amusing people by a public performance.

  A franchise is a special right given or sold by a company to a person or a group of people who are allowed to sell the company's goods or services in a particular place. Franchising is such a business in which the company owning the rights to a particular form of trading licenses them to the franchisees, usually by means of an initial payment with continuing royalties. The main areas of franchising include cleaning services, film processing, print shops, hairdressing and cosmetics, fitness centres, courier delivery, car rental, engine tuning and servicing, and fast food retailing. They are mostly related to consumer services. A franchised store is such a store mentioned above, which is authorized to sell goods or services of a company.

  Producer services are concerned with production and intended to serve producers. They contain accountancy, banking, management consultancy, market research, legal advice, architecture and engineering. Accountancy is the theory or practice of controlling and examining the money accounts of businesses or people. Banking is the business or activity of a bank or a banker. Management consultancy supplies technical assistance and advice to business and government clients. Typically, management consultants identify and investigate problems and opportunities, recommend appropriate actions and help to implement recommendations. Market research is the activity of collecting and studying information about what people want, need, and buy, especially because a company wants to find out whether a new product or idea is likely to be successful before it spends more time, money, or effort on it. Legal advice or legal counsel is the activity of giving people advice about legal affairs. Architecture is the art and science of planning, designing, constructing, and decorating buildings. Engineering is the activities and work involved in planning, designing and constructing machinery, engines, electrical equipment or devices, or roads and bridges.

Business services are newly rising and mainly concerned with business. They contain exhibition or exposition facilities, conference facilities, computing services, advertising and public relations. An exhibition or an exposition is a collection of works of art like pictures and sculptures, or goods, or other things, which is shown in an exhibition centre. Exhibition facilities or exposition facilities refer to the equipment, buildings, and services for holding an exhibition or an exposition. As there is more and more communication among the people, they hold meetings, conferences or discussions to exchange their views and ideas. Conference facilities provide places, equipment and services for people to hold meetings. Computing service comprises the business engaged in software development, production of packaged software, data processing, and the provision of complete computer systems. It also includes the provision of information technology education and training. An advertisement is an announcement in a newspaper, a short film shown on television, or a notice on the wall, about a product or a service, which is aimed at encouraging people to buy them. Advertising is the business or activity of encouraging people to buy goods or services by means of advertisements. Public relations refer to the work of forming in the minds of the general public a favourable opinion of an organization.

The four kinds of services mentioned above are all intended to serve the whole society and also to make profit, so as to accumulate social wealth.

Nonprofits and government services are intended only to serve the whole society but not intended to be lucrative. They are mainly supported by the government for public benefit. They contain national defence, social security, public administration, justice administration, education, public health and social work. National defence is the system and organization of a country's armies, weapons, and military facilities. Its function is to maintain the country's territorial integrity and sovereignty against foreign aggression. Social security is a system by which the government pays money regularly to people who have no other income or only a very small income. Its purposes are to help the people in need, reduce poverty, and promote incentives to work. Public administration is the range of activities connected with organizing and supervising public affairs. Justice administration is the management of the legal system of a country for the purpose of making sure that people obey laws and that punishment is given to those people who break the law. Education is the system of teaching people, usually at a school or college. Public health is the service providing medical care for the public. And social work involves giving help and advice to people who have serious problems of many kinds, for example, to people who are very poor or who live in bad conditions.

While the labour-intensive industry is declining in the present-day world, the knowledge-intensive industry is growing rapidly. The labour-intensive industry is characterized with large inputs of labour and capital instead of knowledge. The knowledge-intensive industry is also called the technique-intensive industry, the high-technique industry, or the high-tech industry. It takes modern science and technology as the main factor of production to give impetus to economic development. Unlike the labour-intensive industry, it no longer uses large inputs of labour and capital but requires advanced and sophisticated scientific knowledge, technology and method. Its employers possess higher levels of education and skills, compared with those in the labour-intensive industry. The electronic industry, the electronic computer industry, the information technology industry, the aviation industry or the aircraft industry, the astronautic industry or the space industry, and the atomic energy industry or the nuclear energy industry all fall into this category.

Words and Expressions

economy *n*. the system according to which the money, industry and trade of a country or region are organized 经济

economic *a*. concerned with economics and with the organization of the money, industry, and trade of a country, region, or social group 经济的 *e.g.* economic system 经济体系;经济制度;economic unit 经济单位

system *n*. a way of working, organizing, or doing sth in which people follow a fixed plan or a set of rules 体系;制度 *e.g.* traditional system 传统制度;market system 市场制度

administer *v*. be responsible for managing and supervising a country, company, institution, etc. 管理;治理 *e.g.* administered system 政府管理的制度

consumption *n*. the act of buying and using things 消费 *e.g.* consumption pattern 消费模式

parentage *n*. the fact of who a person's parents are, what nationality they are, what class they are, etc. 出身;家世

transaction *n*. a piece of business or other activity which is carried out by two or more people negotiating about it, for example, an act of buying or selling sth 交易

caste *n*. a social class or system in any country which is based on dividing people into groups according to their family, rank, wealth, profession, etc. 社会等级;等级制度

obligation *n*. sth that sb must do because they have promised to do it or because it is their duty to do it 义务

shelter *n*. a place where people can stay or live 住所

stagnant *a*. unsuccessful or dull because of no change or development in any way 停滞的 *e.g.* stagnant society 停滞的社会

administrative *a*. concerned with the work of managing and supervising a company, institution, or other organization 行政的 *e.g.* administrative control 行政控制

agency *n*. an administrative organization usu. run by a government 政府分支机构

edict *n*. a public order or instruction given by a government or other authority, which everyone must obey 公告 *e.g.* to issue edicts 发布公告

command *n*. an order which tells people to do sth 命令 *e.g.* to issue commands 发布命令

planning *n*. the process of deciding in detail how to do sth before people actually start to do it 规划 *e.g.* central planning 中央规划

planned economy *n*. an economic system in which production, distribution and consumption are all controlled by the government 计划经济

distribution *n*. the delivering of sth to several people or organizations 流通 *e.g.* distribution of goods 商品流

通；distribution network 流通网络

marketplace *n*. the activity of buying and selling and the places where this occurs 市场

commodity *n*. sth whish is sold for money, such as food, clothing, or machinery 商品 *e.g.* to buy commodities 购买商品

via *prep*. by means of using 通过

barter *n*. exchange of goods for other goods, rather than selling them for money 以物易物；易货 *e.g.* barter economy 易货经济

real goods *also* **concrete goods** *n*. the goods which actually exist 有形商品；实物商品

trader *n*. a person whose job is to trade in goods 商人

introduction *n*. the act of causing sth to exist or be used in a place or system for the first time 引进

medium *n*. a substance or material which is used for a particular purpose or in order to produce a particular effect 媒介

adjust *v*. change sth so that it is more effective or appropriate 调整

sector *n*. all the companies which are involved in a particular area of work or all the companies which are run according to a particular system of ownership or financial control （经济）部门

primary sector *n*. the section of the economy concerned with the extraction of raw materials and the provision of agricultural crops and animal produce 第一部门

industry *n*. branch of production or manufacture 产业；工业；or all the people and the processes which are involved in producing or manufacturing a particular thing 企业；or commercial undertaking which provides services 行业

first industry *n*. the branch of production which is related to farming or agriculture 第一产业

extraction *n*. the act of removing a substance which is contained in another substance, with a machine or instrument or by chemical means 开采；提取；提炼 *e.g.* extraction of raw materials 原材料开采；oil extraction 石油提取；gas extraction 天然气开采

raw material *n*. a natural substance which is used to make sth, for example, in an industrial process 原材料；原料

crop *n*. a plant which is grown regularly and in large quantities on farms, in fields, etc. 作物 *e.g.* agricultural crops 农作物

produce *n*. food or other agricultural material which is grown in large quantities to be sold 农产品 *e.g.* animal produce 动物产品

secondary sector *also* **industrial sector** *n*. the section of the economy mainly concerned with the manufacture of goods 第二部门；工业部门

industrial sector *n*. another way of saying the secondary sector 工业部门

second industry *n*. the branch of production which is related to manufacture 第二产业

service *n*. an organization or system which provides sth that the public needs, esp. transport, communications facilities, or information 服务

tertiary sector *also* **service sector** *n*. the section of the economy concerned with the service industry or the third industry 第三部门；服务部门

service sector *n*. another way of saying the tertiary sector 服务部门

service industry *n*. the branch of economy concerned with services 服务产业

third industry *n*. another way saying the service industry 第三产业

goods-producing sector *n*. the section of the economy concerned with the production of goods, referring to the primary sector and the secondary sector 商品生产部门

agriculture *n*. the practice of farming and the methods which are used to raise and look after crops and animals 农业；农牧业

mining *n*. the industry and activities connected with getting coal, diamonds, gold, etc. from the ground

采矿业

manufacture *n*. the making or production of sth by machine in a factory 机器制造

manufacture *v*. make or produce sth by machines in a factory 机器制造 *e.g.* to manufacture goods 机器制造商品

construction *n*. the building of buildings, roads, bridges, etc. 建筑；建设 *e.g.* construction industry 建筑业

quarrying *n*. the activity of removing a stone or mineral from a quarry by digging, drilling, or blasting 采石

quarry *n*. an open surface which has been dug out of a mountain or a piece of land for the purpose of extracting stone, slate, or some other mineral 采石场；露天矿

forestry *n*. the practice and business of growing and taking care of trees in forests, esp. in order to obtain wood 林业

husbandry *n*. farming, esp. when it is done carefully and well 农牧业

animal husbandry *n*. the practice and business of raising animals 畜牧业

fishing *n*. the business of catching fish 渔业

hunting *n*. the practice and business of hunting wild animals 狩猎

consumer *n*. a person who buys things or uses services 消费者

material economy *n*. the economy which is related to the production of materials 物质经济

immaterial *a*. not having material form; without substance 非物质的

immaterial economy *n*. the economy which is related to the production of things which don't have material forms 非物质经济

distributive service *n*. the service concerned with the distribution of resources and products 流通服务

consumer service *n*. the service concerned with consumption and intended to serve consumers 消费者服务

producer service *n*. the service concerned with production and intended to serve producers 生产者服务

business service *n*. the service concerned with businesses 商务服务

nonprofits service *n*. the service intended to serve the whole society but not intended to be lucrative 非营利服务

government service *n*. the service supported by the government for public benefit 政府服务

logistics *n*. the planning and organization of the distribution of materials 物流

ordering *n*. asking for sth to be brought, made, etc., in return for payment 订货

transportation *n*. carrying people or goods from one place to another 运输

storage *n*. the act of keeping a supply of sth for future use 储存

warehouse *n*. a large building for storing things, esp. things which are to be sold 仓库

warehousing *n*. keeping things in a warehouse 仓储

loading *n*. putting sth which is to be carried on or in a vehicle 装货

unloading *n*. removing sth from a vehicle 卸货

packing *n*. putting sth into packets to be sold 包装

processing *n*. making changes to raw materials industrially in order to make products which can be used or sold 加工

delivery *n*. bringing letters, parcels, or other goods to a place where they are wanted 送货

point of sale *n*. a particular place where things are sold 销售点

rail *n*. one of the two metal bars fixed to the ground on which railway trains run 铁轨 *e.g.* by rail 通过铁路

wholesale *n*. the business of selling goods in large quantities, esp. to shopkeepers 批发

wholesaler *n*. a businessman who sells goods wholesale 批发商

retail trade *also* **retail business**, **retail** *n*. the sale of goods in a shop or a store to customers, for their own use and not for selling to anyone else 零售 *e.g.* retail of goods 商品零售

retailer *n*. a person who sells things by retail 零售商

retail goods *n*. the goods sold in ordinary shops or stores to the public 零售商品

contractor *n*. a person or company that contracts to do work or provide supplies in large amounts, esp. to provide building materials or workers for building jobs 承包商

shop *BrE*. also **store** *AmE*. *n*. a place where things are sold 商店;店铺

department store *n*. a large shop divided into departments, in each of which a different type of goods is sold 百货公司;百货商店

supermarket *n*. a large shop where customers serve themselves with food and other goods needed in the home 超级市场;超市

hypermarket *n*. an extremely large supermarket where people can buy a very wide range of products 大型超级市场;大型超市

chain store *n*. any of a group of usu. large shops of the same kind owned by one organization 连锁商店

shopping *n*. an act or occasion of visiting the shops to buy things 购物

shopping centre *n*. a group of shops of different kinds planned and built together in one area 购物中心

shopping mall also **mall** *n*. a large shopping center, often enclosed, where cars are not permitted 购物城

communications *n*. the systems and processes that are used to communicate or to broadcast information, esp. those that use electricity or radio waves 通讯;交通

telecommunications *n*. the business or process of sending signals and messages over long distances using electronic equipment, for example, radio and telephone 电信;电讯

real estate *n*. immovable property, consisting of land, building, etc. 房地产

real-estate business *n*. the business of selling houses, buildings and land 房地产业

public utility *n*. a public service such as the supply of water, gas or electricity to the home 公用事业

catering *n*. the provision of food and drink for a large number of people 餐饮供应

catering trade *n*. the business of providing food and drink for a large number of people 餐饮业

hotel *n*. a building where people stay, usu. for a few nights, paying for their rooms and meals 饭店;旅店;旅馆;酒店

hotel trade *n*. the business of managing a hotel 旅馆业;酒店业

resort *n*. a place where people regularly go for holidays 度假地;游览胜地

laundry *n*. a place or business where clothes, etc., are washed and ironed 洗衣店

launderette also **laundromat** *AmE*. *n*. a shop where the public can wash their clothes in machines which work when coins are put in them 自助洗衣店

coin-operated washing machine *n*. a washing machine which works when coins are put in them 投币洗衣机

drier *n*. a machine for drying clothes 烘干机

dry cleaning *n*. the action or work of cleaning clothes or other things made of cloth by using a liquid chemical instead of water 干洗

dry-cleaning establishment *n*. a shop where clothes, materials, etc., can be taken to be dry-cleaned 干洗店

repair *n*. mending a machine, a piece of clothing, or other thing which has been damaged or is not working properly 修理

do-it-yourself also **DIY** (*abbrev*.) *n*. the activity of making or repairing things yourself, instead of buying things ready-made or paying a workman to do the work for you 自己动手

DIY shop *n*. a shop in which people can rent tools and buy parts necessary for them to make or fix things themselves "自己动手"商店

travel *n*. making a journey 旅行

travel agency also **travel bureau** *n*. a business which arranges travel, for example, by buying tickets and finding hotel rooms 旅行社

tourism *n*. the business of providing holidays, tours, hotels, etc., for tourists, esp. on their holidays 旅

游业 *e.g.* tourism market 旅游市场

tourist *n.* a person who visits places for pleasure and interest, esp. when he or she is on holiday 旅游者

sightseeing *n.* traveling around, usu. in a city, in order to see the interesting places which tourists usu. visit 观光；游览 *e.g.* sightseeing trip 观光；游览

interesting place *also* **place of interest** *n.* a place which attracts people's attention because it is rather exciting or unusual 名胜

beauty *n.* the fact, quality, or condition of being beautiful 美 *e.g.* natural beauty 自然美

scenic spot *n.* a place which is attractive because it has beautiful views and natural features 景点

appeal *n.* power to move the feelings 魅力

heritage *n.* all the qualities, traditions, or features of life which have been continued over many years and passed on from one generation to another 文化遗产

attraction *n.* sth which people can go to for interest or enjoyment, for example, a famous building, a beautiful piece of countryside, or a concert 吸引人的事物 *e.g.* tourist attraction 旅游景点

museum *n.* a place or building where large numbers of interesting and valuable objects are preserved and studied, and displayed to the public, some of which contain works of art or historical objects, or specimens of plants and stuffed animals 博物馆

art gallery *n.* a place which has permanent exhibitions of works of art in it 美术馆；画廊

historic *a.* important in history, or likely to be considered important at some time in the future 历史性的 *e.g.* historic building 历史性建筑物；historic monument 古迹

theatre *n.* a building with a stage in it, on which plays, shows, and other entertainments are performed for people to go and watch 剧院

facilities *n.* the equipment, buildings, services, etc, which are provided for a particular activity or purpose 设施 *e.g.* business facilities 商业设施

business travel *n.* going from one place to another for the business purpose 商务旅行

share *n.* the part belonging to, owed to, or done by a particular person 份额

market share *also* **share of the market** *n.* the proportion of the total sales of a product which is produced by a company 市场份额

attendance *n.* being present at 出席；参加 *e.g.* attendance at a conference 出席会议

exhibition *also* **exposition** *n.* a collection of such works of art as pictures and sculptures, or goods, or other things in a public place where people can come to look at them 展览会；博览会

exhibition facilities *also* **exposition facilities** *n.* the equipment, buildings, and services for holding an exhibition or an exposition 展览会设施

trade fair *n.* an exhibition where manufacturers show products which they want to sell to people from other industries 交易会

site *n.* a piece of ground which is used or will be used for a particular purpose 场地；场所 *e.g.* business site 商业场所

entertainment *n.* shows, performances, films, etc., which people watch for pleasure 娱乐

franchise *n.* an authority which is given by a company to franchisees, allowing them to sell its goods or services 特许经销权

franchisee *n.* a person or a group of people who are authorized to sell goods or services of a company 有特许经销权者

franchising *n.* a business in which the company owning the rights to a particular form of trading licenses them to franchisees, usually by means of an initial payment with continuing royalties 特许经销

license *v.* give special official permission to or for 特许；许可

royalty *n.* payments made to sb whose invention or property is used by a commercial company 使用费

cleaning service *n.* the activity or work of cleaning the inside of a house or other building and the furniture

in it 保洁服务
film processing *n.* the sequence of chemical reactions, washing and drying involved in treating an exposed film, to produce a permanent visible image which can be safely handled in further operations 胶片冲洗
print shop *n.* a shop where printing or photocopying is done 冲印店；复印店
hairdressing *n.* the occupation of activity of cutting, washing, and styling people's hair 理发业；理发
cosmetic *n.* a substance, such as lipstick or powder, which people, esp. women, put on their face or body to make themselves look more attractive 化妆品
fitness centre *n.* a place where people do exercise to keep fit 健身房
courier *n.* a person who is paid to take a special letter or parcel from one place to another 特快专递人员
courier delivery *n.* the occupation or activity of sending special letters or parcels from one place to another by couriers 特快专递
rental *n.* the occupation or activity of renting goods or services 租赁 *e.g.* car rental 汽车租赁
engine tuning *n.* the adjusting of an engine for the purpose of making it work as well as possible 发动机调试
engine servicing *n.* the examining, adjusting and cleaning of an engine for the purpose of keeping it working efficiently and safely 发动机维修
fast food *n.* food which is easy to prepare, inexpensive, and uniform in taste and quality around the country, as typically sold by nationwide chains, with the McDonald's hamburger as the prototypical fast food 快餐 *e.g.* fast food retailing 快餐零售
franchised store *n.* a store, which is authorized to sell goods or services of a company 专卖店；加盟店
producer *n.* a person, a company, or a country that provides a large supply of sth, esp. sth that is manufactured or grown to be sold to the public 生产者 *e.g.* producer service 生产者服务
accountancy *n.* the theory or practice of keeping or inspecting money accounts 会计学；会计工作
banking *n.* the business or activity of banks or similar institutions 银行业；金融业；银行业务；金融
bank *n.* a business organization which performs services connected with money, esp. keeping money for customers and paying it out on demand 银行
banker *n.* a person who is involved in banking at a senior level 银行家
consultancy *n.* 咨询 *e.g.* management consultancy 管理咨询
market research *n.* the process of collecting information about what products people buy and why they buy these products, usu. done by specialized companies so that they can find ways of increasing sales 市场研究；市场调查
architecture *n.* the art and science of building, including its planning, making, and decoration 建筑学
engineering *n.* the science or profession of planning the making of machines, roads, bridges, electrical equipment, etc. 工程
identify *v.* be able to recognize people or things because they are like other people or things or because they have a particular quality 辨认
investigate *v.* examine all the details of an event or situation in order to find out what happened or what is happening 调查 *e.g.* to investigate problems 调查问题
recommend *v.* suggest that a particular action should be done 建议 *e.g.* to recommend an appropriate action 建议合适的行动
implement *v.* carry out the ideas of a plan, system, law, etc., in order to change or control a situation 实施 *e.g.* to implement recommendations 实施建议
computing *n.* the use of computers, esp. as a job, or in business, industry, or administration 计算机应用
computer *n.* a machine which processes data into information under control of a stored programme 计算机
computing service *n.* the business engaged in software development, production of packaged software, consultancy, processing, the provision of complete computer systems, the provision of information

technology education and training, and independent maintenance 计算机应用服务

software *n*. the programmes which control a computer as opposed to hardware that is the actual machinery of the computer 软件 *e.g.* software development 软件开发；packaged software 成套软件；软件包

data *n*. the raw, unstructured, and unprocessed facts 数据 *e.g.* data processing 数据处理

computer system *n*. the whole set of a computer which consists of an input device, an output device, main memory, and a processor 计算机系统

advertisement *n*. announcement in a newspaper, on television, or on a poster about a product, event, job vacancy, etc. 广告

advertising *n*. the business or activity of encouraging people to buy goods or services by means of advertisements 广告业；做广告

public relations *n*. the part of an organization's work which is concerned with obtaining the approval of the public for what it does 公共关系；公关

accumulate *v*. gather and collect things or make them increase in number and amount, over a period of time 积累 *e.g.* to accumulate social wealth 积累社会财富

lucrative *a*. earning a lot of money, and making large profits 盈利的

benefit *n*. anything that brings help, advantage, or profit 福利 *e.g.* public benefit 公众福利

national defence *n*. a system of armies and weapons of a country for the purpose of maintaining its territorial integrity 国防

weapon *n*. an object such as a gun, a knife, or a missile, which is used to kill or hurt people in a fight or a war 武器

territorial integrity *n*. the state of a country which is united as one whole 领土完整

sovereignty *n*. the complete political power which a country possesses to govern itself 主权

aggression *n*. the political or military activities of a country or group, which constantly makes attacks on other people, esp. people who seem innocent or peaceful 侵略

social security *n*. a system by which the government pays money to people who are unemployed, old, ill, etc. 社会保障

public administration *n*. the management of public affairs 公共管理

education *n*. the process by which a person's mind and character are developed through teaching, esp. through formal instruction at a school or college 教育

public health *n*. the service providing medical care for the public 公众健康；公共卫生

social work *n*. the work done by the government or private organizations to improve bad social conditions and help people in need 社会福利工作

labour-intensive industry *n*. the industry which needs and uses a lot of workers 劳动密集型产业

knowledge-intensive industry *n*. the industry which is characterized with large inputs of knowledge 知识密集型产业

technique-intensive industry *n*. the industry which is characterized with large inputs of technique 技术密集型产业

high technology *also* **high tech** *n*. the practical use of advanced scientific research and knowledge, esp. in relation to electronics and computers, and the development of new advanced machines and equipment 高科技

high-technique industry *also* **high-tech industry** *n*. the industry which involves or results from the use of high technology 高科技产业

impetus *n*. the force which starts an object moving and resists changes in speed or direction once it is moving 刺激；动力

input *n*. sth which is put in for use, 投入 *e.g.* input of labour 劳动投入；input of capital 资本投入

sophisticated *a*. using advanced and complex methods 高级的；复杂的；尖端的 *e.g.* sophisticated scientific knowledge 尖端科学知识

electronic *a.* using or produced by such equipment as radios, televisions and computers, which works by means of an electric current passing through chips, transistors, or valves 电子的 *e.g.* electronic industry 电子工业; electronic computer industry 电子计算机工业

information technology *n.* the theory and practice of using computers to store and analyze information 信息技术 *e.g.* information technology industry 信息技术产业; IT 业

aviation *n.* the operation and production of aircraft 航空; 航空制造

aircraft *n.* a vehicle which can fly, for example, an airplane, glider, or helicopter 航空器

aviation industry *also* **aircraft industry** *n.* the industry which involves the production of aircraft 航空工业

astronautics *n.* the science and technology of space travel 航天

space *n.* the area without boundaries or limits which lies beyond our planet's atmosphere 太空; 宇宙空间

space navigation *n.* travel or flight in space 太空旅行; 宇航

astronautic industry *also* **space industry** *n.* the industry which involves the production of spacecraft 航天工业

atomic energy *also* **nuclear energy** *n.* the powerful force which is produced when the nucleus or the central part of an atom is either split or joined to another atom 原子能; 核能 *e.g.* atomic energy industry 原子能工业; 核能工业

category *n.* a set of people, actions, objects, etc., which all have a particular characteristic or quality in common 类别 *e.g.* to fall into this category 属于这个类别

primitive *a.* belonging to a society of people who live in a very simple way, usu. without industries or a writing system 原始的 *e.g.* primitive people 原始人

farming *n.* the practice or business of growing crops or raising animals on a farm 农业; 农牧业

material industry *n.* the branch of production which produces materials 物质产业

handicraft *n.* an activity, art or craft which involves doing or making things with a person's hands in a skilful way, including pottery, woodwork, embroidery, and weaving 手工业

pottery *n.* the activity or craft of making pots, dishes, and other articles which are shaped from clay and then baked in an oven in order to make them hard 陶器制造; pots, dishes or other objects made out of hardened clay 陶器

woodwork *n.* the activity of making things out of wood, esp. when this is done skillfully or artistically 木工

embroidery *n.* the act or process of sewing designs on cloth or other material 刺绣

weaving *n.* the act or process of making cloth by crossing the threads over and under each other using a loom 编织

loom *n.* a machine which is used for weaving thread into cloth 织布机

handloom *n.* a small loom which is used for weaving by hand 手动编织机

occupation *n.* a job or profession 职业

trade *n.* a particular kind of work that people do, esp. when they have been trained to do it over a period of time as a way of making a living 手艺; the activity of buying, selling, or exchanging goods or services between people, firms, or countries 交易; 贸易; the people engaged in a particular business 行业; 同业; 同行

craftsman *n.* sb who makes things like pottery or carved wooden objects with their skillful hands in their shops 工匠

apprentice *n.* a young person who works, often for a fixed period of time, with a skilful craftsman whose job involves a particular skill, for the purpose of learning the skill as a way of making a living 学徒

master *n.* a skilful craftsman in a particular job, who is qualified to train others 师傅

shop *n.* a place where things are made 作坊; a place like a building or part of a building where things are sold 店铺；商店

commerce *n*. the activities and procedures involved in buying and selling things 商业

efficiency *n*. the quality of being able to do a task successfully and without wasting time or energy 效率 *e.g.* low efficiency 低效率

scale *n*. the size and range of sth, used esp. of sth which cannot be counted or physically measured 规模 *e.g.* small scale 小规模；large scale 大规模

production *n*. the process of manufacturing or growing sth in large quantities in order to provide a supply to be sold to the public 生产

productivity *n*. a measure of the efficiency of a company or country, which is calculated by comparing the amount or value of goods produced with the time and money spent on producing them and the number of workers who produce them 生产力 *e.g.* to raise productivity 提高生产力

industrial revolution *n*. a period of time when machines are invented and factories set up, and the changes which take place during this time 产业革命；工业革命

the Industrial Revolution *n*. a period of time when machines were invented and factories set up, and the changes which took place around 1750 - 1850 in Britain 英国产业革命；英国工业革命

invention *n*. the act of making a machine, process, etc. which has never been made or used before 发明

application *n*. the using of sth in a particular situation 应用

machinery *n*. machines in general 机械；机器

electricity *n*. a form of energy which is used for heating and lighting, and to provide power for machines in houses and factories 电

mass production *n*. the production of sth in large quantities, esp. by using machines to do the work in a factory 批量生产；规模生产

product *n*. sth which is produced and sold in large quantities, often as the result of an industrial process 产品

skillful *a*. being able to do sth very well 有技巧的 *e.g.* skillful craftsman 技艺高超的工匠

skilled *a*. having the knowledge and ability needed to do sth well 技术熟练的 *e.g.* skilled worker 熟练工人

skilled work *n*. the work involving or requiring a certain level of trained ability, used esp. of manual and industrial work 熟练工种

workshop *also* **shop** *n*. a room or a building in a factory, which contains tools or machinery for making or repairing things, esp. using wood or metal 车间；工场

Additional Knowledge

The Economic Progress of Human Society

In human history, primitive people first developed farming on land. While some engaged themselves in agriculture, others made use of their environments and developed animal husbandry, fishing, hunting or forestry. This was the first social division of labour in human society. All these formed the first industry, which belonged to the primary sector of the economy and was a material industry in nature.

Some people who were skillful with their hands separated themselves from farming and started the second social division of labour in human society. As a result, they developed handicraft which was an activity, art or craft needing skill with the hands. Handicraft including pottery, woodwork, embroidery, and weaving at a handloom, became an occupation or a trade. Craftsmen made things such as pottery or carved wooden objects with their skillful hands in their shops. An apprentice learned a trade from a skillful craftsman as his master in a shop for a fixed period of time as a way of making a living.

A craftsman was good at making things, but not necessarily good at selling them. Those who were good at selling things started a new trade or a new occupation. In their shops, they no longer made things, but instead, bought and sold things. They became traders who made a living by trading or exchanging goods. This was the early form of trade, commerce or service.

Craftsmen were not satisfied with their low efficiency and small scale of production by using their hands. Some clever people made simple machines to raise productivity. The Industrial Revolution that first started in Britain gave rise to a new way of production. With the invention and application of machinery and electricity, people manufactured goods and materials on a large scale. Mass production in a factory caused further social division of labour. A skilled worker's job or trade is to deal with only a special part of the product in a workshop or a shop where the manufacturing is done. Handicraft and manufacture form the secondary sector or the second industry, which produces or makes goods and belongs to material economy in nature.

Exercises

I. Explain each of the following:
1) parentage
2) transaction
3) caste
4) planned economy
5) barter
6) real goods
7) distribution
8) consumption
9) primary sector
10) raw material
11) agriculture
12) agricultural crop
13) animal produce
14) secondary sector
15) goods-producing sector
16) tertiary sector
17) mining
18) manufacture
19) construction
20) oil extraction
21) quarrying
22) husbandry
23) forestry
24) fishing
25) hunting
26) service industry
27) distributive service
28) logistics
29) wholesale
30) retail
31) department store
32) supermarket
33) hypermarket
34) shopping centre
35) shopping mall
36) chain store
37) communications
38) telecommunications
39) real estate
40) consumer
41) consumer service
42) catering trade
43) laundry
44) repair

45) do-it-yourself
46) resort
47) travel
48) tourism
49) business travel
50) entertainment
51) franchise
52) franchising
53) franchisee
54) franchised store
55) producer
56) accountancy
57) banking
58) management accountancy
59) market research
60) legal advice
61) architecture
62) engineering
63) business service
64) conference facilities
65) computing service
66) advertising
67) public relations
68) nonprofits service
69) government service
70) national defence
71) social security
72) public administration
73) justice administration
74) education
75) public health
76) social work
77) labour-intensive industry
78) knowledge-intensive industry
79) electronic industry
80) electronic computer industry
81) information technology
82) information technology industry
83) aviation industry
84) astronautic industry
85) atomic energy

II. Give another way or other ways of saying each of the following:
Models: goods → commodities
retail → retail trade, retail business
1) concrete goods →
2) industrial sector →
3) service sector →
4) third industry →
5) shop →
6) mall →
7) laundromat →
8) DIY →
9) travel bureau →
10) interesting place →
11) legal counsel →
12) exposition facilities →
13) high-tech industry →
14) aircraft industry →
15) space industry →

III. Answer the following questions:
1) What are the three contrasting types of economic systems?
2) What fixes a person's social status within the economic system in a traditional society?
3) What is the basic feature of planned economy?
4) What is the difference between planned economy and market economy?
5) Why is it difficult for people to make transactions under barter economy?
6) What is the role that money plays in transactions?
7) What is responsible for adjusting production, distribution and consumption under market economy?
8) What are the three sectors of economy?

9) What is the difference between the industrial sector and the service sector?
10) What does logistics contain?
11) What is the difference between wholesale and retail?
12) What is the difference between a department store and a supermarket?
13) What is the difference between a supermarket and a hypermarket?
14) What does public utility include?
15) What do consumer services contain?
16) What is the difference between a laundry and a launderette?
17) What is the difference between a laundry and a dry-cleaning shop?
18) What does business travel include?
19) What are the main areas of franchising?
20) What is the difference between consumer service and producer service?
21) What do producer services contain?
22) What does computing service comprise?
23) Who supports nonprofits and government services?
24) What are the purposes of social security?
25) What is the difference between the labour-intensive industry and the knowledge-intensive industry?

Lesson Eleven

Income and Expenditure

Employment is the work which a person does in order to earn money for survival. It involves the relationship between the employer and the employee. An employer is a person or a company which gives work to others for payment. An employee is a person who works for someone else or for an organization in return for payment. A self-employed person is a person who works independently for his or her customers or clients and not for an employer.

There is a division of labour in every society. Some people do manual work, manual labour or physical labour by using their hands or physical strength rather than their minds. They are manual workers. Others do mental work and they are mental workers. There is also a distinction between a white-collar worker and a blue-collar worker. The former is an office worker engaged in office work or white-collar work; while the latter is a person engaged in manual work, working with his or her hands. Profession is a type of job which requires special training and also brings a fairly high status, for example, the work connected with law, medicine, or education. Traditional professionals included doctors, lawyers and clergymen, who had long-term special training, won public respect and enjoyed high social status. This group of people are characterized with their service to the public and devotion to society. But they don't create material wealth. People summarize their spirit of service and devotion as altruism. However, in the past few decades, people were discontented with their professional services. Thus they fell in public esteem. Meanwhile, there have appeared a host of new professionals such as administrators, educators, social workers, health-care workers, financial advisors and technicians. There is a tendency towards pluralism. A working woman is a lady who has a job which she is paid to do. A professional woman or career woman is a working woman who has a profession or a career and wishes to work and progress in her job until she retires.

Income is the most general word for the money received over a certain period of time, especially as payment for work like wage or salary, as receipts from trade, or as interest on investments. Regular income is a general word for the money an employer pays to an employee for the regular work or services he has done. Extra income is the additional money someone receives from their extra work, but not from their regular work. Regular income can be wage and salary. A wage is the amount of money which a person or a group of people are paid each week for a particular type of work that they do, usually in cash. Wages are earned by wage-earners who generally do manual or unskilled work. Their wages are based on an hourly, daily or weekly rate or on a certain amount of work done. A living wage is a wage which is large enough to enable a person to buy food, clothing, and other daily necessities. A salary is the money which someone is paid for their job each month, especially when they have a professional or other non-manual job. Salaried employees receive their salaries for their regular employment. Salaries are often paid directly into an employee's bank account, or by cheque. Professional people and those who work in offices receive salary. The word "salary" comes from "salt", and it originally means "money for salt". In Chinese, the equivalent for "salary" is *xinjin*(薪金), which originally means "money for firewood". Fee is the payment or charge to such people as private teachers, school examiners, doctors, lawyers, accountants and surveyors for their professional advice or services. Remuneration is a formal word for the payment or reward someone receives for their work or services. Reward is the money given to someone because they have behaved well, worked hard, or provided a service to the community.

Expenditure is a formal word, which refers to the amount of money that is spent on a particular thing or in a particular situation. Expense is the money spent in doing a specific job or for a specific purpose. Living expenses are the money for providing a person with what is necessary for life. Traveling expenses are the money used for travel, especially the money someone claims back from their employer when they have spent that amount of money on traveling as part of their work. Miscellaneous expenses, miscellaneous charges or miscellaneous fees are the money used for miscellaneous items or purposes, which are apart from the major areas of expenditure. Charge is the money spent on goods or services. For instance, postage charge or postage is the money which people have to pay for sending letters, parcels, etc. by post. Admission charge or entry charge is the money charged for being allowed to enter a building, a society or a school. Admission fee or admission is the amount of money which people have to pay to go into a public place, like a park or museum. A bill is a written statement of money which someone owes for goods or services that they have received. A person has to pay his telephone bill, gas bill and heating bill regularly. Rent is the regular payment for the use of a piece of land, a room, a house, a flat or an apartment, a building, telephone and machinery. A tenant has to pay rent regularly to his or her landlord for the use of land, a room or a building. Rental is the amount of money which people have to pay when they rent something such as a television set or a car. Tuition is the fee paid for the teaching or instruction in a school, a college or a university. Pocket money is the small amount of money used for small personal needs or small expenses. Pocket money can also be a small amount of money given to a child by his or her parents every week. Tip is a small sum of money given to a waiter or a taxi-driver as a personal reward for their service. Most restaurants in Britain and in the United States now include the tip in the price of the meal. But there are also diners who often leave a tip under the plate after eating a meal there.

Revenue is the money which a company or organization receives over a fixed period of time, especially the money which a government receives through taxation. Receipts are the amounts of money received during a particular period by a business company, like a shop or a theatre. Profit is the amount of money gained in business or trade, for instance, when the cost of making something is less than the amount that it is sold for. Tax is the amount of money, which has to be paid by a citizen or a business company to the government for public purposes. Taxes on income include income tax and corporation tax. An individual pays taxes, especially income tax, as a tax-payer. Income tax is payable according to the level of a person's income. The higher the amount of money is earned, the higher the income tax charged. Usually an employer withholds a portion of an employee's wages or salaries for income tax. Corporation tax is the tax paid by a business company on its profits. Taxes on capital include capital gains tax and inheritance tax. Capital gains are the profits made from the sale of investments or property. Capital gains tax is payable by individuals and companies on such profits. Inheritance tax is the tax paid by a person who receives property as heir. In Britain, death duty is the tax, which has to be paid on the money and property that belonged to someone who has died. Now it is called capital transfer tax. Excise duties or excise refers to the government tax on certain goods like beer, spirits and tobacco which are manufactured, sold or used within a country. Customs tariff or tariff is the duty to be paid on imports or exports. But it refers to imports more often than exports. Some countries raise tariff barriers against foreign goods. Customs duties, customs, import duties or duties are the taxes payable to the government on the goods imported from other countries. Duty is a tax, which is paid by people to the government on goods that they buy. Duty-free goods are those goods that are sold at airports, on ships, etc. at a cheaper price than usual because the buyers do not have to pay the tax that is usually paid when the goods are brought into a country. In a duty-free shop, people can buy duty-free goods. Stamp duty is the tax imposed on certain types of legal documents, on which an official stamp is put to show that the tax has been paid. Certain kinds of transfer, like the transfer of shares, are subject to stamp duty. In Britain, rates are a local tax, which has to be paid to local authorities by people who own buildings or rent unfurnished buildings. The money from the rates in an area is used to pay for local services and public facilities.

 Benefit is an amount of money provided by the government to people who need it, especially to those who are ill or unemployed. There are such kinds of benefits as medical benefit, sickness benefit, unemployment benefit and widow's benefit. Allowance is an amount of money allowed or given regularly to someone, usually by the government, in order to help them pay for the things which they need in a particular situation. Clothing allowance is the money given to a person to be spent on clothing. Subsistence allowance is the money to be spent on subsistence, and travel allowance is the money to be spent on travel. Family allowance is a sum of money given to a family regularly by the government for household expenses. Allowance can also be the money which is given regularly to someone, especially a child, for them to spend. Pension is a sum of money paid regularly by the State or by a former employer to people above a certain age, retired people, widowed people, and disabled people. An old-age pension is a regular payment to old-age pensioners who are people above a certain age. Pension can also be a regular payment made by an employer to a retired employee, such as a retirement pension, and an army pension. A pensioner is a person who receives and lives on pension, especially the pension paid by the State to elderly people. In Britain, the pensioners draw or collect their pension regularly from the Post Office. Subsidy is the money paid by the government or other authority to help an industry, to support the arts or other causes needing help, or to keep prices at a desired level. Food subsidies are intended to reduce the price of basic foods. Grant is a sum of money given by the government to an individual or to an organization for particular purposes such as education, welfare, home improvements, etc. Student grant is paid by the government to a student for his or her education. A student who is awarded a grant is called a grant-aided student. Research grant is awarded by the government to an individual for scientific research. Maternity grant is given by the government to a mother with a newly-born baby.

Scholarship is the payment of money to a student by a school or a university so that he may continue his studies in such an educational institution. Usually a scholarship is a yearly grant. Award is the sum of money given according to an official decision made by judges to a person who succeeds in a competition. In Britain, an award can also refer to a grant. That is the money paid to a student at university to help him meet living costs. Prize is the money given to the winner of a competition or a race. A Nobel Prize is one of a set of prizes which are awarded each year to people who have done important work in physics, chemistry, medicine, literature, or economics, or for world peace. This set of prizes were founded according to the will of Alfred Nobel, who was a Swedish chemist, famous for his work on explosives. The prizes are open to men and women of all nationalities for their most deserving work in the above-mentioned fields. Academy Awards is an annual cinema prize in many categories, given since 1927 by the American Academy of Motion Picture Arts and Sciences. The award is a gold-plated statuette, which has been nicknamed "Oscar" since 1931. Nominees are chosen by their peers, for instance, actors nominate actors, and designers nominate designers. The awards ceremony is held and televised each spring. Relief is the money given to poor people, or people in need, as assistance or help. In Britain, the dole is a payment made by the State to unemployed people. It is given at regular intervals, for example, every two weeks. It may also be a weekly payment made from contributions made by workers or employers. So when an unemployed worker is on the dole in Britain, he actually receives an unemployment benefit.

Words and Expressions

income *n.* the amount of money which people earn from their work or business, or the money which they get from other sources such as pension or interest on investments 收入

expenditure *n.* the amount of money which is spent on a particular thing or in a particular situation 支出

employment *n.* the work that a person does in order to earn money for survival 就业

employer *n.* a person or a company that gives work to others for payment; also a company which people work for 雇主

payment *n.* the act of paying money or being paid 支付

employee *n.* a person who is paid to work for another person or for an organization 雇员

self-employed person *n.* sb who organizes their own work or business rather than being employed and paid by another person 自行经营者

manual work *also* **manual labour, physical labour** *n.* the work in which people use their hands or their physical strength rather than their minds 体力劳动

manual worker *n.* sb who works using their hands or their physical strength rather than their minds 体力劳动者

mental work *n.* the work in which people use their minds rather than their physical strength 脑力劳动

mental worker *n.* sb who works using their minds rather than their physical strength 脑力劳动者

office worker *also* **white-collar worker** *n.* sb who works in an office as opposed to sb who works with their hands 坐办公室的人;白领职工;白领

blue-collar worker n. a worker who does manual work as opposed to office work 蓝领职工
office work also **white-collar work** n. the work done in offices or at professional jobs, rather than the hard or dirty work done by hand 办公室工作；白领工作
profession n. a type of job which requires special training and also brings a fairly high status, for example, the work connected with law, medicine, or education 专业
professional n. a person who has received special training for a long time and has got a fairly high status, thus enjoying great respect from the public 专业人员
clergyman n. a member of the priesthood, who is allowed to perform religious services 神职人员
status n. position in society 地位 e.g. social status 社会地位
summarize v. give a summary of 总结；概括
altruism n. concern for the happiness and welfare of other people rather than for one's own 利他主义
be discontented v. phrase be not satisfied with the situation which a person is in 感到不满
a host of phrase a large number of 大量的
administrator n. a person whose job involves helping to organize and supervise the way that a company, institution, or other organization functions 行政人员
educator n. a person whose job is to educate people 教育工作者
social work n. the work which involves giving help and advice to people who have serious problems of many kinds, for example, to people who are very poor or who live in bad conditions 社会福利工作
social worker n. a person whose job is to do social work 社会福利工作者
health-care n. concern for the condition of a person's body or mind 保健
health-care worker n. a person whose job is to take care of people's health 保健工作者
advisor n. a person who is asked to give suggestions to another person or to a group of people about what they should do 顾问 e.g. financial advisor 财政顾问
technician n. a person whose job involves skilled practical work with scientific equipment 技术人员
pluralism n. the existence of a variety of different people, opinions, or principles within the same society, system, or philosophy 多元化
working woman n. a woman who has a job which she is paid to do 劳动妇女
professional woman also **career woman** n. a working woman who has a profession or a career and wishes to work and progress in her job until she retires 职业妇女
customer n. a person who buys sth, esp. from a shop 顾客
client n. a person or company that receives advice or a service from a professional person or organization, usu. in return for payment 委托人
regular income n. the money an employee receives from his/her employer for the regular work or services he/she has done 正常收入
extra income n. the additional money sb receives from their extra work, but not from their regular work 额外收入
wage n. weekly and sometimes daily payment made or received for work or services, and usu. in cash 周工资
wage-earner n. a person who earn wages, usu. a manual worker 挣工资者
living wage n. the lowest wage on which a person can afford a reasonable standard of living 基本生活工资
necessity n. sth, such as food or clothing, which people need to have in order to live or in order to do sth 必需品 e.g. daily necessities 日常必需品；necessities of life 生活必需品
salary n. a monthly and sometimes a quarterly payment made or received for regular employment 月薪
bank account also **account** n. a sum of money kept in a bank or similar institution, which can be added to and taken from 账户
fee n. the amount of money which a person or organization is paid for a particular job or service that they

provide 酬金；服务费

remuneration n. a formal word for the payment or reward sb receives for their work or services 酬金；报酬
private teacher n. a teacher who works alone rather than in a school 私人教师
examiner n. a person who sets or marks an exam 考试官；主考人 e.g. school examiner 学校主考人
accountant n. a person whose job is to inspect or keep accounts 会计师
surveyor n. a person whose job is to survey houses or land 土地勘察员；房产检查员
reward n. the money given or received for a person's work, merit or services 报酬
expenses n. the money that sth costs sb or that they need to spend in order to do sth 费用
living expenses n. the money used for everyday life 生活费
traveling expenses n. the money used for travel 旅费
miscellaneous expenses also **miscellaneous charges**, **miscellaneous fees** n. the money used for miscellaneous purposes 杂费
charge n. the money which sb has to pay for sth they buy or for a service 收费
postage charge also **postage** n. the money spent on sending letters, parcels, etc. by post 邮费；邮资
admission charge also **entry charge** n. the money charged for being allowed to enter a building, a society or a school 入场费；入会费；学费
admission fee also **admission** n. the money charged for being admitted to a public place 入场费
bill n. the written statement of money owed for goods supplied or services rendered 账单 e.g. telephone bill 电话费；gas bill 煤气费；heating bill 取暖费
statement n. a list showing amounts of money paid, received, owing, etc., and their total 结算表；财务报表 e.g. written statement of money 结算表；财务报表
rent n. the amount of money which people pay the owner of a house, a flat, or a piece of land every week or every month in order to be able to use it 租金；房租
tenant n. a person who pays rent regularly to live in a house or flat or who pays rent regularly for the use of land or buildings 房客
rental n. the amount of money which people have to pay when they rent something such as a television set or a car 电视租金；汽车租金
tuition n. the amount of money paid for the teaching or instruction of a subject or subjects in a school, a college or a university 学费
pocket money n. the money for small needs or small expenses, or a small amount of money given to a child 零花钱；零用钱
tip n. a small amount of money given to a waiter or a taxi-driver in order to thank them for their service 小费
revenue n. the income, esp. the total annual income of the State from taxes 税收；收入；岁入
receipts n. the money received by a business company 公司收入
profit n. the amount of money gained in business, esp. the difference between the amount earned and the amount spent 利润
tax n. the money paid by a citizen or a business company to the government for public purposes 税
tax-payer n. a person who pays income tax 纳税人
income tax n. the tax which sb has to pay regularly to the government and which is a certain percentage of their income 所得税
corporation tax n. the tax which companies have to pay on the profits they make 公司税
capital gains n. the profits which people make when they buy sth and then sell it again 资本增益
capital gains tax n. the tax which people have to pay for the profits they make when they buy sth and then sell it again 资本增益税
inheritance tax n. the tax paid by a person who receives property as heir 继承税

inheritance *n.* the money or property which a person receives from sb who is dead 遗产；继承物
death duty *BrE. n.* the tax paid on property after the owner's death 遗产税
capital transfer tax *BrE. n.* the current name of death duty in Britain 资产转移税
excise duties *also* **excise** *n.* a tax which the government of a country puts on goods that are produced for sale in that country 国内货物税
customs *n.* the place at a border, airport, or harbour where people arriving from a foreign country have to declare goods which they bring with them 海关
customs tariff *also* **tariff** *n.* a tax collected by a government on goods coming into or sometimes going out of a country 关税
barrier *n.* sth non-physical that keeps people apart or prevents activity, movement, etc. 障碍 *e.g.* tariff barrier 关税壁垒
customs duties *also* **customs, import duties, duties** *n.* the taxes payable to the government on the goods imported from other countries 进口税
duty *n.* a tax which sb pays to the government on goods that they buy 税
duty-free goods *n.* the goods allowed to come into the country without tax 免税商品
duty-free shop *n.* a shop, for example, at an airport, where people can buy duty-free goods 免税商店
stamp *n.* a piece of paper for sticking to certain official papers to show that tax has been paid 印花
stamp duty *n.* the tax imposed on certain types of legal documents, on which an official stamp is put to show that the tax has been paid 印花税
rates *BrE. n.* the tax on property like land and buildings paid to local authorities for local purposes 地方税
benefit *n.* a payment or a series of payments, usu. made by the government, to sb who is entitled to receive it, for example, because they are ill or unemployed 补助金；救济金 *e.g.* medical benefit 医疗补助金；sickness benefit 疾病救济金；unemployment benefit 失业救济金；widow's benefit 寡妇救济金
allowance *n.* an amount of money allowed or given to a person regularly by the government for personal expenses 补助；or the money given regularly to sb, esp. a child, for them to spend 零花钱
clothing allowance *n.* the money given to a person to be spent on clothing 服装补助
subsistence allowance *n.* the money to be spent on subsistence 生活补助
subsistence *n.* the condition of just having enough food to stay alive 生存
travel allowance *n.* the money to be spent on travel 差旅补助
family allowance *n.* a sum of money given to a family regularly by the government for household expenses 家庭补助
pension *n.* an amount of money paid regularly, esp. by a government or a company, to sb who can no longer earn money by working, esp. because of old age or illness 养老金；退休金；抚恤金 *e.g.* retirement pension 退休金；army pension 战争抚恤金
old-age pension *n.* a regular payment to old-age pensioners who are people above a certain age 养老金
pensioner *n.* a person who receives and lives on pension 领养老金者；领退休金者；领抚恤金者 *e.g.* old-age pensioner 高龄领养老金者
subsidy *n.* the money paid by the government or a society in order to help a company financially or to make sth cheaper for the public 津贴；补贴
food subsidy *n.* the subsidy which is intended to reduce the price of basic foods 食物补贴
grant *n.* the money given by the government for a particular purpose 补助金
student grant *n.* the money which is paid by the government to a student for his education 助学金
grant-aided student *n.* a student who is awarded a grant 领助学金的学生
research grant *n.* the sum of money awarded by the government to an individual for scientific research 科研补助金

maternity grant *n*. the sum of money given by the government to a mother with a newly-born baby 生育补助金

scholarship *n*. the payment of money to a scholar so that he may continue his studies in such an educational institution as a university 奖学金

award *n*. the sum of money given according to an official decision made by judges to a person who succeeds in a competition 奖金

prize *n*. the money given to the winner of a competition or a race 奖金

Nobel Prize *n*. one of a set of prizes which are awarded each year to people who have done important work in science, literature, or economics, or for world peace 诺贝尔奖

Alfred Nobel (1833–1896) *n*. a Swedish chemist, famous for his work on explosives, who died a millionaire 艾尔弗雷德·诺贝尔

Academy Award *also* **Oscar** *n*. an American cinema prize given each year by the American Academy of Motion Picture Arts and Sciences 学院奖；奥斯卡金像奖

academy *n*. a society of people interested in the advancement of art, science, or literature, to which members are usu. elected as an honour 研究院；学会

statuette *n*. a very small statue which is often displayed on a shelf or stand 小塑像 *e.g.* gold-plated statuette 小镀金像；"小金人"

nominee *n*. a person who is nominated for or to sth 被提名者；候选人

peer *n*. a person who is of the same age, social status, ability, etc. as oneself 同辈；同龄人

nominate *v*. suggest sb as a candidate in an election, or a competition, or for a job 提名

ceremony *n*. a set of formal and traditional actions and words, which are performed or spoken at a special occasion such as a wedding or an important public event 仪式 *e.g.* awards ceremony 授奖仪式

televise *v*. broadcast a programme so that it can be seen on television 电视转播

the American Academy of Motion Picture Arts and Sciences *n*. an American society of people who are interested in the advancement of motion picture arts and sciences 美国电影艺术与科学学院

relief *n*. the money, food or clothing which is provided, often from public funds, for people who are very poor or hungry 救济金；救济品

the dole *BrE*. *n*. a weekly payment made by the State to unemployed people; also a weekly payment made from contributions made by workers or employers 失业救济金

on the dole *prep. phrase* registered as unemployed and receiving money regularly from the government 领取失业救济金

taxation *n*. the act of collecting taxes by a government according to income, property, goods bought, etc. 征税 *e.g.* to be subject to taxation 应该纳税

taxable *a*. having to pay a tax on 应纳税的

incentive *n*. sth which encourages people to greater activity 刺激；动力 *e.g.* work incentives 工作动力

savings *n*. the money which a person has saved, esp. in an account at a bank or similar institution 存款；储蓄 *e.g.* to promote savings 推动储蓄

investment *n*. the paying of money into a bank or the buying of shares, in order to receive a profit 投资 *e.g.* long-term investment 长期投资

levy *v*. demand and collect officially 征收 *e.g.* to levy a tax 征税

exempt *a*. free from, not affected or not bound by a particular rule, duty, or obligation 可免除的；可豁免的

exemption *n*. freedom from a particular rule, duty, or obligation 免除；豁免

declare *v*. say how much you have earned so that you can pay tax on it 申报 *e.g.* to declare one's personal income for tax payment 申报个人收入以纳税

estate *n*. the whole of a person's property, esp. left after death 财产；遗产

transfer *n*. the movement of property or land from the control of one person or institution to another 转移
   e.g. lifetime transfer 在世时的转移
spouse *n*. the person sb is married to, that is, a formal word referring to husband or wife 配偶
gift *n*. sth given to sb as a present 礼物；馈赠；赠礼
bequest *n*. the money or property which sb leaves to sb else in their will 遗赠
charity *n*. an organization which raises money for a particular cause, for example, to help people in need or to provide medical facilities 慈善机构
assets *n*. everything a company or an individual person owns, which could if necessary be sold to pay debts 资产 *e.g.* business assets 企业资产
obligation *n*. a condition or influence which makes it necessary for sb to do sth 义务
duty *n*. sth that sb does either because it is part of their job or because it is morally or legally right that they should do it 责任
cunning *a*. having the ability to plan things cleverly in order to achieve what is wanted, often by deceiving or tricking other people 狡猾的
deceit *n*. the behaviour which is deliberately intended to make people believe sth that is not true 欺骗；欺诈
deceitful *a*. behaving in a dishonest way by making other people believe sth that is not true 欺骗；欺诈的
   e.g. deceitful trick 骗人的诡计
trick *n*. a clever act or plan meant to deceive or cheat sb 诡计；花招
trickery *n*. the use of tricks to deceive or cheat people 行骗；耍花招
tax dodging *n*. a cunning and often a deceitful trick which a person uses in order to avoid paying taxes 逃税
tax dodger *n*. a person who avoids an obligation or duty to pay taxes by using trickery or deceit 逃税者

Additional Knowledge

Taxation

Taxation is the system by which a government takes money from the people and spends it on education, health, and national defence. Taxes are the main sources of a country's revenue.

The governments in many countries intend to develop a tax system, which reflects the principles of encouraging employment opportunities and work incentives for everyone, and promoting savings and long-term investment.

The main sources of national revenue are taxes on income and taxes on capital. Taxes on income include personal income tax and corporation tax. Income tax is a personal tax, which is levied on the amount of money a person earns or on the amount of money a person receives from investments. The income of every citizen is taxable, but there are some forms of income which are exempt. The wages, salaries or investment income of a person are subject to taxation. So people should declare their personal income for tax payment. Corporation tax is a tax on the profits of a company. So companies should pay corporation tax on their income and capital gains. But in some countries, the rates of corporation tax are lowered in order to promote greater long-term investment and reduce the tax burden on smaller companies.

Taxes on capital include capital gains tax and inheritance tax. Capital gains tax is a tax on the profits made by selling possessions. Inheritance tax is essentially charged on estates at the time of death and on gifts made within some years of death. Most other lifetime transfers are not taxed. There are several important exemptions. In Britain and the United States, transfers between spouses are exempt, and gifts and bequests to charities, major political parties and heritage bodies are also normally exempt. In general, business assets and farmland are exempt from inheritance tax, so that most family businesses can be passed on without a tax charge.

Paying taxes is an obligation and duty of every citizen. But a few people are found to use a cunning and often a deceitful trick to avoid paying taxes. This kind of illegal act is called "tax dodging". And the person who avoids an obligation or duty to pay taxes by using trickery or deceit is a tax dodger.

Exercises

I. Explain each of the following:
1) income
2) expenditure
3) employment
4) employer
5) employee
6) self-employed person
7) customer
8) client
9) division of labour
10) manual worker
11) mental worker
12) profession
13) professional
14) altruism
15) pluralism
16) working woman
17) receipts
18) wage-earner
19) living wage
20) payment
21) fee
22) remuneration
23) reward
24) expense
25) living expenses
26) traveling expenses
27) miscellaneous expenses
28) charge
29) admission charge
30) admission fee
31) bill
32) telephone bill
33) gas bill
34) heating bill
35) rent
36) rental
37) tuition
38) tenant
39) pocket money
40) tip
41) revenue
42) profit
43) tax
44) income tax
45) corporation tax
46) capital gains
47) capital gains tax
48) inheritance tax
49) death duty
50) excise
51) tariff
52) customs duties
53) duty
54) duty-free shop
55) duty-free goods
56) stamp duty
57) rates
58) benefit

59) insurance policy
60) government funds
61) allowance
62) family allowance
63) pension
64) pensioner
65) old-age pensioner
66) subsidy
67) grant
68) student grant
69) scholarship
70) award
71) prize
72) Nobel Prize
73) Academy Awards
74) relief
75) on the dole

II. Give another way or other ways of saying each of the following:
Model: manual labour → manual work, physical labour
1) white-collar work →
2) white-collar worker →
3) career woman →
4) miscellaneous fees →
5) postage charge →
6) entry charge →
7) admission fee →
8) capital transfer tax →
9) excise duties →
10) customs tariff →
11) import duties →
12) Oscar →

III. Answer the following questions:
1) What is the difference between a manual worker and a mental worker?
2) What is the difference between a white-collar worker and a blue-collar worker?
3) What is profession connected with?
4) What did traditional professionals include?
5) What are traditional professionals characterized with?
6) Why did traditional professionals fall in public esteem in the past few decades?
7) What do new professionals include?
8) What is the difference between regular income and extra income?
9) What is the difference between wage and salary?
10) What is the original meaning of "salt"?
11) Is the tip included in the price of the meal in most American restaurants?
12) Where does a government receive its revenue?
13) What do taxes on income include?
14) How is a person's income tax charged?
15) What do taxes on capital include?
16) Why are duty-free goods cheaper than usual?
17) Please give some examples of different kinds of benefits.
18) Please give some examples of different kinds of allowance.
19) Please give some examples of different kinds of pension.
20) Where do the British pensioners draw their pension regularly?
21) Please give some examples of different kinds of subsidies.
22) Please give some examples of different kinds of grant?
23) What is a Nobel Prize?
24) Who can be the candidates of Nobel Prize winners?
25) Who gives Academy Awards?

26) Who nominate the candidates of Academy Awards?
27) When is the Oscar Awards ceremony held and televised every year?
28) Who are given relief as assistance or help?
29) How often is relief given to those who are in need?
30) What benefit does a British unemployed worker receive?

Lesson Twelve

Commerce and Investment

Money is the means of payment, especially in the form of coins and banknotes, given and accepted in buying and selling. Cash is the tangible and portable money in the form of notes or coins. Hard cash refers to the coins and notes, which is not a cheque or the money promised to pay later. When people buy and sell things, they often pay cash. That is, they pay money in notes or in coins. Paper money is the money in the form of banknotes. A banknote or note in Britain, and a bill in the United States, is a piece of paper money officially issued by the bank, usually by the central bank. It may have a high or low face value. A coin is a piece of metal used as money. It also may have a high or low face value. In everyday life, coins of lower values, together with notes of lower values, are used as small change or change.

In Britain, people may also pay by cheque, while in the United States, people pay by check. A cheque or a check is a special printed form on which one writes an order to a bank to pay a sum of money from his account to another person.

Now more and more people pay by credit card, which is a safe and convenient way to make payments. The credit card is also commonly called the plastic card or the plastic money. It is a card authorizing purchases on credit, that is, to make payments later by the bank. So the holder of a credit card is allowed to buy goods and services on credit.

Currency is the money system in use in a country. It consists of gold currency and paper currency. Hard currency, like gold currency, is the currency that is not likely to fall suddenly in value. Soft currency is the currency that is not convertible into gold or into certain other currencies which are more in demand. A convertible currency is one that can be exchanged for those of other countries. An international currency is a convertible currency that can be exchanged internationally.

International currency is the money system in use in the world. Foreign money is the money of other countries. Foreign exchange is the system of buying and selling foreign money. Exchange rate refers to the relation in value between kinds of money used in different countries. When a currency is appreciating or is being revalued, it is increasing in value. Revaluation is the increase of the value of a currency in relation to other currencies or to gold. When a currency is depreciating or is being devalued, it is decreasing in value. Devaluation is the reduction of the value of a currency in relation to other currencies or to gold.

Price is an amount of money for which something is bought or sold. In a market economy, prices fluctuate freely in response to supply and demand. Take apples for example. When there are more apples available than people want to buy, the price of apples goes down; when there is a shortage, the price goes up. A government exercises some control over prices by various means. Inflation is the action a government takes to increase the amount of money and credit in supply and in circulation in an economy so that prices rise. Hence, inflation also refers to the rise in prices resulting from an increase in the supply of money and credit. When there is an inflationary spiral, there arises an economic situation in which prices and wages rise in turn as the supply of money is increased. Deflation is the action the government takes to reduce the amount of money and credit in supply and in circulation in an economy so that prices can be lowered or kept steady. Sometimes, the government adopts a reflationary policy or takes reflationary measures to increase the amount of money and credit in circulating in an economy so as to restore the economic system after a period of deflation to its previous condition.

  A business company or a company, can also be called a firm, a corporation or an enterprise. As a business or commercial establishment, a company is a group of people united for business or commercial purposes. It can buy and sell property, lend or borrow money, employ people, and enter into contracts. A joint-stock company or a stock company is a company formed by a group of people who carry on a business with money controlled by all. A limited liability company or a limited company is a business company owned by the individuals and organizations that have bought shares in it. If the company gets into debt, the amount which the shareholder will be called on to pay is limited by law, and will be related to the amount of shares the shareholder has. It can be shortened into Limited, whose abbreviated form is Ltd. A public limited company or a public company is a commercial, usually large, company whose shares can be bought and sold by the public on the stock exchange; while a private limited company or a private company is a commercial, usually small, company that does not issue shares to the general public. A large or strong company may merge with a small or failing company. Two small companies may merge into a larger one. And two large companies may merge into an even larger one. The merger of two strong companies has become a tendency. A group company or a group is a set of jointly controlled business companies, which may be the result of a merger. A syndicate is a group of business companies combined to undertake a project. A trust is an association of business companies formed to reduce competition and control prices to their own advantages. In the United States, trusts are illegal. A transnational company or transnational corporation (TNC, for short), which is also called a multinational company or multinational corporation(MNC, for short), is a company that does business in different countries. Though it has substantial operations in many countries, it is controlled from its original home base. This location of activities in many countries is a response to the worldwide distribution of resources, governmental constraints, market opportunities and technology. A company with this wide geographical base is able to retain its status as a major world economic institution. The first transnational corporation in the world is the East India Company. Foreigners may make investments in another country, thus forming foreign-funded companies or foreign-funded corporations. A business company may form a jointly-funded company with a foreign business company, trying to gain profits and taking risks together. People call it a joint venture.

  So far as the ownership is concerned, there are various kinds of enterprises. Ownership shows who has the right to possess an enterprise.

  State ownership shows that the enterprise belongs to the State. A state-owned enterprise is possessed by the State, while a state-run enterprise is managed by those who are entrusted by the State and responsible for the State. So it is actually controlled by the State. Public ownership shows that the enterprise belongs to the public or the people in general, but not to private individuals. In fact, public ownership is the ownership and management of an enterprise by the State, thus it is another way of saying state ownership. Usually the public is represented by the government. Collective ownership is the ownership of land and the means of production by all the members of a community for the benefit of everyone. A cooperative or a co-op is a business or other organization owned and run by those participants with profits shared by them. A collectively-owned enterprise is a business company owned by all its participants collectively. In China, a township-run enterprise or township enterprise is a special type of collectively-owned enterprise run by the participants from the township. Private ownership shows that the enterprise belongs to private individuals, but not to the public. A private enterprise is a business company owned and managed by private individuals.

The common way people make investments is to deposit money in a bank. When they put their savings in a bank, they lend money to it in return for interest, which is the money charged for borrowing money. Generally speaking, keeping money in a bank takes no or few risks. It is a safe way of making profit. When a person deposits his savings in a bank, he first opens a bank account and becomes a depositor. Actually, he lends money to the bank, and the bank borrows money from him. In other words, the bank owes money to the depositor and is in debt to him. So the relation between the depositor and the bank is one between a creditor and a debtor. The depositor may withdraw or draw money from his bank. But there is a difference between deposit account and current account. Deposit account is a type of bank account in which the amount of money in it increases because it earns interest. Fixed deposit or time deposit refers to the money deposited in a bank, not to be withdrawn or drawn without notice, on which interest is payable. Current account is a personal bank account from which someone may take out money at any time using their cheque book or their computerized card. Current deposit or demand deposit refers to the money that can be withdrawn or drawn from the bank without previous notice. If a depositor wants to stop his transaction with the bank, he can close his bank account.

Businessmen and merchants buy and sell spot goods, which are also called spot commodities or spots. They are merchandise on the hands. Spot transaction is an over-the-counter trading which takes place at a spot market. Spots are provided off the shelf. They are available for immediate delivery after sale. Usually spot goods are paid out upon delivery.

Businessmen and merchants also do forward business by dealing in futures, which are agreements to buy or sell financial instruments or physical commodities at a future date. Financial instruments include stocks and shares. Futures goods are physical commodities including steel, oil, grain, rice, coffee, cocoa, sugar and potatoes as a bulk commodity bought for future acceptance or sold for future delivery. As futures are orders for goods, or stocks and shares bought at prices agreed upon at the time of purchase but to be paid for later, it is a time bargain. People humorously say they buy dreams and sell dreams. Futures first appeared in 1679 in Japan. Before the harvest, the farmers and the traders fixed a forward price for the rice in the fields. The traders paid part of the money to the farmers before the harvest. When the farmers brought in the rice, they gave it to the traders and got the unpaid part of the money. In 1780, the traders in Liverpool, England, invented a long-term forward contract. The traders paid part of the money to the farmers who grew and sold cotton. When the harvest came in, the farmers gave out the cotton and got all the money according to the futures contract they had made with the traders. Buying and selling futures as a forward business has become a frequently-seen commercial activity in the world. Those most important futures markets of the world are found in New York, Chicago, London, Pairs, Tokyo and Hong Kong. Among them, Chicago's futures market is the most influential one. The futures markets are full of chances and risks.

Speculation is the business, deal or transaction involving the buying and selling of goods or stocks and shares in the hope of making a profit through changes in their value, but with the risk of losing money. Those who are engaged in speculative activities are speculators. Many people speculate on the stock market, for instance, they speculate in shares or buy shares as a speculation. Others do speculative buying of goods like grain and oil, or do speculative housing.

Real estate, realty, real property or property refers to immovable property, consisting of land and buildings. Real estate also refers to the business of selling houses and land for building. As people make investments in property and gain profit, so real estate has become an important speculation. Some people make profit even through dishonest speculation.

People play games of chance for money. They gamble at cards or on the horse. Gambling is the staking of money on the outcome of a competition. Forms of gambling include betting on sports results, card games, slot machines, and lotteries. Once illegal in many countries, today gambling is a multibillion-dollar operation worldwide and can be addictive. It is an undertaking with a chance of profit and a risk of loss. Some people spend a lot of time gambling in the casino which is a gambling room or a gambling house. A few gamblers may be lucky enough to make some money, but most of them will lose money and even owe heavy gambling debts. The typical American gambler is college-educated and has a white-collar job. Lottery is a way of raising money by selling numbered tickets and giving prizes to the holders of lucky numbers which are selected at random. In many countries, people buy lottery tickets in horseracing, in the hope of making big money. As a game of chance or a guessing game, buying lottery tickets is also a speculative activity in nature.

Words and Expressions

commerce *n*. the activities and procedures involved in buying and selling things 商业

commercial *a*. involving or relating to commerce or business 商业的 *e.g.* commercial establishment 商业机构; commercial purpose 商业目的

money *n*. the coins or banknotes used when people buy sth or pay for a service 钱; 货币

paper money *n*. the money in the form of banknotes 纸币

coin *n*. a small piece of metal used as money 硬币

banknote *also* **note** BrE. *also* **bill** AmE. *n*. a piece of paper money with a particular value, which is officially issued by the bank, usu. by the central bank 钞票

cash *n*. the money in the form of coins and banknotes rather than cheques 现金 *e.g.* to pay cash 付现金

hard cash *n*. the money in the form of coins and banknotes, as opposed to a cheque, a credit card, or the money promised to pay later 现金

tangible *a*. that can be felt by touch; clear and certain; real; not imaginary 可以触摸到的;确凿的;真实的;明确的 *e.g*. tangible money 现金

portable *a*. that can be easily carried or moved 可携带的 *e.g*. portable money 可携带货币

cheque *BrE*. *also* **check** *AmE*. *n*. a piece of paper which people can use instead of cash to pay for things 支票

bank *n*. an institution where people and businesses can keep their money and such services as lending, exchanging, or transferring money are also offered 银行 *e.g*. central bank 中央银行;央行

face value *n*. the amount of money which paper money, coins, investment documents, or tickets are worth, and which is written on them 面值;面额 *e.g*. high face value 高面值;大面额;low face value 低面值;小面额

small change *also* **change** *n*. coins or banknotes of lower values 小面额货币;零钱

order *n*. a small printed paper which can be exchanged for money at a bank or a post office and which is sent to sb 汇票

bank account *also* **account** *n*. a sum of money kept in a bank or similar institution, which can be added to and taken from 账户 *e.g*. to open a bank account 开账户;to close one's bank account 销账户

credit *n*. a system of buying goods or services and paying for them later 赊购制; or the quality of being likely to repay debts and being trusted in money matters 信用;信誉 *e.g*. on credit 赊购

credit card *also* **plastic card, plastic money** *n*. a small plastic card which is used instead of money to pay for goods and services from shops, travel companies, petrol stations, etc., the cost being charged to one's account and paid later 信用卡 *e.g*. to pay by credit card 用信用卡支付

currency *n*. the system of money which is used in a country 通货;币制

gold currency *n*. the system of money in the form of gold 黄金通货

paper currency *n*. the system of money in the form of banknotes 纸通货

hard currency *n*. the currency which is unlikely to lose its value, such as gold currency, and which is considered to be a good one to have or to invest in 硬通货

soft currency *n*. the currency which is not convertible into gold or into certain other currencies that are more in demand 软通货

convertible currency *n*. the money which can be exchanged for that of another country 可兑换货币

international currency *n*. the money system in use in the world 国际货币体系;a convertible currency which can be exchanged internationally 国际货币

foreign money *n*. the money of other countries 外币

foreign exchange *n*. the system by which one country's currency is changed into another country's currency 外汇

exchange rate *n*. the rate at which a sum of money of one country's currency is exchanged for an equivalent sum of money of another country's currency 汇率

appreciate *v*. increase in value 升值

revaluation *n*. the increase of the value of a currency in order that it can buy more foreign currency than before 升值

depreciate *v*. decrease in value 贬值

devaluation *n*. the reduction of the value of a currency, usu. in order to encourage exports and discourage imports 贬值

price *n*. an amount of money for which sth is bought or sold 价格

fluctuate *v*. rise and fall irregularly and suddenly 波动

supply *n*. the act of providing sb with sth 供应; the amount of a commodity or money which can be produced and made available for people to buy 供应量

demand *n*. the need of the public for sth 需求

inflation *n*. a general increase in the prices of goods and services in a country 通货膨胀

circulation *n*. the process of being used by the public 流通

inflationary *a*. relating to inflation or causing inflation 通货膨胀的

spiral *n*. a process of continuous upward or downward movement 螺旋式上升/下降 *e.g.* inflationary spiral 通货急剧膨胀

deflation *n*. a reduction in economic activity which leads to lower levels of industrial output, employment, investment, trade, profits, and prices 经济紧缩；通货紧缩；通缩

deflationary *a*. relating to deflation or causing deflation 通货紧缩的 *e.g.* deflationary policy 通货紧缩政策；deflationary measure 通货紧缩措施

business company *also* **company, firm, corporation, enterprise** *n*. a business organization which sells or produces things or which provides a service that people pay for 公司 *e.g.* failing company 倒台的公司

contract *n*. a formal written agreement between two organizations, two people, etc., which says that one of them will supply goods or do work in an agreed way and for an agreed sum of money 契约；合同 *e.g.* to enter into contracts 签约

joint-stock company *also* **stock company** *AmE*. *n*. a business company which is owned by the people who have bought shares in it 股份公司

limited liability company *also* **limited company, Limited, Ltd.**（*abbrev.*）*n*. a business company in which the shareholders are legally responsible for only a part of any money that it may owe to other people or companies, for example, if it goes bankrupt 有限(责任)股份公司

debt *n*. a sum of money which a person owes another person 债务 *e.g.* in debt to sb 欠……债；heavy debts 重债

liable *a*. tending to happen 倾向于

public limited company *also* **public company** *n*. a commercial, usu. large, company whose shares can be bought and sold by the public on the stock exchange 上市有限股份公司；上市公司

private limited company *also* **private company** *n*. a commercial, usu. small, company which does not issue shares to the general public 不上市有限股份公司；不上市公司

merge *v*. have two things, for examples, two companies joined together or combined as so to make one whole thing 合并；兼并

merger *n*. the joining together of two separate companies, organizations, etc., so that they become one 合并；兼并

group company *also* **group** *n*. a number of separate commercial or industrial companies, which all have the same owner 集团公司；集团

syndicate *n*. a group of business companies formed for business purposes or combined to carry out a project together 辛迪加；企业联合组织

trust *AmE*. *n*. an association of business companies which join together in order to control the market for the particular thing that they produce 托拉斯

transnational company, transnational corporation, TNC（*abbrev.*）*also* **multinational company, multinational corporation, MNC**（*abbrev.*）*n*. a company which has branches and subsidiary companies in many different countries 跨国公司

operation *n*. the work done by the people in a business or organization in a planned way over a period of time or in a particular place 经营；运营；运作 *e.g.* substantial operations 大规模运营

base *n*. a center from which sth is controlled and where plans are made 基地；根据地；大本营 *e.g.* home base 总部

distribution *n*. the sharing out of sth among a particular group 分配 *e.g.* distribution of resources 资源分配

constraint *n*. sth which limits or controls the way people behave or what people can do in a situation 限制；控制 *e.g.* governmental constraint 政府控制
opportunity *n*. a situation which makes it possible for people to do sth that they want to do 机会；机遇；时机 *e.g.* market opportunity 市场机遇
the East India Company *n*. a company which did trade in East Indies, including India, Indochina and the Malay Archipelago in the 17th and 18th centuries 东印度公司
investment *n*. the paying of money into a bank or the buying of shares, in order to receive a profit 投资 *e.g.* to make an investment 投资
foreign-funded company *also* **foreign-funded corporation** *n*. a company or corporation funded by foreign capital 外资公司
risk *n*. a possibility that sth unpleasant or undesirable might happen 风险 *e.g.* to take risks 冒风险
venture *n*. a business operation which involves making investments with a risk of loss or failure as well as a chance of gain or success 风险投资；风险项目
joint venture *also* **jointly-funded company** *n*. a company funded by two or more parties in the hope of getting more money back at a risk of loss or failure 合资公司
ownership *n*. the state of owning sth, esp. sth large such as a business or an area of land 所有制
enterprise *n*. a system of business, esp. one in a particular country 企业体系；企业；a business company or a business firm 企业单位；公司
state ownership *n*. the ownership which shows that the enterprise belongs to the State 国有制
state-owned enterprise *n*. an enterprise which is possessed by the State 国有制企业
state-run enterprise *n*. an enterprise which is managed by those who are entrusted by the State and responsible for the State 国营企业
public ownership *n*. the ownership which shows that the enterprise belongs to the public or the people in general, but not to private individuals 公有制 *syn.* **state ownership** 国有制
collective ownership *n*. the ownership of land and the means of production by all the members of a community for the benefit of everyone 集体所有制
cooperative *also* **co-op** *n*. a business such as a factory, a shop, or a farm, which is jointly owned by the people who run it 合作企业；合作社
collectively-owned enterprise *n*. a business company owned by all its participants collectively 集体所有制企业
township-run enterprise *also* **township enterprise** *n*. a special type of collectively-owned enterprise in China, which is run by the participants from the township 乡镇企业
private ownership *n*. the ownership which shows that the enterprise belongs to private individuals, but not to the public 私有制
private enterprise *n*. an industry and business which is owned by an individual person or group and not supported financially by the government 民营企业；私人企业
deposit *v*. pay a sum of money into a bank account or other savings account, usu. with the intention of leaving it there for some time and getting back some rewards 存款 *e.g.* to deposit money in a bank 在银行存钱
depositor *n*. a person who puts money in a bank 存款人
savings *n*. the money which a person has saved, esp. in an account at a bank or similar institution 积蓄 *e.g.* to put/deposit one's savings in a bank 将积蓄存入银行
interest *n*. a sum of money which is paid as a percentage of a larger sum of money that has been borrowed or invested 利息 *e.g.* rate of interest 利率
owe *v*. need to pay back the money to sb from whom it has been borrowed 欠 *e.g.* to owe money to sb 欠……钱；to owe gambling debts 欠赌债
creditor *n*. a person or a company that sb owes money to 债权人；债主

debtor *n*. a person who owes money to sb else 债务人

withdraw *also* **draw** *v*. take a sum of money from a bank account or savings account in order to spend it or use it 取款 *e.g.* to withdraw/draw money from a bank 从银行取钱

deposit account *n*. a type of bank account in which the amount of money in it increases because it earns interest 定期存款账户

fixed deposit *also* **time deposit** *n*. the money deposited in a bank, not to be withdrawn or drawn without notice, on which interest is payable 定期存款

current account *BrE*. *n*. a personal bank account from which sb may take out money at any time using their cheque book or their computerized card 活期存款账户

current deposit *also* **demand deposit** *n*. the money which can be withdrawn or drawn from the bank without previous notice 活期存款

notice *n*. an announcement or warning in advance that people are going to do sth or sth is going to happen 预先通知 *e.g.* without notice 不预先通知

transaction *n*. a piece of business or other activity which is carried out by two or more people negotiating about it, for example, an act of buying or selling sth 交易 *e.g.* to stop one's transaction with the bank 停止与银行交易

businessman *n*. a person who works in business, for example, a person who runs a commercial or industrial firm 商人；实业家

merchant *n*. a person who buys or sells goods in large quantities, esp. one who imports and exports them 商人

spot goods *also* **spot commodities**, **spots** *n*. merchandise which are bought and sold at once, not at some future time 现货

merchandise *n*. goods which are bought, sold or traded with 货物；商品

spot transaction *n*. an over-the-counter trading which takes place at a spot market 现货交易

spot market *n*. a market where spots goods are bought and sold 现货市场

off the shelf *prep*. *phrase* sold in shops as a standard product which does not have to be specially made or ordered 现成的

forward *a*. relating to the future 面向未来的 *e.g.* forward price 预定的价格；forward contract 预订的合同

forward business *also* **forward buying** *n*. buying of goods at present prices for delivery later 预购

futures *n*. agreements or contracts for goods bought and sold in large quantities at the present price, but not produced or sent until a later time 期货交易；期货 *e.g.* to deal in futures 做期货交易；to buy and sell futures 买卖期货；futures market 期货市场；futures contract 期货合同

instrument *n*. sth used by people as a way of achieving a particular aim 工具 *e.g.* financial instrument 金融工具

futures goods *n*. goods bought and sold in large quantities at the present price, but not produced or sent until a later time 期货商品；期货

bulk commodities *also* **bulk goods** *n*. goods bought and sold in large quantities 大宗货物

bargain *n*. an agreement between two people or groups, esp. in business, in which they agree what each of them will do, pay or receive 交易；协议 *e.g.* time bargain 定期协议

Liverpool *n*. a city in England, U.K. 利物浦

Chicago *n*. a big city in the United States 芝加哥

speculate *v*. buy property, stocks, shares, etc. esp. on a large scale or as a business, in the hope of being able to sell them again at a higher price and make a profit 做投机生意；投机 *e.g.* to speculate on the stock market 在证券市场做投机生意；to speculate in shares 做股票投机生意

speculation *n*. the business, deal or transaction involving the buying and selling of goods or stocks and shares in the hope of making a profit through changes in their value, but with the risk of losing money

投机生意;投机 *e.g.* to buy shares as a speculation 买股票作为投机生意;dishonest speculation 欺诈性投机生意

speculator *n.* a person who are engaged in speculative activities 做投机生意者;投机商

speculative *a.* involving the buying and selling of goods or stocks and shares in the hope of being able to sell them again at a higher price and make a profit, but with the risk of losing money 投机的 *e.g.* speculative activity 投机活动;speculative buying 投机性购买生意;speculative housing 投机性房产生意

real estate *also* **realty, real property, property** *n.* the property in the form of land and buildings, rather than personal possessions 不动产;房地产

real estate *n.* the business of selling houses, buildings and land 房地产业

game of chance *n.* a game with the equal possibility of winning and losing 机遇游戏;风险游戏

gamble *v.* bet money in a game such as cards or on the result of a race or competition, esp. as a regular activity 赌博 *e.g.* to gamble at cards/in card games 赌牌;to gamble on the horse/in horseracing 赌赛马

gambling *n.* the act or habit of betting money, for example, in card games, horseracing, etc. 赌博;an undertaking with a chance of profit and a risk of loss 赌博业

staking *also* **betting** *n.* the risk of one's money on the results of a race or competition 下赌注 *e.g.* staking of money 用钱下赌注;betting on sports results 赌体育比赛结果

card game *n.* a game played by using cards 牌戏

slot machine *n.* a machine from which people can get food or cigarettes by putting coins into a slot in it 自动售货机;or on which people can gamble by putting coins into its slot 吃角子老虎机

billion *n.* a number representing a thousand million 十亿

addictive *a.* unable to stop having, taking or doing 上瘾的

gambling room *also* **gambling house** *n.* a room or house where people play gambling games 赌场

casino *n.* a gambling room or a gambling house where people play gambling games such as roulette 赌场

gambler *n.* a person who gambles regularly, for example, in card games or horseracing 赌徒

lottery *n.* a system in which many numbered tickets are sold, some of which are later chosen by chance and prizes given to those who bought them 博彩;彩票抽奖

numbered ticket *n.* a ticket with a serial number 带序号的票

lucky number *n.* a number which brings sb good luck, for example, giving them prizes 幸运号码

lottery ticket *n.* a ticket with a serial number which might be chosen at random as a lucky number that would make its holder win a prize 彩券;彩票

horseracing *n.* a sport in which horses ridden by jockeys run in races, or a gambling game in which people buy lottery tickets, hoping to win a prize 赛马

guess *v.* form a judgment about sth or risk giving an opinion on it without knowing or considering all the facts 猜测 *e.g.* guessing game 猜测的游戏

stocks *also* **shares** *n.* large parts of the ownership of a company or industry, and which can be bought as an investment 证券;股票 *e.g.* business stocks 公司证券

share *n.* one of the many equal parts into which the ownership of a company can be divided, and which can be bought as an investment 股份;股票

government stocks *also* **government securities** *n.* stocks issued by the government 政府债券

security *n.* a stock, bond, or some other document, which sb has paid money for and which gives them the right to some property 债券

gilts *also* **gilt-edged securities** *n.* stocks usu. issued by the government, which are almost certain to produce interest and can be redeemed or repaid at face value at almost any time, and which originally had gilt edges 金边债券

profitable *a.* likely to make a profit 盈利的

bond *n.* an investment certificate issued by a government or company which shows that a person has lent them an amount of money and that they promise to pay the person a fixed rate of interest 公债；债券 e.g. government bond 政府债券；公债；corporation bond 公司债券；to issue bonds 发行债券

certificate n. an official paper which gives a statement made by an official person that a fact or facts are true 证明书 e.g. interest-bearing certificate 可付利息的证明书

indebtedness n. the state of owing money to sb 债务 e.g. public indebtedness 公共债务；private indebtedness 私人债务

default n. a failure to do sth that a person is legally supposed to do, such as make a payment 违约；不履行债务；不偿还债务 e.g. risk of default 违约的风险；不履行债务的风险；不偿还债务的风险

marketable n. that is able to be sold because people want to buy it 可以出售的

auction n. a public sale of goods or property where people offer higher and higher prices until the goods are sold to the person who offers the highest price 拍卖 e.g. by auction 通过拍卖

loan n. a sum of money which sb borrows for example, from a bank, and which they have to pay back with interest, usu. in weekly or monthly payments 贷款 e.g. to make a loan 贷款；to repay a loan 偿还贷款

funds n. amounts of money which is collected or saved, for example, to help sb or to enable sth to be done 资金 e.g. to raise funds 筹集资金

dividend n. a payment made regularly from the profits of a company to its shareholders, usu. twice a year 红利

shareholder n. an owner of shares in a business company 股东

equities n. ordinary stocks and shares which carry no fixed amount of interest 普通股

stock exchange n. a place where an organization of professional people buy and sell stocks and shares 证券交易所

stockbroker also **broker** n. a person whose job is to buy and sell stocks and shares for people who want to invest money 证券经纪人；股票经纪人

stockbroking n. buying and selling stocks and shares for people who want to invest money 证券经纪；股票经纪

bull market n. a situation on the stock market when the price of shares is likely to rise, allowing people to make a profit by buying at a low price and selling again when the price has risen 牛市

bear market n. a situation on the stock market when people are selling a lot of shares because they expect that the shares will decrease in value and that they will be able to make a profit by buying them again after a short time 熊市

Additional Knowledge

The Stock Market

People often make investments by buying and selling stocks and shares. Government stocks or securities are money lent to the government in return for interest. Buying government stocks is a safe way of making profit with higher interest than bank deposit, thus more profitable. Bond is a printed paper issued by a government or a corporation acknowledging that money has been lent to the government or the corporation and will be paid back with interest. It is an interest-bearing certificate of public or private indebtedness. Government bonds are gilts or gilt-edged securities with no risk of default. As they are marketable and widely traded, they are issued by auction in many countries. The person who invests in bonds is merely making a loan. The bond itself is the borrower's written promise to repay the loan on a certain date and also to pay a certain rate of interest on the borrowed money. The individual who buys corporation bonds does not share in the corporation's profits, but neither does he run the risk of losing money if the stock goes down in value. Central and local governments issue bonds to raise funds for community improvements such as highroads, bridges, schools and hospitals. Corporations may issue bonds to obtain money for expansion. Business stocks are money lent to a business company in return for interest. Buying business stocks is a way of making profit with higher interest than bank deposit, but compared with shares, stocks are less profitable. Shares are any of the equal parts into which the capital of a business company is divided, giving the holder a right to a portion of the profits, including interest and dividend. Interest is the money paid to someone who makes investments. Dividend is the periodical payment of interest on a loan, or the share of profits paid to shareholders in a business company. A shareholder is an owner of shares in a business company. Equities are ordinary stocks and shares that carry no fixed interest. Usually stocks and shares are issued to the public through a stock exchange.

A stock exchange is a financial centre or a stock market where stocks and shares are bought and sold publicly by stockbrokers. They are groups of professional dealers engaged in such business. A stockbroker or a broker buys and sells stocks and shares for his clients. He works to increase their profits through stockbroking. Stock prices often reflect the health of the economy. When business conditions are good, stock prices tend to rise, creating what is called a bull market. When conditions are poor or threatening, prices drop, creating a bear market.

Exercises

I. Explain each of the following:
1) investment
2) commerce
3) money
4) coin
5) banknote
6) cash
7) hard cash
8) paper money
9) high face value
10) low face value
11) cheque
12) credit card
13) currency
14) gold currency
15) paper currency
16) hard currency
17) soft currency
18) convertible currency
19) international currency
20) foreign money
21) foreign exchange
22) exchange rate
23) revaluation
24) devaluation
25) price
26) supply
27) demand
28) inflation
29) inflationary spiral
30) circulation
31) deflation
32) deflationary policy
33) deflationary measure
34) business company
35) contract
36) joint-stock company

37) limited liability company
38) debt
39) shareholder
40) public limited company
41) stock exchange
42) private limited company
43) merge
44) merger
45) group company
46) syndicate
47) trust
48) transnational company
49) multinational corporation
50) the East India Company
51) foreign-funded company
52) risk
53) profit
54) venture
55) joint venture
56) ownership
57) enterprise
58) state ownership
59) state-owned enterprise
60) state-run enterprise
61) public ownership
62) collective ownership
63) cooperative
64) collectively-owned enterprise
65) township-run enterprise
66) private ownership
67) private enterprise
68) participant
69) deposit
70) depositor
71) bank
72) savings
73) bank account
74) credit
75) creditor
76) debtor
77) deposit account
78) current account
79) fixed deposit
80) notice
81) demand deposit
82) businessman
83) merchant
84) spot goods
85) merchandise
86) spot transaction
87) spot market
88) delivery
89) futures
90) futures goods
91) agreement
92) contract
93) financial instrument
94) physical commodities
95) speculation
96) speculator
97) real estate
98) gambling
99) casino
100) lottery

II. Give another way or other ways of saying each of the following:
　　Model: business company → company, firm, corporation, enterprise
　　1) banknote →
　　2) cheque →
　　3) small change →
　　4) bank account →
　　5) credit card →
　　6) A currency is being revaluated. →
　　7) A currency is being devaluated. →
　　8) stock company →
　　9) limited company →
　　10) public company →
　　11) private company →
　　12) group company →
　　13) transnational company →
　　14) multinational corporation →
　　15) foreign-funded corporation →
　　16) jointly-funded company →
　　17) the people in general →
　　18) public ownership →

19) co-op →
20) township enterprise →
21) time deposit →
22) current deposit →
23) spot commodities →
24) real property →

III. Answer the following questions:
1) What are the common forms of money?
2) What does hard cash refer to?
3) What organization issues paper money in a country?
4) Please tell us the different means of payment.
5) What is the difference between hard currency and soft currency?
6) What is the difference between revaluation and devaluation?
7) Why do prices fluctuate freely in a market economy?
8) What will happen to the prices of apples when their supply fails to meet the demand?
9) By what means does a government control prices?
10) Why does a government sometimes adopt a deflationary policy or take deflationary measures?
11) Why has the merger of companies become a tendency?
12) Are trusts legal in the United States?
13) What are the advantages of a transnational company?
14) What is the difference between a foreign-funded company and a joint venture?
15) What is the difference between a state-owned enterprise and a state-run enterprise?
16) What is the difference between public ownership and private ownership?
17) Who represents the people in general?
18) What is the characteristic of a township enterprise in China?
19) Is an independent company a state-owned enterprise or a private enterprise?
20) What do you think is the common way people make investments in China?
21) Why do many people prefer to put their savings in a bank in China?
22) What is the relationship between a depositor and his bank?
23) What is the relationship between a creditor and a debtor?
24) What is the difference between deposit account and current account?
25) What is the difference between fixed deposit and current deposit?
26) What is the difference between spot goods and futures goods?
27) Please give some examples of physical commodities.
28) Are stocks and shares physical goods or financial instruments?
29) Why do people humorously say buying and selling futures is like buying and selling dreams?
30) Where are the most important futures markets of the world located?
31) What does realty consist of?
32) Is real estate a speculative activity?
33) Where do people gamble?
34) What do people gamble at?
35) Is buying lottery tickets a speculative activity?

Lesson Thirteen

Intellectual Property

 People often talk about creativity and its rewards. Imagine that someone has authored a book, written a play, composed a song, designed a product, invented a process, or marketed a product or service under a unique brand name they have conceived. In so doing, they have manifested a form of creativity. In particular, they have manifested a form of creativity, which probably should entitle them to economic reward. Without a system of protective measures, however, the results of their creative efforts could be exploited by anybody without their receiving just compensation. Deprived of economic incentive or economic reward, many individuals would be reluctant or unwilling to labour the long hours and risk the capital necessary to bring their creative ideas to fruition. This matter is concerned with the protection of intellectual property rights.

 Intellectual property, which is also called intelligence achievement property, is an intangible property resulting from inventive activity, for example, patents, designs, trademarks and copyrights. As a kind of incorporeal property, it means that only the individual or the community who has created it can be in possession of its spiritual value by the operation of law. Recognizing the need to nurture and reward creativity so that human society may continue to enjoy the benefits of new products, services, and works of art, the governments in many countries, support creativity and innovation by providing systems which enable the originators of inventions and industrial designs, the proprietors of trademarks, and the owners of copyrights to protect their rights. There are specialized agencies, which are responsible for protecting such intellectual property rights by providing periods of monopoly for those who serve society through their creativity and innovation.

 Intellectual property rights refer to the legal ownership by a person or business of a patent, industrial design, trademark or copyright attached to a particular product or process which protects the owner against unauthorized copying or unauthorized imitation. Such a property right is an important element of product differentiation and confers temporary monopoly advantages to suppliers. The important part of intellectual property is industrial property, which can be classified under the following three headings: patents, industrial designs and trademarks.

 A patent is a governmental grant to an inventor for a limited period of time, which protects his right in an invention. A patentee is a person who obtains or holds a patent. He is given a monopoly right to use, exercise and sell his novel invention, permitting him to exclude others from its exploitation. A patent is granted to the patentee as the true and first inventor of an invention, which possesses utility and novelty. A patent is novel, in the sense that it has never previously been published or publicly used in this country, either by the inventor himself, or by anyone else. Inventions must be something of a tangible or concrete character which has not previously been projected. But one can patent an abstract idea, or some fanciful notion designed for the improvement of the human race. The patentee need not necessarily manufacture it himself. He may sell the right, or lease, or license it, on such terms, within limits, as he chooses to dictate. When two inventors make the same invention independently, and at about the same time, the first to file his patent application at the patent office obtains precedence, and the other gets no patent rights at all in the invention. As a patentee has the exclusive right to manufacture, use and sell his inventions, the heart of his legal monopoly is the right to invoke the State's power to prevent from utilizing his discovery without his consent. Patents play a role in the entire process of technology transfer.

An industrial design is a drawing or an outline from which industrial goods are made. It is intended to be produced in quantity for industrial purposes. A registered design gives the owner a monopoly right in respect of industrial designs, wherein the novelty lies wholly in shape, or in appearance. The test of novelty in an industrial design lies wholly in the appeal to the eye, that is, in the appearance, shape, or configuration of the article, as contrasted with its practical usefulness. A wider and more effective use of design can make a significant contribution to improving competitiveness. The application of good design is paramount in the creation of innovative products, processes and services.

Trademarks are registered marks by which manufacturers and businessmen brand their goods for the purpose of distinction. A trademark is any visible symbol or sign such as a mark, a letter, a number, a picture, a symbol or a name, which is used by a party to identify or distinguish its goods. Trademarks serve multiple purposes. The primary function of a trademark is to indicate the source or origin of a product or service. However, trademarks also serve to guarantee the quality of the goods bearing the mark and, through advertising, serve to create and maintain a demand for the product. So a trademark implies a particular standard of quality, symbolizing the goodwill of the manufacturer and furnishing a means to protect the public from confusion. A trademark is capable of registration only if it contains one of a number of alternative essential features. These include:

1) the name of a company or an individual represented in a special or particular manner;
2) the signature of the applicant or a predecessor in his business;
3) an invented word or invented words;
4) a word or words without direct reference to the quality of the goods; and
5) any other distinctive marks, subject to certain limitations.

A trademark differs from a trade name or a commercial name. Trade names are business names, which are used by businessmen, manufacturers, industrialists, agriculturists, and others to identify their businesses, vocations or occupations. Trade names can also be the names or titles lawfully adopted by persons, companies, associations, unions and other organizations. But they are not subject to registration unless they are actually used as trademarks. In a word, a trademark identifies a product, while a trade name identifies a producer.

A copyright is an exclusive legal right held by the owner of an original work for a certain number of years, to print, publish, sell, broadcast, perform, film or record it wholly or any part of it. While a patentee is an inventor of a machine or a process or of an article of industrial usefulness, an author is a person who invents artistic property. Subject to certain limitations, the author of any literary, dramatic, musical or artistic work has an ownership in his work. This ownership, which is called copyright, gives him the sole right of publication, performance and production. Copyright extends protection to almost everything that is committed to paper, provided it has involved skill and labour and is in some sense original. Copyright also extends to paintings, drawings, charts, plans, photographs, sculpture and architecture. But there is no copyright in an idea.

In Britain, original literary works, including computer programmes and databases, and dramatic, musical or artistic works, films, sound recordings and broadcasts are automatically protected by copyright. This protection is also given to works from countries party to international copyright conventions. The copyright owner has rights against unauthorized copies. In most cases the author is the first owner of the copyright, and the term of copyright in literary, dramatic, musical and artistic works is the life of the author and a period of 70 years after death. For films, the term is 70 years from the last death among the following: the principal director, the author of the screenplay and dialogue, or the composer of music for the film. Sound recordings are protected for 50 years from the year of making or release, and broadcasts for 50 years from the year of broadcast. Performers are also given automatic protection against broadcasting and recording of life performances, and reproduction of recordings. This lasts for 50 years from the year of performance or release of a recording of it.

Those who make unlawful use of other people's patents, trademarks or copyright materials are infringers. Their unlawful conduct is called infringement. Those who take and use someone else's ideas or words unlawfully or without the original author's permission are plagiarists. They plagiarize others' words or ideas as their own, and infringe others' copyright. This conduct is called plagiarism. As a general rule, copyright is infringed by any person who produces or reproduces a substantial part of the copyright work, or any colorable imitation of it, in any material forms, without authority from the owner. But it is, in each case, a question of fact as to whether the infringing material is a substantial part of the work. For example, four lines extracted from a long poem, might in some circumstances be regarded as sufficiently substantial to constitute a legal infringement. It is not, however, an infringement of copyright to make use of extracts from a copyright work for the purpose of review, or fair criticism, or for the purpose of a newspaper summary.

Piracy is robbery carried out by pirates, originally by pirates on the sea but now more usually by people who illegally take other people's work or property. So a pirate is a person, especially in former times, who sailed on the sea around stopping and robbing ships. Now we can refer to someone as a pirate when they take and use someone else's work or property without having the right to do so. When someone is pirating books, videotapes, or cassettes, they are copying, publishing, and selling them without permission or payment. But they have no right to do so because the contents legally belong to someone else. Very often, a lot of pirated versions or illegal versions may appear immediately after a best-selling book or a best seller comes out. Also when a well-known pop star has got a new album published, illegal copies or pirated copies of it will soon be found in the market. And the premiere of a blockbuster will be closely followed by illegally copied videodiscs or pirated videodiscs. It is necessary to carry out a prolonged struggle against piracy on a worldwide scale, so as to protect the interests of the copyright holders.

Each book which is officially published has a special page devoted to its copyright. On the copyright page, we may see the name of the author, the year of publishing, and the name of the publisher:

Copyright © John Smith, 2004

or:

Copyright © 2004, by ... Publishing House
　　　　　　　　　　　　... Publishing Company
　　　　　　　　　　　　... Publishers
　　　　　　　　　　　　... Press

There are various versions of the copyright owner's statement with slight differences on the copyright page:

1) All rights reserved. No part of this book may be reproduced in any form without permission in writing from the publisher.

2) All rights reserved. Printed in the Untied States of America. No part of this book may be used or reproduced in any manner whatsoever without written permission except in the case of brief quotations embodied in critical articles and reviews.

3) All rights reserved. No part of this book may be reproduced in any form without permission in writing from the publisher, except by a reviewer who wishes to quote brief passages in connection with a review written for broadcast or for inclusion in a magazine or newspaper.

4) All rights reserved. Printed in the U.S.A. No part of this publication may be reproduced or transmitted in any form or by any means, electronic or mechanical, including photocopy, recording, or any information storage and retrieval system now known or to be invented, without permission in writing from the publisher, except by a reviewer who wishes to quote brief passages in connection with a review written for inclusion in a magazine, newspaper or broadcast.

5) All rights reserved. No part of this publication may be reproduced, stored in a retrieval system, or transmitted, in any form or by any means, electronic, mechanical, photocopying, recording, or others, without the prior permission of the publisher.

6) All rights reserved. Except for the quotation of short passages for the purposes of criticism and review, no part of this publication may be reproduced, stored in a retrieval system, or transmitted, in any form or by any means, electronic, mechanical, photocopying, recording or otherwise, without the prior permission of the publisher.

7) This book is in copyright. Subject to statutory exception and to the provisions of relevant collective licensing agreements, no reproduction of any part may take place without the written permission of the publisher.

8) Except in the United States of America, this book is sold subject to the condition that it shall not, by way of trade or otherwise, be lent, re-sold, hired out, or otherwise circulated without the publisher's prior consent in any form of binding or cover other than that in which it is published and without a similar condition including this condition being imposed on the subsequent purchaser.

Words & Expressions

creativity *n*. the ability to invent and develop new and original ideas, esp. in an artistic way 创造力;创新 *e.g.* to support creativity 支持创新
creative *a*. able to produce interesting and unusual results in a new and imaginative way 富有创造性的 *e.g.* creative effort 创造性的努力;creative idea 富有创造性的观点
reward *n*. sth that sb is given because they have behaved well, worked hard, or provided a service to the community 报酬;回报 *e.g.* economic reward 经济回报 *syn*. **economic incentive** 经济奖励
reward *v*. give sb sth because they have behaved well, worked hard, or provided a service to the community 酬劳;奖赏;奖励 *e.g.* to reward creativity 奖励创新
author *n*. the person who wrote a piece of writing such as a book, newspaper article, play, poem, etc. 作者
author *v*. write a piece of writing 写作 *e.g.* to author a book 写一本书
authorize *v*. give one's official permission for sth to happen 授权 *e.g.* unauthorized copy 未经授权的复制品;unauthorized copying 未经授权的复制 *syn*. **unauthorized imitation** 未经授权的复制
market *v*. sell sth, esp. in an organized way and on a large scale 营销 *e.g.* to market a product 营销产品
brand name *n*. the name by which a product made by a particular manufacturer is sold 品牌名称
conceive *v*. think of sth and work out how it can be done or put into practice 想出;构思出
protective *a*. designed or intended to protect sb or sth from danger or physical harm 保护性的 *e.g.* protective measure 保护性措施
exploit *v*. use or develop sth fully so as to get profit 利用;开发
exploitation *n*. the full use or development of sth for the purpose of getting profit 利用;开发
just *a*. reasonable and fully deserved by the person who has received a punishment or reward 应得的 *e.g.* just compensation 应得的补偿;应得的赔偿
compensation *n*. the payment which sb claims from a person or an organization that is responsible for sth unpleasant that has happened to them 补偿;赔偿
deprive *v*. take sth away from sb, or prevent them from having it 剥夺;使丧失
incentive *n*. sth which encourages sb to greater activity 刺激;奖励 *e.g.* economic incentive 经济奖励
reluctant *a*. unwilling to do sth and hesitant before doing it 不愿意的;doing sth slowly and without enthusiasm 勉强的
labour *v*. work very hard at sth 艰苦工作 *e.g.* to labour the long hours 长时间艰苦工作
risk *v*. do sth which a person knows might be dangerous or have unpleasant consequences 冒风险 *e.g.* to risk the capital 冒投资风险
fruition *n*. the fulfillment of plans, aims, desired results, etc. 实现 *e.g.* to bring sth to fruition 使实现
intellectual *a*. involving a person's ability to understand or deal with ideas and information 智力的
intellectual property *also* **intelligence achievement property** *n*. an intangible property resulting from inventive activity, for example, patents, designs, trademarks and copyrights 知识资产
intellectual property right *n*. the legal ownership by a person or business of a patent, industrial design, trademark or copyright attached to a particular product or process which protects the owner against unauthorized copying or imitation 知识产权
intangible *a*. that cannot be known by the senses or described 难以触摸到的;难以确定的 *e.g.* intangible property/assets 无形资产 *syn*. **incorporeal property** 无形资产
patent *n*. an official right to be the only person or company allowed to make or sell a new product for a certain period of time 专利;also referring to the document sb is given when they have obtained this right 专利证书 *e.g.* patent right 专利权;patent office 专利机构;专利局
patent *v*. obtain a patent for sth 获得专利 *e.g.* to patent an abstract idea 获得一种抽象观点的专利

patentee *n.* a person who obtains or holds a patent 专利获得者；专利享有者
design *n.* the process and art of creating, planning, and making detailed drawings of sth 设计 *e.g.* registered design 已注册的设计
trademark *n.* a name or symbol which a manufacturer always uses on a product or a range of products, which is usually registered and protected by law 注册商标
copyright *n.* the legal right of the author of a book, the composer of a piece of music, or the publisher to be the only person who is allowed to reproduce it 版权 *e.g.* copyright work 版权作品
incorporeal *a.* without a body; not made of any material substance 无形的 *e.g.* incorporeal property 无形资产
innovation *n.* a new idea or method which is introduced in the way that sth is done or made 新思想；新方法；the introduction of new ideas or methods in the way that sth is done or made 革新；创新
innovative *a.* newly invented or introduced 革新的；创新的 *e.g.* innovative product 创新产品
nurture *v.* take action to encourage the development and success of plans, ideas, or people such as employees 扶持；扶植 *e.g.* to nurture creativity 鼓励创新
originator *n.* a person who first thinks of, begins or causes an action or idea 创始人；发明人
invent *v.* be the first person to think of, or make a machine, process, game, etc. 发明
invention *n.* a machine, device, or system which has been invented by sb 发明物；the act of inventing sth which has never been made or used before 发明；the ability to invent things or to have clever and original ideas 发明才能 *e.g.* to make an invention 发明
inventor *n.* a person who has invented sth 发明人；a person whose job is to invent things 发明家
inventive *a.* having or showing the ability to invent or think in new and different ways 发明的 *e.g.* inventive activity 发明活动
proprietor *n.* a business owner, for example, the owner of a newspaper, a hotel, or a shop 所有人；业主
copying *n.* the act of doing what others do or trying to be like them 模仿；复制
imitation *n.* the act of copying or behaving in the same way as sb else 模仿；复制
differentiation *n.* difference 区别 *e.g.* product differentiation 产品区别
confer *v.* give an honour, a gift, or status to sb 给予；赋予
monopoly *n.* complete control of a particular subject or activity by one person or a group of people, so that other people find it difficult or impossible to compete with them 垄断 *e.g.* monopoly right 垄断权；monopoly advantage 垄断的好处
industrial property *n.* an intangible property for industrial purposes, including patents, industrial designs and trademarks 工业资产
grant *n.* sth given for a particular purpose, esp. money, from the government 补助金
project *v.* make a plan that sth will happen in the future 筹划
fanciful *a.* that is not based on reality 空想的；幻想的 *e.g.* fanciful notion 空想的念头
utility *n.* the degree of usefulness 功用
novelty *n.* the quality of being different, new, and unusual 新奇；新颖
dictate *v.* state what must happen in certain circumstances 要求；支配
file *v.* make a request officially 正式提出 *e.g.* to file one's patent application 正式提出专利申请
application *n.* a formal request to be allowed to do sth 申请 *e.g.* patent application 专利申请
applicant *n.* a person who formally asks to be given sth such as a job or a place at a college or university 申请人
precedence *n.* the order of priority which is given to sb 优先
invoke *v.* use the power or law to justify what a person is doing 求助于；援用
consent *n.* permission given to sb to do sth by a person who has authority over them 同意；许可
technology *n.* the knowledge dealing with scientific and industrial methods and their practical use in industry

技术

technology transfer *n.* the change of the ownership of technology, from a person or institution to another 技术转让

industrial design *n.* a drawing or an outline from which industrial goods are made 工业设计

configuration *n.* an arrangement of a group of things or parts 配置

article *n.* a particular object or item 物品

paramount *a.* more important than anything else 最重要的

predecessor *n.* a person who held a position before sb else 前任

trade name *also* **commercial name** *n.* a business name, which is used by businessmen, manufacturers, industrialists, agriculturists, and others to identify their businesses, vocations or occupations 厂名;店名

business name *n.* the name of an organization which produces and sells goods or which provides a service 企业名称

manufacturer *n.* a person or a group of people who own a business that makes goods in large quantities 制造商

industrialist *n.* a person who owns or controls large amounts of money or property in industry 实业家

agriculturist *n.* a person who is an expert on agriculture and who advises farmers 农业专家

vocation *n.* a profession or career which sb feels that they are especially suitable to do 职业;业务

association *n.* a group of people who have joined together because they have a common occupation, aim, or interest 协会;社团

subject *a.* affected by sth or made to experience it 受……影响的;需要……的 *e.g.* subject to registration 需要登记;需要注册;governed by 受……约束的 *e.g.* subject to certain limitations 受某些局限性约束的;subject to statutory exception 受法定的例外情况约束的;depending on 取决于 *e.g.* subject to the condition that... 取决于下列条件

registration *n.* the recording of sth such as a person's name or the details of an event in an official list or record 登记;注册

artistic property *n.* an intangible property resulting from artistic creation or artistic activity 艺术资产

computer programme *n.* a set of instructions which a computer uses in order to perform a particular operation 计算机程序

database *n.* a collection of data which is stored in a computer in a way that enables people to get information out of it very quickly 数据库

party *n.* a person who is one of the people involved in sth such as a legal dispute or the signing of a contract or agreement 一方

be party to *v. phrase* be involved in a particular action, agreement, etc. and therefore partly responsible for it 参与 *e.g.* to be party to international copyright conventions 参与国际版权公约

convention *n.* a list of rules of behaviour which is agreed between groups or countries （国际间的）公约 *e.g.* international copyright convention 国际版权公约

director *n.* a person who decides how a play, film, or television programme is to be performed or made 导演 *e.g.* principal director 总导演

screenplay *n.* the script of a film 电影剧本

unlawful *a.* illegal 非法的;违法的 *e.g.* unlawful conduct 违法行为;to make unlawful use of 非法利用

infringe *v.* interfere with other people and disallow them the freedom they are entitled to 侵犯 *e.g.* to infringe others' copyright 侵犯别人的版权

infringer *n.* a person who makes unlawful use other people's rights 侵权者

infringement *n.* the unlawful conduct of an infringer to interfere with others' rights 侵权 *e.g.* legal infringement 合法的侵权

plagiarize *v.* take and use others' words or ideas as one's own and infringe others' copyright 剽窃;抄袭

plagiarist *n*. a person who takes and uses sb else's ideas or words unlawfully or without the original author's permission 剽窃者；抄袭者

plagiarism *n*. the conduct of taking and using others' words or ideas as one's own without the original author's permission 剽窃；抄袭

criticism *n*. a comment which expresses disapproval of sth or sb 批评；a comment, often written, which expresses an opinion or judgment of a book, play, work of art, etc. 批评文章 *e.g.* fair criticism 公正的批评

summary *n*. a short written or spoken account of sth, which gives the important points but not the details 摘要 *e.g.* newspaper summary 报纸摘要

piracy *n*. robbery carried out by pirates, originally by pirates on the sea 海盗行为；illegal taking of other people's work or property 盗版；盗取资产

pirate *n*. a person, esp. in former times, who sailed on the sea around stopping and robbing ships 海盗；a person who takes and uses sb else's work or property without having the right to do so 盗版者；盗取资产者

pirate *v*. copy, publish, and sell a book, videotape, or cassette without the permission of the copyright holder 盗版

pirated version *also* **illegal version** *n*. an illegally copied version 盗版

pirated copy *also* **illegal copy** *n*. an illegally copied version 盗版

best-selling *a*. very popular 畅销的 *e.g.* best-selling book 畅销书

best seller *n*. a book of which a great number of copies has been sold *syn.* best-selling book 畅销书

pop star *n*. a well-known singer of pop songs 通俗歌星

album *n*. a record which usu. has about 25 minutes of music, speech, etc. on each side 专辑；唱片集

premiere *n*. the first public show of a new film 首映式；the first performance of a new play 首次公演

blockbuster *n*. a very popular and successful film because of the exciting or sensational events shown in it 大片

videodisc *n*. a round piece of plastic, like a record, from which recorded pictures can be played back in the same way as from a videotape 影碟 *e.g.* illegally copied videodisc；pirated videodisc 盗版影碟

copyright page *n*. a special page in an officially published book, which is devoted to its copyright 版权页

publishing house *n*. a business which publishes books 出版社

publishing company *n*. a company which publishes books 出版公司

publisher *n*. a person who publishes books 出版商；a business which publishes books 出版社

press *n*. a business for printing, and sometimes also for selling books, magazines, etc. 出版社 *e.g.* Peking University Press 北京大学出版社；Oxford University Press 牛津大学出版社

reserve *v*. keep sth for a particular person or purpose 保留 *e.g.* to reserve the right 保留权利

whatsoever *a*. used after a noun group in order to strongly emphasize a negative statement or a statement which includes the word "any" 不论什么

quote *v*. repeat a phrase or passage from a book, poem, play, etc. 引述；引用 *e.g.* to quote a brief passage 引用一段短文

quotation *n*. a phrase or passage from a book, poem, play, etc. 引语；引文 *e.g.* brief quotation 简短引文

embody *v*. include 收录

critical *a*. relating to the work of a critic 批评的 *e.g.* critical article 批评文章

reviewer *n*. a person who gives opinions of a new book or a play 评论家

publication *n*. a book, or a magazine which has been published 出版物

retrieval *n*. the process of getting back information from a computer system 检索 *e.g.* retrieval system 检索系统

photocopying *n*. making a copy of a document by using a photocopier 复印

prior *a*. existing, happening, coming, or planned, done, or experienced before a particular time 事先的

  e.g. prior permission of the publisher 出版商事先允许;prior consent 事先同意
statutory *a*. fixed or controlled by law 法定的 *e.g.* statutory exception 法定的例外情况
binding *n*. the cover of a book 书的封面
impose on *v. phrase* use one's authority to force a condition or rule to be kept on people 强加于
subsequent *a*. existing or happening at a later time than sth else 随后的
purchaser *n*. buyer 购买者;买家
component *n*. one of the parts or features from which sth is created, made, or produced 组成部分
know-how *n*. the knowledge of the methods or techniques of doing sth, esp. sth scientific or technical 实际知识;专门技能
end product *n*. sth which is produced or achieved by means of a particular activity or process 最终产品
state-of-the-art *a*. the best available because of using the most modern techniques and technology 使用先进技术的 *e.g.* state-of-the-art item 使用先进技术的物品;state-of-the-art system 使用先进技术的系统
entity *n*. a complete, separate thing which is not divided and which is not part of anything else 实体
specification *n*. a detailed description of features in the design or composition of a machine, a building, materials, etc. 规格;说明书 *e.g.* specification for a part 零件规格
piece-part *n*. one of the individual parts or sections which make up an object, esp. a part of section that can be removed 部件 *e.g.* piece-part construction 部件构造
integration *n*. the combination of things so that they are closely linked 整合 *e.g.* system integration 系统整合
autonomous *a*. able to make one's own decision about what to do rather than being influenced by sb else or told what to do 独立自主的 *e.g.* autonomous production capability 独立自主的生产能力
handover *n*. an act of passing sth, esp. power or responsibility, from one person or group to another 移交
illustration *n*. sth such as an example or a story which is used to explain a point or make it clear 实例;例证
hint *v*. suggest in a very indirect way that sth is true 暗示

Additional Knowledge

Technology Transfer

  The two components of the term "technology transfer" might be defined as follows:
  Technology is the understanding and application of scientific knowledge, technical information, know-how, critical materials, unique manufacturing equipment, end products, and test equipment essential to research, develop, produce, and use state-of-the-art items or systems.
  Transfer is the communication of information materials, or equipment, from a sender to a receiver. The sender is the entity or person who possesses desired data or materials, while the receiver is the entity or person who obtains the data or materials.
  The varying perceptions in communications between individuals are fundamental to technology transfer. For instance, let's consider the differing understanding by citizens of the United States and the People's Republic of China when "technology transfer" is mentioned. The Chinese understand this two-word phrase to mean the transfer of specifications for a part, a system, or a product, in return for money or access to Chinese markets, or other rights.
  In their understanding, no U.S. technical personnel would be needed nor would the Chinese slowly evolve from piece-part construction, to system integration, to final

autonomous production capability. Technology transfer to China may simply be a handover. A U.S. technical individual or manufacturer, however, would interpret "technology transfer" to mean a long-term learning process involving scientists, technicians, and managers from both countries working toward a future goal of Chinese autonomous production capability for one product or similar sets of products.

Naturally, a payment for these activities is expected by both parties, but this illustration also hints at a larger issue: How much, and what should we be willing to transfer? What protections are necessary for long-term national interests?

Exercises

I. Explain each of the following:
  1) intellectual property
  2) creativity
  3) reward
  4) brand name
  5) compensation
  6) intellectual property right
  7) patent
  8) patentee
  9) design
  10) industrial design
  11) trademark
  12) copyright
  13) intangible property
  14) monopoly
  15) industrial property
  16) precedence
  17) technology transfer
  18) registration
  19) predecessor
  20) trade name
  21) business name
  22) artistic property
  23) computer programme
  24) database
  25) convention
  26) director
  27) screenplay
  28) infringer
  29) infringement
  30) plagiarist
  31) plagiarism
  32) videotape
  33) cassette
  34) best seller
  35) pop star
  36) album
  37) premiere
  38) blockbuster
  39) videodisc
  40) publisher

II. Give another way or other ways of saying each of the following:
  Models: television set → television
          movie → film; motion pictures
  1) author a book →
  2) economic reward →
  3) unwilling →
  4) intelligence achievement property →
  5) incorporeal property →
  6) proprietor →
  7) unauthorized copying →
  8) commercial name →
  9) best-selling book →
  10) pirated copy →
  11) illegal version →
  12) illegally copied videodisc →

III. Give the corresponding adjective and noun(s) of each of the following verbs:
  Model: create → creative; creativity/creativeness/creator

1) exploit →
2) protect →
3) produce →
4) reproduce →
5) invent →
6) originate →
7) operate →
8) innovate →
9) limit →
10) permit →
11) exclude →
12) publish →
13) project →
14) prevent →
15) compete →
16) industrialize →
17) identify →
18) perform →
19) record →
20) extend →
21) include →
22) direct →
23) imitate →
24) infringe →
25) plagiarize →
26) review →
27) criticize →
28) quote →
29) connect →
30) collect →

IV. Give the opposite of each of the following:
Model: good → bad
1) tangible →
2) concrete →
3) willing →
4) authorized →
5) lawful →
6) legal →

V. Answer the following questions:
1) What will happen to a person's creative efforts, if there isn't a system of protective measures?
2) Why do we need to nurture and reward creativity?
3) How do the governments in many countries support creativity?
4) How shall we classify industrial property?
5) What is the important part of intellectual property?
6) What is the right of a patentee?
7) In what sense is a patent novel?
8) Who obtains precedence when two inventors make the same invention independently?
9) What is the essence of a patentee's legal monopoly?
10) Where does the novelty of an industrial design lie?
11) What are the functions of a trademark?
12) What is the difference between a trademark and a trade name?
13) Under what circumstances is a trade name subject to registration?
14) What is the difference between a patentee and an author?
15) Is there any patent in an abstract idea? Is there any copyright in an abstract idea?
16) What is the original meaning of a pirate?
17) What is a copyright page?
18) What can we see on the copyright page?
19) Can you give different ways of saying "publishing house"?
20) Is it necessary for a critic to ask for permission from the author of a book when he quotes brief passages in connection with a book review?

Lesson Fourteen

The Educational System

Education is the teaching or training of people, especially in schools, and colleges to improve their knowledge and develop their skills.

Before a child is old enough to go to school, it receives pre-school education or early childhood education. The children of pre-school age may stay at home, being taken care of and educated by their parents or grandparents. A pre-school child may also be cared for in a nursery, a child-care centre, or a day-care centre when its working mother is at work. Before the very young children go to school, they may also go to nursery school or kindergarten where they are separated from their parents, playing and sharing with other children of the same age, and following the directions of a teacher. The children are also introduced to skills and information that will help them later with their study, life and work. For example, they learn the colours and the alphabet. They also learn how to write their names, to count to ten, to work with art supplies, and to enjoy books. Pre-school education is considered beneficial to pre-school children for their future growth and development. The availability of pre-school education varies from area to area, and parents often have to pay for it.

The first stage of education is primary education. School-age children in Britain go to school when they are five, while children in the United States go to school at the age of six. The first academic institution that a child attends is called a primary school in Britain and an elementary school, a grade school or a grammar school in the United States. In this kind of school, elementary subjects are taught for the first six to eight years of a child's education. When the children enter first grade, they become first-graders. They begin to receive their primary education, learning to read, write and do arithmetic. A grade is a division or an academic level of a school which is based on the age of the pupils. To complete each grade requires an academic year which starts from September and ends in next June.

In Britain and the United States, parents are required by compulsory school attendance law to see that their children receive full-time education, at school or elsewhere between the age of five and sixteen in Britain and between the age of six and eighteen in the United States.

Most of the pupils receive free education from public funds, while the others attend independent schools financed by fees paid by their parents.

In Britain, pupils usually transfer from primary school to secondary school or high school at the age of eleven. Then they begin to receive their secondary education, which is the second stage of their education. They usually stay at secondary school or high school until they are eighteen. In the United States, pupils receive their secondary education in a high school. In some school systems, elementary school includes grades one to eight. The next four years are called high school, which includes grades nine to twelve. In some other school systems, there are three divisions: elementary school including grades one to six, junior high school including grades seven to nine, and senior high school including grades ten to twelve. The Chinese counterpart of a British secondary school or an American high school is a middle school, which can be divided into a junior middle school and a senior middle school.

In Britain, a comprehensive school is a secondary school for all children, and it is not a private school. In this kind of school, pupils of all abilities are taught from the age of eleven. A grammar school is a different kind of secondary school, which provides more academic education for children over the age of eleven. Formerly, a grammar school was for the pupils who were specially chosen to study for examinations which may lead to higher education.

A school is usually a place where children go to be educated. There are different kinds of schools. A state school in the United Kingdom or a public school in the United States is tax-supported and controlled by local officials, in which education is free. A private school or an independent school is one with no publicly aided funds, in which education is not free. Some private schools in Britain and America are supported by various religious groups. A coeducational or mixed school is one with both boys and girls studying together in the same class. Such a school enables girls to prove that they possess as much intellectual potential as boys. But there are still a few single-sex schools which are exclusively for boys or girls. A day school is a school whose pupils attend only during the day, returning home at night and at weekends. And a boarding school is usually a private one, where pupils live as well as study during term time. And many boarding schools are single-sex schools.

In Britain, a preparatory school, and also called a prep school, is a private school for pupils up to the age of thirteen, where they are made ready to attend a school for older pupils, especially a public school. In the United States, a preparatory school or a prep school is a private school that makes pupils ready for college.

Most children go to state schools. Some children go to independent schools run by private organizations, for which their parents have to pay high fees. These parents think that their children can receive a better education at a private school where there is a better quality of education. In the United States and Scotland, a public school is a free local school, controlled and paid for by the state, for children who study there but live at home. But in England, a public school is actually a private fee-paying secondary school where children usually live as well as study. Many celebrated public schools have a long history. Winchester College was founded in 1394, Eton College in 1440, and Harrow School in 1571. Traditionally, most public schools were for boys only, because until the 19th century people did not think it suitable for girls to be sent away to school. Cheltenham Ladies College, founded in 1853, was the first girls' public school. In the past few decades, some of the old-established boys' public schools have also started to accept girls as pupils.

In a school, children have to study such core subjects as English, mathematics and science. They also have to study the foundation subjects like technology, geography, history, art, music and physical education. Older children take a foreign language. A school can also be a place where particular subjects or skills are taught for adults, but not for children. For instance, adults can attend a driving school where they learn how to drive a car, or go to a language school where they study a foreign language. Adults can also go to evening school or night school to learn a particular subject or skill. In British English, a school-leaver is a young person who has just left school and is looking for a job or doing his or her job. In American English, a high school graduate or a graduate is a young person who has successfully completed high school and received a certificate or diploma.

Education in a university or college is called tertiary education or higher education. A university is an educational institution of the highest level, where degrees are given. The students at a university receive higher education or tertiary education. Usually, a college is an educational institution where students can study after they leave school, but it is not a university. However, it is a school for higher education, especially in a particular subject or professional skill, for instance, an agricultural college, a teachers' training college, a law college or an art college. Sometimes in a university, a college is an independent institution, which has its own teachers, students and buildings. For instance, Oxford University and Cambridge University in Britain both have their own colleges. In Britain, a technical college, and also called a tech, is a college providing courses in practical subjects, art, social studies, etc., for students who have left school. And in Britain, a polytechnic, or informally called a poly, is a college of higher education providing training and often degrees in many subjects, especially those which prepare people for particular jobs in science and industry.

In the United States, there are two thousand universities and colleges. They have great differences in quality and reputation. Among them, the famous ones are a group of eight old private northeastern universities commonly known as "the Ivy League". The best known of all is Harvard University and Yale University. They occupy a position in American university life rather like Oxford and Cambridge in Britain. Several other institutions such as Princeton University and Columbia University are closely following them in eminence.

Usually, campus refers to the area of land, which contains the main buildings of a university or college such as the administration offices, lecture rooms, libraries, laboratories, sports facilities, and some living accommodation for students. In some universities, the students live on campus. A campus university is one in which all the buildings are in the same area, often outside a town.

In Britain, a small percentage of students go on to higher education. Many of them go to university and study for a bachelor's degree, while others study for a certificate or diploma at a college of further education. An undergraduate is a student at a university or college who has not yet taken his or her first degree. It is a bachelor's degree, such as a BA or a BSc. BA stands for Bachelor of Arts. A Bachelor of Arts refers to a person with a first degree from a university, usually in an arts or social science subject. BSc stands for Bachelor of Science. A Bachelor of Science is a person with a first degree from a university in a science subject. In British English, a fresher or a freshman is a first-year student at college or university; while in American English, a freshman can be a student in the first year at a high school, college or university. In American English, a sophomore is a second-year student in a university or a student in the second year of a course in a college or high school. In British English, a junior is a pupil at a junior school; but in American English, a junior can be a student of the third year in a four-year course at high school or university. In American English, a senior is a student of the last year in a high school or university course. A major is a student studying a chief or special subject at a university. For example, an English major is a student who studies English as the chief subject when doing a university degree.

A graduate is in the sense of a graduate student, a postgraduate or a postgraduate student, who has a first degree from a university and is studying or doing research at a more advanced level for a higher degree than a first degree. A master's degree like an MA, an MSc, an MBA or an MPA, is a higher degree than a bachelor's degree and usually takes one or two years to complete in Britain and America. MA stands for Master of Arts, while MSc stands for Master of Science. A Master of Arts refers to a person with a master's degree from a university, usually in an arts or social science subject; while a Master of Science is a person with a master's degree from a university in a science subject. MBA stands for Master of Business Administration, while MPA stands for Master of Public Administration. A Master of Business Administration refers to a person with a master's degree in business administration; while a Master of Public Administration refers to a person with a master's degree in public administration.

A doctor's degree, doctoral degree or doctorate is the highest academic or honorary degree by a university. A person who is studying for a doctor's degree is called a doctoral student or a doctoral candidate. And a person who has been awarded a doctor's degree is called a doctor. PhD is an abbreviation for "Doctor of Philosophy", which is a degree awarded to people who have done advanced research into a particular subject and have written an account of it. A Doctor of Philosophy is a person who has got a PhD. A person with a doctoral degree can do post-doctoral research or post-doctoral studies. People who are engaged in such programmes will not get a degree.

In the era of knowledge economy, everybody should form the concept of lifelong education. People should study and renew their knowledge so long as they live. Further education is the education for people who have left school, but not at a university. However, further education classes can be held at a local college. Most courses at such a college train people in a particular skill and combine periods of study with work experience.

Some people return to education later in life and attend evening classes run by adult education institutes. Adult education is the education provided for adults outside the formal educational system. Many adults attend evening classes and try to study some special subjects, or improve their foreign language. Open learning schemes enable people to obtain recognized qualifications, such as a degree from the Open University or a qualification in accountancy, without having to leave their jobs.

The Open University is a university in Britain that runs degree courses on the radio and television for students who do not have the proper qualifications and want to study part-time or mainly at home. Students send their work by post to their tutors.

Vocational education is connected with the skills people need to do a particular job. Vocational training is aimed at preparing a person for a job.

Technological developments, such as the Internet, are changing the way the world's people communicate and the way organizations operate. The means of education tends to be diversified. Long-distance education, computer-aided instruction, E-learning, and online education provide people with more opportunities and facilities to receive education.

Words & Expressions

education *n.* the process by which a person's mind and character are developed through teaching, esp. through formal instruction at a school or college 教育

pre-school education *n.* the care and education received by the children before they reach the age when they have to go to school 学龄前教育

early childhood education *n.* the care and education received by the children in the early time of their life during which they are too young to go to school 早期儿童教育

pre-school age *n.* the period of time before the children reach the age when they have to go to school 学龄前时期

pre-school child *n.* a child who has not yet reached the age when it has to go to school 学龄前儿童

nursery *n.* a place where very young children are looked after while their parents are at work, shopping, etc. 托儿所

child-care centre *n.* a place where very young children are looked after while their parents are at work, shopping, etc. 托儿中心

day-care centre *n.* a place where very young children are looked after in the day time when their parents are at work 日托中心

school *n.* a place where people are educated 学校

nursery school *n.* a school for young children who are between three and five years old 幼儿园;幼稚园

kindergarten *n.* a school for young children who are not yet old enough to go to primary school 幼儿园;幼稚园

learn *v.* gain the knowledge of 学;学习;学会;学到 *e.g.* to learn the colours 学会认颜色;to learn the alphabet 学会认字母

count *v.* say all the numbers one after another up to a particular number 数;计数 *e.g.* to count to ten 数到十

art supplies *n.* things needed for painting or drawing 绘画用品

primary education *n.* the first stage of education 初等教育

academic *a.* concerning education in schools, colleges, and universities, esp. work which involves studying and reasoning rather than practical or technical skills 学习的;学术的 *e.g.* academic institution 学习机构;学术机构

primary school *BrE. n.* a school in Britain for children between five and eleven years old (英国)小学

elementary school *also* **grade school, grammar school** *AmE. n.* a school where children are taught for the first six or eight years of their education (美国)小学

grade *AmE. n.* a class or a group of classes in which all the children are of a similar age in an American school 年级

first-grader *AmE. n.* a first-year pupil at the age of six in an elementary school in the United States 一年级小学生

arithmetic *n.* the part of mathematics which is concerned with the addition, subtraction, multiplication, and division of numbers 算术 *e.g.* to do arithmetic 做算术

academic year *n.* a school year which starts from September and ends in next June 学年

compulsory school attendance law *n.* the law according to which parents are required to send their children to school 义务教育法

full-time education *n.* the education received for the whole of each normal working week rather than for part of it 全日制教育

free education *n*. the education received without paying the fees 免费教育

private school *also* **independent school** *n*. a school which is not supported financially by the government and which parents have to pay for their children to go to 私立学校

independent school *also* **private school** *n*. a school which does not receive money from the government 不靠政府资助的学校；私立学校

secondary school *BrE. n*. a school for students between the ages of eleven or twelve and eighteen（英国）中学

secondary education *n*. the second stage of education 中等教育

high school *n*. a school in Britain for students aged between eleven and eighteen（英国）中学；a school in the United States for students aged between fifteen and eighteen（美国）中学

junior high school *n*. an American high school including grades seven through nine（美国）初中

senior high school *n*. an American high school including grades ten through twelve（美国）高中

middle school *n*. the Chinese counterpart of a British secondary school or an American high school, which can be divided into junior middle school and senior middle school（中国）中学

junior middle school *n*. a Chinese middle school which contains the first three grades（中国）初中

senior middle school *n*. a Chinese middle school which contains the second three grades（中国）高中

comprehensive school *n*. a secondary school in Britain for children of all abilities and social backgrounds（英国）综合中学

grammar school *n*. a kind of secondary school in Britain which provides more academic education for children aged between eleven and eighteen who have a high academic ability（英国）语法学校；文法学校；a school where children are taught for the first six or eight years of their education（美国）小学

high school graduate *also* **graduate** *AmE. n*. a student who has successfully completed high school and received a certificate or diploma（美国）中学毕业生

school-leaver *BrE. n*. a young person who has just left school and is looking for a job or doing his or her first job（英国）中学毕业生

higher education *also* **tertiary education** *n*. the education received at universities and colleges 高等教育

state school *BrE. n*. a non-fee-paying school in the United Kingdom which is run by the government and controlled by local officials（英国）公立学校

public school *AmE. n*. a school in the United States which is tax-supported and controlled by local officials（美国）公立学校

coeducational school *also* **mixed school** *n*. a school with both boys and girls studying together in the same class 男女合校

single-sex school *n*. a school exclusively for boys or girls 单一性别学校（男生学校；女生学校）

potential *n*. the range of abilities and talents which a person was born with, although these abilities and talents may not be in full use yet 潜能 *e.g.* intellectual potential 智力潜能

day school *n*. a school where all the pupils go home in the evening and do not live at the school 走读学校

boarding school *n*. a school where some or all of the pupils live as well as study during term time 寄宿学校

preparatory school *also* **prep school** *BrE. n*. a private school in Britain, where pupils are educated until the age of eleven or thirteen and made ready to attend a public school or other secondary school（英国）中学预科学校

preparatory school *also* **prep school** *AmE. n*. a private school in the United States, which makes pupils ready for college（美国）大学预科学校

public school *BrE. n*. a private fee-paying secondary school in Britain, esp. in England, where children usually live as well as study in term time（英国）公学

Winchester College *n*. a British public school founded in 1394 温彻斯特学院

Eton College *n*. a British public school founded in 1440 伊顿公学;伊顿学院
Harrow School *n*. a British public school founded in 1571 哈罗公学
Cheltenham Ladies College *n*. the first British girls' public school founded in 1853 彻尔滕纳女子学院
core subject *n*. a subject which children have to study in a school, such as English, mathematics and science 核心科目;主科
foundation subject *n*. a subject which children have to study in a school, such as technology, geography, history, art, music and physical education 基础科目;副科
driving school *n*. a school where instructors are employed to teach people how to drive a car 驾驶学校
language school *n*. a school where people study a foreign language 语言学校
evening school *also* **night school** *n*. a school where educational classes are held for adults who learn a particular subject or skill in the evening or at night 夜校
university *n*. an educational institution where students study for degrees and where academic research is done 大学
college *n*. an educational institution where students study for qualifications or do training courses after they leave school; or one of the separate institutions which a university is divided into in Britain 学院
agricultural college *n*. an educational institution belonging to a university, where agriculture is taught 农学院
teachers' training college *n*. an educational institution belonging to a university, where teachers are trained 师范学院
law college *n*. an educational institution belonging to a university, where law is taught 法学院
art college *n*. an educational institution belonging to a university, where art is taught 艺术学院
Oxford University *also* **Oxford** *n*. one of the oldest and most famous British universities, which was founded in the 12th century 牛津大学
Cambridge University *also* **Cambridge** *n*. one of the oldest and most famous British universities, which was founded in the 13th century 剑桥大学
technical college *also* **tech** *n*. a college of further education in Britain, which provides courses in practical subjects, art, social studies, etc., for students who have left school (英国)技术学院
polytechnic *also* **poly** *n*. a college of higher education in Britain, where students can go after leaving school in order to study academic subjects at various levels up to degree level or to train for particular jobs (英国)理工学院
the Ivy League *n*. a group of eight important old private universities in the northeastern part of the United States 常春藤联盟
Harvard University *also* **Harvard** *n*. one of the oldest and most famous American universities, which was founded in 1636 哈佛大学
Yale University *also* **Yale** *n*. one of the oldest and most famous American universities, which was founded in 1701 耶鲁大学
Princeton University *also* **Princeton** *n*. one of the most famous American universities, which was founded in 1749 普林斯顿大学
Columbia University *also* **Columbia** *n*. one of the most famous American universities, which was founded in 1754 哥伦比亚大学
campus *n*. the area of land where the main building of a university is 校园
administration office *n*. an office for the group of people in a company, institution, or other organization, which manages and supervises it 行政办公室
facilities *n*. the buildings, equipment, and services which are provided for a particular activity or purpose 设施 *e.g.* sports facilities 体育设施
living accommodation *n*. a room or building to stay or live in 住处;住所
campus university *n*. a university in which all the buildings are in the same area, often outside a town 校园

大学

certificate *n*. an official document which sb receives when they have successfully completed a course of study or training 结业证书

diploma *BrE*. *n*. a document showing that sb has successfully completed a course of study or passed an examination （英国）结业证书

diploma *AmE*. *n*. a document showing that a student has successfully completed his/her college or university education, which is not as high as a degree （美国）毕业证书；文凭

further education *BrE*. *n*. the education of people who have left school and who are not at a university or college of higher education 继续教育 *e.g.* a college of further education 继续教育学院

undergraduate *n*. a student at a university or college who is doing a programme for a first degree 本科生

degree *n*. a course of study at a university, which sb takes or the qualification which sb gets when they have passed the course 学位 *e.g.* university degree 大学学位

first degree *n*. a bachelor's degree, such as a BA or a BSc 学士学位

bachelor's degree *n*. a first degree, such as a BA or a BSc 学士学位

Bachelor of Arts *also* **BA**（*abbrev.*）*n*. a person with a first degree from a university, usu. in an arts or social science subject 文学士

Bachelor of Science *also* **BSc**（*abbrev.*）*n*. a person with a first degree from a university in a science subject 理学士

fresher *also* **freshman** *BrE*. *n*. a first-year student at university or college （英国）一年级大学生

freshman *AmE*. *n*. a student in the first year at a high school, college or university （美国）一年级中学生；一年级大学生

sophomore *AmE*. *n*. a student in the second year of a course in a college or high school （美国）二年级中学生；二年级大学生

junior *BrE*. *n*. a pupil at a junior school （英国）小学生

junior school *BrE*. *n*. a school in England or Wales for children between the ages of about seven and eleven, or the part of a primary school which teaches children of this age （英国）小学

junior *AmE*. *n*. a student of the third year in a four-year course at high school or university （美国）三年级中学生；三年级大学生

senior *AmE*. *n*. a student of the last year in a high school or university course （美国）毕业班中学生；毕业班大学生

major *n*. a student studying a chief or special subject at a university 专业学生；主修专业的学生

English major *n*. a student who studies English as the chief subject when doing a university degree 英语专业学生；主修英语专业的学生

graduate *also* **graduate student**, **postgraduate**, **postgraduate student** *n*. a student who has a first degree from a university and is studying or doing research at a more advanced level 研究生

master's degree *n*. a university degree such as an MA and an MSc, which is a higher level than a first degree and usu. takes one or two years to complete 硕士学位

MA *also* **Master of Arts** *n*. a higher level than a first degree in an arts or social science subject, which usu. takes one or two years to complete in Britain and America 文学硕士学位

MSc *also* **Master of Science** *n*. a higher level than a first degree in a science subject, which usu. takes one or two years to complete in Britain and America 理学硕士学位

Master of Arts *n*. a person with a master's degree from a university, usu. in an arts or social science subject 文学硕士

Master of Science *n*. a person with a master's degree from a university in a science subject 理学硕士

MBA *also* **Master of Business Administration** *n*. a master's degree in business administration 工商管理硕士学位

MPA *also* **Master of Public Administration** *n.* a master's degree in public administration 公共管理硕士学位
Master of Business Administration *n.* a person with a master's degree in business administration 工商管理硕士
Master of Public Administration *n.* a person with a master's degree in public administration 公共管理硕士
doctor's degree *also* **doctoral degree, doctorate** *n.* the highest academic or honorary degree by a university 博士学位
doctoral student *also* **doctoral candidate** *n.* a person who is studying for a doctor's degree 博士生
doctor *n.* a person who has been awarded a doctor's degree 博士
PhD *also* **Doctor of Philosophy** *n.* a degree awarded to people who have done advanced research into a particular subject and have written an account of it 哲学博士学位
Doctor of Philosophy *n.* a person who has got a PhD 哲学博士
post-doctoral research *also* **post-doctoral studies** *n.* the programme done by a person with a doctor's degree 博士后研究
era *n.* a continuous period of time which is considered as a single unit because it has a particular feature that makes it notable 时代 *e.g.* era of knowledge economy 知识经济时代
knowledge economy *also* **knowledge-based economy** *n.* the type of economy which is based on the production, distribution and application of scientific and technological knowledge 知识经济
concept *n.* an idea or abstract principle which relates to a particular subject or to a particular view of that subject 理念
lifelong *a.* existing or happening for the whole of a person's life 终生的 *e.g.* lifelong education 终身教育
renew *v.* replace sth old with sth new 更新 *e.g.* to renew one's knowledge 更新知识
evening class *n.* an educational class for adults, which is held in the evening 夜校班
adult education *n.* the education provided for adults outside the formal educational system 成人教育 *e.g.* adult education institute 成人教育学院
qualification *n.* an official record of achievement which sb gets when they have successfully completed a course of training or passed an exam 资格证书;合格证书 *e.g.* recognized qualification 承认的资格证书
open learning scheme *n.* an learning plan or programme offered to any adult student who wants to obtain a recognized qualification, such as a degree from the Open University 开放学习计划
the Open University *n.* a non-residential university offering degree and other courses for adult students of all ages in Britain, the European Union, Gibraltar, Slovenia and Switzerland 开放大学
course *n.* a series of lessons or lectures on a particular subject, which usu. includes reading and written work that a student has to do 课程 *e.g.* degree course 学位课程
tutor *BrE. n.* a member of staff at a British university or college who teaches small groups of students or gives individual students general help and advice（英国）导师
vocational education *n.* the education connected with the skills people need to do a particular job 职业教育
vocational training *n.* the training aimed at preparing a person for a job 职业培训
long-distance education *n.* the education provided over a long distance by means of radio, TV and the Internet 远程教育
computer-aided instruction *n.* the teaching with the help of the computer 计算机辅助教学
Internet *n.* the worldwide network of computer links, which allows computer users to connect with computers all over the world, and which carries e-mail 互联网;因特网
E-learning *n.* the learning provided by using such electronic devices as radio, TV and the Internet 电子学习
online education *n.* the education offered on line which provides people with more opportunities and facilities to education 在线教育;网上教育
Oxbridge *n.* a colloquial term used to refer to the universities of Oxford and Cambridge 牛津-剑桥大学
New College *n.* a college founded in 1379 at Oxford University 新学院

All Souls College *n.* a college founded in 1437 at Oxford University, which is unique in having no undergraduates but only fellows 万灵学院

fellow *n.* a member of a college or university engaged in scientific research and usu. combining his work with lecturing 研究人员；教员

Magdalen College *n.* a college founded in 1458 at Oxford University 莫德琳学院

Christ Church *n.* a college founded in 1546 at Oxford University 基督教堂学院

King's College *n.* a college founded in 1441 at Cambridge University 国王学院

St John's College *n.* a college founded in 1511 at Cambridge University 圣约翰学院

Magdalene College *n.* a college founded in 1542 at Cambridge University 玛格德琳学院

Trinity College *n.* a college founded in 1546 at Cambridge University 三一学院

court *also* **courtyard** *n.* a flat open area of ground which is surrounded by buildings or walls 庭院

the Oxford and Cambridge Boat Race *n.* an annual rowing competition between the universities of Oxford and Cambridge, which takes place on the first Saturday in April every year 牛津-剑桥大学划船比赛

the River Thames *also* **the Thames** *n.* the most important river of Britain, which passes Oxford, Windsor and London 泰晤士河

Additional Knowledge

Oxbridge

Oxbridge is a colloquial term used to refer to the universities of Oxford and Cambridge, considered together and separately from all other British universities. The two universities are the oldest and most famous universities in Britain. They are jointly regarded as being academically superior to other British universities and as enjoying and giving special privilege and prestige.

Oxford University was founded in the 12th century. There are at present 35 colleges, of which three are exclusively for female students and the rest take both men and women students. Among the best-known colleges, New College was founded in 1379; All Souls College was founded in 1437, which is unique in having no undergraduates but only fellows; Magdalen College was founded in 1458; and Christ Church was founded in 1546. The city of Oxford, although considerably more industrialized than Cambridge, is popular with tourists because of the many beautiful medieval buildings at Oxford University.

Cambridge University was founded in the 13th century. There are at present 28 colleges, of which only one is exclusively for men students and two are exclusively for women students. Among the best-known colleges, King's College was founded in 1441; St John's College was founded in 1511; Magdalene College was founded in 1542; and Trinity College was founded in 1546, which is famous for its large court and excellent library. Cambridge University has made the city of Cambridge an internationally famous tourist centre.

On the first Saturday in April every year, the Oxford and Cambridge Boat Race takes place on the River Thames in London. This annual rowing competition is between crews from the two oldest universities in Britain, founded in the 13th century.

Exercises

I. Explain each of the following:

1) education
2) early childhood education
3) pre-school child
4) nursery
5) child-care centre
6) day-care centre
7) nursery school
8) kindergarten
9) school-age child
10) primary education
11) primary school
12) grade school
13) grade
14) first-grader
15) academic year
16) compulsory school attendance law
17) full-time education
18) free education
19) independent school
20) secondary education
21) secondary school
22) junior high school
23) senior high school
24) junior middle school
25) senior middle school
26) comprehensive school
27) private school
28) higher education
29) state school
30) coeducational school
31) single-sex school
32) day school
33) boarding school
34) preparatory school
35) core subject
36) foundation subject
37) driving school
38) language school
39) evening school
40) school-leaver
41) high school graduate
42) certificate
43) diploma
44) university
45) degree
46) college
47) agricultural college
48) teachers' training college
49) law college
50) art college
51) Oxford University
52) Cambridge University
53) technical college
54) polytechnic
55) campus
56) campus university
57) bachelor's degree
58) undergraduate
59) Bachelor of Arts
60) Bachelor of Science
61) fresher
62) sophomore
63) senior
64) major
65) English major
66) graduate student
67) postgraduate
68) master's degree
69) Master of Arts
70) Master of Science
71) doctoral degree
72) doctoral candidate
73) doctor
74) Doctor of Philosophy
75) further education
76) evening class
77) adult education
78) open learning scheme
79) the Open University
80) qualification
81) lifelong education
82) course
83) tutor
84) vocational education
85) vocational training
86) Internet

87) long-distance education
88) computer-aided instruction
89) E-learning
90) online education

II. Give another way or other ways of saying each of the following:
   Model: pre-school child → child of pre-school age
   1) pre-school education →
   2) elementary school →
   3) school year →
   4) first-year pupil →
   5) secondary school →
   6) tertiary education →
   7) mixed school →
   8) prep school →
   9) independent school →
   10) night school →
   11) high school graduate →
   12) tech →
   13) poly →
   14) first degree →
   15) fresher →
   16) second-year student from a university →
   17) postgraduate student →
   18) doctorate →
   19) doctoral student →
   20) post-doctoral studies →

III. Tell what each of the following stands for:
   Modal: Prof → Professor
   1) BA →
   2) BSc →
   3) MA →
   4) MSc →
   5) PhD →

IV. Answer the following questions:
   1) What kind of education does a pre-school child receive?
   2) Who take care of and educate the children of pre-school age when their working mothers are at work?
   3) Where can the children of pre-school age be taken care of and educated?
   4) What does a pre-school child do in a nursery school?
   5) Why is pre-school education considered beneficial to pre-school children?
   6) Do the pre-school children from various areas in Britain receive education in the same manner?
   7) When do the British and American school-age children start to go to school respectively?
   8) What do the pupils learn at primary school or elementary school?
   9) When does an academic year start and end?
   10) When do the British and American children receive full-time education according to compulsory school attendance law?
   11) When do the British pupils usually transfer from primary school to secondary school?
   12) When do the British students leave secondary school?
   13) What is the difference between the two American school systems?
   14) What is the Chinese counterpart of a British secondary school or an American high school?
   15) What is the difference between a British grammar school and an American grammar school?
   16) What is the advantage of a comprehensive school in Britain?
   17) What is the difference between a British public school and an American public school?

18) What does a coeducational school enable girls to prove?
19) What is the difference between a day school and a boarding school?
20) What is the difference between a British prep school and an American prep school?
21) Why do some parents send their children to a private school?
22) Can you give the names of some of the famous British public schools?
23) What is the name of the first British girls' public school?
24) Why didn't public schools for girls appear until the 19th century in Britain?
25) Please give the names of some core subjects in a British or American school.
26) Please give the names of some foundation subjects in a British or American school.
27) Is there any difference between a British freshman and an American freshman?
28) Is there any difference between a junior in British English and a junior in American English?
29) What is the difference between a bachelor's degree and a master's degree?
30) What is the highest academic degree by a university?
31) What is the difference between a doctoral candidate and a person with a doctor's degree?
32) What is the aim of further education?
33) Why do many adults attend evening classes?
34) What are open learning schemes intended to do?
35) How do technological developments change the means of education?

Lesson Fifteen

Mass Media

Mass media are carriers of information, which traditionally include television, radio and newspapers. They play a central role in people's daily life in every country, with the functions of informing, educating, questioning, challenging, and entertaining. Technological advances have made mass communications inexpensive and immediately available to everyone. The British and American people spend more time absorbing the products of the mass communications media than in any other activity except working and sleeping.

Various television channels offer a mixture of news and current affairs, documentaries, educational programmes, children's programmes, drama, light entertainment, films, sports, and religious programmes. Nearly every household in Britain and America has at least one television set. People spend an average of 25 – 30 hours a week watching television.

In Britain, there are two main radio and television broadcasting companies. They are the British Broadcasting Corporation, or BBC; and the Independent Television Commission, or ITC. BBC broadcasts television and radio programmes. It has been under government control since 1927, but free to manage its own policy and decide the content of its programmes. BBC1 is its main television channel, which transmits mostly programmes of general interest such as news, current affairs, sports, light entertainment and children's programmes. BBC2 is its second television channel, which transmits mainly programmes that are more specialized than those of BBC1, such as documentaries, travel programmes, serious plays, concert performances, programmes on leisure interests, and international films. ITC is responsible for licensing and regulating commercial television services including cable television and satellite television services, whether delivered by digital or analogue technology. It has three commercial terrestrial television services, including ITV Channel 3, ITV Channel 4 and ITV Channel 5. They are all funded by advertising and sponsorship.

In the United States, there is no government-owned television network. Public television stations and commercial television stations coexist. Funds to operate public television come from donations by individuals and industries and, to a small degree, from the government. Public television stations offer a wide variety of high-quality entertainment and information without the annoying interruptions of commercials. People highly praise public television for its imaginative, appealing shows which help children learn basic reading concepts, valuable psychological insights, English and foreign languages. Besides, fine dramatic and musical presentations, award-winning movies, and intelligent discussions of national problems often take up the evening hours on public television. For those who seek self-improvement via TV, there are "how-to" shows in the daytime and evening, which teach cooking, skiing, sewing, guitar-playing, yoga, and dozens of other skills. College courses are also offered on public television, which give academic credit to enrolled listeners.

Commercial television in America attempts to please a vast audience of all age groups and educational levels by presenting entertainment, which can be understood by all. A typical day's commercial TV listing includes news and weather, interview shows, sports, cartoons and other children's shows, family situation comedies, melodramatic serials, movies, mysteries, westerns, and musical reviews. On commercial TV, the goal of attracting more audiences leads to a great deal of sports coverage and generally inadequate analysis of the national and international situation. Many adults in the United States are annoyed by the simplicity and triteness of most shows from commercial television.

Radio stations transmit all types of news, current affairs, music, drama, education, sports and a range of features programmes. Many years ago, families gathered around one big living-room radio. Today, almost everyone takes a small, lightweight cassette player like a Walkman with them so that they can listen to MP3 while they are walking or cycling here and there, or sitting on the bus. Because of the development of television, radio is no longer the major source of home entertainment. But the British and American people still spend many hours every week listening to radio. They turn to radio when they want the latest news quickly. Many stations broadcast up-to-the-minute news every half-hour. People tend to listen to radio for short periods. In an effort to hold audiences, many radio stations appeal to special interests. Some offer an all-news or all-music format; others broadcast professional sporting events. There are two types of radio broadcasting—AM and FM. AM is an abbreviation for amplitude modulation; while FM is an abbreviation for frequency modulation. AM is a system of broadcasting in which the strength of the sound waves varies and sometimes the sounds provided for the listener are not always very clear. FM is a method of transmitting radio waves which can be used to broadcast high quality sound. It can produce a wider range of sounds and can also broadcast in stereophonic sound. FM has now become increasingly popular. So many radios are equipped to receive both AM and FM.

More and more advanced technology has been applied to television transmission. Direct broadcasting by satellite or DBS for short, is now available in most countries. Television can be transmitted directly by satellite into people's homes. The signals from satellite broadcasting are received through specially designed aerials or "dishes", that is, satellite dishes or dish antennas. Most services are paid for by subscription.

Cable services are delivered to consumers through underground cables and are also paid for by subscription. Cable television or cable TV is a television system in which a high antenna and one or more dish antennas receive signals from distant and local stations, electronic satellite relays, etc., and transmit them by direct cable to the receivers of persons subscribing to the system. Cable TV allows subscribers to enjoy a variety of programmes and entertainment not available on network television. Broadband cable systems can carry between 30 and 65 television channels using analogue technology, as well as a full range of telecommunications services. Analogue technology includes terrestrial broadcasts, satellite television and channels delivered to cable operators by landline or videotape. But analogue technology will be replaced by digital technology, which can support up to 500 television channels. Interactive services such as video-on-demand, home shopping, home banking, security and alarm services, e-mail and high-speed Internet access are also possible on cable. Besides, cable can additionally supply television services tailored specifically for local communities.

A newspaper is a publication consisting of a number of large sheets of folded paper, on which news, articles, advertisements, and other information is printed. Newspapers, at national, regional and local level, offer readers great diversity of content. National newspapers carry news and features covering events in the capital and of national and international interest. In Britain, they are often described as quality papers or popular papers on the basis of differences in style and content. A quality paper is a daily or Sunday newspaper directed at educated readers who want full information on a wide range of public matters. Quality papers are normally broadsheet or large-sheet in format. They contain detailed news coverage and comment, authoritative editorials, a wide range of topical features written by experts in their fields, arts and literary reviews and much professional advertising. A popular paper is a daily or Sunday newspaper whose content and format are designed to appeal to people wanting news of a more entertaining character, presented more concisely. Emphasis is put on personal stories, especially when sensational, or involving a figure in the public eye, and importance is also given to sports and to entertaining features such as cartoons. Most popular papers are tabloid or small-sheet in format. They have brief and direct news reports and a large number of photographs. The style of English is often colloquial or conversational, with much use of slang, nicknames, and catchy headlines often in large, bold letters. Most cities and towns throughout Britain and America have their own regional or local newspapers. They mainly include stories of regional or local attraction. But the daily regional or local newspapers also cover national and international news, but they are often looked at from a local viewpoint.

Morning newspapers giving national and international news are distributed every morning nationwide. For instance, Britain is such a small country that it is possible for all the major daily papers to be printed in London, and such leading cities as Manchester and Glasgow during the night and be dispatched by train or lorry to the tip of Scotland and the end of Cornwall in time for breakfast the following morning. An evening newspaper usually comes out in the late afternoon and is read by people in the evening. Many cities and towns also have their own evening newspapers. A daily newspaper or a daily is a newspaper which is published every day of the week except Sunday. Daily newspapers contain news, stock market reports, sports coverage, fashions, recipes, medical information, advice on child care, and want ads. Besides, most daily papers also include television listings, film and TV reviews, and chess and bridge columns. A Sunday newspaper is a newspaper which is published on Sunday. Many newspapers are printed in colour and most produce colour supplements as part of the Sunday paper, with articles on travel, food and wine, and other leisure topics.

A magazine is a publication with a paper cover which is issued regularly, usually weekly or monthly, and which contains articles, stories, photographs and advertisements. Thousands of different magazines are published in Britain and the United States. Magazines are generally defined as business and professional titles, and consumer titles. The former category provides special groups of people with materials of relevance to their working life. Consumer titles appeal to the general public and provide readers with leisure-time information and entertainment. Within the latter category, there are general consumer titles, which have a wide appeal; and consumer specialist titles, which are aimed specifically at groups of people with particular interests and hobbies, such as motoring, gardening, fishing, stamp-collecting, photography, and classic music. Literary and political journals cater for a more academic readership. Women's magazines traditionally enjoy large readerships. They carry articles on fashions, cookery, home decoration and how to cope with family problems. Most include longer serial stories and romantic short stories too. In recent years, there has been an upsurge in the market for men's general interest magazines. There are magazines filled with stories and photographs about famous entertainers. Digest magazines consist largely of selected or abridged articles, which are reprinted from other publications.

Since industries in Britain and the United States prefer to advertise where they will reach the largest number of potential customers, the newspapers, magazines, and broadcasting stations do everything they can to hold the largest audience possible. Most newspapers, magazines and radio stations have many advertisements, which help to pay for their production. The same is true for commercial television. For instance, ITV in Britain had its first advertisement in 1955, which showed a tube of toothpaste frozen into the middle of a block of ice. But the British Broadcasting Corporation does not allow advertising on its radio or television channels. It receives its money from fees paid by TV owners for their licences. Lord Reith, the first Director-General of BBC, insisted that BBC should be a public service and that it should educate as well as entertain. This high standard has always been maintained.

Generally speaking, the communications media in Britain and the United States are private businesses operated for profit. What newspapers, magazines, radio, and TV present to the public is largely influenced by three factors—the owners' opinions, the advertisers' best interests, and the attitudes of the public.

The Internet is among the most far-reaching of recent developments in electronic communications. It plays a new and increasing important role in the provision and dissemination of information and entertainment. Broadly, it is a loose collection of computer networks around the world. It links hundreds of thousands of academic, government, military and public computer systems, giving hundreds of millions of people access to a wealth of stored information and other resources. No one owns it, and there is no centralized controlling or regulating body.

The system dates from the 1960s, when it began life in the military and academic communities in the United States. It has only assumed widespread significance in commercial and consumer terms over the last decade. It is the World Wide Web(WWW or Web) that has given the Internet its user appeal and accessibility. The Web consists of tens of millions of web pages or websites on the Internet, which can be viewed by a browser, which is a programme that provides a window in a computer screen on which pages are displayed. Users can move from page to page in search of whatever information or service they are after.

Words & Expressions

mass media *also* **media** *n.* newspapers, radio and television regarded as a group 大众媒体；媒体
carrier *n.* a vehicle or device which is used for carrying things or people 载体
information *n.* knowledge in the form of facts, news, etc. 信息
communication *n.* the activity of process of giving information to other people, using signals, such as speech, body movements or radio signals 传播；交流；交际
communications *n.* 通讯；通信 the systems and processes that are used to communicate or to broadcast information, esp. those that use electricity or radio waves *e.g.* mass communications 大众通讯；communications media 通讯媒体；mass communications media 大众通讯媒体
television *n.* a system of sending pictures and sounds by electrical signals over a distance so that people can receive them on a television set in their home 电视
channel *n.* a specific wavelength which is used to receive the television or radio programmes that are broadcast by a particular TV or radio station 频道 *e.g.* television channel 电视频道
current affairs *n.* political and social events which are of international importance or interest and which are discussed in newspapers and on radio and television programmes 时事 *e.g.* current affairs programme 时事节目
documentary *n.* a film, or a radio or television programme which provides factual information about a particular subject 纪实影片；纪实节目
programme *BrE also* **program** *AmE n.* a play, show, talk, etc. which people listen to on radio or watch on television 节目 *e.g.* educational programme 教育节目；children's programme 儿童节目；religious programme 宗教节目；travel programme 旅游节目
drama *n.* a serious play for the theatre, radio or television 戏；剧
light *a.* entertaining people without making them think very deeply 轻松的 *e.g.* light entertainment 轻松的娱乐节目
entertainment *n.* a performance which people watch for pleasure 娱乐活动；娱乐节目 *e.g.* TV entertainment 电视娱乐节目
television set *also* **television** *n.* a piece of electrical equipment which consists of a box containing a special electronic tube with a screen in front of it, on which people can watch programmes with sounds and pictures 电视机
radio broadcasting *n.* sending out of a radio programme by radio waves 无线电广播 *e.g.* radio broadcasting company 无线电广播公司
television broadcasting *n.* sending out of a TV programme by radio waves 电视广播 *e.g.* television broadcasting company 电视广播公司
British Broadcasting Corporation *also* **BBC** (*abbrev.*) *n.* a British organization which broadcasts programmes on radio and television 英国广播公司
Independent Television Commission *also* **ITC** *n.* a British TV-broadcasting organization which is funded by advertising and sponsorship 独立电视公司
Independent Television *also* **ITV** (*abbrev.*) *n.* a group of several British commercial television channels, which are controlled by ITC 英国独立电视
broadcast *v.* send out a programme by radio waves, so that it can be heard on radio or seen on television 播放 *e.g.* to broadcast a radio programme 播放无线电节目；to broadcast a television programme 播放电视节目
BBC1 *n.* the main television channel of BBC BBC 一台
BBC2 *n.* the second television channel of BBC BBC 二台

commercial television *n.* the television financed by the broadcasting of commercial advertising between programmes 商业电视 *e.g.* commercial television service 商业电视服务

television network *n.* a television company or a group of companies which usually broadcast the same programmes at the same time in different parts of the country 电视网

network television *n.* the broadcasting of TV programmes at the same time by several different television stations 网络电视

cable television *also* **cable TV** *n.* a television system in which signals are sent along wires to people's television sets after they have been transmitted to a central receiver 有线电视 *e.g.* cable television service 有线电视服务

satellite television *n.* a television system in which signals are sent to people's television sets via a satellite and received by a satellite dish on their houses 卫星电视 *e.g.* satellite television service 卫星电视服务

digital technology *n.* the technology related to communications circuits in which the information is transmitted in the form of trains of pulses, with speech and vision converted into code before such transmission where most data is already in suitable form 数字技术;数码技术

analogue technology *n.* the technology related to any form of transmission of information where the transmitted signal's information-bearing characteristic is varied in direct proportion to the intensity of the sound, or the brightness of pictures, etc., which is desired to communicate 模拟技术

terrestrial television *n.* a television system in which signals are sent to people's television sets via the landline used to connect places in communications 地面电视 *e.g.* terrestrial television service 地面电视服务

ITV Channel 3 *n.* the main television channel of ITV ITV 三台

ITV Channel 4 *n.* the second television channel of ITV ITV 四台

ITV Channel 5 *n.* the third television channel of ITV ITV 五台

fund *v.* provide money for 提供资金 *e.g.* funded by advertising 通过做广告筹集资金

advertising *n.* the activity of telling people about products and making them seem attractive so that people want to buy them 做广告 *e.g.* professional advertising 做专业广告

sponsorship *n.* the financial support which is given to sb by a sponsor 赞助

public television *AmE n.* the television in the United States, whose funds come from donations by individuals and industries and, to a small degree, from the government 公共电视 *e.g.* public television station 公共电视台

donation *n.* sth which sb gives to a charity or other organization that they wish to support 捐赠

commercial *n.* an advertisement which is broadcast on radio or television 商业广告

imaginative *a.* easily able to think of and form pictures or ideas of things which are different, interesting, or exciting, esp. things that do not exist in real life 富于想象力的

appealing *a.* pleasing and attractive 有吸引力的 *e.g.* appealing show 有吸引力的节目

skiing *n.* moving of people wearing skis and using a pair of long sticks to push themselves along, esp. as a sport or a holiday activity 滑雪

guitar *n.* a musical instrument that is made of wood and usu. has six strings, which is played by plucking or strumming the strings 吉他 *e.g.* guitar-playing 吉他演奏

yoga *n.* a type of exercise in which sb moves their body into various positions, and which helps them to become fitter, improve the way they breathe, and relax their mind 瑜伽功

credit *n.* the successful completion of a part of a higher education course 学分 *e.g.* academic credit 学分

enroll *v.* take in a person officially as a member of a group 招收 *e.g.* to enroll a student 招收学生

age group *n.* all the people in a place or organization who were born during a particular period of time 年龄组

TV listing *n.* a list of TV programmes 电视节目单

interview *n*. a conversation in which a well-known person talks to a reporter about the interesting or important things that they do, which is published in a newspaper or a magazine, or broadcast on radio or on television 访谈 *e.g.* interview show 访谈节目

cartoon *n*. a film in which the characters and scenes are drawn rather than being real people and objects 卡通片;动画片

situation comedy *n*. a type of comedy, esp. on radio or television, which shows the characters in amusing situation that were similar to everyday life 情景喜剧

mystery *n*. a story in which strange things happen that are not explained until the end 疑案推理故事

western film *also* **western** *AmE. n*. a film about life in the west of America in the 19th century 西部片

melodrama *n*. a story or play in which a lot of exciting, tragic, or serious things happen and in which people's emotions are very exaggerated 传奇剧

serial *n*. a story in a newspaper or magazine, or on radio or television which appears in a number of parts at regular times, such as once a day or once a week 连续剧;连载小说 *e.g.* melodramatic serial 传奇连续剧

review *n*. an article written in a newspaper or a magazine, or a talk given on radio or television, to express the author's opinion of a book, play, art exhibition or music 评论 *e.g.* musical review 音乐评论;arts review 艺术评论;literary review 文学评论;movie review 电影评论;TV review 电视评论

coverage *n*. the reporting in a newspaper or magazine, or on television or radio, of a particular activity or subject 报道 *e.g.* sports coverage 体育报道

simplicity *n*. the fact that sth is uncomplicated and can be understood easily 简单

triteness *n*. being dull and not original of ideas, remarks, and stories, because they have been told too many times 陈腐;老一套

radio station *also* **broadcasting station** *n*. a building with equipment for broadcasting programmes, which is used by a radio company 无线电台;广播电台;电台

feature *n*. a special programme on radio or television which is not part of a series, and which is usu. about a serious subject 专题节目 *e.g.* a range of features programmes 一系列专题节目;entertaining feature 娱乐专题节目

living room *n*. a room of a house, in which people sit and relax, but do not usu. eat 起居室

Walkman *n*. the trademark of a small cassette player with very light headphones which people carry around so that they can listen to music while they are walking, cycling, sitting on the bus, etc. 随身听

cassette player *n*. a machine which is used for recording cassettes and sometimes also playing them 卡式录音/像机;卡式放音/影机

format *n*. the way and order in which sth is arranged and presented 格式 *e.g.* all-news format 全新闻格式;all-music format 全音乐格式

sporting event *also* **sports event** *n*. a planned and organized occasion, for a sports match 体育比赛

AM *also* **amplitude modulation** *n*. a system of broadcasting in which the strength of the sound waves varies and sometimes the sounds provided for the listener are not always very clear 调幅 *e.g.* AM radio 调幅收音机

FM *also* **frequency modulation** *n*. a method of transmitting radio waves which can be used to broadcast high quality sound 调频

radio wave *n*. the form in which radio signals are thought to travel 无线电波

stereophonic sound *also* **stereo sound** *n*. the sound directed through two different speakers in a system of sound recording, broadcasting and receiving, which give an effect of greater reality 立体声

transmission *n*. the broadcasting of radio or television programmes 播送 *e.g.* television transmission 电视播送

direct broadcasting by satellite *also* **DBS** (*abbrev.*) *n*. a method of broadcasting television programmes by which signals are directly sent to people's television sets via a satellite and directly received by a satellite dish on their houses 卫星直接播送

signal *n.* a series of radio waves, light waves, electrical impulses, etc., which carry information of some kind 信号

aerial *BrE. n.* a device made of metal rods or wire, which is often attached to the outside of buildings, vehicles, radios and television sets, with the function of receiving or sending out radio or television signals 天线

antenna *AmE. n.* aerial in American English 天线 *e.g.* TV antenna 电视天线

dish antenna *also* **dish** *n.* an aerial or antenna in the form of a dish 碟形天线；"大锅"

satellite dish *n.* a piece of equipment which people need to have on their houses in order to receive satellite television 卫星碟形天线；卫星碟

subscription *n.* the arrangement by which people pay an amount of money regularly in order to receive copies of a newspaper or a magazine, or watch satellite television 订阅

cable service *n.* the service delivered to consumers through underground cables and paid for by subscription 有线服务

cable *n.* a bundle of wires inside a rubber or plastic covering, along which electricity flows or electronic signals are passed 电缆 *e.g.* underground cable 地下电缆

relay *n.* a piece of equipment which receives radio or television signals from one place and sends them on to another place 转播设备 *e.g.* satellite relay 卫星转播设备

broadband cable *n.* a cable which is capable of operating with consistent efficiency over a wide range of frequencies 宽带 *e.g.* broadband cable system 宽带系统

telecommunications *n.* the technology of sending signals and messages over long distances using electronic equipment such as radio, telephone and mobile phone 电讯；电信 *e.g.* telecommunications service 电讯服务；电信服务

landline *n.* a specific route on land used in communications when it connects places 地面线路

videotape *n.* the magnetic tape which is used to record the frequencies in an electric signal that are then converted into pictures on television 录像带

interactive service *n.* the service in which the user and the television communicate directly with each other, which includes video-on-demand, home shopping, home banking, security and alarm services 互动服务

video-on-demand *also* **VOD** (*abbrev.*) *n.* a kind of interactive service in which television programmes are available when the user needs them or asks for them 视频点播

home shopping *n.* the shopping which people do by ordering goods from their homes, using catalogues, television channels, or the Internet 家庭购物

home banking *n.* the banking business activity which people do from their homes, using television channels or the Internet 家庭银行

security *n.* safety from possible harm or loss 安全 *e.g.* security service 安全服务

alarm *n.* an automatic device which warns people of sth unpleasant or dangerous that might happen 警报 *e.g.* alarm service 警报服务；alarm system 警报系统

e-mail *also* **electronic mail** *n.* a system by which messages are sent by electronic means, without the use of paper 电子邮件

access *n.* the opportunity or right to use or see sth 使用机会；使用权 *e.g.* Internet access 互联网入网；互联网接入

tailor *v.* make sth like a plan or system suitable for a particular purpose by changing its details 使……适应特定需要

newspaper *n.* a publication consisting of a set of large folded sheets of paper, which contains news, articles, advertisements, and other information 报纸

national newspaper *n.* the newspaper distributed on a nationwide scale, which carries news and features covering events in the capital and of national and international interest 全国性报纸

quality paper *n.* a daily or Sunday newspaper which is generally thought to give serious accounts of the news and reports on business matters, industry, culture, and society 高级报纸；严肃报纸；大报

broadsheet *also* **large-sheet** *BrE n.* sth such as a newspaper or advertisement, which is printed on one large sheet of paper 宽幅报纸；宽幅广告

authoritative *a.* having a lot of knowledge or understanding of a particular subject 权威的

editorial *n.* an article in a newspaper which gives the opinion of the editor or publisher on a topic or item of news 社论 *e.g.* authoritative editorial 权威社论

topical *a.* concerning or relating to events which are happening at the present time 当前关注的；热门话题的

feature *n.* a special article in a newspaper or magazine, usu. one that does not deal with an actual news event 专题报道 *e.g.* topical feature 当前关注的专题报道

popular paper *n.* a daily or Sunday newspaper which is aimed at the needs or tastes of ordinary people and not the specialists in a particular subject 大众报纸；通俗报纸；小报

sensational *a.* intended to produce strong feelings of shock, anger, or excitement 耸人听闻的；煽情的

figure *n.* a well-known and important person 人物

in the public eye *prep. phrase* known about by everyone and often mentioned on television, in newspapers, etc. 广为人知的

tabloid *also* **small-sheet** *n.* a small sized newspaper in which the news stories and articles are short, usu. with a lot of photographs 通俗小报

report *n.* an account of sth which is published in a newspaper or magazine or on radio or television 报导 *e.g.* news report 新闻报导

colloquial *a.* suitable for ordinary, informal, or familiar conversation 口语的

conversational *a.* commonly used in conversation 会话的

slang *n.* very informal language which includes new and sometimes not polite words, and meanings, and which is often used among particular groups of people, and is usu. not used in serious speech or writing 俚语

catchy *a.* easy to remember 容易记的

headline *n.* the title of a newspaper story, printed in large letters at the top of the story, esp. on the front page 大标题；通栏标题 *e.g.* sensational headline 耸人听闻的通栏标题

bold letter *n.* a letter which is thicker and looks blacker than an ordinary printed letter 黑体字母

regional newspaper *n.* a newspaper published in a region out of the capital of a country, which mainly includes stories of regional attraction 地区性报纸

local newspaper *n.* a newspaper published in an area like a city or town, which mainly includes stories of local attraction 地方报纸

morning newspaper *also* **morning paper** *n.* a newspaper published and distributed every morning 晨报

daily newspaper *also* **daily paper**, **daily** *n.* a newspaper published from Monday to Saturday of the week 日报

Manchester *n.* a big city in England, U.K. 曼彻斯特

Glasgow *n.* a big city in Scotland, U.K. 格拉斯哥

Cornwall *n.* a place in the southwest extremity of England, U.K. 康沃尔

evening newspaper *also* **evening paper** *n.* a newspaper which usu. comes out in the late afternoon and is read by people in the evening 晚报

stock market *n.* an organization of professional people who buy and sell stocks and shares 证券交易所；the trading activity of the stock buyers and sellers 证券交易；the place where the stock buyers and sellers do

business 证券市场；股市 *e.g.* stock market report 股市报表
fashion *n.* an activity, attitude, way of behaving, etc. which is popular with a lot of people at a particular time 时尚；the styles of clothing which change quickly as people's ideas and tastes change 时装
recipe *n.* a list of ingredients and a set of instructions telling people how to mix and cook the ingredients in order to make a particular dish 烹调术；菜谱；食谱
ad *n.* an informal word for advertisement 广告 *e.g.* want ad 招聘广告；small ad 小广告；newspaper ad 报纸广告
column *n.* a vertical section of print on the page of a newspaper, magazine, etc. 栏目 *e.g.* chess and bridge column 国际象棋与桥牌栏目
Sunday newspaper also **Sunday paper** *n.* a newspaper which is published on Sunday 星期日报
supplement *n.* a separate part of a newspaper or a magazine, often dealing with particular subjects 增刊；副刊 *e.g.* colour supplement 彩色增刊
leisure *n.* the time when people are not working and they can relax and do things that they enjoy doing 休闲
topic *n.* a particular subject which people talk about or write about 话题
magazine *n.* a sort of book with a paper cover and usu. large pages, which contains written articles, photographs, and advertisements, usu. on a special subject or for a certain group of people, and which is printed and sold every week or month 杂志 *e.g.* fashion magazine 时装杂志
cover *n.* the outside part of a book or a magazine 封面 *e.g.* paper cover 纸封面；book cover 书封面；cover story 封面故事；cover girl 封面女郎
issue *v.* publish a newspaper or a magazine 出版；发行
weekly *n.* a newspaper or magazine which is published once a week 周报；周刊
monthly *n.* a magazine which is published once a month 月刊
title *n.* a particular book or magazine 特定类型书籍；特定类型杂志
business title *n.* a particular book or magazine for business people 商务类书籍；商务类杂志
professional title *n.* a particular book or magazine for professionals 专业类书籍；专业类杂志
consumer title *n.* a particular book or magazine for consumers 消费类书籍；消费类杂志 *e.g.* general consumer title 一般消费类书籍；一般消费类杂志；consumer specialist title 专门消费类书籍；专门消费类杂志
hobby *n.* sth that people enjoy doing in their spare time 业余爱好
motoring *n.* the activity relating to cars and the people who drive them 汽车驾驶
gardening *n.* the art of growing plants in a garden 园艺
journal *n.* a magazine which is published regularly and devoted to a particular profession, trade or subject 期刊 *e.g.* literary journal 文学期刊；political journal 政治期刊
women's magazine *n.* a magazine which is exclusively for women 妇女杂志
cookery *n.* the activity of cooking and preparing food 烹饪 *e.g.* cookery book 烹饪书；食谱
home decoration *n.* the art of making a room or a building look more attractive with furniture, wallpaper, and ornaments 家居装饰
short story *n.* a piece of prose fiction which is only a few pages long 短篇小说
romantic short story *n.* a short story describing or presenting love or a love affair 短篇爱情小说
serial story *n.* a story in a newspaper or magazine, which appears in a number of parts at regular times, for example, once a week or once a day 连载小说
upsurge *n.* a sudden and serious increase in sth 高潮
entertainer *n.* a person whose job is to amuse and please audiences, for example by telling jokes, singing, or dancing 演艺人员
digest *n.* a collection of written things, which are put together and published again in a more concise form

文摘 *e.g.* digest magazine 文摘杂志

abridge *v.* make a book, play, article, or other piece of work shorter by removing some parts of it 删节；节略 *e.g.* abridged article 节略的文章

licence *n.* an official document which gives a person permission to do, use, or own sth 许可证；执照 *e.g.* television licence 电视许可证；driving licence 驾驶执照

Lord Reith (1889-19?) *n.* John Charles Walsham Reith, the first Director-General of BBC, who took an active part in the early days of broadcasting in 1922, and who was knighted in 1927 雷思勋爵

the World Wide Web *also* **the WWW, the Web** *n.* a computer system which links documents and pictures into a database that is stored in computers in many different parts of the world and that people everywhere can use 万维网

web page *also* **page** *n.* a set of data or information which is designed to be viewed as part of a website 网页 *e.g.* to display a page 显示网页

website *n.* a set of data and information about a particular subject which is available on the Internet 网站 *e.g.* the Internet website 互联网网站

browser *n.* a piece of computer software which people use to search for information on the Internet, esp. on the World Wide Web 浏览器

window *n.* one of a number of areas into which a computer's screen can be divided, each of which is used to show a particular type of information 视窗 *e.g.* a window in a computer screen 计算机屏幕上的视窗

Hollywood *n.* the place in Los Angeles, the United States, where a large number of films are made 好莱坞；or the part of the American film industry which makes Hollywood films 好莱坞电影业

movie *also* **film, motion pictures** *n.* moving pictures shown on a screen, esp. at a cinema, which tell a story, or sometimes show a real situation or series of events 电影 *e.g.* American movie 美国电影；black-and-white movie 黑白影片；movie industry 电影业；to shoot motion pictures 拍电影；motion picture-making 电影制片；motion pictures corporation 电影公司

Los Angeles *n.* a city and port in southern California, the United States 洛杉矶

world war *n.* a war which involves countries all over the world 世界大战 *e.g.* World War I 第一次世界大战

golden days *n.* the days in which a person is happy and does best work 黄金时代；好日子

legendary *a.* very famous, with many stories told about a person or place 出名的

film studio *also* **studio** *n.* the buildings where a film company has its main offices and produces films 电影厂 *e.g.* Hollywood studio 好莱坞的电影厂

20th Century-Fox *n.* an American movie production company founded in 1935 二十世纪福克斯电影公司

Metro-Goldwyn-Mayer *also* **MGM** (*abbrev.*) *n.* the largest Hollywood studio founded in 1924 米特罗-高尔德温-梅耶电影公司；米高梅电影公司

Paramount *n.* one of the major studios of Hollywood's Golden Age 派拉蒙电影公司

United Artists *also* **UA** (*abbrev.*) *n.* a Hollywood film production and distribution company founded in 1919 联艺电影公司

Disney *n.* an animation studio in Hollywood, which was founded in 1923 迪斯尼动画制片厂

Columbia Pictures *also* **Columbia** *n.* an American film production and distribution company founded in 1924 哥伦比亚电影公司

Warner Brothers *n.* a film distribution company founded in 1910, which was incorporated into a movie studio in 1932 华纳兄弟公司

be in business *v. phrase* be currently operating and trading 在营业中

star *n.* a very successful and famous actor, actress, musician, or sports player 明星 *e.g.* Hollywood star 好莱坞明星

Greta Garbo (1905-1990) *n.* a Hollywood actress of the 1940's and 1950's, better known for her looks and stardom than her acting ability 葛丽泰·嘉宝

Marlen Dietrich (1901 – 1992) *n.* a famous American actress 玛琳·黛德丽

Charles Chaplin (1889 – 1977) *n.* a famous American filmmaker and actor 查理·卓别林

Gary Cooper (1901 – 1962) *n.* a famous American actor 加里·库珀

immortal *a.* famous and likely to be remembered for a long time 不朽的

film a movie *v. phrase* use a camera to take moving pictures which can be shown on a screen or on television 拍电影

location *n.* a place away from a studio where a film or part of a film is made 外景拍摄地 *e.g.* on location 在外景拍摄地

script *n.* the written version of sth which is spoken or performed, such as a play, film, or television programme 剧本；脚本

lease *v.* allow sb else to use the property in return for regular payments according to an official agreement 出租

glamour *n.* the charm and excitement which seems to surround an interesting, fashionable, and attractive person, place, or job 魅力

Beverly Hills *n.* an expensive residential area of Los Angeles, which is well-known for being the home of many movie stars and continues to carry a glamour image to the present 贝弗利山

movies house *AmE. also* **cinema** *BrE. n.* a place where people go to watch films for entertainment 电影院

screen *n.* a flat, vertical surface on which a picture is shown 屏幕 *e.g.* television screen 电视屏幕

Additional Knowledge

Hollywood

The term "Hollywood" stands symbolically for American movies.

Hollywood is a district in the city of Los Angeles, California, the United States. Movies were first made in Hollywood before World War I. Since 1911, it has been the centre of the U.S. movie industry. The constant sunshine and mild climate of southern California made it an ideal site for shooting motion pictures. Hollywood's fame and fortune reached its peak in the 1930s and 1940s, the golden days of the black and white movies.

Hollywood has been the home to many legendary film studios such as 20th Century-Fox, Metro-Goldwyn-Mayer(MGM), Paramount, United Artists, Disney, Columbia, and Warner Brothers. Most of the famous motion pictures corporations of the 1930s and 1940s, like MGM, Columbia and Warner Brothers are still very much in business. Great Hollywood stars like Greta Garbo, Marlen Dietrich, Charles Chaplin, Gary Cooper, and many others, have become immortal.

Hollywood is no longer the heart of the world's movie industry. Most movies today are filmed on location, that is to say, in the cities, in the countryside, and in any part of the world that the script demands. The Hollywood studios are still standing, but most of them have been leased to television networks. About 80% of all American TV entertainment comes from Hollywood.

Yet Hollywood has not lost all its glamour. Many movie stars own homes there, or in the neighbouring Beverly Hills and many other communities near Hollywood.

Above all, Hollywood has the glamour of the past. It is a name which will always be associated with motion picture-making. And for many years to come the old Hollywood movies will be shown again and again in movies houses and on television screens all over the world.

Exercises

I. Explain each of the following:
1) mass media
2) carrier
3) communication
4) communications
5) television channel
6) current affairs
7) documentary
8) drama
9) light entertainment
10) the British Broadcasting Corporation
11) the Independent Television Commission
12) commercial television
13) cable television
14) satellite television
15) digital technology
16) analogue technology
17) terrestrial television
18) advertising
19) sponsorship
20) public television
21) donation
22) commercials
23) skiing
24) guitar-playing
25) yoga
26) cartoon
27) family situation comedy
28) mystery
29) western
30) melodramatic serial
31) radio station
32) feature
33) living room
34) cassette player
35) Walkman
36) amplitude modulation
37) frequency modulation
38) radio wave
39) stereophonic sound
40) television transmission
41) direct broadcasting by satellite
42) aerial
43) antenna
44) dish antenna
45) satellite dish
46) satellite relay
47) network television
48) telecommunications
49) videotape
50) interactive service
51) video-on-demand
52) home shopping
53) home banking
54) security service
55) alarm service
56) electronic mail
57) Internet access
58) public matter
59) broadsheet
60) format
61) news coverage
62) editorial
63) tabloid
64) colloquial
65) conversational
66) slang
67) catchy headline
68) bold letter
69) regional newspaper
70) local newspaper
71) magazine
72) stock market

73) fashion
75) television listing
77) column
79) leisure
81) professional title
83) hobby
85) the Internet
87) web page
89) browser

74) recipe
76) programme
78) supplement
80) business title
82) consumer title
84) home decoration
86) the World Wide Web
88) website
90) a window in a computer screen

II. Give another way or other ways of saying each of the following:
   Models: television set → television
             movie → film; motion pictures
   1) mass media →
   3) sports event →
   5) aerial →
   7) e-mail →
   9) small-sheet →
   11) ad →

   2) radio station →
   4) stereo sound →
   6) dish antenna →
   8) large-sheet →
   10) daily paper →
   12) the Web →

III. Tell what each of the following stands for:
   Modal: TV → television
   1) BBC →
   3) ITV →
   5) FM →
   7) VOD →

   2) ITC →
   4) AM →
   6) DBS →
   8) the WWW →

IV. Answer the following questions:
   1) What do mass media traditionally include?
   2) What are the functions of mass media?
   3) What are the influences technological advances have made upon mass communications?
   4) Do the British and American people spend a lot of time watching TV?
   5) What programmes do various television channels provide?
   6) What are the two main radio and TV broadcasting companies in Britain?
   7) What programmes does BBC1 transmit?
   8) What programmes does BBC2 transmit?
   9) What is ITC responsible for?
   10) What are the three commercial terrestrial television services of ITC?
   11) Is there any government-owned television network in the United States?
   12) Where does American public television get its funds?
   13) Is American public television interrupted by commercials?
   14) Why do the American people highly praise their public television?
   15) In what way is television beneficial to those who seek self-improvement?
   16) What do the "how-to" shows on television teach in the United States?
   17) Does American public TV provide enrolled listeners with college courses?
   18) What is commercial television in America intended to do?

19) What does a typical day's commercial TV listing include?
20) Do American adults enjoy watching shows from commercial television?
21) Is radio still the major source of home entertainment?
22) Why do many people still listen to radio?
23) How do many radio stations make efforts to hold audiences?
24) What are the two types of radio broadcasting?
25) Why are so many radios equipped to receive both AM and FM?
26) What is the advantage of cable television, compared with network television?
27) What is the advantage of the broadband cable system?
28) What is the advantage of digital technology, compared with analogue technology?
29) Give some examples of interactive services.
30) What is the difference between a newspaper and a magazine?
31) What is the difference between a national newspaper and a regional newspaper or local newspaper?
32) What is the difference between a quality newspaper and a popular newspaper?
33) What is the difference between a daily newspaper and a Sunday newspaper?
34) What is the difference between a morning newspaper and an evening newspaper?
35) Where is London?
36) Where is Manchester?
37) Where is Glasgow?
38) Where is Cornwall?
39) What is the difference between a consumer title and a business or professional title in defining magazines?
40) What is the difference between a general consumer title and a consumer specialist title?
41) What is the difference between a magazine and a journal?
42) What is the difference between a women's magazine and a men's general interests magazine?
43) What is a digest magazine?
44) Why do most newspapers, magazines, and broadcasting stations have so many advertisements?
45) Why does BBC not allow advertising on its radio and television channels?
46) Where does BBC receive its funds?
47) What high standard has BBC always maintained?
48) What are the three factors that influence the content of the communications media?
49) What is the role that the Internet plays in the provision and dissemination of information and entertainment?
50) Who owns the Internet?

Lesson Sixteen

Network Culture

A computer network, or simply a network, is a collection of computers connected to each other. The network allows computers to communicate with each other and share resources and information. The Internet is an international computer network providing electronic mail and information for computer users around the world. People call it a network of networks.

A Web site, alternatively, a web site or a Website, is a collection of Web files on a particular subject that includes a beginning file called a home page. For example, most companies, organizations, or individuals that have Web sites have a single address that they give you. This is their home page address. From the home page, you can get to all the other pages on their site. A Web site can be confused with a Web server. A server in this context is a computer that holds the files for one or more sites. A very large Web site may reside on a number of servers located in many different geographic places.

A Web page is a resource of information that is suitable for the World Wide Web and can be accessed through a web browser. Web pages are actually what make up the World Wide Web.

E-mail, short for electronic mail and often abbreviated to e-mail, email or simply mail, is the exchange of computer-stored messages by telecommunications. Next to the post office, the telephone and the FAX machine, e-mail has become an integral part of business and personal communication today. By using an e-mail, people can compose, send, receive and store messages over electronic communication systems. Companies that are fully computerized make extensive use of e-mail because it is fast, flexible, and reliable.

Online chat is an electronic communications technology that allows people to talk to each other in real time over the Internet, but is primarily meant to refer to direct one-on-one chat or text-based group chat. You can join online chat rooms and chat with your friends and meet new people. The term chat room, or chatroom, is primarily used by mass media to describe any form of synchronous conferencing, occasionally even asynchronous conferencing.

Online services and bulletin board services can provide a variety of forums. In these forums, participants with common interests can exchange open messages. An online forum is open to all interested people and designed to enable and encourage an open debate on issues related in the information society. As a forum is a place where the discussions on related topics are made, you will see the listing of topics when you enter a forum. Each topic contains the original message and, if applicable, replies to that message. After you log in, you can open a new topic, post a new topic, or contribute a post on the web to tell others about your ideas on an issue you are interested in. If you want to answer an existing topic, you are required to make a registration. Of course, you can simply view a topic or read a thread. Online forums are also commonly referred to as Internet forums, Web forums, newsgroups, message boards, discussion boards, discussion groups, discussion forums, bulletin boards, or simply forums.

Instant messaging, often shortened to "IM" or "Iming", is the exchange of text messages through a software application in real time. In other words, it is a form of real-time communication between two or more people based on typed text. The text is conveyed through computers connected over the Internet. As instant messaging boosts communication and allows easy collaboration, it has become popular with young people because of its speed, ease of use, and privacy. Instant messaging differs from ordinary e-mail in the immediacy of the message exchange and also makes a continued exchange simpler than sending e-mail back and forth.

A blog, which is a contraction of the term "web log", is actually a website, usually maintained by an individual with regular entries of commentaries, descriptions of events, or other materials such as graphics or videos. To blog, which is used as a verb, means to maintain or add content to a blog. Many blogs provide commentaries or news on a particular subject while others function as more personal online diaries. A typical blog combines a text with images, and links to other blogs, web pages, or media related to its topic. The first feature of a blog is that its entries are commonly displayed in reverse-chronological order. The second feature is its unfiltered content. If somebody filters or edits the author, it's no longer a blog. The third feature is its comments. The ability for readers to leave comments in an interactive format is an important part of many blogs. The flip, informal, ironic tone is also common to bloggers. Besides, a hypertext links to the world outside the blog. And the bloggers tend to excerpt chunks of an attributed text, sometimes at length, from other sources. Most blogs are primarily textual, although some focus on art (artlog), photographs (photoblog), sketches (sketchblog), videos (vlog), music (MP3 blog), or audio (podcasting), which are part of a wider network of social media.

Microblogging is a type of blogging. It is a new form of communication in which users can describe their current status in short posts distributed by instant messages, mobile phones, email or the Web. People use microblogging to talk about their daily activities and to seek or share information. A microblog differs from a traditional blog in which its content is typically much smaller in size.

A blog community is basically a group of people who visit a particular blog and use the same blogging platform. This term can also be used to describe group blogs, in which members do not run individual blogs but rather all contribute to the same blog. So blog communities are not bound by country borders. They can connect bloggers sharing the same interest and discussing the same subject from different cities, countries or continents.

Chat, instant messaging and blogging facilities have been at the core of web communication, which enables you and your business to have better communication and task management.

The Internet also has such applications as remote login, file transfer and information search. Remote login is an act to access a native computer from the other computer on the network when you are connected to the Internet. Remote login occurs when a user connects to an Internet host to use its native user interface. File transfer refers to the act of transmitting files over a computer network. So it is possible to copy files from one computer on the Internet to another. And vast numbers of articles, databases, and other information are also available in this way.

Information search is looking for the information you need on the Internet with the help of a search tool or a search engine. If you're trying to find a particular page on the Internet, you can use one of the many available online search engines. A search engine is a software programme that searches documents for specified keywords and returns a list of the documents where the keywords were found. The search engines allow you to look for information in many different ways—some engines search titles or headers of documents on the web, others search the documents themselves, and still others just search other indexes or directories.

With the availability of computers and the Internet, people can study for many different qualifications—including online degrees—using online education. Online education refers to any form of teaching or learning that takes place through a computer network. Online education uses latest computer technology to deliver courses over the Internet. Instead of traveling to a college campus to attend lectures and meet tutors face-to-face, they can access this over the Internet.

The most common function used in online education is e-mail that allows students and teachers to send messages to each other. In addition, most networks also provide conferencing capabilities that let participants conduct multi-person discussions either in real time or on the basis of asynchronous conferencing. Earning an online degree has become easier than ever. Students can access changes to the syllabus and assignments by visiting a course page, communicate easily with lecturers and fellow students with e-mail, and join in discussions using message boards.

These days, lots of people can do their shopping in the comfort of their own home with the help of the Internet. Online shopping is becoming more and more popular for a number of reasons. It saves a lot of time, money and effort to buy goods on line since you do not have to go to the shops in person. You can purchase almost any product imaginable with just a few clicks of your mouse. As some customers are worried about the security and reliability of the Internet, they are reluctant to shop on line. But as online shopping has become more widespread, these worries have begun to disappear. Though many Internet users still have security worries, it hasn't slowed down the ever-increasing numbers of online shoppers.

Internet addiction has long been recognized as a social problem, which can have a devastating effect on peoples' health. Internet addicts log onto the Internet for long periods of time every day and reduce interpersonal communication and make the Internet a priority more important than family, friends and work. Students may waste too much of their youth in front of a computer screen. Adults may lose their most important years for career development. Young people are at risk of becoming addicted or dependent on the Internet, when they can't control their time spent on line. Many teenagers are addicted to the Internet and their devotion to the cyber world has created serious negative effects in their school and home lives. If their Internet access is cut off, they react strongly and some even experience physical illness. Internet addiction is now a serious public health issue that should be officially recognized as a clinical disorder.

Cyber crime, or computer crime, refers to anything done in the cyber space with a criminal intent. It consists of specific crimes dealing with computers and networks. These could be either the criminal activities in the conventional sense or could be activities, newly evolved with the growth of the new medium. Cyber crime includes acts such as hacking, uploading obscene content on the Internet, sending obscene e-mails and hacking into a person's e-banking account to withdraw money.

Computer viruses are small software programmes that are designed to spread from one computer to another and to interfere with computer operation. A virus might corrupt or delete data on your computer, use your e-mail programme to spread itself to other computers, or even erase everything on your hard disk. Computer viruses may be programmed by hackers or crackers. A hacker uses or changes the information in other people's computer systems without their knowledge or permission while a cracker gains unauthorized access to the data held on a computer system. Some people say the basic difference between a hacker and a cracker is that the former builds things, while the latter breaks them. Fortunately for us, there are a number of software programmes available to prevent, detect and kill computer viruses. So we must learn how to kill computer viruses, discover the best antivirus software, do a system's restore, and wipe out unnecessary files that hog on our computers. With the popularity of the Internet, it is increasingly difficult to guarantee the network security. Sometimes the network was breached because of hackers' visit. A firewall is an effective measure of network security. It is a set of related programmes, located at a network gateway server, which protects the resources of a private network from users who are from other networks.

As the computer can store and handle huge amounts of data, the Internet is characterized with the capacity to provide vast amounts of messages. But the voluminous information found on the Internet is often mixed with false, distorted and even spiteful messages. Another feature of the Internet is its anonymousness. Because of its anonymousness, people can vent what they feel without revealing their identity. The anonymousness of the Internet determines that people would not have their reputation damaged even if they created a disturbance intentionally on the web. Being real-time in nature, the Internet can spread information instantaneously. As a result, the Internet has become an important platform for people to express their ideas. But quite a lot of netizens are superficial in thinking and in expressing themselves. Besides, the Internet has the advantage in its quick search for needed information and in its hyperlink with other web pages, web sites and viewers. These characteristics have turned the Internet into a centre of information collection and distribution.

A netizen, also known as a cybercitizen, is a person actively involved in online communities. The word "netizen" is formed by "net" and "citizen". Netizens use the Internet to engage in activities of the extended social groups of the internetworks. They give and receive viewpoints, furnish information, foster the Internet as an intellectual and social resource, and make choices for the self-assembled communities. Generally, a netizen can be any user of the worldwide, unstructured forums of the Internet. Netizens are Internet users who utilize the networks from their home, workplace or school. They try to be conducive to the Internet's use and growth. Netizens, who know about and use the network of networks, usually have a self-imposed responsibility to make sure that it is improved in its development while encouraging free speech and open access.

  Network culture is also called cyberculture. Cyber means imaginary space, which is created when the electronic devices communicate, like network of computers. Network culture refers to the forms of culture that are heavily influenced by communication using global networks. It is the developed culture, which has sprung up around the use of the Internet for communication, entertainment, work and business.

  Network culture is characterized with openness, independence and interactivity. The openness of network culture lies in that people can publish and access all kinds of content on the web, ranging from the most banal to the most controversial. For most people, the independence of network culture means that they can read, watch and listen to anything they like, and they are almost free to do whatever they want to do on the web. For ordinary people, the interactivity of network culture implies that they can place something on the web and receive responses.

Words and Expressions

computer network *also* **network** *n*. a set of computers that are connected to each other and can be used to send or share information or messages 计算机网络；网络

Web site *also* **web site, Website, site** *n*. a collection of Web pages, images, videos or other digital assets, which is hosted on one or more web servers, *usu*. accessible to the general public 网站

file *n*. a related collection of record in data processing 文件

home page *n*. the main page of a Web site, which serves as an index or table of contents to other document stored at the site 主页

Web server *also* **server** *n*. a specialized computer that stores and manages information and acts as a hub to connect other computers and devices 网络服务器；服务器

Web page *also* **web page, webpage** *n*. a resource of information that is suitable for the World Wide Web and can be accessed through a web browse 网页

web browser *also* **browser** *n*. a software application which enables a user to display and interact with texts, images, videos, music, games and other information typically located on a Web page at a website on the World Wide Web or on a local area network 网络浏览器；浏览器

E-mail *also* **electronic mail, e-mail, email, mail** *n*. a system in which people send messages by electronic means from one computer to another via a network 电子邮件

online *a*. performed on equipment directly under the control of the central processor, while the user remaining in communication with the computer 在线的，网上的 *e.g.* online chat 网上聊天

real time *n*. point of time at which you deal with data from outside sources as rapidly as you receive them 即时

chat room *also* **chatroom** *n*. a site on the Internet where people can exchange messages about a particular subject 聊天室

synchronous conferencing *n*. communication between human beings facilitated by networked computers at the same time and speed 同步会议

asynchronous conferencing *n*. communication between human beings facilitated by networked computers not at the same time and speed 非同步会议

instant message *also* **real-time message** *n*. the message (text, audio, or video) you exchange with another person over the Internet in real time 即时信息

instant messaging *also* **IM** (*abbrev*.), **Iming** (*abbrev*.) *n*. a form of real-time communication between two or more people based on the typed text 即时通讯

electronic bulletin board *also* **bulletin board, bulletin board service, BBS** *n.* a computer system that allows people to read each other's messages and post new ones 电子布告栏;布告栏;公告板服务

forum *n.* a discussion group where users can interact through a series of posts typically contained within threads 论坛

online forum *also* **Internet forum, Web forum, discussion forum** *n.* a web application for holding discussions and posting user-generated content 在线论坛;互联网论坛;网上论坛;讨论区

newsgroup *n.* a specialized forum where users with a common interest can put information and opinions about a particular subject so they can be read by everyone who looks at the site 新闻讨论组

message board *also* **discussion board** *n.* an Internet site where people can post and read messages, *usu.* on a specific topic or an area of interest 留言板;讨论板

discussion group *n.* any system that supports group messaging such as a shared mailbox, a bulletin board system, or possibly a mailing list, used to publish messages on some particular topics 讨论组

log in *v. phrase* gain access to a computer system, *usu.* by giving a special word or name so that the computer can check whether someone is allowed to use it 登录

login *n.* a combination of personal information such as a name and password or an ID number and security code that authenticates an Internet user's identity 登录

remote login *n.* the capability of an Internet user's access to other computers on the network 远程登录

make a registration *v. phrase* record one's name in an official list 注册

topic *n.* a particular subject that you write about or discuss 话题 *e.g.* open a new topic, post a new topic, contribute a post on the web 发帖子; answer a topic, reply a topic 回帖子;跟帖子; view a topic, read a thread 看帖子;查帖子

information society *n.* a society in which economic and cultural life is critically dependent on information and communications technologies 信息社会

privacy *n.* the state of being alone and not watched or disturbed by other people 隐私

blog *also* **web log, weblog** *n.* a web site that displays in chronological order the postings by one or more individuals and *usu.* has links to comments on specific postings 博客;网络日志

blog *v.* write entries in, add material to, or maintain a web log 撰写博客

blogger *n.* one who writes an entry for a web site 博客;撰写网络日志的人

hypertext *n.* a text stored in a computer system that contains links that allow the user to move from one piece of text or document to another 超文本 *e.g.* a hypertext link on the Internet 互联网上的超文本链接

artlog *n.* a form of art sharing and publishing in the format of a blog, but differentiated by the predominant use of and focus on art work rather than a text 艺术博客

photoblog *also* **photolog, fotolog** *n.* a form of photo sharing and publishing in the format of a blog, but differentiated by the predominant use of and focus on photographs rather than a text 照片博客

sketchblog *n.* a form of sketch sharing and publishing in the format of a blog, but differentiated by the predominant use of and focus on sketches rather than a text 图片博客

vlog *n.* a form of video sharing and publishing in the format of a blog, but differentiated by the predominant use of and focus on videos rather than a text 视频博客

MP3 blog *n.* a type of blog in which the creator makes music files, normally in the MP3 format, available for download MP3 博客

podcasting *also* **personal optional digital casting** *n.* a way to receive audio broadcasts through the Internet using an automatic "feed" in a process called "subscribing" 播客;个人自选数字广播

microblogging *n.* the act of posting short messages to the Web 微型博客;微博

blog community *n.* an online community where people can share information with other users by writing a blog post, and find information by reading other users' blogs 博客社区

group blog *n*. a working group of writers who write about the same topics, and are intended to give voice to a diversity of voices within their community 群体博客;团体博客

interface *n*. a device or a system that unrelated entities use to interact 接口;界面

file transfer *n*. the movement of one or more files from one location to another 文件转移;文件传送;文件传输

database *n*. a collection of data that is organized so that its contents can easily be accessed, managed, and updated 数据库

information search *also* **Internet search, online search** *n*. a search on the Internet for the information that is needed 信息搜索;网上搜索

search tool *also* **search engine** *n*. a computer programme that performs searches for Web sites based on the words that you designate as search terms 搜索工具;搜索引擎

index *n*. a collection of all the significant terms that are found in a particular field of all the documents in the database 索引

directory *n*. a database specifically designed for information searching and browsing 目录

title *n*. a name given to a label or context that is displayed to the user 题目 *e.g.* set the title of the displayable 设置可显示组件的题目

header *n*. a unit of information that precedes a document 标题

online degree *n*. the degree awarded by an accredited online university to students in various fields 网上学位

online education *n*. education conducted at a distance, *usu*. in the form of courses or instructional units through the Internet 网络教育

syllabus *n*. a list of topics, books, etc. that students should study in a particular subject at school or college 教学大纲

course page *n*. the content of a course that can be seen on a computer screen 课程网页

online shopping *also* **Internet shopping** *n*. a way to let the consumer to buy goods on line, but without going outside 网上购物;互联网购物

mouse *n*. a small hand-held device connected to a computer by a wire, with buttons which one presses to give commands to the computer 鼠标

click *n*. a press of a computer mouse to do a computer operation 点击

Internet addiction *n*. an impulse control disorder that does not involve the use of an intoxicating drug and is very similar to pathological gambling 网络成瘾症

Internet addict *n*. one who suffers from emotional problems such as depression and anxiety-related disorders and often uses the fantasy world of the Internet to escape unpleasant feelings or stressful situations psychologically 网络成瘾者

cyber world *n*. the world of computers and communications, which implies today's fast-moving, high-technology world 计算机网络世界

cyber crime *also* **computer crime** *n*. a crime that is done through the use of a computer 网络犯罪;计算机犯罪

upload *v*. transmit data from a computer to a bulletin board service or a network 上载;上传 *e.g.* 在互联网上传淫秽内容 upload obscene content on the Internet

obscene *a*. connected with sex in a way that most people find offensive 淫秽的;色情的 *e.g.* obscene book 淫秽书籍; send obscene e-mails 发送淫秽的电子邮件

hack *v*. secretly find a way of looking at and/or changing information on sb else's computer system without permission (黑客)非法侵入 *e.g.* hack into sb's e-banking account to withdraw money 非法侵入某人电子银行账户取钱

hacker *n*. one who tries to break into computer systems, esp. in order to get secret information 黑客

cracker *n*. one who breaks into or otherwise violates the system integrity of remote machines, with malicious intent 骇客

computer virus *also* **virus** *n*. instructions that are hidden within a computer programme and are designed to cause faults or destroy data 计算机病毒;病毒

software *n*. a general term for various kinds of programmes used to operate computers and related devices 软件

programme *n*. a specific set of ordered operations for a computer to perform 程序

hard disk *n*. part of a hard disk drive, that stores and provides relatively quick access to large amounts of data on an electromagnetically charged surface or set of surfaces 硬盘

antivirus software *also* **antivirus** *n*. a software programme that is designed to identify and kill a known or potential computer virus 反病毒软件;杀病毒软件

network security *n*. the provisions made in an underlying computer network infrastructure, policies adopted by the network administrator to protect the network 网络安全

firewall *n*. a part of computer system designed to block unauthorized access while permitting outward communication 防火墙

gateway *n*. a network point that acts as an entrance to another network 网关

worm virus *also* **worm** *n*. a self-replicating computer programme 蠕虫病毒

Trojan horse *also* **trojan** *n*. a type of computer virus disguised as a programme 特洛伊木马病毒;木马病毒

anonymousness *n*. the state of having one's name unknown to the public 匿名性

identity *also* **ID** (*abbrev.*) *n*. who sb is 身份 *e.g.* reveal one's identity 暴露身份

platform *n*. a place for people to express their opinions publicly 平台

hyperlink *n*. a place in an electronic document on a computer that is linked to another electronic document 超链接 *e.g.* hyperlink with other web pages 与其他网页的超链接;click on the hyperlink 点击超链接

cyber *a*. connected with electronic communication networks, esp. the Internet 网络的 *e.g.* cyber space 网络空间;cyber café 网吧

netizen *also* **cybercitizen** *n*. a citizen of the Internet, or one who uses networked resources 网民

internetwork *n*. an interconnected system of networks, esp. computer networks 互联网络

network culture *also* **cyberculture** *n*. the culture that has emerged, or is emerging, from the use of computer networks, as for communication, entertainment and business 网络文化

openness *n*. freedom from being hidden or limited 公开性

independence *n*. freedom from being connected with, controlled by or influenced by others 独立性

interactivity *n*. capability of acting on or influencing each other 互动性

Internet predator *n*. one who uses the Internet to prey on other people, *usu.* young teens 网上掠夺者;网上行骗者

victim *n*. one who has been injured or tricked 受害者;受骗者

Additional Knowledge

What is Instant Messaging?

Instant messaging, or IM in Internet slang, consists of sending real-time messages to another Internet user. Instant messaging is comparable to chatting in your own private chat room, with only those people you choose to invite. You can create a list to keep track of welcome guests and alert you when one of them sends you a message.

Instant messaging is a bit more private than a typical chat room, and it is a much faster and simpler way to communicate than using e-mail. Since instant messaging allows users to communicate in real time, they can respond quickly to questions or comments. Instant messaging is a great way to stay in touch with family members and friends while saving money on your long distance phone bills.

As with any online activity, caution should be exercised with messaging. It is not a good idea to add people to your list unless you know something about them. Children should be supervised carefully when instant messaging is going on, and they should never add anyone to their list or agree to be added to anyone else's list without approval from their parents. Internet predators have been known to use instant messaging as well as chat rooms to seek out victims, so while instant messaging may seem safer, it is not without risks. It is also possible to obtain viruses, worms, and Trojan horses through messaging, so you should take care when accepting any files. Also, don't type anything that you wouldn't want shared with others, since instant messages can be captured and the text can be saved. Even though messaging sessions seem private, they are really not any more secure than your average e-mail. Instant messaging can be a lot of fun and it is a great way to communicate, but like anything else, it should be used with care.

Exercises

I. Explain each of the following:
1) file
2) home page
3) web page
4) web browser
5) e-mail
6) online
7) real time
8) chat room
9) instant messaging
10) online forum
11) topic
12) electronic bulletin board
13) message board
14) discussion group
15) newsgroup
16) remote login
17) information society
18) privacy
19) weblog
20) blogger
21) hypertext
22) microblogging
23) blog community
24) interface
25) database
26) information search
27) search tool
28) online education
29) online shopping
30) Internet addict
31) cyber world
32) computer virus
33) software
34) programme
35) hard disk
36) antivirus software
37) network security
38) firewall
39) gateway
40) hyperlink

II. Give another way or other ways of saying each of the following:
Models: trojan → Trojan horse
E-mail → electronic mail, e-mail, email, mail

1) Web site →
2) Web page →
3) instant message →
4) electronic bulletin board →
5) online forum →
6) message board →
7) blog →
8) photoblog →
9) podcasting →
10) information search →
11) search tool →
12) online shopping →
13) cyber crime →
14) netizen →
15) network culture →

III. Give the words or word groups in this text, which are formed by the given word or prefix:
Model: e- → e-mail, e-banking
network → computer network, internetwork, global network, private network, gateway server network, network culture, network security
1) cyber →
2) hyper- →
3) Internet →
4) online →
5) web →

IV. Tell what each of the following stands for:
Model: email → electronic mail
1) IM →
2) Iming →
3) BBS →
4) ID →
5) netizen →

V. Answer the following questions:
1) What is a computer network?
2) Why do people call the Internet a network of networks?
3) How do you differ a web site from a web server?
4) By what means can people communicate with each other from a long distance?
5) Why has e-mail been used so extensively now?
6) What can the netizens do in an online chat room?
7) What is the difference between synchronous conferencing and asynchronous conferencing?
8) What can the netizens do in an online forum?
9) What are you required to do before you reply a topic?
10) Why has instant messaging become so popular with young people?
11) In what way does instant messaging differ from ordinary e-mail?
12) What is the relationship between a blog and a website?
13) What are the characteristics of a blog?
14) Are blog communities bound by country borders?
15) Why is it possible to copy files from one computer on the Internet to another?
16) In what ways do the search engines allow people to look for information?
17) How can a person obtain an online degree?
18) Why is online shopping becoming so popular with the netizens?
19) Why is Internet addiction recognized as a clinical disorder as well as a social problem?
20) Can you give some acts that are considered as cyber crime?

21) What is the difference between a hacker and a cracker?
22) What harms can viruses do to the computers?
23) Why is a firewall considered as an effective measure of network security?
24) What can a netizen do on the web?
25) What is network culture characterized with?

Lesson Seventeen

Religion (I)

Ancient people were curious about various natural events, such as the sun, the moon, the stars, the wind, the rain and the seasons. They also wanted to know the origin of human beings. But it was difficult for them to give scientific answers. Our ancestors thought there existed a supernatural ruling power living in the heaven. It was the creator and controller of the universe, who gave man a spiritual nature which continued to exist after the death of the body. The ancient people showed respect and awe for this supernatural ruling power and imagined that it was in the form of a human being.

The worship for the supernatural ruling power developed in two ways. Some ancient people made up stories to explain the mystery of the natural events and the origin of man. These stories originated in ancient times were handed down from generation to generation, forming myths. The study or science of these myths is mythology.

Other ancient people believed in the existence of the supernatural ruling power in the form of human beings who lived somewhere in the sky. They were supernatural beings or celestial beings. Just like human beings, they were divided into two sexes: male and female. A god can refer to a supernatural being in general, and a male one in particular. A goddess is a female god. God in big letter refers to the Supreme Being in various religions, especially in Christianity, Judaism and Islam. It is considered as the creator and ruler of the universe. Religious people show reverence and respect for gods and goddesses who are thought holy, divine, and sacred. A religion is a particular system of belief in a god or gods and the activities and behaviours that are connected with this system. Some scholars make religious studies. The study or science of the nature of God and of the foundations and formations of religious beliefs is theology.

Theism is the belief in the existence of a god or gods while atheism is the belief that no god exists. Pantheism is the belief that God is everything in nature and the universe and that everything in nature and the universe is God. Polytheism is the belief in and worship of more than one god. And monotheism is the belief that there is only one God.

In the world there are three geographical areas where religions were originated. They are India, China and Japan, and the Middle East. In India, such religions as Hinduism, Sikhism, Buddhism and Jainism were originated. Hinduism is an Indian religion characterized by belief in destiny and reincarnation. Destiny refers to the power that some people believe decides what will happen to them in the future. Reincarnation refers to the belief that after someone dies their soul enters a new human or animal body and lives again. As Hinduism is also characterized by worship of several gods, it is polytheism. Sikhism is the religion of the Sikhs in India which was separated from Hinduism in the 16th century and is based on a belief in only one God. It upholds religious toleration, equality and fraternity, and opposes worship of idols. The Golden Temple in Amritsar in India is the holy place of the

Sikhs. Jainism is a religion of India that is against violence towards any living things.

In China, Confucianism and Taoism were originated. Confucianism was founded by Confucius. Chinese scholars think Confucianism is only a school of philosophical thought for it is a belief in Confucius as a philosopher and a teacher; while Western scholars think it is a religion for Confucius was worshiped from generation to generation in the temple. Taoism is another important school of philosophical thought developed in ancient China on the basis of the writings of Lao Zi(or Lao Tzu, transcribed by foreign scholars). This way of thought emphasizes a natural and simple way of life. Taoism, as a school of philosophical thought, advocates Tao, which is the natural force that unites all things in the universe. In ancient China, Taoism was also developed into a religion which believes that people should lead a simple, honest life and not interfere with the course of natural events. In later times, it was concerned with magic and good fortune.

In Japan, Shinto or Shintoism was originated. It was the ancient religion of Japan that has gods who represent various parts of nature, and gives great importance to people who died in the past.

In the Middle East, Zoroastrianism, Judaism, Christianity and Islam were originated. Zoroastrianism was an ancient Persian religion founded by Zoroaster, the Persian religious reformer who lived about 6th century B.C. Judaism is the religion of the Jews or the Jewish people. This Jewish religion is based on *the Old Testament of the Bible*, *the Talmud*, and the later teachings of the Rabbis who were Jewish religious leaders, especially those who are in charge of a synagogue, that is, a building where Jews meet to worship or to study their religion, and who are qualified to teach Judaism, or who are experts on Jewish laws. *The Talmud* is the collection of writings that make up Jewish laws which governs the religious and non-religious life of Orthodox Jews. There are three major denominations in Judaism, which are Orthodox, Conservative and Reform. During the Sabbath, which is observed from sundown Friday until sundown Saturday. Orthodox Jews do not ride or conduct business. Jewish tradition imposes certain dietary restrictions, prohibiting pork and certain seafoods and forbidding the serving of milk products at meals which include meat or poultry. But Reform Judaism does not impose these restrictions.

The three great religions of the world include Buddhism, Islam and Christianity. Buddhism is an Asian religion based on the teachings of the North Indian philosopher Gautama Siddartha in the 6th century B.C. As the founder of Buddhism, he was called Sakya-Muni by the Buddhists, which means the sage of Sakya. The Buddhists also address him Buddha respectfully. Buddhism is an old religion but is still influential in the world. As early as in 2 B.C., Buddhism was introduced to China. Zen Buddhism or Zen is a Japanese form of Buddhism introduced from China. It states that one must look inside oneself for understanding rather than depend on learning through religious writings, and aims for enlightenment which is the state of freedom from desire and suffering, leading to union with the spirit of the universe. It stresses the importance of meditation, through which people carry out the practice at emptying the mind of thought or fixing the attention on one matter. Zen is now very popular in the Western world.

Islam is the Muslim religion based on the teachings of Muhammad, which can also be spelt as Muhammed, Mohammad or Mohammed. This Muslim religion teaches that there is only one God. Allah is the name of God in Islam. As the founder of the Muslim religion, Muhammad is considered as His Prophet or the Prophet, who teaches religion and claims to be inspired by Allah. Among Muslims and among Arabs of all faiths, a Muslim, a Moslem, a Muhammadan or a Mohammedan is a believer of Islam and a follower of Muhammad. Islam can also be called Islamism, Muhammadanism, Muhammedanism, Mohammadanism or Mohammedanism. Some people refer to Islam when they are talking about all the countries where Islam is the main religion. As Muhammad was born in Mecca, a city in Saudi Arabia, it has become the holiest city and the spiritual centre of Islam. All Muslims face towards Mecca when they say their daily prayers. Every year, hundreds of thousands of Muslims from various countries go to Mecca to pay their tributes to Muhammad, the founder of Islam. They are pilgrims who make their pilgrimage to Mecca. The sacred book of the Muslims is *the Koran*, which is written in Arabic, containing the Prophet Muhammad's revelations. They are signs or explanations from Muhammad about God's nature and purpose.

The English-speaking countries are generally considered as Christian countries where many people believe in Christianity. Christianity is the religion based on the life and teachings of Jesus Christ. He is the founder of Christianity. According to the doctrine of Christianity, the Trinity is the union of the three forms of God as one God. The three forms of God are the Father, the Son and the Holy Spirit. Jesus Christ is the Son of God. The holy book of Christianity *is the Bible*, which consists of *the Old Testament* and *the New Testament*. The former tells the history of the Jews and their beliefs, while the latter is concerned with the teachings of Jesus Christ and his earliest followers. Christianity is very influential ideologically among the English-speaking people. A Christian is a believer of Christianity.

There are a few important festivals in the West in connection with Jesus Christ. Christmas is a festival in celebration of the birth of Jesus Christ on December 25. Virgin Birth refers to the birth of Christ, which Christians believe to have been caused by God rather than by ordinary sexual union. Jesus Christ was born in human form of the Virgin Mary at Bethlehem which was six miles to the south of Jerusalem in Palestine, in the early days of the Roman Europe. Jerusalem is the holy place of Islam, Judaism and Christianity. Jesus Christ appeared as a prophet with miraculous powers. He had a band of disciples of whom twelve were chosen by himself to spread his teachings. They were called Apostles. They were often sent out by Jesus Christ to spread his teaching and message to the world. Later, he was betrayed by one of his disciples, Judas, and was persecuted by the Roman Governor. Now Judas is often used in a derogatory sense to refer to a traitor or a disloyal person who betrays his friends and secretly helps their enemies.

Jesus Christ was put to death by being nailed on a cross or being crucified. It is called the Crucifixion of Jesus Christ. The model of the Cross with the figure of Jesus Christ on it is called a crucifix. In this way, he made atonement for human sin. After three days, he rose from the dead and ascended visibly into Heaven. This is called the Resurrection of Jesus Christ. Easter is another important Christian festival, which commemorates the Resurrection of Jesus Christ. Now it is fixed on the first Sunday after the second Saturday in April. According to Christian belief, resurrection also refers to the return of all dead people to life at the end of the world.

His apostles established the Christian Church. A church can be a building used for public Christian worship. A church can also mean a sect or a denomination of Christianity, that is, a particular group of Christians who have their own beliefs, clergy, and forms of worship. The Church can refer to the Christian religion regarded as an established institution or to all Christians regarded as a group. St. Paul carried Christianity to Rome, which later adopted it as the official religion.

The Roman Catholic Church was the first main branch of Christianity. Roman Catholicism is the faith of the Roman Catholic Church. A Roman Catholic or a Catholic is a member of the Roman Catholic Church, who acknowledges the supremacy of the Pope. The Pope is the leader of the Roman Catholic Church. He is directly addressed as Your Holiness. He is indirectly addressed as His Holiness the Pope. The papal government is the headquarters of the Roman Catholic Church, which is located in the Vatican City. The Vatican City is a small city within Rome. The Vatican may refer to the Pope's residence in Rome or the papal government. The Pope is also the Bishop of Rome at the same time. A bishop is a senior clergyman in charge of the work of the Christian Church in a city or a district. The Pope is elected by the Sacred College which consists of 70 members who are called Cardinals. A Cardinal is a senior Roman Catholic priest who elects the Pope. A Catholic priest or a Catholic father is a person appointed to perform religious duties and ceremonies in the Roman Catholic Church.

A monastery or a monastic house is a building in which monks live as a secluded community. They live together under religious vows. A prior is the head of a monastery. A priory is a monastery governed by a prior. An abbey is a building in which monks live or used to live as a community under an abbot in the service of God. An abbot is the head of an abbey or a monastery. A monk is a member of a religious community of men who live together in a monastery of the Roman Catholic Church apart from the rest of society and who have made solemn promises, especially not to marry and not to have any possessions. A brother, with brethren as its plural form, is a member of a religious order, especially a monk. A friar is a monk of certain Roman Catholic religious orders which refer to a state of being a priest or other person permitted to perform Christian services and duties. And he works with people in the outside world rather than living in retreat. A friary is a building in which friars live.

A convent, a nunnery or a house of nuns is a building in which nuns live as a secluded community. They live together under religious vows. A prioress is the head of a convent. A priory can also be a convent governed by a prioress. An abbey can also be a building in which nuns live as a community under an abbess in the service of God. An abbess is the head of a convent or a nunnery. A nun is a woman who, usually after taking religious vows, lives a secluded life in the service of God, with other women in a convent or a nunnery. A sister is a nun or a member of certain female religious orders.

Words & Expressions

religion n. a particular system of belief in a god or gods and the activities and behaviours that are connected with this system 宗教

natural event *n.* existence or happening such as the sun, the moon, the stars, the wind, the rain and the seasons, which are not caused or controlled by people 自然现象

human being *n.* a man, woman or a child, not an animal 人

ancestor *n.* a person from whom one is descended, esp. one who lived a long time ago 祖先 *syn.* **forefather** 祖先

man *n.* referring to the human race or human beings in general, instead of a single male person 人类 *syn.* **mankind, humankind, humans, human beings, human race** 人类 *e.g.* the origin of man 人类起源

supernatural *a.* of creatures, forces and events which are believed by some people to exist or happen, or to be caused by the powers of spirits, gods and magic, although they are impossible to explain by scientific laws 超自然的 *e.g.* supernatural ruling power 超自然的统治力量

heaven *n.* a place where God or the gods are supposed to live; or a place of complete happiness where the souls of good people are believed to go after they die 天堂；极乐世界

universe *n.* the whole of space, including all the stars and planets, and all other things that exist in it 宇宙

awe *n.* a feeling of respect mixed with fear and amazement 敬畏

worship *n.* strong usu. religious feelings of love, respect and admiration, esp. when shown to God or a god 崇拜

mystery *n.* a strange secret nature or quality of sth which cannot be explained or understood 奥秘 *e.g.* the mystery of the natural events 自然现象的奥秘

myth *n.* an ancient story which was made up to explain natural events or to justify religious beliefs 神话

mythology *n.* the study or science of myths 神话学 *e.g.* Greek and Roman mythology 希腊罗马神话

being *n.* a living thing, esp. a person 生命体（尤指人）*e.g.* human being 人；supernatural being 超自然生命体（神）；Supreme Being 至高无上的上帝

celestial *a.* of the sky or the heaven 天上的 *e.g.* celestial being 天神

god *n.* a being or spirit that is believed in many religions to have power over a particular part of the world or nature; a supernatural being in general, and a male one in particular 神

God *n.* the being or spirit that is worshipped as the creator and ruler of the universe, esp. in the Christian, Jewish and Muslim religions 上帝；主

goddess *n.* a female being or spirit that is believed in many religions to have power over a particular part of the world or nature; a female god 女神

Christianity *n.* the religion which is based on the teachings of Jesus Christ and on the belief that he was the Son of God 基督教

Judaism *n.* the religion of the Jewish people, which is based on *the Old Testament of the Bible*, and on the Jewish book of laws and traditions 犹太教

Islam *also* **Islamism, Muhammadanism, Muhammedanism, Mohammadanism, Mohammedanism** *n.* the religion of the Muslims, which teaches that there is only one God and that Muhammad is His Prophet 伊斯兰教

Muslim *also* **Moslem, Muhammadan, Mohammedan** *n.* a person who believes in Islam and follows its founder Muhammad, and lives according to its rules 穆斯林

holy *a.* belonging or relating to a god or goddess 神圣的 *syn* **divine, sacred** 神的

theology *n.* the study of religion and God 神学

theism *n.* the belief in the existence of a god or gods 有神论；有神教

atheism *n.* the belief that there is no god 无神论；无神教

pantheism *n.* the belief that God is everything and that everything is God 泛神论；泛神教

polytheism *n.* the belief in and worship of more than one god 多神论；多神教

monotheism *n.* the belief that there is only one God 一神论；一神教

Hinduism *n.* an Indian religion which has many gods and teaches that people live again after they die 印度教

destiny *n*. the power which decides the course of events and decides what will certainly happen in the future 天命

reincarnation *n*. the belief that after sb dies his spirit will be born again and live in the body of another person or animal 转世

Sikhism *n*. the religion of the Sikhs in India which was developed from Hinduism in the 16th century and is based on a belief in only one God 锡克教

Sikh *n*. a person who believes in the Indian religion of Sikhism and follows its teachings 锡克教徒

religious toleration *n*. allowing the existence of religious variety 宗教宽容

fraternity *n*. friendship between groups of people 友爱

idol *n*. an image worshipped as a god 偶像 *e.g.* worship of idols; idol worship 偶像崇拜

the Golden Temple *n*. the holy place of the Sikhs, located in Amritsar in India 金庙

Amritsar *n*. the holy town of the Sikhs, located in the northwest of India 阿姆利则

Buddhism *n*. an ancient Asian religion which teaches people that the way to end suffering is by overcoming their desires 佛教

Buddhist *n*. a person who believes in Buddhism 佛教徒

Gautama Siddartha (565 – 486 B.C.) *n*. a North Indian philosopher in the 6th century B.C., the founder of Buddhism 乔答摩·悉达多

Sakya-Muni *n*. another way the Buddhists address Gautama Siddartha, which means the sage of Sakya 释迦牟尼

Buddha *n*. another way the Buddhists address Sakya-Muni respectfully 佛祖;佛陀;佛

Jainism *n*. an Indian religion which is against violence towards any living things 耆那教

Confucianism *n*. a Chinese school of thought which teaches that one should be loyal to one's family, friends and rulers and treat others as one would like to be treated 儒家;儒教

Confucius (551 – 479 B.C.) *n*. an ancient Chinese philosopher and teacher, the founder of Confucianism 孔子

Lao Zi *also* **Lao Tzu** *n*. an ancient Chinese philosopher, the founder of Taoism 老子

Taoism *n*. a Chinese school of thought and also a religion developed in ancient China teaching a simple way of life and the principle of not trying to change the natural course of events, also in later times concerned with magic and good fortune 道家;道教

Tao *n*. the natural force which unites all things in the universe, according to Taoism 道

Shinto *also* **Shintoism** *n*. the ancient religion of Japan, including the worship of gods that represent various parts of nature, and of the past members of one's family 神道教

Zoroastrianism *n*. an ancient Persian religion founded by Zoroaster, the Persian religious reformer who lived about 6th century B.C. 琐罗亚斯德教

Persia *n*. the old name of Iran 波斯(伊朗的旧称)

Persian *a*. relating to Persia 波斯的

Jew *n*. a person who believes in and practises the religion of Judaism 犹太教徒;a member of the Jewish people who lived in ancient times in the land of Israel, some of whom now live in the modern state of Israel, and others in various countries throughout the world 犹太人

Jewish *a*. relating to the Jews 犹太的 *e.g.* the Jewish people 犹太人民;the Jewish religion 犹太教

Orthodox Jews *n*. one of the three major denominations in Judaism 正统派犹太教徒

Conservative Jews *n*. one of the three major denominations in Judaism 保守派犹太教徒

Reform Jews *n*. one of the three major denominations in Judaism 改革派犹太教徒

the Old Testament *n*. the first part of *the Bible*, containing Jewish writings, mostly about the history of the Jewish people 《旧约全书》

the New Testament *n*. the second part of *the Bible*, dealing with the life of Jesus Christ and with Christianity in the early Church《新约全书》

the Talmud *n*. the collection of writings that make up Jewish laws about religious and non-religious life《塔木德经》

Rabbi *n*. an established Jewish priest 拉比（犹太教宗教领袖）

synagogue *n*. a building where Jews meet for religious worship 犹太教堂

sect *n*. a group of people that has separated from a larger group and has a particular set of religious or political beliefs 派别 *e.g.* religious sect 宗教派别

denomination *n*. a religious group which is part of a larger religious body 教派

Sabbath *n*. the day of the week when members of some religious groups, esp. Jews and Christians, do not work; Saturday, kept as a day of rest and worship by Jews and some Christians; or Sunday, kept as a day of rest and worship by most Christian churches 安息日

sundown *n*. sunset 日落

dietary *a*. eating special kinds of food 特别饮食的；忌口的

Zen Buddhism *also* **Zen** *n*. a Japanese form of Buddhism introduced from China 禅宗；禅

enlightenment *n*. the state of freedom from desire and suffering, leading to union with the spirit of the universe, according to Buddhism 彻悟

meditation *n*. the practice of training the mind and body to become less active for certain regular periods, esp. so as to be able to think deep religious thoughts 坐禅

Muhammad *also* **Muhammed**, **Mohammad**, **Mohammed** (570-632) *n*. the founder of Islam, who is considered as Allah's Prophet, His Prophet or the Prophet 穆罕默德

prophet *n*. a person who is believed to be chosen by God to say the things that God wants to tell people 先知 *e.g.* the Prophet Muhammad 先知穆罕默德

Allah *n*. the name of God in Islam 安拉；真主

Mecca *n*. a city in Saudi Arabia, the birthplace of Muhammad, and the holiest city and the spiritual centre of Islam 麦加

Saudi Arabia *n*. a country in the Middle East 沙特阿拉伯

the Koran *n*. the sacred book of the Muslims, which is written in Arabic and forms the basis of the religion of Islam《古兰经》

Arabic *n*. a language spoken by the Arab people who live in the Middle East and in parts of North Africa 阿拉伯语

revelation *n*. the making known of the truth by God 启示

Jesus Christ *n*. the founder of Christianity, the Son of God 耶稣基督

Trinity *n*. the union of the three forms of God as one God, according to the doctrine of Christianity 三位一体

the Father *n*. one of the three forms of God 圣父

the Son *n*. one of the three forms of God 圣子

the Holy Spirit *n*. one of the three forms of God; God in the form of a spirit 圣灵

Christian *n*. a believer of Christianity 基督徒

Christmas *n*. a festival in celebration of the birth of Jesus Christ on December 25 圣诞节

Virgin Birth *n*. the doctrine that Jesus was miraculously conceived by the Virgin Mary 圣灵感孕；童贞女之子

Virgin Mary *also* **the Blessed Virgin**, **Virgin** *n*. mother of Christ 童贞女马利亚

Bethlehem *n*. the birthplace of Jesus Christ, which was six miles to the south of Jerusalem in Palestine, in the early days of the Roman Europe 伯利恒

Jerusalem *n*. the holy place of Islam, Judaism and Christianity 耶路撒冷

disciple *n*. a person who believes, supports and uses the ideas of his leader or superior 门徒 *e.g.* Jesus and his disciples 耶稣及其门徒

Apostle *n*. any of the 12 followers of Jesus Christ chosen by him to spread his teaching and message to the world 使徒

Judas *n*. one of Jesus Christ's 12 disciples, who betrayed him 犹大; a disloyal person who secretly helps the enemies of his friends 叛徒

Roman Governor *n*. a person who was responsible for the political administration of a region in the Roman Empire 罗马总督

cross *n*. an upright post with a bar crossing it near the top, on which people were tied or nailed and left to die as a punishment in ancient times 十字架 *e.g.* Jesus Christ was put do death by being nailed on a cross. 耶稣基督被钉在十字架上处死。

the cross *n*. the shape of a cross as the sign of the Christian faith 十字 *e.g.* He made the sign of the cross. (= He made a hand movement down and across the chest.) 他在胸前画十字。

crucify *v*. kill sb by tying and nailing him to a cross and leave him there to die 将……钉在十字架上

Crucifixion *n*. the death of Jesus Christ by being tied and nailed to a cross and left there 耶稣基督蒙难

crucifix *n*. a cross with a figure of Jesus Christ on it 带耶稣基督像的十字架

make atonement *v. phrase* atone; make repayment for a crime or a sin 救赎 *e.g.* By being crucified, Jesus Christ made atonement for human sin. 耶稣基督被钉在十字架上,以此为人类罪恶救赎。

sin *n*. behaviour which is considered to be very bad and immoral 罪 *e.g.* human sin 人之罪; original sin 原罪

Resurrection *n*. the event in which Jesus Christ came back to life three days after he had been crucified 耶稣基督复活

Easter *n*. an important Christian religious festival when Christians celebrate the Resurrection of Jesus Christ 复活节

church *n*. a building in which Christians worship 教堂; one of the groups of people within the Christian religion, who have their own beliefs, clergy, and forms of worship 教会; 教派

the Christian Church *also* **the Church** *n*. the Christian religion regarded as an established institution or to all Christians regarded as a group 基督教会

saint *n*. a dead person who has been officially recognized by a Christian church as deserving special honour, because their life was very good or holy 圣徒

Saint *also* **St.** (*abbrev.*) *n*. a title before a saint's name 圣

St. Paul *n*. the co-founder (with St. Peter) of the Christian church, who carried Christianity to Rome 圣保罗

Rome *n*. capital of the Roman Empire 罗马

Roman Catholic Church *n*. the first main branch of Christianity, whose leader, the Pope, rules from Rome 罗马天主教会

Roman Catholicism *also* **Catholicism** *n*. the faith of the Roman Catholic Church 天主教教义

Roman Catholic *also* **Catholic** *n*. a member of the Roman Catholic Church, who accepts the Pope as its leader 天主教徒

Pope *n*. the head of the Roman Catholic Church 教皇

Your Holiness *n*. a title directly addressed to the Pope 教皇陛下

His Holiness the Pope *n*. a title indirectly addressed to the Pope 教皇陛下

papal government *n*. the headquarters of the Roman Catholic Church, which is located in the Vatican City 教廷

Vatican City *n*. a small city within Rome 梵蒂冈城

the Vatican *n*. the group of buildings in Rome in which the Pope lives and where the central administration of the Roman Catholic Church has its offices 梵蒂冈

clergy *n*. the people who are members of the priesthood and who are allowed to perform religious services in a particular church or temple, esp. in the Christian church 全体神职人员

clergyman *n.* a male member of the clergy 神职人员;牧师

cardinal *n.* one of the members of the clergy of high rank in the Catholic church who elect the Pope and advise him 红衣主教;枢机主教

Sacred College *n.* a group of 70 Cardinals who elect the Pope and advise him 枢机主教团

Catholic priest *also* **Catholic father** *n.* a person appointed to perform religious duties and ceremonies in the Roman Catholic Church 神甫;神父

monastery *also* **monastic house** *n.* a building or a collection of buildings in which a group of monks live as a secluded community 男修道院

monk *n.* a member of a male religious community 僧侣

prior *n.* the head of a monastery 男修道院长

priory *n.* a monastery governed by a prior 男修道院

abbey *n.* a church with buildings attached to it in which monks or nuns live or used to live as a community under an abbot or an abbess in the service of God 修道院

abbot *n.* a monk who is in charge of the other monks in an abbey or a monastery 修道院长

brother (**brethren** *plural*) *n.* a male member of a religious order, esp. a monk, who belongs to a religious institution such as a monastery 修士

friar *n.* a male member of a Catholic religious order 修士

friary *n.* a building in which friars live 男修道院

convent *also* **nunnery**, **house of nuns** *n.* a building in which nuns live as a secluded community 女修道院

prioress *n.* the head of a convent 女修道院长

priory *n.* a convent governed by a prioress 女修道院

abbess *n.* the head of a convent or a nunnery 女修道院长

nun *n.* a member of a female religious community like a convent or a nunnery 修女

sister *n.* a nun or a member of a female religious order 修女

Christmas Day *n.* December 25th, the central day of the Christmas season, on which people celebrate Christmas, give each other cards and presents, and eat special food 圣诞日

Christmas season *also* **Christmas time** *n.* a period of time which traditionally begins on Christmas Eve and continues until Twelfth Night 圣诞节期间

Christmas Eve *n.* December 24th, the day before Christmas Day 圣诞夜;圣诞前夕

Boxing Day *n.* December 26th, the day after Christmas Day, on which people used to have the custom of giving Christmas boxes, or gifts of money, to servants and tradesmen 节礼日

Twelfth Night *n.* January 6th, the twelfth day after Christmas Day, which is the traditional end of the celebrations of Christmas and the New Year 第十二夜

church service *n.* a formal religious ceremony which is held on a particular occasion or at a particular time in the church 教堂仪式

Christmas stocking *n.* a stocking traditionally hanging up at the head of a child's bed for Santa Claus to fill with presents during the night 圣诞之袜

Father Christmas *also* **Santa Claus** *n.* an imaginary old man with a red coat and a long white beard who, children believe, visits them and brings presents at Christmas 圣诞老人

Santa Claus *n.* another name for Father Christmas 圣诞老人

family reunion *n.* a party attended by members of the same family, who have not seen each other for a long time 家庭聚会

Christmas dinner *n.* a traditional midday meal, which usually includes roast turkey and Christmas pudding with mince pies, and accompanied by wine 圣诞午餐

Christmas pudding *n.* a special pudding which is made from dried fruit, spices and suet, and eaten at

Christmas 圣诞布丁

pudding *n*. a sweet dish cooked with flour, milk, eggs, fruit and other ingredients, and usu. served hot 布丁 *e.g.* Christmas pudding 圣诞布丁

holly *n*. a tree with bright red berries and shiny, dark green, prickly leaves, which is often used to decorate houses at Christmas 冬青树

cracker *n*. a hollow cardboard tube covered with coloured paper and usu. containing a small toy and a paper hat, which makes a sharp sound when pulled apart at a party or a meal, esp. at Christmas dinner 彩色拉爆

Christmas card *n*. a greeting card sent to a person's family member, relative or friend at Christmas 圣诞卡

Christmas tree *n*. a fir tree or an artificial tree that looks like a fir tree, decorated with small, brightly-coloured lights and balls, and put somewhere in the house at Christmas 圣诞树

Additional Knowledge

Christmas

The Christmas season traditionally begins on Christmas Eve and continues until Twelfth Night.

December 24th, the day before Christmas Day, is Christmas Eve. It is a traditional time for parties. Many work places, including shops and banks, close earlier than usual. In the late evening, many people go to a church service. Children, on going to bed, traditionally hang up a Christmas stocking at the head of their bed for Santa Claus to fill with presents during the night. Santa Claus, or called Father Christmas, is an old man with a red coat and a long white beard who, children believe, brings presents at Christmas. Actually, this role is often played by a child's parent.

Christmas Day, December 25th, is the central day of the Christmas season and a traditional family reunion day. On this day, many people attend a church service, open their presents and eat a Christmas dinner. Christmas dinner is a traditional midday meal, which usually includes roast turkey and Christmas pudding with mince pies, and accompanied by wine. Christmas pudding is a rich steamed pudding containing fried fruit, spices and often brandy, served as part of a Christmas dinner and traditionally decorated with a small piece of holly planted in the top. People often pull crackers and wear the paper hats contained in them throughout the meal.

At Christmas time, people send Christmas cards to each other. The Christmas card usually has a picture on the front and a message inside. Decorating the Christmas tree is part of the Christmas festivities. It is a special tree put somewhere in the house. Usually it is a fir tree decorated with small, brightly-coloured lights and small coloured glass ornaments. Now people also use an artificial tree which looks like a fir tree as the Christmas tree, for the sake of environmental protection.

The day following Christmas Day, December 26th, is Boxing Day. Officially, if December 26th is a Sunday, December 27th will be Boxing Day. It was formerly the custom to give Christmas boxes, or gifts of money, to servants and tradesmen on this day. Today, many people still give an annual Christmas gift to regular callers such dustmen and paperboys.

The twelfth day after Christmas Day, January 6th, is Twelfth Night. It is the traditional end of the celebrations of Christmas and the New Year. On this day, Christmas decorations are usually taken down, as are Christmas cards that have been on display since Christmas Day or earlier.

Exercises

I. Explain each of the following:
1) ancestor
2) supernatural ruling power
3) supernatural being
4) celestial being
5) human being
6) Supreme Being
7) religion
8) theism
9) pantheism
10) atheism
11) Hinduism
12) Sikhism
13) Buddhism
14) Jainism
15) destiny
16) reincarnation
17) Confucianism
18) Shinto
19) Zoroastrianism
20) Judaism
21) *the Old Testament*
22) *the New Testament*
23) Christianity
24) Islam
25) Rabbi
26) Sabbath
27) Buddha
28) Zen
29) Allah
30) Muslim
31) Mecca
32) *the Koran*
33) Arabic
34) pilgrim
35) revelation
36) Christian country
37) the Trinity
38) Christmas
39) Virgin Mary
40) Jerusalem
41) Apostles
42) the Crucifixion of Jesus Christ
43) the Resurrection of Jesus Christ
44) Easter
45) the Christian Church
46) the Roman Catholic Church
47) Roman Catholicism
48) Pope
49) papal government
50) the Vatican
51) the Sacred College
52) Cardinal
53) Catholic priest
54) monastery
55) prior
56) abbot
57) monk
58) brethren
59) friar
60) sister

II. Give another way or other ways of saying each of the following:
Models: origin of human beings → origin of man
holy → divine, sacred
1) female god →
2) worship of many gods →
3) belief in only one God →
4) Shinto →

5) believer of Buddhism →
6) Zen →
7) Muhammad →
8) believer of Christianity →
9) be nailed on a cross →
10) Roman Catholic →
11) Catholic father →
12) monastic house →
13) house of nuns →
14) head of an abbey →
15) head of a convent →

III. Fill in the blanks:
Model: Confucius is the founder of _____.
→Confucius is the founder of Confucianism.
1) Zoroaster is the founder of _____.
2) Sakya-Muni is the founder of _____.
3) Muhammad is the founder of _____.
4) Jesus Christ is the founder of _____.

IV. Answer the following questions:
1) Give some examples of natural events.
2) How were myths formed?
3) What is the difference between god and God?
4) What is the difference between mythology and theology?
5) Where are the three geographical areas where religions were originated?
6) What religions were originated from India?
7) What is the holy town of the Sikhs in India?
8) Where were Confucianism and Taoism originated?
9) Who was Lao Zi?
10) What religions were originated in the Middle East?
11) What is Judaism based on?
12) What are the three major denominations in Judaism?
13) What are the three world religions?
14) Who was Gautama Siddartha?
15) When was Buddhism introduced to China?
16) Is Islam monotheism or polytheism?
17) Where was Muhammad born?
18) What is the language of the Arab people?
19) Where is Saudi Arabia?
20) What are the three forms of God?
21) Who is Son of God, according to the doctrine of Christianity?
22) What is the holy book of Christianity?
23) What does Virgin Birth refer to?
24) Where was the birthplace of Jesus Christ?
25) Who was Judas? What does Judas refer to in a derogatory sense?
26) What is a crucifix?
27) When do the Christians observe Easter?
28) Who established the Christian Church?
29) Who carried Christianity to Rome?

30) What are the three main branches of Christianity?
31) Who is the leader of the Roman Catholic Church?
32) Where is the papal government located?
33) What is a bishop?
34) What is a priory?
35) What is an abbey?
36) What is a friary?
37) What is a nunnery?
38) What is a prioress?
39) What is an abbess?
40) What is a nun?

Lesson Eighteen

Religion (II)

In 1054, Christianity was split into two branches: the Roman Catholic Church and the Eastern Orthodox Church. Each of them says it follows the older, and the more traditional practice of Christianity strictly. The latter is also called the Orthodox Church. This branch of the Christian Church is found in Eastern Europe, including Greece, Turkey, Russia and some other Balkan countries, which no longer recognizes the Pope as its head, but recognizes the Patriarch of Constantinople, that is the present Istanbul in Turkey, as its head bishop. A patriarch is a high-ranking bishop in the Roman Catholic Church and the Eastern Orthodox Church. The Orthodox Church in Greece is called the Greek Orthodox Church, or the Greek Church.

In the 16th century, the German Protestant reformer Martin Luther (1483 – 1546), a poor minister, led a movement to protest against the assumption of supremacy in spiritual matters by the Roman Catholic Church. He also translated *the Bible* into German. This 16th-century European Protestant movement led by Martin Luther for the reform of the Roman Catholic Church was called the Reformation, which resulted in the establishment of the Reformed or Protestant Churches. Protestantism is the third main branch of Christianity. It is a system of belief of the Protestants. A Protestant is a member of any of the Christian bodies that separated from the Roman Catholic Church in the 16th century, or of their branches formed later. A most important religious reformer after Martin Luther in the 16th century in Western Europe was John Calvin (1509 – 1564). He was a French religious reformer, an authoritative spokesman of the Protestant movement, and the author of the epoch-making book entitled *the Institutes of the Christian Religion*. For twenty years he held away in Geneva, and for so long he was regarded as the head of the Reformed Churches in Scotland, Switzerland, Holland and France.

The Protestants include all Christian bodies in the West other than the Roman Catholic Church. The main sects or denominations of Protestantism are the Church of England, the Methodists, the Baptists, the Congregationalists, the Presbyterians, the Lutherans and the Reformed Church or the Calvinists. But some sections of the Church of England, object to being classed as Protestants.

The Methodist Church is a Protestant Church that believes in Methodism. Its teaching, organization and manner of worship were started by John Wesley (1703 – 1791). A Methodist is a Christian who follows the teachings of John Wesley.

The Baptist Church is a Protestant Church that believes in Baptism by the immersion of a person at an age when he or she is old enough to understand what the ceremony means. Baptism is a ceremony which marks the admission of someone into the Christian Church either by dipping them in water or by sprinkling them with water as a sign that they have become spiritually pure, and often giving them a name. When a person is baptized, he or she is admitted into a specific Christian Church and given a Christian name. A Baptist is a Christian who believes that baptism is necessary for a Christian, and that it should happen only to someone who is old enough to understand the meaning of the ceremony.

The Congregationalist Church is a union of Protestant churches in which individual congregations are responsible for their own affairs. Congregation refers to a group of people who regularly attend a particular church for religious worship, usually excluding the priest and choir. A choir is an organized group of singers that perform in church services. A Congregationalist is a member of the Congregationalist Church. Congregationalism is the beliefs and practices of the Congregationalists.

The Presbyterian Church is a Protestant Church, especially a church of the National Church of Scotland governed by a body of official people called elders or presbyters who are all equal in rank. The National Church of Scotland is also called the Presbyterian Church of Scotland. An elder or a presbyter refers to an official in a Presbyterian Church. A Presbyterian is a member of the Presbyterian Church. Presbyterianism is the beliefs and practices of the Presbyterians.

The Lutheran Church is a Protestant Church named after Martin Luther. A Lutheran is a member of the Lutheran Church. Lutheranism refers to the beliefs and practices of the Lutherans, on the basis of Martin Luther's thought.

The Reformed Church refers to the churches in Switzerland, Holland, Scotland and elsewhere, which accepted the doctrines of John Calvin. Calvinism is John Calvin's Christian religious teachings. A Calvinist is a follower of Calvinism. The Calvinists are a group of Christians who follow the teachings of John Calvin.

The Church of England, which is also called the Anglican Church, is the established Protestant Church in England. An established church is legally recognized as the official church of the State. The Church of England is an episcopal church, which is governed by a bishop or by bishops. Influenced by the Reformation led by Martin Luther in the 16th century, the Church of England became the established church in England. Henry VIII (1491 - 1547), the king of England from 1509 to 1547, declared himself to be Supreme Head of the Church of England in 1534. He wanted a divorce from his first wife Catherine of Aragon (1485 - 1536) who was a Roman Catholic and failed to give birth to a son to him. But he was refused by the Pope. His second wife Anne Boleyn (1507 - 1536) also failed to give him a son. But she gave him a daughter called Elizabeth, who became the Queen later. However, he was not happy about Anne and promptly had her head chopped off.

In 1662, some Protestants in England separated themselves from the Church of England and formed the Free Churches and the Nonconformist Churches. The Free Church is a church that does not follow the teachings or practices of such established churches as the Roman Catholic Church and the Anglican Church. The Nonconformist Church refers to the sect that does not conform to the beliefs and practices of the Church of England. Among the Free Churches and the Nonconformist Churches are the Methodists, the Baptists, the Congregationalists and the Presbyterians. They have simple religious services or ceremonies, with no bishops or archbishops. They are more independent and less related to each other. Some of them even have no ceremonies, no candles and no private confessions.

The Church of England is the official state religion of England. The Monarch is the "Supreme Governor", that is, the temporal leader of the Church of England. And the Monarch must always be a member of the Church of England and promise to uphold it. The Church of England, with its own church districts, can be divided into two provinces: Canterbury and York. They are respectively governed by two archbishops: the Archbishop of Canterbury and the Archbishop of York. The former is the spiritual leader of the Church of England, and also the Primate of All England, while the latter is the Primate of England. An archbishop is a bishop of the highest rank, responsible for a large church district. A bishop is a senior clergyman who is in charge of a cathedral as the central church in a diocese. A cathedral is the chief church in a diocese, under the charge of a bishop. A diocese is a bishop's district for which he is responsible. Clergy refers to the people who have been ordained as priests or ministers of the Christian Church. A clergyman or a priest is a person appointed to perform religious duties and ceremonies in the Christian Church, especially in the Church of England. He is between a bishop and a deacon, in charge of a parish with its own church and clergyman within a diocese. So a parish is a clergyman's or a priest's district for which he is responsible. An ecclesiastic is a formal or old-fashioned word for a priest or a clergyman in the Christian Church. A minister is a clergyman, especially in the Protestant churches. As a clergyman of the Church of England, a rector is in charge of a parish from which he receives his income directly. A rector can also be head of a church or a religious community in the Roman Catholic Church. A vicar is a clergyman of the Church of England, who is in charge of a parish and who looks after the spiritual needs of people in his parish. A curate is a clergyman of the Church of England, who helps the rector or vicar in charge of a parish. A deacon is a person ranking below a priest in the Church of England. A deacon can also be a lay person who deals with church business affairs in the Nonconformist churches. As a member of the Christian Church, a layman is involved with it. But he is not a clergyman or priest. So he does not belong to the clergy.

In the English-speaking countries like Britain and the United States, everyone is supposed to have the right to religious freedom without interference from the community or the State. Religious organizations and groups may own their own property, conduct their rites and ceremonies, run schools, and promote their beliefs in speech and writing, within the limits of the law. There is no religious bar to the holding of public office. But the last few decades have seen an increasingly diverse pattern of religious belief. And there have been fewer church-goers who regularly attend services. But religion still provides the customs and ceremonies that mark life's most important events, including birth, coming of age, marriage and death. Churches are not only places where prayers are recited and ceremonies are conducted; they are also community centres where educational, cultural, social and philanthropic activities are held.

There are so many races in Britain and America, because so many people have arrived as immigrants that it is possible to find a place of worship for almost all the different world religions. There are several non-conformist groups of the Christian Church too. In the 17th century, George Fox, an Englishman, found that it was difficult to pray in church because the sermon and hymns kept disturbing his thoughts. He decided that he felt nearer to God when he was walking in the fields. He interrupted church services to tell people about his feeling and was often put in prison for being so noisy. Gradually, he discussed religion with a few of his friends and formed a group called the Society of Friends. While they were sitting quietly together people said they quaked or shook with emotion. From this the Society of Friends was given the nickname "Quakers". But they are far from being cowards. They are opposed to war and violence and have supplied leaders for all kinds of philanthropic work. Many Quakers have been seen as very brave and helpful when people are in trouble.

  A pagan or a heathen is a person who is not a believer in any of the world's chief religions like Christianity, Judaism and Islam. It refers to a person who is neither a Christian, a Jew, nor a Muslim. Formerly, a pagan referred to a person who did not believe in Christianity. Paganism is the beliefs and practices of pagans. A temple is a building used for the worship of a god or gods, in non-Christian religions. A Buddhist temple is a building used for the worship of Buddha. It is under the charge of a Buddhist abbot. Buddhist monks live a secluded life in a Buddhist monastery while Buddhist nuns live a secluded life in a Buddhist convent or a Buddhist nunnery. A lay Buddhist or a Buddhist layman is a Buddhist who worships Buddha at home. A lama is a Tibetan or Mongolian Buddhist monk. A lama temple is a building where Tibetan or Mongolian Buddhist monks live a secluded life. A Taoist temple is a building where Taoist priests live and do their religious practices. A Taoist priest is a man who lives and does his religious practices in a Taoist temple.

Words & Expressions

the Eastern Orthodox Church *also* **the Orthodox Church** *n*. the Christian Church found in Eastern Europe, including Greece, Turkey, Russia and many Balkan countries 东正教；正教

Balkan countries *n*. countries on the Balkan Peninsula, including Greece, Turkey, Yugoslavia, Rumania, Bulgaria, Albania, etc. 巴尔干国家

Constantinople *n*. the former capital of the Turkish Empire, and the present Istanbul in Turkey 君士坦丁堡

Istanbul *n*. port and former capital of Turkey until 1923 伊斯坦布尔

patriarch *n*. a high-ranking bishop in the Roman Catholic Church and the Eastern Orthodox Church 宗主教；牧首

the Patriarch of Constantinople *n*. the head bishop of the Eastern Orthodox Church 君士坦丁堡宗主教；东正教牧首

the Greek Orthodox Church *also* **the Greek Church** *n*. the Orthodox Church in Greece 希腊正教会；希腊教会

Martin Luther (1483 – 1546) *n*. the German Protestant reformer of the 16th century 马丁·路德

minister *n*. a member of the clergy, esp. in Protestant churches 牧师

reformer *n*. a person who tries to improve sth such as a law or a social system 改革家 *e.g.* religious reformer 宗教改革家

the Reformation *n*. the 16th-century European Protestant movement led by Martin Luther, in which a large section of the Christian Church broke away from Rome 宗教改革运动

the Reformed Church *n*. the churches in Switzerland, Holland, Scotland and elsewhere, which accepted the doctrines of John Calvin 归正会；归正宗

the Protestant Church *n*. the Christian bodies in the West other than the Roman Catholic Church 新教教会

Protestantism *n*. the third main branch of Christianity, which was formed in the Reformation led by Martin Luther in the 16th century 新教

Protestant n. a member of any of the Christian bodies which separated from the Roman Catholic Church in the 16th century, or of their branches formed later 新教徒

John Calvin (1509-1564) n. a French religious reformer after Martin Luther, and the author of *the Institutes of the Christian Religion* 约翰·加尔文

the Institutes of the Christian Religion n. a book written by John Calvin《基督教原理》

Geneva n. a city in Switzerland 日内瓦

the Methodist Church n. a Protestant Church that believes in Methodism 卫理公会

Methodism n. the beliefs and practices of the Methodists 循道宗

John Wesley (1703-1791) n. an English religious leader and the founder of Methodism 约翰·卫斯理

Methodist n. a follower of the teachings of John Wesley 循道宗信徒；卫理公会教徒

the Methodists n. the group of Christians who follow the teachings of John Wesley and who have their own branch of the Christian church and their own kind of worship 循道宗

the Baptist Church n. a Protestant Church that believes in Baptism 浸会

Baptist n. a member of a Christian group which believes that baptism should be only for people old enough to understand its meaning and that they should be covered completely with water 浸礼宗信徒；浸会教徒

the Baptists n. the group of Christians who believe that baptism is necessary for a Christian, and that it should happen only to sb who is old enough to understand what they are doing 浸礼宗

the Congregationalist Church n. a union of Protestant churches in which individual congregations are responsible for their own affairs 公理会

Congregationalism n. the beliefs and practices of the Congregationalists 公理宗

congregation n. a group of people who regularly attend a particular church for religious worship, usu. excluding the priest and choir 教堂会众

choir n. an organized group of singers that perform in church services 唱诗班

Congregationalist n. a member of the Congregationalist Church 公理宗信徒；公理会教徒

the Congregationalists n. the group of Christians in a Protestant branch in which each local church governs its own affairs 公理宗

the Presbyterian Church n. a Protestant Church, esp. a church of the National Church of Scotland governed by a body of official people called elders or presbyters who are all equal in rank 长老会

elder *also* **presbyter** n. an official in a Presbyterian Church 长老

Presbyterianism n. the beliefs and practices of the Presbyterians 长老宗

Presbyterian n. a member of the Presbyterian Church 长老宗信徒；长老会教徒

the Presbyterians n. the group of Christian of a Protestant church governed by a body of official people of equal rank 长老宗

the National Church of Scotland *also* **the Presbyterian Church of Scotland** n. the established Protestant Church in Scotland, and the official state religion of Scotland 苏格兰国教会

the Presbyterian Church of Scotland n. the established Protestant Church in Scotland, which is also called the National Church of Scotland 苏格兰长老会

the Lutheran Church n. a Protestant Church named after Martin Luther 路德宗；信义会

Lutheranism n. the beliefs and practices of the Lutherans, which are based on the thinking of Martin Luther 路德宗

Lutheran n. a member of the Lutheran Church 路德宗信徒；信义会教徒

the Lutherans n. the group of Christians who believe in Lutheranism 路德宗；信义宗

Calvinism n. John Calvin's Christian religious teachings 加尔文宗

Calvinist n. a follower of Calvinism 加尔文宗信徒

the Calvinists n. the group of Christians who follow the teachings of John Calvin 加尔文宗

the Church of England *also* **the Anglican Church** n. the established Protestant Church in England, and the official state religion of England 英国国教会

the Anglican Church n. the established Protestant Church in England, which is also called the Church of England 圣公会

established church n. a church which is legally recognized as the official church of the State 国教

episcopal a. belonging to a bishop or bishops, in connection with the activities, duties and responsibilities 主教的；主教团的

episcopal church n. a church governed by a bishop or by bishops 主教教会

King Henry VIII (1491–1547) n. the king of England from 1509 to 1547, who declared himself to be Supreme Head of the Church of England in 1534 亨利八世

Catherine of Aragon (1485–1536) n. King Henry VIII's first wife, who was a Roman Catholic 阿拉贡的凯瑟琳

Anne Boleyn (1507–1536) n. King Henry VIII's second wife, who was the Mother of Queen Elizabeth 安妮·博林

the Free Church n. a church which does not follow the teachings or practices of such established churches as the Roman Catholic Church and the Anglican Church 自由教会

the Nonconformist Church n. the Protestant sect which does not conform to the beliefs and practices of the Church of England 不从国教者教会

confession n. the act of telling God or a priest about one's own sins so as to be forgiven, in a confessional box which is a small room in a church 忏悔

the Supreme Governor n. the temporal leader of the Church of England 至高元首

primate n. the archbishop of a country or a particular region 首主教；大主教

cathedral n. the chief church in a diocese, under the charge of a bishop 主教座堂

diocese n. a bishop's district for which he is responsible 主教教区

parish n. a clergyman's or a priest's district for which he is responsible 堂区；牧师教区

ecclesiastic n. a formal or old-fashioned word for a priest **minister** n. a clergyman, esp. in the Protestant churches 神职人员；牧师

rector n. a clergyman of the Church of England, in charge of a parish 牧师

vicar n. a clergyman of the Church of England, in charge of a church 牧师

curate n. a clergyman of the Church of England, who helps a parish priest 助理牧师

deacon n. a person ranking below a priest in the Church of England and also a lay person who deals with church business affairs in the Nonconformist churches 执事；助祭；辅祭；会吏

layman n. a member of the Christian Church, but not a clergyman or priest 平信徒

religious freedom n. the right to believe in a religion, carry out religious activities and express religious opinions, without interference from the community or the State 宗教自由

rite n. a series of words and actions which has a fixed order and which is used for a special religious purpose 宗教仪式

church-goer n. a person who regularly attends services in a church 按时到教堂做礼拜的教友

prayer n. a set form of words which is said during a religious service 祈祷辞 e.g. to recite prayers 念诵祈祷辞；to say the Lord's Prayer 念诵主祷文

community centre n. the place of a community where educational, cultural, social and philanthropic activities are held 社区中心

George Fox (1624–1691) n. the founder of the Quakers 乔治·福克斯

sermon n. a talk on a religious subject which is given by a member of the clergy as part of a church service 布道；讲道

hymn n. a song which Christians sing in order to praise God or the saints 赞美诗；圣歌

the Society of Friends n. a religious sect founded in 1652 by George Fox 公谊会

Quakers *n.* the nickname of the Society of Friends 贵格会；教友派

pagan *also* **heathen** *n.* a person who is not a believer in any of the world's chief religions like Christianity, Judaism and Islam 异教徒

paganism *n.* the beliefs and practices of pagans 异教信仰

temple *n.* a building used for the worship of a god or gods, in non-Christian religions 寺庙；庙宇 *e.g.* Buddhist temple 佛寺

Buddhist abbot *n.* a person who is in charge of a Buddhist temple 方丈

Buddhist monk *n.* a man who lives a secluded life in a Buddhist monastery 和尚；佛僧

Buddhist monastery *n.* a building or a collection of buildings, usu. situated away from towns and cities, in which a group of Buddhist monks live together and do their religious practices 寺院；僧院

Buddhist nun *n.* a woman who lives a secluded life in a Buddhist convent or a Buddhist nunnery 尼姑

Buddhist convent *also* **Buddhist nunnery** *n.* a building or a collection of buildings, usu. situated away from towns and cities, in which a group of Buddhist nuns live together and do their religious practices 尼庵

lay Buddhist *also* **Buddhist layman** *n.* a Buddhist who worships Buddha at home 居士

lama *n.* a Tibetan or Mongolian Buddhist priest or monk 喇嘛

lama temple *n.* a building where Tibetan or Mongolian Buddhist monks live a secluded life and do their religious practices 喇嘛寺；喇嘛庙

Taoist temple *n.* a building where Taoist priests live and do their religious practices 宫观；道宫；道观

Taoist priest *n.* a man who lives and does his religious practices in a Taoist temple 道士

prehistoric *a.* relating to the time in history before information was written down 史前的 *e.g.* prehistoric times 史前时期

tread *v.* step on sth, or press one's foot on it 踏；踩 *e.g.* to tread the earth 踏上地球

game *n.* wild animals or birds which are hunted or killed for sports and sometimes cooked and eaten 猎物；野味 *e.g.* wild game 猎物

attributable to *a.* caused by 归咎于

be attributed to *v. phrase* be caused by 归咎于

superhuman *a.* extraordinary and beyond the powers or experience of an ordinary person 超人的

superanimal *a.* beyond the powers of animals 超动物的

persecution *n.* cruel and unfair treatment of a person or group, esp. because of their political or religious beliefs 迫害

abominable *a.* very unpleasant, very bad, or very poor in quality, used to show strong disapproval 恶劣的；极坏的 *e.g.* abominable cruelty 极端残酷

ritual *n.* a religious service or other ceremony, which involves a series of actions usu. performed in a fixed order 宗教仪式 *e.g.* compelling rituals 引人入胜的宗教仪式

impulse *n.* a sudden wish to do sth 冲动 *e.g.* religious impulse 宗教冲动

Additional Knowledge

The Origin of Religion

Religion is one of the things, which distinguishes man from the other animals. No group of human beings has ever been discovered which did not have religious beliefs. Religion is so old that its origins are hidden in the darkness of prehistoric times, when our early ancestors trod the earth. But as prehistoric men left no written records behind them, we can only speculate about what they believed. They survived by hunting, fishing and gathering wild fruits, and crucial factors in their survival were outside their control. They needed a continuing supply of game and fruit every year, which depended on the annual cycle of nature, the birth of young animals and fresh vegetation in the spring. The continuance of each human group similarly required the birth of children to replace the adults who died. Early man may have sensed a pattern, an order in nature, not attributable to men or animal, and so attributed to unseen powers, superhuman and superanimal. Religions have taught men and women how to lead their lives on the earth and have given them hope for a happier life after death. They have supported human beings in times of danger, pain, bewilderment and despair. They have inspired nobility, self-sacrifice, courage and endurance, and they have also inspired wars, persecutions and abominable cruelty. They have created compelling and magnificent rituals and a massive wealth of literature, architecture, art, music and philosophy. Great civilizations have grown up round religions and even in the modern world, when the religious impulse is supposed to be dying, it is in fact vigorously expressing itself in new forms and disguises.

Exercises

I. Explain each of the following:
1) the Eastern Orthodox Church
2) Balkan countries
3) the Patriarch of Constantinople
4) Martin Luther
5) the Reformation
6) Protestantism
7) Protestant
8) John Calvin
9) the Reformed Church
10) the Church of England
11) the Methodists
12) the Methodist Church
13) the Baptists
14) the Baptist Church
15) the Congregationalists
16) the Congregationalist Church
17) the Presbyterians
18) the Presbyterian Church
19) elder
20) the National Church of Scotland
21) the Lutherans
22) the Lutheran Church
23) the Calvinists
24) choir
25) established church
26) the Free Church
27) the Nonconformist Church
28) confession
29) the "Supreme Governor" of the Church of England
30) temporal leader
31) spiritual leader
32) the Archbishop of Canterbury
33) the Archbishop of York
34) cathedral
35) diocese
36) parish
37) clergy
38) clergyman
39) deacon
40) ecclesiastic
41) minister
42) rector
43) vicar
44) curate
45) religious freedom
46) church-goer
47) the Society of Friends
48) Quakers
49) paganism
50) temple

51) Buddhist monk
52) Buddhist monastery
53) Buddhist nun
54) lama
55) Taoist priest

II. Give another way or other ways of saying each of the following:
Models: origin of human beings → origin of man
holy → divine, sacred
1) the Eastern Orthodox Church →
2) denomination →
3) presbyter →
4) the Presbyterian Church of Scotland →
5) the Anglican Church →
6) heathen →
7) Buddhist convent →
8) Buddhist layman →

III. Fill in the blanks:
Model: Jesus Christ is the founder of _____.
→ Jesus Christ is the founder of Christianity.
1) Martin Luther is the founder of _____.
2) John Calvin is the founder of _____.
3) John Wesley is the founder of _____.
4) King Henry VIII is the founder of _____.
5) George Fox is the founder of _____.

IV. Answer the following questions:
1) When was Christianity split into the Roman Catholic Church and the Eastern Orthodox Church?
2) Please name some countries where the Eastern Orthodox Church is found.
3) Where was Constantinople?
4) What is a patriarch?
5) What is the name of the Orthodox Church in Greece?
6) Who led the European Protestant movement for the reform of the Roman Catholic Church in the 16th century?
7) What is the third main branch of Christianity?
8) Who is the author of *the Institutes of the Christian Religion*?
9) Where is Geneva?
10) Please name some of the main sects of Protestantism.
11) What does congregation refer to?
12) What is the established Protestant Church in England?
13) What is an episcopal church?
14) Who declared himself to be Supreme Head of the Church of England in 1534?
15) Do the Baptists have bishops and archbishops?
16) Are the Congregationalists and the Presbyterians related to each other?
17) What is the official state religion of England?
18) Who is the temporal leader of the Church of England now?
19) What are the two provinces of the Church of England?
20) Who is the spiritual leader of the Church of England?
21) Who is the Primate of All England? And who is the Primate of England?
22) What is a bishop? What is an archbishop?

23) What is a layman? Does a layman belong to the clergy?
24) Why are there so many races in Britain and America?
25) Is a pagan a Christian?
26) Who is in charge of a Buddhist temple?
27) Who live in a Buddhist nunnery?
28) What is a lay Buddhist?
29) What is a lama temple?
30) Who is in charge of a Taoist temple?

Partial Answers to Exercises

Lesson One

II. Tell what each of the following stands for:
  1) L1 → first language
  2) L2 → second language
  3) TESL → Teaching English as a Second Language
  4) ESP → English for Special Purposes
  5) BrE. → British English
  6) AmE. → American English
  7) IT → information technology
  8) PC → personal computer
  9) CBD → central business district
  10) UFO → unidentified flying object

III. Give another way or other ways of saying each of the following:
  1) English-speaking population → English-speaking people
  2) Chinglish → Chinese English
  3) Anglo-Saxon → Old English
  4) Old Continent → European Continent; the Continent
  5) ordinary language → natural language

Lesson Two

II. Tell what each of the following initial letters stands for, and tell whether it is an initialism or an acronym:
  1) U. K. → the United Kingdom of Great Britain and North Ireland (initialism)
  2) U. N. → the United Nations (initialism)
  3) U. S. A. → the United States of America (initialism)
  4) IRC → International Red Cross, the Red Cross (initialism)
  5) WTO → World Trade Organization (initialism)
  6) NATO → North Atlantic Treaty Organization (acronym)
  7) GRE → Graduate Record Examination (initialism)
  8) TOEFL → Test of English as a Foreign Language (acronym)
  9) IOC → International Olympic Committee (initialism)
  10) IRO → International Refugee Organization (initialism)

III. Fill in the blanks:
  1) A Czech is a person from <u>Czech</u>, whose official language is <u>Czech</u>.
  2) A Turk is a person from <u>Turkey</u>, whose official language is <u>Turkish</u>.
  3) A Portuguese is a person from <u>Portugal</u>, whose official language is <u>Portuguese</u>.
  4) A Dane is a person from <u>Denmark</u>, whose official language is <u>Danish</u>.
  5) A Swede is a person from <u>Sweden</u>, whose official language is <u>Swedish</u>.
  6) A Russian is a person from <u>Russia</u>, whose official language is <u>Russian</u>.

7) A Greek is a person from Greece, whose official language is Greek.
8) A German is a person from Germany, whose official language is German.
9) A Slovak is a person from Slovakia, whose official language is Slovak.
10) A Finn is a person from Finland, whose official language is Finnish.
11) A Romanian is a person from Romania, whose official language is Romanian.
12) A Pole is a person from Poland, whose official language is Polish.
13) A Frenchman is a person from France, whose official language is French.
14) A Dutch is a person from Holland, whose official language is Dutch.
15) A Spaniard is a person from Spain, whose official language is Spanish.

IV. Fill in the blanks:
1) Wales has English and Welsh as its official languages.
2) Canada has English and French as its official languages.
3) Belgium has French, Dutch and German as its official languages.
4) Switzerland has French, German and Italian as its official languages.

V. Give another way or other ways of saying each of the following:
1) the Commonwealth → the British Commonwealth of Nations, the British Commonwealth
2) the Celtic languages → Celtic
3) the Gaelic language → Gaelic
4) the Continent → the European Continent; the Old Continent
5) the Channel → the English Channel
6) the Atlantic → the Atlantic Ocean
7) the New Continent → the American Continent; the New World
8) the States → the United States
9) the Pacific → the Pacific Ocean
10) American Indian → Native American; Amerindian
11) African American → American Black; Afro-American
12) Oceanica → Oceania
13) Eastern country → Oriental country
14) the Red Cross → International Red Cross

Lesson Three

II. Give the original form of each of the following pet names:
1) Betty → Elizabeth
2) Bill → William
3) Bobby → Robert
4) Dick → Richard
5) Eddie → Edward
6) Fred → Frederick
7) Lizzie → Elizabeth
8) Mike → Michael
9) Sam → Samuel
10) Tom → Thomas

III. Tell which of the following is a surname of Scottish origin, which of the following is a

surname of Welsh origin, and which of the following is a surname of Irish origin:
1) Campbell → a surname of Scottish origin
2) Edwards → a surname of Welsh origin
3) Fraser → a surname of Scottish origin
4) Jones → a surname of Welsh origin
5) McArthur → a surname of Scottish origin
6) Williams → a surname of Welsh origin
7) Owen → a surname of Welsh origin
8) Stuart → a surname of Scottish origin
9) MacDonald → a surname of Scottish origin
10) Mulligan → a surname of Irish origin

IV. Tell what each of the following initial letters stands for:
1) IMF → International Monetary Fund
2) WHO → World Health Organization
3) FAO → Food and Agriculture Organization of the United Nations
4) UPU → Universal Post Union
5) WMO → World Meteorological Organization
6) ILO → International Labour Organization
7) ICAO → International Civil Aviation Organization
8) IMO → International Maritime Organization
9) UNDP → Untied Nations Development Programme
10) UNICEF → United Nations Children Fund

Lesson Four

II. Give another way or other ways of saying each of the following:
1) the expectation of life → life expectancy
2) mortality rate → mortality; death rate
3) minor child → dependent child
4) large family → big family
5) contraceptive method → contraceptive technique
6) single-parent family → one-parent family; lone-parent family
7) Double Income, No Kids → Dual Income, No Kids; dink
8) dinky → Double Income, No Kids Yet; Dual Income, No Kids Yet
9) Women's Lib → Women's Liberation
10) kinfolk → kin; kindred
11) close kin → near kin; near relative; near relation, close relative; close relation
12) distant kin → remote kinfolk; distant relative; distant relation
13) relative on one's father's side → paternal relative
14) relative on one's mother's side → maternal relative

Lesson Five

II. Give the converse word for each of the following words:
1) king → queen
2) emperor → empress

3) Crown Prince → Crown Princess
4) reigning queen → Prince Consort
5) nobleman → noblewoman
6) peer → peeress
7) marquis → marquise; marchioness
8) count → countess
9) viscount → viscountess
10) baron → baroness

III. Look at the following list of words and find out which are members of the royalty, and which are members of the nobility:
1) Members of the royalty: monarch, king, queen, emperor, empress, consort, prince, princess, crown prince, crown princess, queen dowager, empress dowager, imperial concubine
2) Members of the nobility: noble, nobleman, noblewoman, aristocrat, peer, peeress, duke, duchess, marquis, marquise, earl, count, countess, viscount, viscountess, baron, baroness, baronet

Lesson Six

II. Give another way or other ways of saying each of the following:
1) the Upper Chamber → the Upper House
2) the Lower House → the Lower Chamber
3) the House of Lords → the Lords; the House
4) the House of Commons → the Commons Chamber; the Chamber of Commons; the Commons; the House
5) Law Lords → Lords of Appeal
6) Lord High Chancellor → Lord Chancellor
7) MP → Member of Parliament
8) proposed law → bill
9) the party in power → the ruling party
10) the opposition party → the opposition
11) Backbench MP → Back Bencher
12) the House of Representatives → the House

III. Fill in the blanks:
1) The British Parliament consists of two houses, which are <u>the House of Lords</u> and <u>the House of Commons</u>.
2) The U. S. Congress consists of two houses, which are <u>the Senate</u> and <u>the House of Representatives</u>.
3) The members of the House of Lords consist of Lords <u>Spiritual</u> and Lords <u>Temporal</u>.
4) In the United States, the judicial branch consists of the <u>federal</u> courts, which are the <u>District</u> Courts, where trials are conducted; the Courts of <u>Appeals</u>; and the <u>Supreme</u> Court.

IV. Look at the following words and find out which are related to the British Parliament and which are related to the U. S. Congress:

1) The British Parliament: Parliament, House of Lords, Lords Spiritual, Archbishop of Canterbury, Archbishop of York, Lords Temporal, Lords of Appeal, Lord High Chancellor, House of Commons, Speaker, Member of Parliament, MP, frontbench, Front Bencher, backbench, Back Bencher, crossbench, crossbencher, parliamentarian, Houses of Parliament, Parliament Square, Westminster
2) The U. S. Congress: Congress, Senate, senator, House of Representatives, Speaker, Congressman, Congresswoman, Capitol

Lesson Seven

II. Give another way or other ways of saying each of the following:
   1) the electoral system → the voting system
   2) voter → elector; constituent
   3) cast one's vote → record one's vote
   4) vote by post → postal vote
   5) proxy vote → vote by proxy
   6) balloting → voting
   7) vice-presidential candidate → running mate of the presidential candidate

III. Fill in the blanks:
   1) An elector is a member of the <u>electorate</u>.
   2) A constituent is a member of the <u>constituency</u>.
   3) A Republican is a member of the <u>Republican Party</u>.
   4) A Democrat is a member of the <u>Democratic Party</u>.
   5) A senator is a member of the <u>Senate</u>.
   6) An Electoral College elector is a member of the <u>Electoral College</u>.

Lesson Eight

II. Give another way or other ways of saying each of the following:
   1) the Home Secretary (U.K.) → the Secretary of State for Home Affairs
   2) the Defence Secretary (U.K.) → the Secretary of State for Defence
   3) the Chancellor (U.K.) → the Chancellor of the Exchequer
   4) the State Secretary (U.S.) → the Secretary of State
   5) government department → department
   6) appellate court (U.S.) → court of appeal
   7) municipality → municipal government
   8) coup → coup d'état
   9) stage a coup → launch a coup
   10) coalition → coalition government

III. Fill in the blanks:
   1) 10 Downing Street in London is the official residence of the <u>Prime Minister</u>.
   2) 11 Downing Street in London is the official residence of the <u>Chancellor of the Exchequer</u>.
   3) The White House is the official residence of the <u>American President in Washington D. C.</u>

IV. What does each of the following stand for?
   1) Downing Street can be used to refer to <u>the British Prime Minister or the British</u>

Government.
2) Whitehall can be used to refer to <u>the British Government itself</u>.
3) The White House can be used to refer to <u>the American President or his advisers</u>.

Lesson Nine

II. Give another way or other ways of saying each of the following:
1) conventions → conventional law
2) Justice of the Peace → magistrate
3) law-enforcement official → judiciary official
4) turn down the appeal → reject the appeal
5) violate the law → break the law; disobey the law; cheat the law
6) death penalty → capital punishment
7) legal counsel → legal advice
8) civil court of law → civil court
9) abide by the law → keep the law; obey the law; follow the law; comply with the law
10) ensure → make sure

Lesson Ten

II. Give another way or other ways of saying each of the following:
1) concrete goods → real goods
2) industrial sector → secondary sector
3) service sector → tertiary sector
4) third industry → service industry
5) shop → store
6) mall → shopping mall
7) laundromat → launderette
8) DIY → do-it-yourself
9) travel bureau → travel agency
10) interesting place → place of interest
11) legal counsel → legal advice
12) exposition facilities → exhibition facilities
13) high-tech industry → high-technique industry
14) aircraft industry → aviation industry
15) space industry → astronautic industry

Lesson Eleven

II. Give another way or other ways of saying each of the following:
1) white-collar work → office work
2) white-collar worker → office worker
3) career woman → professional woman
4) miscellaneous fees → miscellaneous expenses; miscellaneous charges
5) postage charge → postage
6) entry charge → admission charge
7) admission fee → admission

8) capital transfer tax → death duty
9) excise duties → excise
10) customs tariff → tariff
11) import duties → customs duties; customs; duties
12) Oscar → Academy Award

Lesson Twelve

II. Give another way or other ways of saying each of the following:
1) banknote → note; bill
2) cheque → check
3) small change → change
4) bank account → account
5) credit card → plastic card; plastic money
6) A currency is being revaluated. → A currency is appreciating.
7) A currency is being devaluated. → A currency is depreciating.
8) stock company → joint-stock company
9) limited company → limited liability company
10) public company → public limited company
11) private company → private limited company
12) group company → group
13) transnational company → transnational corporation; TNC
14) multinational corporation → multinational company; MNC
15) foreign-funded corporation → foreign-funded company
16) jointly-funded company → jointly-funded corporation
17) the people in general → the public
18) public ownership → state ownership
19) co-op → cooperative
20) township enterprise → township-run enterprise
21) time deposit → fixed deposit
22) current deposit → demand deposit
23) spot commodities → spot goods; spots
24) real property → real estate; realty; property

Lesson Thirteen

II. Give another way or other ways of saying each of the following:
1) author a book → write a book
2) economic reward → economic incentive
3) unwilling → reluctant
4) intelligence achievement property → intellectual property
5) incorporeal property → intangible property; intangible assets
6) proprietor → business owner
7) unauthorized copying → unauthorized imitation
8) commercial name → trade name
9) best-selling book → best seller

10) pirated copy → illegal copy
11) illegal version → pirated version
12) illegally copied videodisc → pirated videodisc

III. Give the corresponding adjective and noun(s) of each of the following verbs:
1) exploit → exploiting; exploited; exploitation
2) protect → protective; protection
3) produce → productive; producer; product; production
4) reproduce → reproductive; reproduction
5) invent → inventive; inventor; invention
6) originate → original; originator; originality
7) operate → operative; operator; operation
8) innovate → innovative; innovation
9) limit → limited; limitation
10) permit → permissive; permission
11) exclude → exclusive; exclusion
12) publish → publishing; publisher; publication
13) project → projective; projector; projection
14) prevent → preventive; prevention
15) compete → competitive; competitor; competition
16) industrialize → industrial; industrialized; industralist; industry; industrialization
17) identify → identical; identity; identification
18) perform → performer; performance
19) record → recording; recorder
20) extend → extensive; extension
21) include → inclusive; inclusion
22) direct → directive; director; direction
23) imitate → imitative; imitator; imitation
24) infringe → infringer; infringement
25) plagiarize → plagiarist; plagiarism
26) review → reviewer; review
27) criticize → critical; criticism
28) quote → quotation
29) connect → connection
30) collect → collective; collection

IV. Give the opposite of each of the following:
1) tangible → intangible
2) concrete → abstract
3) willing → unwilling
4) authorized → unauthorized
5) lawful → unlawful
6) legal → illegal

Lesson Fourteen

II. Give another way or other ways of saying each of the following:
1) pre-school education → early childhood education
2) elementary school → grade school, grammar school
3) school year → academic year
4) first-year pupil → first grader
5) secondary school → high school
6) tertiary education → higher education
7) mixed school → coeducational school
8) prep school → preparatory school
9) independent school → private school
10) night school → evening school
11) high school graduate → graduate; school leaver
12) tech → technical college
13) poly → polytechnic
14) first degree → bachelor's degree
15) fresher → freshman
16) second-year student from a university → sophomore
17) postgraduate student → graduate, graduate student, postgraduate
18) doctorate → doctor's degree; doctoral degree
19) doctoral student → doctoral candidate
20) post-doctoral studies → post-doctoral research

III. Tell what each of the following stands for:
1) BA → Bachelor of Arts
2) BSc → Bachelor of Science
3) MA → Master of Arts
4) MSc → Master of Science
5) PhD → Doctor of Philosophy

Lesson Fifteen

II. Give another way or other ways of saying each of the following:
1) mass media → media
2) radio station → broadcasting station
3) sports event → sporting event
4) stereo sound → stereophonic sound
5) aerial → antenna
6) dish antenna → dish
7) e-mail → electronic mail
8) large-sheet → broadsheet
9) small-sheet → tabloid
10) daily paper → daily newspaper; daily
11) ad → advertisement

12) the Web → the World Wide Web, the WWW
III. Tell what each of the following stands for:
1) BBC → British Broadcasting Corporation
2) ITC → Independent Television Commission
3) ITV → Independent Television
4) AM → amplitude modulation
5) FM → frequency modulation
6) DBS → direct broadcasting by satellite
7) VOD → video-on-demand
8) the WWW → the World Wide Web

Lesson Sixteen

II. Give another way or other ways of saying each of the following:
1) Web site → web site, Website, site
2) Web page → web page, webpage
3) instant message → real-time message
4) electronic bulletin board → bulletin board, bulletin board service, BBS
5) online forum → Internet forum, Web forum, discussion forum
6) message board → discussion board
7) blog → web log, weblog
8) photoblog → photolog, fotolog
9) podcasting → personal optional digital casting
10) information search → Internet search, online search
11) search tool → search engine
12) online shopping → Internet shopping
13) cyber crime → computer crime
14) netizen → cybercitizen
15) network culture → cyberculture

III. Give the words or word groups in this text, which are formed by the given word or prefix:
1) cyber → cyber space, cyber world, cyber crime, cybercitizen, cyberculture
2) hyper- → hypertext, hyperlink
3) Internet → Internet forum, Internet host, Internet user, Internet addiction, Internet addict, Internet access
4) online → online chat, online chat room, online service, online forum, online diary, online search, online search engine, online degree, online education, online shopping, online shopper, online community
5) web → World Wide Web, web site, web file, web server, web page, web browser, web forum, web log, web communication

IV. Tell what each of the following stands for:
1) IM → instant messaging
2) Iming → instant messaging
3) BBS → bulletin board service

4) ID → identity
5) netizen → net citizen

Lesson Seventeen

II. Give another way or other ways of saying each of the following:
   1) female god → goddess
   2) worship of many gods → polytheism
   3) belief in only one God → monotheism
   4) Shinto → Shintoism
   5) believer of Buddhism → Buddhist
   6) Zen → Zen Buddhism
   7) Muhammad → Muhammed; Mohammad; Mohammed
   8) believer of Christianity → Christian
   9) be nailed on a cross → be crucified
   10) Roman Catholic → Catholic
   11) Catholic father → Catholic priest
   12) monastic house → monastery
   13) house of nuns → convent; nunnery
   14) head of an abbey → abbot
   15) head of a convent → prioress

III. Fill in the blanks:
   1) Zoroaster is the founder of <u>Zoroastrianism</u>.
   2) Sakya-Muni is the founder of <u>Buddhism</u>.
   3) Muhammad is the founder of <u>Islam</u>.
   4) Jesus Christ is the founder of <u>Christianity</u>.

Lesson Eighteen

II. Give another way or other ways of saying each of the following:
   1) the Eastern Orthodox Church → the Orthodox Church
   2) denomination → sect
   3) presbyter → elder
   4) the Presbyterian Church of Scotland → the National Church of Scotland
   5) the Anglican Church → the Church of England
   6) heathen → pagan
   7) Buddhist convent → Buddhist nunnery
   8) Buddhist layman → lay Buddhist

III. Fill in the blanks:
   1) Martin Luther is the founder of <u>Protestantism</u>.
   2) John Calvin is the founder of <u>Calvinism</u>.
   3) John Wesley is the founder of <u>Methodism</u>.
   4) King Henry VIII is the founder of <u>the Church of England</u>.
   5) George Fox is the founder of <u>the Society of Friends or the Quakers</u>.

References

Cottle, Basil. *The Penguin Dictionary of Surnames*. London: Penguin Books. 1967.
Crystal, David. *English as a Global Language* 英语:全球通用语[M]. 北京:外语教学与研究出版社;Cambridge: Cambridge University Press 剑桥大学出版社. 2001.
Graddol, David. *The Future of English?* [M] London: British Council. 1997.
Reaney, Percy Hide. *A Dictionary of English Surnames*. London: Routledge. 1991.
Room, Adrian. *The Cassell Dictionary of First Names*. London: Cassell Publishers Limited. 1995.
Room, Adrian. *Dictionary of Britain*. Oxford: Oxford University Press. 1986.
Tiersky, Ethel & Martin Tiersky. *The USA Customs and Institutions* [M]. New York: Regents Publishing Company, Inc. 1975.
Trudgill, Peter & Jean Hannah. *International English* Third edition 英语:全球通用语 [M]. 北京:外语教学与研究出版社;Edward Arnold (Publishers) Limited 爱德华·阿诺德出版社. 2000.
裘克安. 英语与英语文化 [M]. 长沙:湖南教育出版社. 1993.
任继愈. 宗教词典. 上海:上海辞书出版社. 1981.